THE HISTORY OF

LOUIS THE SEVENTEENTH.

His Life—His Suffering—His Death.

VOLUME I.

LOUIS XVII.

FROM THE MINIATURE TAKEN BY DUMONT, THE QUEEN'S PAINTER, TWO MONTHS PRIOR TO HIS INCARCERATION IN THE TEMPLE.

LOUIS XVII.

His Life—His Suffering—His Death:

THE CAPTIVITY

OF THE ROYAL FAMILY IN THE TEMPLE.

BY A. DE BEAUCHESNE.

TRANSLATED AND EDITED BY W. HAZLITT, ESQ.

EMBELLISHED WITH VIGNETTES, AUTOGRAPHS, AND PLANS.

VOLUME I.

NEW YORK:

HARPER & BROTHERS, PUBLISHERS,

329 & 331 PEARL STREET,

FRANKLIN SQUARE.

1853.

CONTENTS OF VOLUME I.

BOOK SIXTH.

THE TEMPLE.

BOOK SEVENTH.

THE REPUBLIC PROCLAIMED BEFORE THE TEMPLE.

BOOK EIGHTH.

THE GREAT TOWER OF THE TEMPLE.

BOOK NINTH.

THE KING'S TRIAL.

BOOK TENTH.

THE REGICIDE.

APPENDIX.

LIST OF ILLUSTRATIONS, FAC-SIMILES, &c.

INTRODUCTION.

> "The tyrannous and bloody act is done—
> The most arch deed of piteous massacre
> That ever yet this land was guilty of."
>
> SHAKESPEARE: Richard III., Act iv., Sc. 3.

I.

LOUIS OF FRANCE, the seventeenth of the name, lived only ten years, two months, and twelve days. He bore the title of king only beneath the thatched roofs of La Vendée, and within the tents of an exiled nobility. A few words, then, might seem to suffice for the narration of his life.

But that life, so brief in its days, was so protracted in its torments, that we have needed some time and infinite courage to trace it. If we have not here one of those existences of kings or of heroes which have led the destiny of their age, and weighed potently in the balance of the world, we have at least one of those existences of martyrs, the most deserving of a respectful pity on account of their wretchedness, and the most interesting by the very mysteries of their death. Thus we cannot do justice to the sad and painful charm we have experienced in threading this labyrinth, where truth was so close to error, and whence we could only extricate ourselves by carefully collecting the half broken threads of a thousand reminiscences, and by availing ourselves of all the further light that might be shed upon our labours. We discovered, at the commencement of our researches, how it was that public opinion had never been definitively fixed upon the point, apparently imperceptible, but in reality considerable, of the death of a child. Both France and Europe witnessed, but from a distance, the drama of the Tower of the Temple; they saw not all the scenes; they only learned the lamentable catastrophe in such a manner as to lead them almost to doubt its reality. Before the veil which enveloped the tragic end of the son of Louis XVI., we are not astonished to hear it said, with the warmth of firm conviction, that the young victim issued alive from his prison; men, indeed, admitted that a child really died in the Temple, but they added, that whether it was the son of our King, no one can prove; that the physicians, indeed, affirmed his death, but not his identity; that as it was never known how the man in the iron mask came into the world, so it would never be known how the child of the Temple had quitted it; and that the tomb of the one must remain as mysterious as the cradle of the other.

II.

It was, therefore, natural that impostors should put themselves forward in the face of the world as the heirs to a sacred and glorious name. Independently of some ephemeral pretensions with which the tribunals were not called upon to occupy themselves, we have, since the beginning of this century, seen four candidates gravely come forward, and in turns vividly excite the public attention. Hervagault, Mathurin Bruneau, Naündorff, Richemont, all of them men perfectly unlike one another, have in turns played the same part with so much firmness, so much apparent candour, such consistency and daring, that they have succeeded in gaining over a few consciences, and in unsettling a great many others. That which is incredible is that which ever most seduces credulity. Probability is little heeded by men, and the imagination, allured by the extraordinary, requires, so to speak, to be astounded in order to believe. As for ourselves, we have also been fain to be on our guard against our own wishes, against the instinct of our nature, which leads us on toward the regions of the marvellous. We should have taken pleasure in allowing a poetical mystery to soar over the ruins of the Temple; but we have examined too narrowly all the circumstances of that fearful episode, not to find poetry fade away before a sad and mournful reality. Born amid the tempest, which for more than a century so many different causes had been collecting about his race and his country, the infant whose life we have undertaken to write was destined to see his father and mother pay the debt of the faults of the past, and himself to vanish in the storm after them; doubtless so that innocence might march by the side of virtue, amid the expiatory victims of the revolution. This conviction has with me all the character of an authentic and demonstrated certainty. Woe to me if my mind, in possession of the truth, were to allow my pen to lie! I have spared no pains, no researches, no study, to arrive at that truth. I have gone back to the source of all the facts already ascertained; I have put myself in communication with all the persons now living to whom the chances of their position, or the duties of their office, opened the gates of the Temple; I have had much information to gather, many errors to rectify; I was particularly acquainted with Lasné and Gomin, the two last keepers of the Tower, in whose arms Louis XVII. expired It is not, then, traditions collected by children from the lips of their fathers that I have consulted, but rather the reminiscences of eye witnesses—reminiscences religiously preserved, despite of years, in their memories and in their hearts. For twenty years I have been turning up the ruins of the Temple, seeking there some wreck of unrecorded suffering, some memorials of unrecorded calamities. For twenty years I have been raising stone upon stone of that tower of sacrifice and expiation, whence saints were led to another punishment, and kings to another crown! For twenty years I have shut myself up in that Tower; I have lived there. I have traversed its staircases, its chambers, all its corners; I have re-peopled all these; I have listened to all their sighs, all their sobs; I have read the tortures written on the walls, the pardons left as a farewell; I have heard the echoes that repeated them; and from the top of that Tower, as from the top of a rock, I have seen all the crimes piling up, like waves, and breaking around.

III.

I find myself, then, in a position to describe, from personal inquiry, and with certainty, the least circumstance of the events which I relate. I shall bring to my recital the most exact impartiality, hazarding nothing that is doubtful, but resolute to say that which I believe to be true. If among the new details which these memoirs contain, there be some that seem improbable in the very excess of their atrocity, let it not be forgotten that I have them from the very mouths of the actors and witnesses, and that I should fail in my duty if I were to seek to extenuate them, to give them more credit. Not having the ambition of the historian, I must at least preserve the fidelity of the narrator.

I have lived long years absorbed in the memory of my subject. I have had for this unhappy prince the veneration that I should have for my own son. Insensible to the movement of peoples, and to the transformation of society, I only demanded from that terrible period of the revolution, what had relation to that little head on which I had concentrated my most vivid and most tender faculties. I cannot describe the pious avidity, the unbroken patience, with which I have applied myself to seize, amidst the riot of the storm of revolution, the feeble murmur of that life so short, of those joys so brief, of those miseries so lingering, of that death so cruel.

Thus, I have been obliged to enter into the most minute developments of all that concerns them, not scrupling to derogate from historic gravity, and being persuaded, on the contrary, that in the life of an infant, where there are no great actions to relate, the most circumstantial details should not be neglected; and that the very drama in which they are enveloped communicates interest to them. Some learned botanist devoted a whole volume to recount the life, peculiarities, and habits of a little flower amidst the immense subjects which the kingdom of nature. to which it belonged, presented. The Dauphin of France has been to me that little flower, amid the immense events of the revolution.

Often obliged to retrace, from the reign of his father, the events with which his frail childhood was mixed up, I have endeavoured to do so as succinctly as possible, and only in order that we might not lose sight of its labyrinthine intrigues, its complicated changes of fortune, its chain of catastrophes; I shall be excused then, if I glance over important matters, to dwell upon matters apparently slight and ephemeral. A simple narrator of what I have collected, I have not aimed at dramatic movements or picturesque effects; I have been equally on my guard against complaisant credulity, which admits everything, without proof, and against prejudiced incredulity, which rejects everything, without examination I have desired to reach the limits of the truth, but have feared to pass them. I have even restrained, as far as was in my power, the expressions of a sentiment, which will ever nourish in my mind recollections and regrets; my object not being to say how I loved this child, but to show how worthy he was of being loved.

Many passages requiring notes, I have thought it better not to introduce these notes into the narrative, of which they would have impeded the course, but I have placed them, some at the bottom of the pages; others, I have removed to the end of each volume; yet my hands still remain full of official documents, almost all of them unpublished, which, if need were, would confirm the scrupulous exactitude of my narrative. Those which I produce, will, I hope, satisfy the reader; he will find there, like me, with the aid of his conscience, infallible inductions, positive evidences, undeniable vouchers. He will see what weight gross and unexplained fallacies can have against the irrefragable documents which I oppose to them; and he will think, I also hope, that I supply to history, not only the certitude, but also the material, authentic proof that the Dauphin of France, son of Louis XVI., really died within the Temple.

Too many royal heads have been given to the tempest, on the high roads of Europe: let us leave the peace of their tomb to those whom God has been pleased o save from exile, even though by death.

Let it not be supposed that I have dug amongst these ruins, or raised up the stones of this edifice, to supply fuel for the passions of the day; still less do I pretend to plead a cause Party spirit should grow gentle when it approaches the tomb of kings; it should be extinct over the cradle of an infant. I trust that the impulses of my heart, have never blinded my reason. I have remembered that the guilty were dead, that they had appeared before the justice-seat of God; I have remembered also, the pardon that descended from the scaffold of a King, and from that of a Queen, and of the magnanimous amnesty of one of the orphans of the Temple.

So far as I could, I have stated the facts without judging them; I have suppressed in myself all the feelings of indignation that crowded the heart at the aspect of so much cruelty conspiring against innocence, of so much violence against feebleness. I will leave the facts to speak for themselves; those facts speak so loud that it needs not for me to add anything by the futile murmur of my opinion. It is not for me to accuse, or to curse; I will relate the things, and display the men.

This is not a funeral oration, not a lamentation issuing from the fatal tower, not an invective hurled against the crimes of the revolution; it is a history, in all the simplicity of its recitals, in all the candour of its facts and its frankness.

IV.

We have little to say as to the plan and arrangement of this work. The life of the Dauphin of France, afterwards Louis XVII., is its centre and its unity. The narrative begins and ends with that.

Around the life and sufferings of this young and unfortunate prince, are developed, as a first and living girdle, the trials, the fall, the misfortunes, the captivity, and the hapless end of the other members of the royal family.

The general events of the revolution press around this inner zone; the scene changes often; the drama is opened at Versailles,—is transferred to the Tuileries after the 5th and 6th of October,—quits the Tuileries for Varennes,—returns to the Tuileries for the terrible days of the 20th June and 10th August,—traverses, for an instant, the hall of the National Assembly,—and enters the Temple, where the catastrophe is accomplished.

The first volume contains the facts represented by these two words, which sum up a long history: *Versailles and the Temple.*

It commences with the recital of the last days spent by the royal family at Versailles; it closes with the first period of the abode of the royal family at the prison of the Temple, taking the reader to the foot of the scaffold of Louis XVI.

The second volume opens after the death of the King, that is to say, with the reign of Louis XVII., hapless reign, that had for its throne, a truckle-bed, for its palace a prison, and knew no other crown than that of martyrdom.

The void expands by degrees around him: first of all, he has lost the King his father.

Soon comes the execution of the Queen.

Then begin those indescribable days, which, nevertheless, we have undertaken to narrate, in which the good King Louis XVI., who had hitherto to his life's end, been his son's preceptor, is succeeded, in the conduct of that education, by Simon the cobbler, as he had for heirs in the government of France, Marat, Danton, and Robespierre.

Then, the chapters are divided in the names of the keepers into whose hands successively passed this poor life, fading, afar from the pure air and rays of the sun, in the heavy atmosphere of prison.

Simon from the 3rd July, 1793 to 30 Nivôse, year II. (19th January, 1794).

After Simon, an interregnum in the gaol, and from the 19th January to the 27th July, 1794, more than six months of lugubrious solitude, and most cruel abandonment.

Then Laurent, to 10th Thermidor, year II. (28th July, 1794).

Gomin, assistant to Laurent, from 18th Brumaire, year III. (8th November, 1794), to 9th Germinal, year III. (29th March, 1795).

Lasne, assistant to Gomin, from 11th Germinal, year III (31st March, 1795,) to the close.

Then come the last illness, the agony, and the death.

The first volume may, as we have said, be summed up in two words, *from Versailles to the Temple.*

Two words again suffice to sum up the second volume, *from the Temple to the Tomb.*

Yet, after having told by what gate, at once sad and sacred, all those that had entered the Temple quitted it, we should deem ourselves failing in our mission, and frustrating the just expectations of the reader, if, in a third portion, we were to omit the story derived from new and special documents, how Marie Thérèse of France, she alone of all its victims whom the Temple restored alive, quitted it, leaving behind her so many dear and mournful recollections.

Then, as the interest is communicated from the drama to the theatre, or, to speak more correctly, as the sacrifice consecrates the altar; after having related how the captivity of all the prisoners of the Temple terminated, it will remain for us to say, in a very few words, how the prison itself came to its end; for the downfall of the Temple is connected with the history of the royal captivity. There were men of the revolution, upon whom the shadow of that edifice fell as a reproach, and who resolved its destruction. As often happens at the close of long processes, men wish to get rid of a witness who has seen too much, and spoken too loud

The end of the Temple, after the end of Louis XVII., will close the narrative of this lamentable legend, wherein all perishes, even the monument which had afforded as a theatre its sombre walls and its lugubrious towers.

LOUIS THE SEVENTEENTH.

BOOK FIRST.

VERSAILLES.

27TH MARCH, 1785—6TH OCTOBER, 1789.

Birth and baptism of the Duke of Normandy—Joy of the people—Popularity of Louis XVI.—His virtues, his qualities, and his defects—Letter to the Duke de la Vrillière—Suppression of abuses—Glance at the position of matters—The churching of the Queen—Journey to Cherbourg—Death of the eldest son of Louis XVI.—The Duke of Normandy assumes the title of Dauphin—Description of him—Anecdotes—The King and Queen superintend the education of their son—The young prince's taste for flowers—His love for his mother—His answer to a courtier—A visit that he received—The revolution announces itself—The day of the 14th July—Madame de Tourzel, governess of the royal children—Portrait of the Queen—The days of the 5th and 6th October.

LOUIS CHARLES of France and Bourbon, second son of Louis XVI., King of France, and Marie Antoinette Josèphe Jeanne of Lorraine, Archduchess of Austria and Queen of France, was born at the château of Versailles, on the 27th March, 1785, at five minutes before seven in the evening.

Contrary to the ancient usage which delayed for some years the baptism of the royal children of France, he was baptised on the very day of his birth, at half-past eight, by the Cardinal de Rohan, Bishop of Strasbourg, grand almoner, and the Abbé Brocquevielle, vicar of Versailles. He had for his godfather Louis Stanislas Xavier, Count de Provence, Monsieur, the King's brother, and for his godmother, Marie Charlotte

Louise of Lorraine, Archduchess of Austria, Queen of the Two Sicilies, represented by Madame Elizabeth.*

He received the title of Duke of Normandy, which no son of France had borne since the fourth son of Charles VII. The King, followed by all the court, went to the chapel of the château, where *Te Deum* was sung. After the ceremony, M. de Calonne, minister of finance and grand treasurer, brought to the new-born prince the insignia of the order of the Holy Ghost.

Towards nine o'clock, beautiful fireworks were displayed on the Place d'Armes, in the presence of the King and all the court.

Louis XVI. then directed the grand master of the ceremonies to go and inform his good town of Paris that God had accorded him a second son. Lettres de cachet were transmitted, according to custom, to all the leading personages in the church, in the army, and in the parliament. Joy spread itself from one end of the great city to the other, and soon from one end of the great kingdom to the other. The cannon of the Bastille responded to the cannon of the Invalides. Everywhere spontaneous illuminations, the ringing of bells, the acclamations of the people, manifested the love of France for a king who, in the flower of his youth, found his happiness in the happiness of the people.

Never, in fact, had monarch ascended the throne with intentions more pure and upright than those of Louis XVI. He had not merely the taste, his was a passion, for goodness. It was with him an inexpressible satisfaction to feel himself beloved by his people, a cruel suffering to see that love diminishing. Hence the so deserved popularity that he enjoyed at the commencement of his reign. He had proceeded at once to the measures which he himself deemed the best calculated to obtain that affection, and to those which others suggested with a view to the same end; and it was not simply without hesitation, it was with joy and delight, that he reformed the abuses which he discovered, or which were pointed out to him,

* See Appendix.

Versailles ce 26 7bre 1774.

Par une disposition du feu Roy, dans le bail des Fermes, les Fermiers Generaux sont tenus de payer au Controleur general 50000 lt par année de leur bail, M. l'abbé Terray s'est fait payer par année le pot de vin du dernier bail, et ce n'est pas sans indignation que j'ai appris, qu'il s'etoit fait payer, par une ordonnance au porteur du 23 Janvier dernier, 300000 lt pour le bail qui commencera au 1er Octobre prochain, Je vous ecrit Monsieur pour que vous leur mandiez de ma part de les faire reporter au Tresor Royal n'ayant rien a y pretendre et ce le plustost possible.

Louis

A Monsieur le Duc de la Vrilliere.

even where the suppression of those abuses exhausted his exchequer, and lessened the splendour of his throne.

He was more especially indignant against those peculations, or that misconduct, which, by impoverishing the public treasury, augmented the already heavy burdens of the people; and one of his first proceedings, after his accession, was to command the reparation of an act of this class, by writing to the Duke de la Vrillière a letter to that effect.*

France loudly applauded this vigilant probity. She hailed at once useful reform—the abolition of personal serfdom within the royal domain—the substitution for the *corvée*, or compulsory highway labour, of a general rate, to which the King required that his own domains should be subjected equally with the rest of the kingdom—the imposts that weighed down agriculture diminished by a prince who had towards the labouring population the affection of Henry IV.—torture expunged from the code—civil rights restored to the Protestants—the port of Cherbourg opened on the coast towards England, and that of Port Vendres on the coast towards Spain—the fleets of France unfolding on the waves once more, with distinction, the flag of Duquesne, of Duguay-Trouin, of Jean Bart; and young America, springing forth to independence under the shadow of the old *fleur-de-lys* standard. The people then, full of enthusiasm for a king whose greatest consolation it was to alleviate their sufferings, ran to inscribe on the pedestal of the statue of Henry IV., "*Redivivus*," while the most influential voices of Europe announced for the nascent reign mighty destinies.

"Versailles, 26th Sept., 1774.

* "By an order of the late king, respecting the leases of farms, the chief farmers are obliged to pay yearly 50,000 livres to the comptroller-general, according to their leases. M. the Abbé Terray having made the premium of the last lease payable yearly, it was not without displeasure that I heard he had obtained, on the 23rd January last, by an *ordonnance au porteur* (cheque to be paid to the bearer), 300,000 livres on account of the lease commencing on the 1st October next. I write to you, Monsieur, that you may announce to him, on my part, that he return it to the Royal Treasury as soon as possible, having nothing there to claim. (Signed) "LOUIS."

"To M. the Duke de la Vrillière."

Yet he who should have confronted the endowments, the character, and the spirit which the King had received from Heaven, with the wants, the aspirations, and, above all, with the difficulties and vices of the time, would have seen in the future grave complications. Louis XVI. was a prince profoundly honest, thoroughly attached to his duties, of a mind enlightened, but not audacious, and of a temperament, strong in the presence of misfortune, but the passive courage of which, ready to accept peril, was not combined with that active courage which surmounts it. He had accurate perception, but a distrust of himself which neutralised the justness of perception that God had bestowed on him. Brought up remote from public business during the reign of his grandfather, Louis XV., he was impressed with a profound sense of his inexperience. He would have been an admirable king to exercise, in tranquil times, under laws long established, a power wisely limited and regulated by uncontested institutions; for he had a thorough appreciation of and taste for the good, and was one of those men with whom there is but one difficulty—that of knowing their duty; for, once knowing it, they perform it. But he was in a position where his qualities were destined to be scarcely less fatal to him than his defects, for the position was one which demanded both qualities and defects of precisely the contrary character to those which he possessed.

It was an age of renovation and change, prepared by the current of the philosophical ideas of the entire eighteenth century. What was more dangerous still, the spirit of the times was at once innovating and theoretical by reason of the long suspension of the States-general, which had left the nation a stranger to its own affairs. Men only saw the end without perceiving the difficulty of the means; and, not seeing the difficulty, they thought everything possible.

The very bodies which, by their nature, seemed destined to moderate the movement,—the nobility, and a great portion of the clergy,—were deeply impressed with the new ideas; so that the counterpoise was wanting to this political rationalism, which passed not only abuses, but institutions themselves, through the sieve of their free examination.

The intellectual movement at Paris moved the world. The echoes of Europe and of America responded to the voice of French philosophy.

More daring, yet less wise than Montesquieu, Beccaria attacked in Milan the vicious forms of the old legislation.

Alfieri at Florence, Schiller at Weimar, became the Tyrteis of their country.

Chatham, in the English parliament, inaugurated modern policy.

Philosophy had illuminated with a dubious but brilliant light all the summits of society. Rousseau, Diderot, Helvétius, Voltaire, dangerous apostles, had filled the world with their disciples. The generality of the movement augmented its intensity.

All imaginations were on fire, and there was in all minds an ardent aspiration for the remodelling of social order. It was observed in the spirit of the sages, in the instincts of the people ; and men discerned in the air those certain signs which announce great changes. There was in Europe no superior spirit that belonged to the past. A few mediocrities kept their ground motionless, under the shade of the old institutions.

The torrent of grievances which had swollen during centuries was about to burst its banks. 1789 issued from the bosom of France ; a revolution sprung from the manners, ideas, hopes, and illusions of all !

To guide this movement to its legitimate good, avoiding the rocks scattered along its path, and to prevent it from passing beyond that goal, required a mind far-sighted and prompt in its decisions, with a strong will, a vigorous hand either to innovate, notwithstanding imprudent resistance, or to stay innovation within reasonable limits, despite all impulsion ; and even then it is not certain that, with all these qualities, anyone would have succeeded, so great were the difficulties, so intoxicated were men's minds, so corrupt, let us add, were their hearts.

But Louis XVI. had not one of the qualities that the circumstances demanded. Too pure to understand the wicked perversity of men, too feeble to dominate them, he had benevolence without will, courage without decision.

Like a too fond father, unhappy at having to scold his child, he regarded with profound charity the vices and ambitions which crawled along at his feet. He was well educated, but one science was wanting, that science most needful to him—the science of government. Virtuous, he feared not calumny, for he felt at the bottom of his heart, in the testimony of his intentions, the justification of his actions. That candour of conscience itself was fated to turn against him; no life is above calumny: intrigues and pamphlets were about to heap around him all kinds of vulgar and paltry hostilities, capable of making a giant reel. His heart was firm, but his mind was timid; so that, instead of foreseeing and directing events, he followed them, which inevitably tended to bring him to ruin, for ideas led events to the attack of the principles on which French society had heretofore reposed—hereditary succession, the royal sovereignty, religion.

To complete his misfortune, Louis XVI. with so many virtues, had two defects of character dangerous at all times, but mortal at the period wherein God had created him. The first of these was, that he was unable to resist, for any length of time, a movement of opinion; instead of making it serve him, as sailors make use of the wind, to advance in a previously determined direction, he soon came to serve it; it was no longer merely a motive force which he employed for his own purposes, it was his compass. The second was, that he constantly sacrificed his own ideas, which were for the most part sound and just, to those of the persons who were presented to him as able men. It was thus that he successively permitted Turgot, Brienne, Carnot, Necker, &c., to experimentalize with their ideas, though he had himself the most legitimate doubts as to the practical efficacy of their systems. This distrust of himself necessarily rendered his policy the sport of adventurous experiments, and of reactions still more dangerous than the experiments themselves. One illustration will suffice to depict this turn of his mind and his heart. On his accession to the throne, Louis XVI. recalled the old parliaments which the chancellor Maupeou had dissolved; he fully comprehended the inconveniences that would arise from this recall, but he replied to one of his ministers, a friend of the Dauphin, his father, who reminded him of them: "I know it all very well, my dear Du Muy, but I will and must, first of all, make myself beloved by my people." This mode of reasoning, and especially of acting, was calculated to carry a man very far indeed, and far indeed did it carry Louis XVI. at a time when the wind of innovation had set in, and when the people were successively attaching their hopes to every fresh chimera. From the recall of the parliaments, it led him to the convocation of the notables; from the convocation of the notables, to the assembling of the States-general, to the doubling of the Tiers Etat, to the confusion of orders, to the Constituent Assembly, to the 15th July, to the 5th and 6th October, and lastly, step by step, to the fatal term.

Already the new ideas were beginning to ferment. Nine days after the birth of the Duke of Normandy (5th April, 1785), there was read at the Royal Academy of Inscriptions and Belles Lettres a memoir on the narrative, by the ancient and modern historians, of the accession of Hugh Capet to the throne. The author seemed to have proposed to himself to prove that Hugh received the crown by the free consent of the nation. This theme was elaborated by the encyclopedists, through whose utopias the possibility of a fourth dynasty was perceptible. But these ideas of innovation which fermented in the bosom of the lettered world, had not descended into the street: royalty tranquilly preserved its happy course beneath a cloudless sky. On the 24th May, Marie Antoinette came to Paris to thank God for her confinement, and the people for their affection. She there received for herself and her infant the benedictions of God and the acclamations of the people.

These acclamations accompanied the King even still more emphatically in a journey which next year (21st June, 1786), he made to Cherbourg, to visit the immense works he had ordered in that military port, destined to look in the face a great people, at that time our enemy. Louis XVI. had drawn out a detailed plan of the route he intended to pursue, exhibiting the châteaux and principal habitations of the notables, with, in each case, an indication of the name of the individual and of the services which he had rendered to the public. The worthy people who had occasion to approach him were amazed to find that the King knew not only their names, but the particulars of their life and their family associations. Their enthusiasm was augmented still more by the manifest astonishment of the courtiers. Louis XVI. accordingly brought back from this journey gentle emotions, which he frequently afterwards recalled, and applauded himself for having given to the second of his sons the name of that fine province. "My little Norman," he would often say, as he pressed the boy in his arms, "thy name will bring thee happiness."

We have seen under what auspices that existence opened, which seemed marked out for such high and such happy destinies. The future soon held out to him still more magnificent promises. The Dauphin (Louis Joseph Xavier François), born at Versailles on the 22nd October, 1781, died at Meudon, on Thursday, 4th June, 1789. He was a charming child, who announced the finest qualities of heart and head. The whole kingdom regretted him. The States-general, in session for the last month, became the interpreters of the public grief. In the sitting of the same day, the Tiers Etat directed the speaker to present to their majesties the expression of the profound affliction with which the death of the Dauphin had

Letter from Madame Elizabeth to "Bombelle."

(In order to preserve the style of the original, this letter has been translated literally, which will account for the inaccuracies.)

This 25th June, 1787.

"Your relations will have informed you that sophia died the day after I wrote to you, the poor little creature had a thousand reasons for dying, and nothing could have saved it; I think it a consolation. My niece has been charming; she has evinced an extraordinary degree of feeling for her age, and which is very natural, her poor little sister is very happy, she has escaped every peril, my indolence would have been gratified if, younger, I had shared her fate, to console myself for it I have nursed her with great care, hoping that she would pray for me: I count upon it much. If you knew how pretty she was when dying, it is incredible the very evening before she was white and rosy, not thin, in a word—charming; if you had seen her you would have become attached to her; as for me, though I knew her but little, I was truly sorry, and I almost weep when I think of her; your sister has been all that one could desire, and everybody praises her, she has been very much fatigued, and your poor mother also; but all is well. I wish it were the same with your cough, be sure and keep the promise you made me to take care of yourself, I ask it of you as a favour my dear heart. Think much of your friends, that will give courage to think of yourself; friendship, you see, my dear Bombelle, is a second life, which supports us in this lower world. The portrait of M. de fourqueuse is striking. The council is named; it is the council of state and Messrs. dormesor, and de lambert, the four comptrollers of finance, Messrs. de forges, de la boulaie, blondel, de la milliere or la miniere I don't know his name well, Messrs. de nivernois et and malserbe, minister of state, this latter is terribly changed since you saw him; M. de Briene has the command of Bordeaux, M. de caraman at provence, and M. de Bouillé at metz. If I have already told you all this news or you have learned it from other quarters, you will skip all that. Monsieur and the Count d'artois went to the parliament on friday, and to-day, to have the edicts registered, several are registered, others for which they have named commissioners. The sacrifice I proposed to make, as regards my horses, has not been accepted. I cannot conceal from you that that has much pleased me, and so much the more as I am going to the hunt at rambouillet to-morrow with the Duchess de duvas; the Queen will come there to supper, that is another great pleasure for me, for she is very kind to me at this moment, we are to go together to st. cyr, which she calls my bower, she calls Montreuil my little trianon. I accompanied her to hers the other day without any suite, and she paid me every possible attention, she had prepared one of those surprises in which she excels, but we were occupied mostly there in weeping over the death of my poor little niece.

"I am very glad that you are a little disabused concerning your hero, he is very far from being worthy of your sentiment. They do well, very well, to spoil Bitche: in the first place you can do nothing in it; you know very well that he must be an indifferent subject; it cannot be otherwise, for I love him; and you know it is the clearest proof that can be given. How is constance? Does the physician still give hope? Adieu my little dear, I have been interrupted, which makes me conclude. I embrace you, and love you with all my heart.

"ELISABETH MARIE."

Superscribed "For Bombelle."

apelle Montreuil mon petit trianon. que été un sun sans aucune suitte ces jours derniés avec elle et il ny a pas dattention quélle ne ny est montrée, elle y avoit fait preparé une de ces surprise dans quoi elle excelle, mais ceque nous y avons fait le plus cést de pleurés sur la mort de ma pauvre petite niece.

je suis bien aise que tu revienne un peu sur le compte de ton heros, il est loin d'être digne de ton sentiment. on fait bien et tres bien, de gater Bitche, d'abort tu ny peut rien, tu sais bien qu'il doit être mediocre sujet, cela est impossible autrement parceque je l'aime, et tu sais que c'est la preuve la plus claire que l'on en puisse donner.

comment va constance, le medecin donne t'il toujour de l'esperance. adieu ma petite jai été interrompue ce qui me fait finir je tembrasse, et t'aime de tout mon coeur. Elisabeth Marie

Pour Bombelle

tout monde. le portrait de Mr de fourqueux est frapant le conseil est nomé, c'est celui d'état et Mrs dormesson, et de lambert, les postes intendans de finances Mrs de forges, de la boulaie, blondel, et de lamilliere ou luminiere, je ne sais pas bien son nom, Mrs de nivernois et de malserbe ministre d'état, ce dernier est terriblement changés depuis que tu ne la vue; Mr de Brienne a le comandement de Bordeaux, Mr de caraman provence, et Mr de Bouillé a metz si je tai deja dit toutes ces nouvelles ou que tu les sache d'autre part, tu sautera tout cela. Mr et le Cte d'artois ont été au parlement vendredi, et aujourd'hui, pour faire enregistrés les édits, il y en a plusieurs qui le sont, d'autre pour lesquelles on a nomées des commissaires. l'on a point acceptés le sacrifice que j'avois proposé de faire pour mes chevaux, je ne puis te dissimuler que cela m'a fait un vrais plaisir, et j'en jouis d'autant plus, que je vais demain a la chasse a rambouillet avec la Dsse de duras, la Reine y viendra soupés, cela me fait un tres grand plaisir, car elle est fort bien pour moi en ce moment, nous devons allés ensemble a St cyr qu'elle apelle mon berceau, elle

ce 25 juin 1787

tes parents t'auront mandés que sophie est morte le lendemain que je t'ai écrit, la pauvre petite avoit mille raison pour mourire et rien n'auroit pue la sauvez je trouve que c'est une consolation; Ma nièce a été charmante, elle a montrée une sensibilitée extraordinaire pour son age, et qui étoit bien naturel, sa pauvre petite soeur est bien heureuse, elle a échapée a tous les perils, ma paresse se seroit très bien trouvées de partagés, plus jeune son sort, pour m'en consoler je l'ai bien soignés, esperant qu'elle prieroit pour moi, j'y compte beaucoup; si tu sçavois comme elle etois jolie en mourant, c'est incroyable la veille encore elle étoit blanche et couleur de rose, point maigrie, enfin charmante, si tu l'avoit vue tu t'y serois attachée, pour moi quoique je l'aie peu connue, j'ai été vraiment fachée, et je suis presque atendrie lorsque j'y pense, ta soeur a été parfaite, et tout le monde en a fait l'éloge, elle a été bien fatiguée et ta pauvre mere aussi, mais tout cela va bien. je voudrais qu'il en fut autant de ta tante, tiens bien la parole que tu me donne de te menagés je te la demande en grace mon coeur, pense beaucoup a tes amis cela te donnera le courage de t'occupés de toi, l'amitié vois tu ma chere Bombelle, est une seconde vie qui nous soutient en ce penetrated the assembly; and the nobles, on the motion of the Duke de Chatelet, resolved in like manner, by a unanimous vote, to send a deputation to the King and Queen, to declare their deep sympathy with their majesties' grief.

In the sitting of the Tiers Etat next day, Bailly proposed that they should go and sprinkle holy water on the body of the young prince, and the motion was unanimously agreed to. Yet, according to several contemporaries, whose testimony is of great weight—among others, M. Ferrand in his "*Eloge de Madame Elizabeth*"—the Tiers Etat manifested, on the very occasion of this death, the extent of the pretensions which they entertained. Two hours after the loss of his son, Louis XVI., who had shut himself up in his closet that he might weep freely, was informed that the speaker of the Tiers Etat insisted upon coming in, though so perfectly aware of the death of the young prince. The King exclaimed: "There are, then, no fathers in the Chamber of the Tiers Etat!" and ordered him to be admitted.

Would it not appear as though there was in the date of the birth and of the death of this prince, destined for the throne, something prophetic and fatal? He was born on the 22nd October, 1781; the celebration of his baptism was postponed till the 21st January of the following year; the old States-general, in desuetude since the time of Richelieu, prefaced their labours by attending the obsequies of the heir of the monarchy, who seemed thus to withdraw into the tomb, in order to avoid a lamentable destiny.

Already, in 1787, the Queen had lost a female infant—Sophie Hélène Béatrix of France, born at Versailles, 9th July, 1786—and the letter of Madame Elizabeth, reproduced in this volume, manifests how deeply this loss had been felt by the royal family.

The death of these two children was the first link in the chain of afflictions reserved for the royal house. The infancy of the Duke of Normandy had, up to the month of June, 1789, passed, as it were, unheeded; the death of his elder brother then directed upon him the eyes and the hopes of France, and imposed on him that title of Dauphin, which subjects a prince to the apprenticeship and obligations of future royalty. But he was as yet too young to comprehend how deeply he had to regret his brother. Happy age! He could not yet appreciate the royal and terrible heritage to which this loss, according to all appearance, was to condemn him, in a distant future; and of all the fraternal inheritance, his infantile fancy only apprehended the immediate possession of a pretty little dog, which, after having belonged to the Dauphin, now came to him, in his turn, and which answered to the name of Moufflet.

Louis XVI., who distributed his affections equally among his children, bestowed upon the Duke of Normandy that especial, if not exceptional interest, which a king owes to him whose birth calls him to occupy, after himself, the supreme rank. The Queen, on her part, applied to him her most attentive, her most assiduous care; determined, as she was, to be the teacher, as well as the mother of her son.

He was at this time rather more than four years old. His frame was well-shaped and graceful; his forehead broad and open, his eyebrows arched; his large, blue eyes, fringed with long chestnut lashes, were of an angelic beauty, beyond my powers of description; his complexion, dazzlingly fair, was blended with a brilliant bloom; his hair, dark chestnut, curled naturally and fell in thick ringlets on his shoulders; he had the vermillion mouth of his mother, and, like her, a small dimple on the chin. His physiognomy, at once noble and gentle, recalled the dignity of Marie Antoinette, the amiability of Louis XVI. All his movements were full of grace and vivacity; there was in his manners, in his mien, an exquisite distinction, a sort of childish fondness which charmed all who approached him. His mouth never opened but to give utterance to the most amiable *naïvetés*. You admired him when you saw him, you loved him after you had heard him speak. Children and princes are generally full of themselves; but this prince had the selfishness neither of princes nor of children, who are kings in their own way. He always thought, not of himself, but of others; he was tender towards those who loved him, attentive to those who spoke to him, conciliatory towards those who visited him, polite to every one. These excellent qualities were tempered, however, by a singular vivacity and impatience. He ill-endured the rule of the female attendants to whose charge he was committed, and combatted, with the utmost vigour of his age, the rule established as to the hours of his rising and his going to rest; his indocility, however, at once disappeared on the approach of his mother.

The reason of this was, that he found in her the ascendancy of authority, as well as the influence of affection. He had for her, accordingly, at once love and respect. That exalted and tender tutoress knew how to fashion his character, and to correct his faults without inflicting pain. Having undertaken the management of his instruction, previous to his passing under the care of preceptors, there were no means to which she did not have recourse for the purpose of bringing within his reach the elements of early knowledge. First lessons in reading having nothing in themselves attractive, she did not present them to him as a serious duty; she applied herself to render them an object of taste and desire. She read, or had read to him, those simple tales, those artless moralities, which the genius of La Fontaine, the talent of Perrault and Berquin have placed within the scope of childhood; it was in the form of recreation that his first lessons came to him. These readings developed the sense and sagacity of the young pupil; he listened with the utmost attention, and his animated physiognomy reflected all the varying incidents of the littte drama presented to his notice. Expressions of more or less vivid admiration would escape him at points which he clearly understood, and appreciated as admirable; at passages which he comprehended but indistinctly or not at all, his forehead would be clouded with reverie, his eyes express hesitation; and then would follow a hundred questions, characterised by the most charming *naiveté*, original remarks, and ingenious reflections that repeatedly surprised his auditors, and inspired them with the loftiest and most gratifying idea of the intellectual development of the royal child.

The sensibility of his heart, the delicacy of his soul, corresponded with the perspicuity of his mind, the nobleness of his character. After the familiar conversations which always followed these readings, the Queen would generally place herself at the piano or harp, and that which she had been doing in order to create within her son a taste for reading, she would now do to inspire him with a taste for music; she would play to him little expressive airs which she had learned or composed for him, and it was manifest from the movements of the child's head, and his radiant features, that his ears and his soul were alike open to the charm of harmony. One evening, at St. Cloud, his mother was singing, accompanying herself, the melody in the "*Ami des Enfants:*"

"Dors, mon enfant, clos ta paupière,
Tes cris me déchirent le cœur;
Dors, mon enfant, ta pauvre mère
A bien assez de sa douleur."

This couplet, and the words, "Your poor mother," sung with exquisite expression, as they had been, vividly moved the heart of the Dauphin, who, silent and motionless, in his little arm-chair, was all eyes and ears beside the piano. Madame Elizabeth, who was present, surprised to see him so quiet, said laughingly, "By my faith, there's Charles asleep." At once raising his head, he exclaimed with an agitated voice, "Ah, my dear aunt, could any one sleep when mamma is singing?"

There was a boy whose precocious qualities and heroic death*

* This expression will not appear exaggerated to those who know with what patience, with what grandeur of soul, this unhappy child, who was to

had left in the memory of the royal family, and of France, a memento and a sorrow of which the Marquis de Pompignan had rendered himself at once the interpreter and the consoler by writing, with touching simplicity, "The Life of the Duke of Burgundy, son of the Grand Dauphin, and eldest brother of Louis XVI."

It was in this book, consecrated to the praises of a child who died at nine years old, after sufferings of the most painful kind, supported by extraordinary courage, that Louis Charles learned to read. Strange coincidence! Louis XVI., when a young man, had, as a study of the English language, translated the life of Charles I., and the Dauphin, a child, had before him, as an introduction to reading, the life of the last Duke of Burgundy! It was thus that, in the study of the past, the future, as in a dismal mirage, was reflected to both father and son.

This book was not only with Louis Charles matter for reading, it was also matter for emulation. The ingenious conversation and the early virtues of the youthful uncle were vividly appreciated by the youthful nephew. Equally excited by head and heart to the desire to imitate him, he inquired whether he resembled him at all in face; and when the portrait of the young Duke was given to him, exceedingly well painted on a bon-bon box, he contemplated it for some time, with a sort of astonishment, and then kissing it with an air of grave reverie, said: "How could my little uncle, so young, have managed to acquire so much knowledge, so much wisdom?"

Louis XVI., contrary to established custom, formed no household for his son; he feared that, in surrounding him with a number of officers, gentlemen, and domestics, he might

serve as a model for him whose life we are now sketching, supported unprecedented sufferings. It is in speaking of him that a contemporary says, "A long illness developed still more his rare qualities; the result of that cruel malady deprived France of him, and at nine years old he died the death of a hero."—*Portrait de feu Monseigneur le Dauphin.* Paris, 1766.

expose him to the maleficial influences of flattery. It was his desire that everything about the young prince should be such as should only inspire him with the love of virtue and glory.

The heir of the throne had for his governess the Duchess de Polignac, the particular friend of the Queen; and for his preceptor, the Abbé Devaux, who, for several years past, had been instructing Madame Royale, his sister, in religion, history, reading, mythology, and geography. But while giving a preceptor to his son, it may be said that Louis XVI. reserved to himself the pleasing functions of chief tutor, for it was, throughout, to be a plan traced by himself, that was to be exactly pursued in this so important education. In assuming this elevated tutorage, the King said to the Queen: "It is to second you that I occupy myself with our child; for I have not the pretension that I can in any way do better than you have done thus far. I shall esteem myself happy if my efforts at all correspond to your own, and if I make Charles one day fulfil all the promises which he has given under your direction." In this respect, at least, the King might esteem himself happy, for never had the affection of a father, the pride of a mother, settled on a little head more worthy of both the one and the other.

"The Dauphin," says the virtuous Hue, in his *Dernieres Années de Louis XVI.*, "had received from Heaven a celestial countenance, a precocious capacity, a feeling heart, the germ of the greatest qualities. In his tenderest years this prince excited admiration by the grace and shrewdness of his repartees. How many instances might I not cite of this.

"One day, while studying his lesson, he began to whistle, or, rather, to hiss; he was reprimanded for it, and when the Queen came, she also scolded him. 'Mamma,' replied he, 'I was saying my lesson so ill, that I hissed myself.' Another day, in the garden of Bagatelle, carried away by his vivacity, he was about to dash through a bush of rose-trees. I hastened to him: 'Monseigneur,' I said, holding him back, 'one of those thorns might wound your face, or even destroy your eye-sight.' He turned round, and said to me, with an air equally noble and decided, 'Thorny ways lead to glory.'"

Informed by M. Hue of this reply, the Queen immediately sent for the Dauphin, and said to him: "My son, you have cited a maxim perfectly true in itself, but which you have not applied correctly. There is no glory in endangering your eyes, merely for the pleasure of running about and playing. To destroy a pernicious animal, to rescue a person from peril, to expose one's own life in order to save that of another person, that may be called glory; but what you were going to do is simply heedlessness and imprudence. Before you talk of glory, my dear, wait till you are old enough to read the history of your ancestors, and of the French heroes, such as Du Guesclin, Bayard, Turenne, D'Assas, and many others, who defended France and our crown at the price of their blood." Given with all the fervour of tenderness, with the authority of reason, this grave lesson made a profound impression on the heart of the young prince, who at first blushed, and then, seizing his mother's hand, impressed a kiss upon it, saying, with a graceful pertinence, "Well, dear mamma, I will make it my glory to follow your counsels and to obey you."

Never did child more tenderly love his mother, and there is no proof of affection of which he did not avail himself. He had remarked that she was fond of flowers; and every morning his first occupation was to run, simply with a *femme de chambre* and the faithful Moufflet, into the gardens of Versailles, and gather a bouquet, which he would place upon the Queen's toilette-table, before she had risen. Every day there was a fresh harvest of flowers, and every day the happy mother was enabled to see that the first act of her son was for her, as well as his first prayer. When unfavourable weather prevented him from going out, and consequently from gathering his bouquet, he would say with vexation, "I am displeased with myself; I have not this morning earned mamma's first kiss."

The King observed, with sincere happiness and tender solicitude, the affectionate disposition of his son, and his pious veneration for his mother. He took pleasure in superintending his exercises; he examined his copy-books; he questioned him constantly; he observed him at his games, in order the more thoroughly to appreciate his tastes and his character. He rejoiced to find in him inclinations so gentle and so pure, so well calculated to develope his corporal strength; and it was to cultivate in him this taste and to encourage these tendencies, that he assigned to his especial use a plot of ground in front of the royal apartments, on the terrace of the château, and provided him with a rake, a spade, a watering-pot, and other gardening implements.

It was here that the prince passed all his leisure moments in the intervals of his lessons; it was his pride to be the only gardener of his little *parterre*, which was among the best kept in the park. "My father gave me this garden; he did so, that I might take charge of it myself," said he, one day. Then he added, after a brief pause, and with a charming air: "But I am only the farmer; the produce is for mamma." It was for him a great delight to watch the growth and the blossoming of the shrubs he had tended and watered; and his morning bouquets seemed to him all the prettier after he came to form them with flowers grown in his own domain. A lord of the court, seeing him one day digging his border with such energy that the perspiration rolled down his cheeks, said to him: "You are very simple to fatigue yourself in this manner, Monseigneur; why do you not speak to one of the gardeners; he would finish the work for you in a few minutes?" "It is very possible," replied the boy, "but these flowers I must and will grow myself; they would be less agreeable to mamma, were they cultivated by any one else."

The engaging manner, and the precocious intellect of the Dauphin, became known beyond the precincts of the court;

and there were spread abroad many anecdotes of the amiable young prince which excited a general desire to see and know him. A schoolmistress, who had a noted establishment at Paris, came one day for this purpose to St. Cloud, and solicited from a lady of the court, with whom she was acquainted, permission to pay her respects to the Dauphin, with three of her pupils who accompanied her. The Queen instantly granted this favour, and to enhance its value, proffered to receive the schoolmistress and her pupils herself, and present them to her son. The three young ladies and their mistress trembled with emotion, but the imposing dignity of the Queen attired itself in gentle affability, in order to reassure them. Before withdrawing, the schoolmistress requested, for her pupils, permission to kiss the hand of the royal infant; the latter at once met the wish with a grace all the more charming that it seemed embarrassed and almost humiliated by the concession. Then, having withdrawn his little hand which the three girls had kissed, he advanced, of his own accord, to their mistress, who was standing respectfully apart, and with an exquisite discrimination of the age and the quality of the individuals, said to her, raising his radiant brow: "And you, Madame, kiss me on the forehead."

If this interview, these words, convey an idea of the young prince's tact, the following anecdote will exhibit his sense of justice. He had, in one of his walks, carried off a flute belonging to a page in attendance upon him, and roguishly hidden it in a yew tree on the terrace. Informed of this little trick, the Queen thought it necessary to punish the author, not this time in his own person, but in that of an object of his affection; poor Moufflet bore the brunt of its master's roguery; the companion of all his sports, it was treated in this case as his accomplice, and condemned, in his stead, to be placed under arrest. Confined in a dark cupboard, deprived of its liberty, and of the presence of its young master, the poor animal began to scratch at the door, and to growl, cry, and yelp with all its might. Its lamentations pierced the heart of the real culprit, who, full of compassion for his dear dog, went overwhelmed with affliction to the Queen: "But, mamma, it is not Moufflet who did wrong," said he; "it is not Moufflet, therefore, who ought to be punished; pray release him, and I will take his place." The favour was granted, and the young prince, taking the place of the innocent animal, condemned himself to imprisonment, and underwent it for even longer than the prescribed term. Nor was this all: in the solitude of the closet, he reflected upon his conduct, and said to himself, that if his fault was expiated, it was not repaired; and accordingly, the first use he made of his liberty was to go to the garden, take the flute from its concealment, and restore it to his young companion.

One would justly esteem, in the commonest peasant's son, such a mode of thinking and of acting; how much more laudable does it not appear in the son of a King, subjected, notwithstanding the utmost paternal precautions, and by the very force of things, to the flatteries of an obsequious train.

Prophetic alarms soon mingled with the gratulations which saluted the royal cradle; already dark rumours were heard. Nascent convulsions announced sombre events; faults committed, economical theories rashly essayed, imprudences induced by the inexperience of the King, concessions wrested from his weakness, disastrous deaths, tumultuous movements, had dissipated the hopes which had shed a lustre on the opening of his reign. Financial and political difficulties were about to swoop down upon France. Four years before, Louis XVI. had traced out to La Perouse, his route across the ocean; the King and the mariner had bid each other adieu; La Perouse departed for those distant shores, whence he was never to return; the King departed for that ocean of revolutions, whence he, too, was never to return. The eighteenth century had disjointed all the bases of the ancient social order, and had prepared, by daring innovations, the storms which were to signalise its last years.

While the passions were thus agitating the assemblies, and making their way into the streets, the Dauphin, little disturbed by the noise around him, and heeding it only as it seemed to disquiet his mother, tranquilly passed his hours of recreation in his garden, following with the most attentive interest the development of his flowers, and observing, on the evening before, those of which he designed to form the bouquet next morning. One day, in a moment of abstraction, he put some *soucis* (marygolds)* with the other flowers; perceiving them at the moment he was about to present the bouquet, he immediately removed them, saying: "Ah, mamma, you have enough of them elsewhere."

Another day, Louis XVI. having called to him, and said: "You know to-morrow is a grand day, your mamma's birthday; you must prepare an extraordinary bouquet, and you must, moreover, compose for yourself the compliment with which you accompany your gift." "Papa," he replied, "I have a fine *immortelle* (elychrysum) in my garden; it will be at once my gift and my compliment. In presenting it to mamma, I shall say: 'May mamma resemble my flower.'"

Let us now cast a rapid glance beyond the abode and the garden, in which the last happy days of this child were gliding away; for the revolution will soon knock at the gates of the château of his fathers.

On the 17th June, 1789, the deputies of the Tiers Etat, to whom the double representation had been accorded, proclaimed the unity of the States-general, and usurped the title of National Assembly. It is best to grant to political assemblies that which they are disposed to take: the most fatal of all errors, after having refused to them rights which they have achieved, is to commence against them a resistance which you have not the will or the power to carry out. By such a course you reveal to them at once the secret of your ill will and of

* The term also means *cares*, *anxieties*.

their force, and passion then impels them so much the more to abuse the one as they think they perceive everywhere the trace of the other. This was precisely the dangerous path entered upon when Louis XVI., who had essayed to dissolve, after the sitting of the 23rd June, the Assembly of the Tiers Etat, began to give way before the sitting at the *Jeu de Paume.*

On that day, the question between royalty and revolution was mooted: all equilibrium was destroyed between royalty and the Assembly, which was now mistress of the situation, and in which the Tiers Etat, which appreciated at once its force and its injury, had gained a preponderating influence. Thenceforth, there was no progressive, orderly, temperate ameliorations; peaceable and regular reform gave place to revolution. The Assembly was resolved to dominate royalty, and it knew how to effect the object; but in order to exercise this domination, it was necessary to make an appeal to the irregular force of the streets, and, to emancipate itself from authority, to accept the aid, and, ere long, the yoke of the multitude.

Under the influence of this situation, which began to develope itself, France became an arena of gladiators; the intelligence from the provinces daily announced the conflagrations of châteaux and of archives, seditions and assassinations; the effervescence of men's minds was at its height. The King essayed to take some measures of security; he ordered the advance of 10,000 troops, who were distributed between Paris and Versailles; the tribune resounded with the formidable clamours of Mirabeau, and the dismissal of the troops was demanded. On the 11th July, M. Necker quitted the ministry and exiled himself; M. Necker owed his popularity less to useful acts than to innovating words, adapted for flattering the masses; the crown had little sympathy with him, as may well be conceived. Seneca tells us, that "to please princes, one must render them many services, and speak little to them." Necker had done precisely the reverse of this. On the evening of the 12th, the news of his departure circulated:

Paris grew amazed, indignant—the signal for explosion was given—the theatres were deserted—the shops were closed—the cafés were filled—the streets resounded with the hum of many voices—the Palais-royal was crowded—the busts of the Duke d'Orleans and of M. Necker were carried thither in triumph! Camille Desmoulins, then intoxicated with the favours of that revolution which afterwards marched him as one of its victims, distributed green cockades, and was the first to call to arms; the clubs descended into the streets, the tocsin sounded, fire was set to the barriers, everyone was in motion, the howl of fury was raised, all Paris was in a blaze: the revolution was on foot.

The military were displayed, but to no purpose; the soldiers were without order, and would not act; the regiment of Gardes Françaises went over to the insurgents. Sedition grew with its success, it told over its numbers, it adjusted itself; it observed that the green cockade, adopted the evening before, was of the same colour as the livery of the Count d'Artois; it proscribed it, and adopted the tri-coloured riband—blue, red, and white. The people rushed to the Invalides, took possession of the weapons, and marched upon the Bastille (14th of July, 1789); taken as soon as attacked, the fortress of dark legends was overrun by an innumerable populace who massacred the governor and some disarmed invalids. M. de Flesselles, provost of the merchants, was killed with a pistol shot; Bailly succeeded him, but under the title of Mayor of Paris. The King proceeded to the National Assembly; the troops were dismissed; the Marquis de Lafayette was directed to organize the National Guard. Returning on foot to the château, the King showed himself in the balcony, the Queen and her children by his side, and acclamations saluted them; thence, repairing to the chapel, the royal family sought, at the foot of the altar, some alleviation of their afflictions. On the 14th July, the revolution was accomplished; everything turned, in fact, against power, which, at the outset, had allowed it to be seen that it was not in a position to defend itself. Woe to the weak in revolutions, as, after battles, woe to the vanquished! Each resistance, ill calculated, and ill sustained, involved a retrograde step; the retreat of royalty was soon to become a rout.

In these critical circumstances, the King and the Queen saw, without regret, the withdrawal from about them of many of their subjects who had seemed most closely attached to their persons; they even carried their abnegation so far as to induce several of their attendants to quit them; and this was the commencement of the emigration. The family of Polignac enjoyed favours too signal not to have excited envy; and there was no family which calumny would with the greater malignity have denounced to the fury of the populace. The Queen ordered the Duchess of Polignac to depart; the duchess would not consent. "You wish, then, to augment my anxieties," said Marie Antoinette, "and to give me additional torture." Madame Polignac had not yielded to the friend, but she obeyed the Queen; under the pretext of going to the waters, she retired into Switzerland, and thence into Austria. As the governess of the children of France may not be absent from her charge, the duchess on her way sent in her resignation; and Marie Antoinette selected the Marchioness de Tourzel to fulfil the functions, so important at any time, but perilous at this; the disasters which afterwards overwhelmed the royal family were a cruel trial for Madame de Tourzel, whose courageous fidelity so nobly justified the words in which the Queen had announced to her her appointment. "I confide to virtue that which I had before entrusted to friendship."

At a time when calumny represented her as wholly abandoned to pleasure and frivolous amusements, Marie Antionette devoted the greater part of the day to her duties as a mother. Her children were scarcely ever out of her sight; at ten in the morning an under-governess brought them to her, and it was in her presence that they went through their lessons with their different masters. The disquietudes, the apprehensions of an imminently menacing future, served but to increase in her that active superintendence, that tender care, which had been her happiness, and now became her consolation.

As we are still at Versailles, let us sketch a portrait of the Queen in her last happy days; for the happy days of this so calumniated Queen—calumniated in her own time by hostile politicians, and since by historians—are about to close for ever.

She was not proud; but, habituated to dominate all around her, she had a sort of ingenuous consciousness of her position, exempt from anything like haughtiness, which, of itself, rendered her superior to other women.

The illusory grandeur in which she had been lulled from her infancy, the admiration of the people, the glorious memory of her ancestors, the thought that she was seated on the fairest throne in the universe, all this constituted for her a pedestal, which placed the heads of the crowd on a level with her feet.

Her charming face and figure, her grace, her intellect seemed, not less than her rank, to give her access to the sphere of happy mortals; her fresh girlhood glided away amid enchantments, her youthful womanhood amid the delightful illusions of pure and gentle sentiments.

Never had she witnessed, with insensibility, the sight of unhappiness; she went whither her heart directed her, and her heart ever directed her towards the suffering.

Her destinies, lofty as they were, never soared so high as to isolate them from the happy level of the common affections; her royal heart loved to expand its tenderness in the bosom of friendship.

It was not only in the days of peril and of calamity that the touching qualities of Marie Antoinette manifested themselves.

Long before she had undergone any outrage from man or from fate, while yet all around her was happiness, her soul was already the asylum of the most serious meditations, of the most generous sentiments.

That age of philosophy, that age of fallacious intelligence, of dangerous light, received, in its later years, a pure and beneficent ray from that young Queen whom infamous pamphlets pursued even amid the glory of martyrdom; royalty, about to expire, she re-invested, for a passing moment, with its elegant gaiety, and its chivalry.

Unfortunately the Queen was, when she ascended the throne, as inexperienced as the King himself; everything was turned against her, her good qualities equally with her defects, the graces of her intellect equally with the errors of her judgment, the joyousness of her humour, the simplicity of her manners, the vivacity and the constancy of her friendships.

Calumny fastened itself upon her as its prey; it darkened her every step, it envenomed her every word, it poisoned her every action, and sowed around her those furious hatreds which, in the end, were to crush her.

On the 17th July, the King, despite ominous warnings, resolved to keep the promise he had made to go to Paris, and he entered his carriage for that purpose at eleven o'clock, after bidding the most touching adieus to his family. The Queen, trembling for her husband's life, passed the whole day in the most poignant alarm; her children did not quit her for an instant; the Dauphin went constantly to the window, anxious to be the first to announce his father's return. "He will come back, mamma," he kept saying, "he will come back; my father is too good for any one to seek to harm him." At length the King returned; he rushed from the carriage to embrace his wife and his children; Versailles was full of joy; the people crowded into the marble court, bearing willow branches decorated with ribands, which, in the obscurity of night, presented the appearance of olive branches. Demanded by the joyous transports of this multitude, the King appeared twice in the balcony with his family. Yet this happiness could not make him forget the alarm and anxieties of the day: the storm he had left behind him at Paris, menaced, from day to day, to burst upon Versailles.

For a long time past the factions had been watching an opportunity for attempting a *coup-de-main.* A banquet was given by the King's Gardes-du-Corps, in the theatre of the château, to the officers of the regiment of Flanders, who had come to garrison at Versailles (1st October, 1789); and this banquet was, for a moment, honoured with the presence of the royal family. This circumstance immediately received a calumnious interpretation at the hands of the intriguers, and served them as a pretext for giving the signal of insurrection; the most mendacious statements were circulated, accusations were raised, the popular rage let loose, a troop of furies paraded the capital, crying, "Bread! bread!" The drums beat, the tocsin sounded, the populace of the faubourgs rose, and put itself in motion (5th October); women with dishevelled hair and disordered attire, and drunken men, led the procession, which swelled in numbers with each street that it passed through. The ringleaders, armed with hatchets and knives, mixed with the National Guard, and surrounded M. de Lafayette, whom they compelled to head them on their march to Versailles. At six o'clock, through a thick fog, there was seen advancing along the Avenue de Paris, this multitude of women, who served as the advance-guard of the Parisian multitude;—approaching the château they sent forward a deputation. Louise Chabry, who had been appointed spokeswoman, stammered out a few words about the misery and poverty of the people, and seemed ready to faint, so eminently did the calm mien and steady gaze of the King impress her with stupefaction and respect. "My friends," said his Majesty, "if you are unhappy, it is not my fault; I am still more so than yourselves. I will give orders to the keepers of the granaries at Corbeil and Etampes to deliver all the corn and flour they can spare. May these orders be better obeyed than those I have hitherto issued." These women, hired to curse, proffered their blessing to the King; come to menace death, they departed, crying "*Vive le Roi!*" To this unexpected shout responded exclamations of hatred and rage without; and poor Louise Chabry, who knew not that the demand for bread was a mere pretext, would have been hanged at the lamp-post, had not some Gardes-du-Corps, forcing their way through the throng, wrested her from the wretches who were about to assassinate their dupe.

Meanwhile, all around the palace swelled the raging waves of Mægeras which crime had collected in the lowest sinks of Paris to impel them on Versailles; next, bodies of hideous men in tatters, armed with hatchets, knives, sticks, pikes,—troops collected from prison cells to increase the army of the revolution; and then the regular columns of the Parisian National Guard, having at their head a chief who, driven on by the movement, seemed to lead it,—an honest man, but full of illusions, and vacillating to a degree; who passed his life in the preparation of results which he would have wished to avert, and in astonishment at witnessing consequences, to which he was wholly opposed, issue from causes to which he had been instrumental.

Lafayette, then, had come to the succour of his king, whom he wished to save, and whom he feared to strengthen. Yet he reassured himself and reassured the King; he answered, on his head, for the safety of the whole château, issued various orders, placed sentinels, harangued the National Guard, and then retired to the Hotel de Noailles to take some repose. But crime sleeps not; and before daybreak (6th October, 1789) it had forced the gates of the palace, taken possession of the apartments of the royal family, massacred the Gardes-du-Corps who defended the corridor leading to the chamber of the Queen. Frustrated in their rage, the ruffians cut to pieces the bed whence Marie Antoinette had just made her escape, half-naked. Trembling for the life of his son, the King had rushed to the chamber of the precious child, taken him in his arms, passed, to avoid the assassins, along a subterranean corridor, where his taper went out and left him in the dark, and then felt his way to his apartment, where he found the Queen, who, with a dressing-gown over her shoulders, had just taken refuge there; he also found there Madame Royale, Monsieur, Madame Elizabeth, and the Marchioness de Tourzel. Thus united, the royal family awaited with less fear the fate that menaced them.

M. de Lafayette at length made his appearance, and, having cleared the palace, solicited the King, in the name of the people, to go and fix his residence from that day at Paris, depicting to him, in alarming colours, the dangers of a refusal. Meanwhile, the crowd of ruffians who had been ejected from the interior, collected in the courtyard of the palace, where, with loud cries, they demanded the King. The attendants, justly alarmed, conjured the sovereign not to comply with this desire; but the King, rejecting all prudential considerations, showed himself on the balcony, and himself announced that he was about to depart for Paris with all his family. "Let the Queen show herself," exclaimed a number of voices;—the Queen advanced, holding in one hand the Dauphin, in the other, Madame Royale. At this sight the cries redoubled: "The Queen alone! No children! The Queen alone!" The King essayed to speak, but the clamour drowned his voice; he retired, leading both the Queen and the children. The vociferations proceeded: "The Queen! No children! The Queen alone! The Queen!" Without permitting herself to be intimidated by the menacing intentions which this cry conveyed, the Queen, having transferred the children to their father, advanced into the balcony, alone, intrepid, menaced by earth, forsaken, as it almost seemed by Heaven; she crossed her hands on her bosom, and gazed with a majestic look upon the multitude: the people, struck with admiration, applauded—sedition was stupefied.

Returning to the King, Marie Antoinette said to him with

emotion, clasping her son to her bosom, "Promise me, Sire, I conjure you, in the name of all you hold most dear, for the safety of France, for your own, for that of this loved child, promise me, oh promise me, that if such an occurrence as this again presents itself, and that you have the means to withdraw from it, you will not omit to employ those means." These words deeply affected the King, who, without replying, passed into the adjoining chamber.

The preparations for departure were rapidly made; when they became known, the National Assembly decreed that it was inseparable from the monarch, and that it would follow him to Paris.

At one o'clock, Louis XVI., the Queen, the Dauphin, Madame Royale, Madame Elizabeth, and the Marchioness de Tourzel got into their carriages, having for their strange escort, trains of artillery, drunken ruffians armed with pikes and sticks and daggers, covered with mud and blood, and reeling with wine; women equally intoxicated, with hair dishevelled, some riding on the cannon, or behind the soldiers, some with cuirasses on, some armed with guns and sabres, and all vociferating obscene songs or ferocious imprecations. The royal children were amazed at the fury and wickedness of the people, whom they had been taught to love. Then came two hundred of the Gardes-du-Corps, disarmed, and without hats or belts, each led between two grenadiers; then some of the Cent-suisses, dragoons, and soldiers of the regiment of Flanders; and, in the midst, cannon loaded with grape-shot. The livid heads of Deshuttes and Varicourt, the two young Gardes-du Corps, who, at the outset of the attack on the château, had suffered themselves to be massacred rather than abandon their post, were carried at the end of pikes, by two men—if such a title can justly be given them—who, at the village of Sèvres stopped to have the hair curled and powdered. Between these bleeding trophies was seen Nicholas Jourdan, a man with a long black beard, who was employed as a model at the academy of painting and sculpture, and who now, with bare arms, glaring eyes, his face and hands red with the blood in which he had washed them, marched along, brandishing his hatchet, still humid with gore, and glorying in the surname of *Coupe-Tête* which had that day been given him

Events continued to advance in the same direction; with every collision royalty lost ground, lost strength, lost chances. It receded on 27th June, 1789, it receded on 17th July, it receded on 5th and 6th October, when it recalled M. Necker to power; and now it was being led to Paris, to that city where not only was it in no condition to resist the Assembly, but where the Assembly itself was no longer in a condition to resist the irregular forces of the revolution.

It was not until after nearly seven hours' march, that this convoy of royalty reached Paris from Versailles. The people at their windows contemplated with stupor the indescribable scene. "Fear nothing now," cried the women of the funereal escort; "no more poverty: we bring you the baker, the bakeress, and the baker's boy."

It was in this fashion that Lafayette transferred Louis XVI into the hands of Bailly. Bailly said to the King: "Sire, this is a great day, in which your Majesty comes to your capital accompanied by your august spouse, and with a prince who will be as good and as just as Louis XVI. himself." He then, in the name of Paris, of which he was mayor, expressed the hope that his Majesty would establish his permanent residence in his capital. The King replied: "It is ever with pleasure and with confidence that I find myself among the inhabitants of my good city of Paris." Bailly, in repeating this reply to those who had been too far apart to hear it, omitted the word confidence. "Repeat, *with confidence*," said the Queen.

As the strange procession of this wine-stained and blood-stained multitude, bringing back the royal family as the booty of the day, passed along the quay which borders the garden of the Tuileries, a young man of classic profile and eagle eye, exclaimed, with a gesture of contemptuous indignation, "What! has the King no cannon to sweep away this scum?"

This young man, himself predestined one day to sweep away the revolution, was called Napoleon Bonaparte.

BOOK SECOND.

THE TUILERIES.

6TH OCTOBER, 1789—20TH JUNE, 1791.

Observation of the Dauphin on entering the Tuileries—Efforts and illusions of the King—Menaces and outrages—Progress of the Revolution—Walks of the Dauphin—His sister's first communion—The garden of the terrace along the water—Anecdotes—The Dauphin's charity—The federation—Civil constitution of the clergy—Revolutionary intolerance—Violences offered to the King.

LOUIS XVI. came to occupy the château of the Tuileries, which, uninhabited almost continuously since 1655, had become dismantled of even the most ordinary necessaries; the furniture was dilapidated, the tapestry worn and faded, the apartments dark and dismal. "Everything is very ugly here, mamma," said the Dauphin, as they entered. "My dear," replied the Queen, "Louis XIV. lived here, and found it comfortable; we must not be more fastidious than he."

The presence of the royal family seemed for an instant to restore tranquillity to Paris. Louis XVI. sent for the Subsistence Committee, who were surprised to find in the King, combined with all the solicitude of a father, the information of a wise administrator; measures were instantly adopted for provisioning the capital, and for the re-establishment of public order. Louis XVI. imagined that he had only to combat an evanescent aberration; he endeavoured to regain the hearts of the people; he visited the charitable establishments, went through the Faubourgs on foot, and announced to the indigent class the gratuitous redemption of all articles of clothing that were then in pawn.

These hopes were of brief duration. There were systematic hostilities labouring in the dark, exciting every passion, every prejudice against the royal family; moreover, the masses were at once animated by that spirit of revolution which produces fermentation in them, and by the rage arising from the sense of their sufferings, and the excitement given to their hate.

From the traditionary idea of the royal power in France, they regarded the King as the cause of all their evils, as the obstacle to the realization of their hopes; thus the King still bore the responsibility of an authority which he no longer possessed.

Odious calumnies circulated more than ever against the King, and especially against the Queen. The factions hired, excited, and hallooed on a populace, which, from time to time, came beneath the windows of the château, vociferating insults, abuse, and obscenity. They dared more: they sent to the throne, under the title of deputies, persons belonging to the lowest dregs of the people. The ministers wished to refuse them admission, but the King and the Queen directed that access to the palace should be given to all. The worthy orator of this troop ventured, one day, to denounce, in the most insulting and most disgraceful terms, the Queen, who was present with her son. "You are mistaken," said the King, "the Queen and I have none of the intentions you attribute to us; we act altogether in concert, and solely with a view to the public benefit." The deputation had scarcely quitted when the Queen burst into a passion of tears; a mother is doubly insulted when she is insulted in the presence of her child.

To these daily outrages were superadded the restraint of scarcely veiled captivity. The royal family never quitted Paris, and only walked at certain hours in the garden of the Tuileries; the people being excluded at these times, the populace and even the soldiers, would say coarsely: "The King is let out."

Some noble hearts grew indignant at this constraint, at this degradation of royalty; everyone knows with what facility the people pass from hatred to pity. A deputation of the municipality, headed by the Mayor of Paris, waited on the King themselves to suggest that he should resume the exercise of hunting, the long habit of which had rendered it almost a matter of necessity with him. The King replied, however. "It was with me less a pleasure than a regimen, the effect of which was beneficial to my health; at present, the gravity of public affairs does not even permit me to think of it, much less to regret it."

Though the ringleaders of the events of 5th and 6th October were almost all known, and their impunity certain, the court of the Châtelet took official cognizance of the affair, and appointed commissioners to inquire into it, who presented themselves before the Queen to receive her evidence as to the outrages committed on the morning of the 6th. Her Majesty replied, "I saw all, I knew all, I have forgotten all."

Some new aliment was required for the excitement of men's minds. The Red Book was discovered, and made the most of. This famous register of secret expenditure, which had been in the custody of the Comptroller-General of Finance, became, from its very nature, matter for the vague and mendacious assumptions, and for the satirical imagination of the pamphleteers, who suppose whatever they do not know, and say whatever they suppose. The National Assembly loudly demanded the examination of this book, and then ordered it to be printed. The public read with avidity; but perceived not as yet the real abyss in which the treasures of France were about to be engulphed.

Anarchy pervaded the provinces; landed properties were devastated, châteaux burned; the laws were without force, the magistrates without authority. At Paris, the provisioning was interrupted by the factious; the supply of bread became inadequate to the daily wants of the people. A general insurrection was projected for 19th October; seduced and intimidated by the conspirators, most of the bakers omitted to bake any bread on the night previous. Some few disobeyed the order,—their shops were attacked and pillaged. One of them, named François, was branded with the title of aristocrat, and hanged at a lamp-post by the populace, who, a few days afterwards, required the condemnation and execution of the Marquis de Favras, accused of anti-revolutionary connivings with the Count de Provence.

The disorders of that day revealed to all the powers the dangers of anarchical fury. The National Assembly proposed the re-establishment of martial law; and, after a vehement opposition, the proposition was adopted. After a while there was another lull of the popular effervescence. The renewed supply of provisions, and repeated acts of royal benevolence seemed to revive better sentiments in the people. The National Assembly, meeting, of its own accord, the public opinion of the day, resolved upon offering to the King and Queen a public testimony of respect. Without being either invited or expected, it presented itself spontaneously at the château of the Tuileries, headed by its president, M. Freteau. The King, who had received no notice of this proceeding, manifested extreme satisfaction. From the King's apartment, the Assembly passed to that of the Queen. "Madame," said the President, "the first wish of the National Assembly on its arrival in the capital, was to present to the King the tribute of its respect and attachment; it could not resist so natural an opportunity of offering to you also its most cordial and most respectful sentiments. Receive them, Madame, such as we proffer them: warm, earnest, sincere. It would be a high satisfaction to the National Assembly to contemplate in your arms the illustrious child, the scion of so many kings tenderly cherished by their people, the heir of Louis IX., of Henry IV., of him whose virtues now constitute the hope of France. Never will he or the authors of his life enjoy so much prosperity as we wish them."

"I am touched, as I ought to be," replied Marie Antoinette, "with the sentiments expressed towards me by the National Assembly. Had I been aware of its intentions, I would have received it in a manner more worthy of it." Then, taking in her arms the heir of the throne, she presented him to the Assembly. The cries of "*Vive le Roi! Vive la Reine! Vive le Dauphin!*" repeated with enthusiasm, snatched the Queen, for a moment, from the sense of her misfortunes.

Meanwhile the National Assembly pursued, without interruption, the preparation of the Constitution. On February 4th, 1790, the King, in compliance with the advice of M. Necker, proceeded to the Assembly, and in a remarkable speech, claimed its co-operation in enlightening the nation as to its true interests. The following are passages in this speech which are connected, at all events indirectly, with our subject. "I also should have losses to set forth, were I, amid the supreme interests of the state, to dwell upon personal considerations; but I find a compensation that suffices for me, a full and complete compensation in the augmentation of the nation's happiness; it is from the bottom of my heart that I express this sentiment.

"I will defend them, and maintain the constitutional liberty of which the general wish, in entire accordance with my own, has consecrated the principles. I will do more; and in concert with the Queen, who shares all my sentiments, I will early adapt the mind and the heart of my son to the new order of things, which circumstances have brought about; I will habituate him from his childhood to be happy in the happiness of the French people, and ever to recognise, despite the language of flatterers, that a wise constitution will preserve him from the dangers of inexperience, and that a just liberty adds new value to the sentiments of love and fidelity, of which the nation, for so many centuries, has given to its kings such touching proofs.

"By what fatality, when tranquillity was becoming re-established, have new disorders spread through the provinces? By what fatality have fresh excesses been committed there? Join with me in suppressing them, and let us apply all our efforts to prevent criminal violence from sullying these days in which the happiness of the nation is being prepared. You, who can exercise such influence, in so many ways, upon the public power, enlighten on their true interests the people whom men are misleading, the good people I so love, and by whom, they who seek to console me for my sorrows, assure me I am beloved."

Here the emotion of the Assembly interrupted Louis XVI.

The King's attitude, his language, his accent, all so eminently paternal, moved, for a moment, every heart. After a brief reply from the President (M. Bureau de Puzy), he quitted the Chamber amid universal applause, and was reconducted to the Tuileries by a deputation of the Assembly. The Queen, with the Dauphin in her hand, came to meet him.

"I share," she said, addressing the deputation, "all the sentiments of his Majesty; I concur with heart and spirit in all that emanates from his love for his people. Here is my son; I will constantly hold up to him, for his example, the virtues of the best of fathers; I will teach him, from his earliest youth, to respect public liberty, and to maintain the laws, fervently hoping that he may one day be their firmest support."

Alas! these movements of enthusiasm and effusion were but brief halts between the stages of revolution; anarchy soon resumed its march, and made up for lost time by advancing with giant strides. The Assembly decreed the sale of all the property of the clergy, the suppression of the religious orders, the spoliation of the churches; it decreed that civil constitution of the clergy, which soon involved the persecution of the faithful priests, and became the primary cause of the insurrection, which later broke out in La Vendée; it decreed the abolition of nobility, the suppression of titles, armorial bearings, and liveries. The spirit of revolt passed the seas, convulsed our colonies, armed the blacks against the whites, the slaves against the masters; the plantations became a prey to conflagration—blood flowed in torrents.

At Paris, the revolution was not calmed by its triumph. The feelings excited by the dearness of corn, the scarcity of provisions, assumed the form of an intense hatred of royalty, whose powerlessness remained responsible for everything. The rigours of a disastrous winter became an accusation against it; an upright and benevolent king was rendered chargeable with the inclemencies of nature. The dealers in corn were denounced to the popular indignation as forestallers and monopolists; all commercial speculation was stayed by the fear of being charged with starving the people. The fear of the evil aggravated the evil itself.

Almost permanently confined to the apartments of the château, it may be readily imagined how the Dauphin regretted Versailles. He sometimes, however, was driven out in a carriage with his governess, and on Thursdays, always paid a visit to the Marquise de Leyde, who possessed, in the Faubourg Saint Germain, a fine mansion with a large garden. Here he found flowers, air, and liberty, and moreover, one or two children of his own age, who ran about and played with him. One day, at hide and seek, the Prince took it into his head to climb by a ladder into a loft at the end of the garden; the ladder, badly placed, slipped, but was checked in its progress by a border of box which surrounded a flower bed. The officer who was in charge of the royal child, and who was directed not to lose sight of him, was but two steps off, but having turned his head for a moment, on looking round again, he missed the young rogue. Casting his eyes towards the loft, he saw the Prince at the top of the ladder, and apparently in danger of falling; however, the little fellow held on till the ladder stayed its movement, and then quietly descended, triumphantly counting each step as he passed it.

The amusements of Louis Charles became fewer and fewer, but he did not complain. Still, on the 7th April, 1790, he said to Madame de Tourzel: "I am very sorry I have not got my garden. I should have gathered two beautiful bouquets to-morrow morning, one for mamma, the other for my sister." That morrow was the day on which Madame Royale partook of her first communion. In the morning, the Queen led her to the King's chamber. "My daughter," said she, "kneel to your father, and ask his blessing." Madame knelt; her father raising her, said: "It is from the bottom of my heart, my child, that I bless you, imploring heaven to grant you grace to appreciate the solemn act you are about to perform. Your heart is innocent and pure in the eyes of God; your prayers cannot be otherwise than acceptable to him. Offer them, then, in behalf of your mother and of your father. Pray that he may endow me with the grace necessary to secure the happiness of those over whom he has given me the Empire, and whom I must consider as my children. Pray that he will deign to preserve in this kingdom, the purity of religion; and remember, my daughter, that this holy religion is the source of happiness, and our sustentation in the adversities of life. Think not that from those adversities you are secure; you are very young, but you have already more than once seen your father heavily afflicted. You know not, my child, to what you may be destined by providence; whether you will remain in this kingdom, or whether you go to dwell in another. But wherever the hand of God leads you, remember that it behoves you to edify by your example, and to do good whenever the opportunity for doing good shall present itself. But, above all, my child, succour and solace the poor and the unhappy with your utmost power; God only placed us in the rank we occupy, to labour for their happiness, to console them in their afflictions. Now proceed to the altar where you are awaited, and pray the God of mercy that you may never forget the counsels of a tender father."

I shall, I am sure, be pardoned for having yielded to the pious impulse to transcribe these affecting words, which M. Hue has preserved: as the narrator of the life of the Dauphin of France, I shall not be called upon to relate the exhortations which his father would have addressed to him on that day of solemnity in the life of all Christians, but I am consoled for it by repeating those which produced so profound an impression on the heart of Madame Royale, his sister.

The Dauphin, at the desire of the Queen, was present at the ceremony, which impressed all the royal family with the most grateful emotions.

Some days afterwards fearful rumours circulated; it was said that a plot had been formed to carry the château by main force. One night several gun-shots were heard; the King rose and hurried to the Queen's apartment,—she was not there; he went to the Dauphin's room, and there he found Marie Antoinette clasping her son in her arms: "Madame, I have been seeking you, and have been most uneasy." "Sire," replied the Queen, "I was at my post."

This incessant agitation, however, did not prejudice the regular instruction, the normal instruction of the Dauphin. He was taught religion, writing, history, arithmetic, geography, botany. M. de la Borde, formerly first *valet-de-chambre* to Louis XV., had arranged, for the study of the last named science, a herbal which excited the young prince's especial attention. He was trained, at the same time, to bodily exercises, to dancing, and to tennis; and no child ever exhibited, at these exercises and games, more grace, agility and address.

There was within the boundaries of the Tuileries, at the extremity of the terrace, on the water-side, a little garden surrounded by a hawhaw, close to a small house occupied by the Abbé Davaux, the Dauphin's tutor. It was thought that the Dauphin might here find what he had left at Versailles, and resume an exercise adapted to his tastes and promotive of his health. This little plot of garden was accordingly assigned to him, and he took possession of it with avidity. He reared rabbits there; he cultivated flowers. This plot has since been raised to the level of the terrace; but it is the same garden, thus altered, reconstructed, and enlarged, which, later, Napoleon consecrated to the King of Rome; Charles X. to the Duke de Bordeaux; and Louis Philippe to the Count de Paris. How much instruction has been conveyed on this little angle of ground, so soon abandoned by its young proprietors! One died in a prison, at ten years old; another, while in his cradle, was whirled away by the storm, and only lived to learn the name of his father, and to gaze, before he died, on his sword; the third and the fourth driven, like the two others, before the tempest, still drag on the existence of exiles in the cities of Austria and of England. And what tears had not these children—who, themselves, are so much entitled to our pity,—to shed for their fathers! one died on the scaffold; another under the knife of an assassin; a third was dashed to pieces on the highway; and lastly, the greatest of all by his genius, was bound, like Prometheus, to a rock, where the gnawing recollections of the past consigned him slowly to the tomb.

When he visited his new garden, the prince was usually accompanied by a detachment of the National Guard, on service at the Tuileries. For some days past he had been learning the use of arms, and he himself ordinarily wore the uniform of the National Guards. He was proud of his escort, and his frank and open countenance ingenuously bespoke his happiness. His brow seemed free from all disquieting thoughts. When his train was limited, the prince would invite them to enter his garden with him. One day, when so great a number had accompanied him that they were obliged to remain outside, the prince said to them: "Excuse me, gentlemen; I am very sorry that my garden is so small, since it deprives me of the pleasure of receiving you all." He then hastened to offer flowers to whomsoever approached the fence and seemed to take any interest in his amusements.

Another day,—and this anecdote will show that the grace of his manners and the kindliness of his nature were blended with a certain chivalrous vivacity, which seemed to justify the ancient device of the House of Bourbon, *Bonté et Valeur,*—before quitting the château to proceed to his little garden, he had practised the musket exercise. At the moment of departure, the officer of the National Guard on duty said to him: "Monseigneur, as you are going out, surrender me your musket." The Dauphin roughly refused. Madame de Tourzel having reprimanded him for this vivacity, he replied: "If the gentleman had said: *give* me your musket, that would have been all very well,—but surrender it!" On learning his son's reply, the King exclaimed: "Always so abrupt, so mettlesome! yet I like to see that he discriminates the value and meaning of terms."

There had been formed in Paris a company of quite young lads, under the designation of *Regiment du Dauphin*. It was the Abbé Antheaume who had conceived the idea of this company, and proposed to the King its formation. The citizens of Paris had defrayed almost all the expenses, and furnished all the members. "I was one of this troop," says M. Antoine, in his *Vie du jeune Louis XVII.*, "and we were admitted frequently to manœuvre in presence of the young prince. At our first visit, we found him in his garden, surrounded by several young noblemen. 'Will you be colonel of this regiment,' said one of them to him. 'Yes,' replied the Dauphin; 'I like my garden *grenadiers* (pomegranate trees) very much, but I had rather be at the head of these living grenadiers.' "Good-bye, then, to the flowers and bouquets for your mamma!' 'No, I can still look after my flowers. No doubt, many of these young gentlemen have also little gardens; well, they will love the Queen, after the example of their colonel, and mamma will have, every day, a whole regiment of bouquets.' Our acclamations," adds M. Antoine, " manifested to him the love we bore to his august parents."

The boys composing this little battalion were select children. It was natural that they should exhibit deference towards the son of their King. Beyond this, however, the prince's preceptor would admit of no concession; they were formally prohibited from succumbing to their *comrade* The King had said: "I would have companions for my son, to excite his emulation, but not little flatterers to humour him in everything." Meanwhile this troop which, in the outset, formed only a nucleus of 150 to 200 *men*, augmented daily. After M. Antheaume had announced in the public journals the royal authorisation he had received, many families hastened to place their children's names on the *rôle* of this beardless regiment, and to defray the cost of their equipment. This equipment was the uniform and arms of the French guard in miniature, including the white gaiters and the three cornered hat.

It became necessary to discipline this little army, now become very numerous, and which had assumed with pride the name of *Royal Dauphin.* Officers were selected from its ranks, the selection being made, as a rule, according to age and to advancement in military instruction. The acting colonel, (for the Dauphin had only the title of colonel,) was a charming young man of seventeen, whose father was a tailor under the Piliers des Halles, near the house in which Molière was born. There was great emulation among the recruits, from time to time, as to who would exhibit the greatest capability in military exercises. Twice a week, the *Royal Dauphin* formed in front of the house of tho Abbé Antheaume, who lived in the narrow street, since widened, which joined the Rue Montmartre to the court of the Messageries Royales; and thence, with drums beating, and the object of general attention, they would march to the Clos Saint Lazare, at the top of the Faubourg Saint Denis, the Abbé Antheaume at their head, and there manœuvre under the direction of a regular military instructor. After two hours' exercise, the regiment would march back whence they came, and there dispersing, return to their quarters, that is to say, to their parents' houses.

The regiment had, from the first, its post in all the ceremonies in which the Dauphin appeared; but its pretensions soon enlarging, it demanded to be considered as being on an equal military footing with the National Guard. "There are no longer any children," said M. Lafayette; "we have all of us seen so many old men with the vices of youth, that it is well to see youth with the virtues of men." The *Royal Dauphin* now assumed quite an important attitude. It was permitted to occupy three posts of honour: the Château, the Hotel of the Mayor of Paris, in the Rue des Capucines, now No. 12 in that street—and the Hotel of the Commander-in-Chief of the National Guard, in the Rue de Bourbon. When the detachment mounted guard, and defiled in front of the Tuileries, the young soldiers always received marks of approbation from the royal family, who would watch them from the balcony of the clock-tower. The King would salute their flag affectionately, and the Dauphin gave his comrades repeated proofs of his delight and sympathy.

But there is no perfect success. If the *Royal Dauphin* had their partisans, they had also their detractors. No popularity endures at Paris, not even that of childhood. Public malice there soon discerns in everything a ludicrous or a ridiculous aspect. The little regiment received the nickname of the *Royal-Bonbon*. "They feed you with a spoon!" cried some. "No, they eat with their beaks, the little Maine ducks," cried others,* and these jests would not slightly exasperate the nascent warriors. Gradually all thoughts became turned towards war, and, step by step, the military spirit, so potent in France, had taken possession of the brain of even children ten years

* The French guards were called in derision *Canards du Maine*, because, in one of the last wars, they had been compelled, in a retreat, to cross the Maine swimming.

old. It was not enough for the *Royal-Dauphin* to parade with the troops of the line, and the National Guard; to see its little sentry-box, side by side, with their great sentry-box, at the three posts which it militarily occupied night and day; it insisted on further claims to the public respect; it demanded to have, like the elder regiments, its pass-words, its order of the day, a demand clearly out of the question, and which was refused accordingly.

Moreover, there was a man who, in imitation of M. Antheaume, formed a regiment of boys, designated the *Epaulettes Blanches*, or the regiment of Henri IV., from the circumstance of their assembling at the Pont Neuf. This competition led to warm altercations between the rival boy-regiments, and these to several duels, in which three children were wounded with the bayonet, and a fourth received a very dangerous sabre-cut. Nothing further was needed—not to calm the effervescent brains of the apprentice-soldiers—but to cool the warlike zeal of their parents, who, without any previous consultation, came to the unanimous resolution that the time was really come when they must issue an order of the day, and this order of the day was the dissolution of the *Royal-Dauphin.*

The funeral of Mirabeau was one of the most imposing public ceremonies in which our youthful militia figured. Two months afterwards, we find them mixed up with the excitement produced by the flight of the King to Montmédy. When the générale was beaten throughout Paris, the little drummers of this militia took their part in it.* A few days after this they were

* Alexander Piccini, composer of music, (born at Paris, September 17, 1779, died at Baden-Baden, March 30, 1850,) has told me that, when a corporal in the *Royal Dauphin,* he was on guard at the hotel of the Mayor of Paris on the night of the 20th June, 1791; that he saw at one o'clock in the morning, a lady, entirely clothed in white, issue from the hotel, cross the court, and go out into the street; that six or seven hours afterwards, he heard, in common with everyone else, the news of the departure of the royal family; but that he has never been able to explain to himself the mysterious apparition he witnessed in the court of the hotel.

disbanded. The tragedies in the streets were becoming too serious to allow children to take a share in them.

But let us not anticipate events. The Dauphin now, whenever he repaired to his little garden, always found on his way some of his comrades with their mothers; he would salute the former with cordiality, the latter with kindness. He would listen to them, for it was in his nature to be gentle, and more than once he had money given to such of them as came to tell him that their families were in want. One day, a poor mother came to him amid his flowers, and entreated him to ask a favour for her: "Ah! Monseigneur," said she, "if I were to obtain this favour, I should be as happy as a queen!" The prince, who had stooped to pick some china-asters, rose, looked at the petitioner with a mournful air, and said: "Happy as a queen! Ah! I know a queen who does nothing but weep."

He charged himself with the poor woman's memorial, and when she returned, next day, all impatience, to his little garden: "I have an answer for you," said the child, and, radiant with joy, he drew from his pocket a piece of gold wrapped in paper; "that is from mamma," said he, "and this is my present," giving her a large bouquet.

This precious disposition to do good was tenderly fostered in him, both by his father, who regarded beneficence as one of the bases of education, and by his mother, who omitted no occasion to impress upon him that princes are born to be the protectors of the unfortunate, the terrestrial providence of the indigent. And it was not to fine-sounding words and glowing theories that Marie Antoinette limited the lessons of charity. Ever ready to bring example in aid of precept, distress and misfortune were never made known to her but she instantly sent succour and consolation. She made her son a participator in her good works, both towards the poor in the hospitals, and towards those poor still more miserable, whose tears flow in the frigid solitude of the garret or the cellar. Followed by two footmen with large open purses, the little prince himself took out pieces of silver money, which he gave to each orphan. He seemed joyous to the bottom of his heart, at the happiness which his presence and his liberality diffused in the hospital, and not less moved with the blessings which were showered upon him and his mother as they passed on.

A particularity worthy of remark is, that he manifested himself, under all circumstances, especially sensible to the misery of children about his own age. When he went to his garden, he always requested the guards, to give free access to all such, that he might talk with them, give pieces of money to those who were very much in need, and flowers to the rest. Every time he left the Foundling Hospital, he expressed his regret at leaving it so soon. "Mamma, mamma, when shall we come back again?" he would say to the Queen, as they got into the carriage that was to convey them to the Tuileries. May it not be suggested, observing in him so much sympathy for unfortunate children, that there was in his commiseration a sort of presentiment, that something revealed to him that he himself would be one day poor, miserable, and abandoned?

There is nothing more persuasive than family example, nothing more felicitously contagious than sentiments of love, honour, beneficence, breathed from one's earliest years in the maternal atmosphere. The young heir to the throne put aside the greater portion of his pocket-money, which he kept in a pretty little coffer that had been given to him by his aunt Elizabeth, the habitual purveyor of his modest treasure, and the ardent co-operatrix in his charity. Louis XVI., who was not, at first, in the secret, saw his son, one day, gravely occupied in counting crowns, which he then carefully ranged in piles in his coffer. "What, Charles," said the King seriously, "are you hoarding like the misers?" Disconcerted at this appellation of miser, the boy at first blushed, but immediately recovering himself, said, with a joyous air and softly cadenced voice:

"Yes, papa, I am a miser, but it is for the poor Foundlings. Ah! if you were to see them, they are truly piteous." The King took in his arms the young almoner, and tenderly embracing him, said: "In that case, my child, I will help you to fill your coffer!"

Time advances; events advance still quicker than time. On the 14th July, 1790, the anniversary of the Taking of the Bastille, the civic festival of the general federation of France, was celebrated in the Champ-de-Mars.

The generation of 1789 were fond of those great festivals which make a whole people live with the same life, which make all hearts palpitate in unison. This theatrical side of the revolution intoxicated the souls of that multitude—at once actor and spectator of these ceremonies. The people awaited these new tables of the law, on which the philosophy of the 18th century had written its decalogue, with as much impatience as the Hebrews awaited, in the desert, the sacred law which God sent them on Sinaï. It seemed as though order, peace, liberty, progress, prosperity, everything, was to be found in this constitution; and France, forgetting that she had lived fourteen centuries, thought that only from 14th July, 1790, was her life to date. All the provinces were largely represented in that vast concourse. The King took the oath to the new Constitution; innumerable hands were raised after his, in token of fidelity; cannon roared, trumpets sounded, acclamations were heard in every direction; the Queen, who was placed in a gallery above the throne, took the Dauphin in her arms, and presented him, as it were, to the people, to the army, to the whole nation: the child instinctively raised his innocent hands, as if to invoke the blessing of Heaven on France; enthusiasm was at its height; and assuredly the prophet would have seemed very mad indeed, who should have announced to the spectators of that festival, the deluge of calamities about to pour down upon the whole empire. During the sojourn of the Federates at Paris, the garden and the courts of the Tuileries resounded with *vivats* and benedictions; the trees of the garden and the walls of the palace, were covered with emblems of fidelity and sympathy. The Dauphinese deputies, offered, in especial, the most affectionate homage to the Dauphin, and the manner in which the royal infant received them, made it evident that notwithstanding his extreme youth (five years and some months), he thoroughly appreciated these tokens of sensibility, and was proud of bearing the name of a province in which such sentiments still subsisted.

Notwithstanding the good-will of the Federates, anarchy spread through the kingdom. The public powers were subjected to the incessant denunciations of the new powers, compelled to submit either to constant insult or to retirement, M. Necker withdrew from the administration of affairs, never to return. The National Assembly gloried in the fall of this idol, hurled from his pedestal; the provinces looked on with indifference. Mesdames, the King's aunts, determined also to depart, and to repair to Rome; they were arrested, for several days, at Arnay-le-Duc, on account of their not having a passport from the Assembly: the revolution already began to practise the laying of hands on royal personages. The King's authority was daily more contested, and his liberty more restricted. Mirabeau died, *carrying with him*, as he himself expressed it, *the last shreds of the monarchy*. In this old enemy, the King lost an auxiliary; but would he not have been impotent for good, having been so potent for evil? Such was the opinion of Madame Elizabeth: "I do not think," she wrote to her friend Madame de Raigecourt, "that it is by the hands of men without principles and without virtue that God will save us."

Holy week approached. Fearing that he should be unable to fulfil at Paris the exercises of religion to which these days are consecrated, Louis XVI. prepared to pass Easter fortnight at St. Cloud, alleging the need to breathe the country air, after a painful indisposition, from which he had scarcely recovered. The leading conspirators hereupon published through the city, that under pretext of this journey were hidden projects of escape; they stated that the King had dismissed his ordinary confessor because he had taken the oath. They thus stirred up the populace of Paris, at once so unbelieving and so credulous, to demand that the King should not depart, but should frequent his parish church and receive the communion from the hands of the constitutional *curé*. "They want," wrote Madame Elizabeth to her friend, "to force the King to send away the priests of his chapel, or to make these take the oath, and to celebrate his Easter service in the parish church. This was the cause of yesterday's insurrection: the journey to St. Cloud was a mere pretext. The guard altogether disobeyed M. de Lafayette and his officers. Fortunately, nothing serious occurred. The King spoke with firmness and goodness, and was quite himself."

The course of these events was this: the King had, to meet the public rumours renounced his project, but on the representation of MM. Bailly and de Lafayette, he had resumed them, and at eleven o'clock in the forenoon, got into his carriage with his family; the carriage was immediately surrounded by an immense crowd. A body of mutinous soldiers closed the gates of the château and rushed to the carriage, menacing, and levelling their bayonets at the horses. "The King shall go," cried M. de Lafayette, "though I employ force, and spill blood to secure his departure." But resistance continued; force was not employed against it, and the King, after sitting two hours in the carriage, amidst an incessant struggle, and exposed, himself and his family, to the grossest insults, renounced his journey, rather than involve one portion of the National Guard in a fight with the other, and returned to his apartments, or rather to his prison.

The Dauphin, who, like all children, was fond of change, and had framed a thousand pleasant projects of amusement for the period of his stay at St. Cloud, was extremely afflicted at this disappointment. To divert his mind from the thought, the Abbé Devaux, on returning to his study, placed in his hands a volume of Berquin's *Ami des Enfants;* the young prince opened it casually, and, all astonishment, exclaimed: "Here is a coincidence, M. l'Abbé; look at this title: how curious! "The Little Prisoner."

Next day the King repaired to the National Assembly. "Gentlemen," said he, "I come amongst you with the confidence which I have always manifested towards you. You have been informed of the resistance opposed yesterday to my departure for Saint Cloud. I did not choose that this resistance should be put a stop to by force, because I feared to occasion acts of rigour against a misguided multitude, who imagined they were acting in favour of the very laws they were infringing; but to prove that I am free is important to the nation, essential for the authorization of the sanction I have given to your decrees. I am resolved, therefore, for this powerful motive, to persist in my journey to St. Cloud, and the National Assembly must see the necessity of my doing so."

This proceeding, which involved the imminent risk of confirming both within and without the kingdom, the too well founded opinion of the King's captivity, was very embarrassing to the National Assembly; and the President, accordingly, merely replied that agitation was inseparable from the progress of liberty, but that all hearts were for the King, and that as the King desired the happiness of his people, the people sought the happiness of their King.

The King did not go to St. Cloud. Nay more; finding that the animosity grew daily more fierce against the Catholic priests who had not taken the oath, he invited the ecclesiastics who composed his chapel, to remove from about his person. These concessions did not satisfy the intolerance of the factions. They required that on the 24th April, Easter Sunday, the King and the Queen should go to St. Germain l'Auxerrois, the parish church of the palace, and hear mass celebrated by the constitutional pastor, the dispossessor of the old curé, who had remained faithful to the principles laid down by the episcopal body, and which the Pope had solemnly proclaimed in his Brief of the 10th July, 1790.

Not being compelled to such concessions, Madame Elizabeth declared that on Easter Sunday, she would hear mass from her own chaplain in the chapel of the château. In abominable placards, affixed against the very walls of the gallery adjoining her apartments, she was threatened with insult and outrage, should she fail to accompany the King to his parish church. She heeded not these menaces, further than to abstain from receiving the communion. "I looked forward," she wrote, "to the happiness of receiving the sacrament on Holy Thursday, and on Easter day, but circumstances deprived me of that happiness; I feared to be the occasion of disturbance in the palace."

It was in vain that, at the expense of his authority, and even of the just scruples of his conscience, Louis XVI. essayed to re-establish peace and tranquillity in his kingdom; by his patience and his goodness, far from reanimating in the hearts of his people, that love for which he was so earnest, he only multiplied recriminations and calumnies. Perversion became every day more and more blind, defections more audacious, exactions more intolerable. The Queen could not look out of the window without incurring some insult, some outrage. The yoke became so heavy that nothing remained but absolutely to sink under it, or to throw it off. Moreover, the revolution, which hitherto had only attacked Louis XVI. in his rights as a monarch, his dignity as a prince, and his liberty as a man, was now directing against him an attack still more injurious: by the civil constitution of the clergy and by the fanatical intolerance of the Assembly, which laid its hands on the censer as on the sceptre—it had attacked him in his duties as a Christian. On the 10th July, 1790, the Pope had written to the King: "Were it in your disposition to renounce even the rights inherent in the royal prerogative, you have no right to alienate in the least degree, or to abandon that which is due to God, and to the church, of which you are the eldest son." On the 15th September in the same year, the Pope had intimated to the King, in a second letter, that the civil constitution of the clergy was "contrary to the fundamentals of the Catholic religion;" and in a last brief, addressed to the cardinals, on 13th April, 1791, the Pope had denounced as schism, the oath taken to the civil constitution of the clergy.

The revolution had thus assailed, in Louis XVI., a force of which it had not been aware. The King had made every sacrifice, the prince had accepted every trial, the man nad patiently suffered every insult, the Christian rose erect.

BOOK THIRD.

JOURNEY TO VARENNES.

20TH—26TH JUNE, 1791.

Repugnance of the King to this journey—Plan of Mirabeau—Correspondence with M. de Bouillé—Preparations for escape—M. de Fersen—Surveillance exercised at the Château—Details of the interior—The royal family leave the Tuileries—Disguises and names adopted on the journey—Bondi—Claye—Montmirail—Châlons—The King is recognised—St. Menehould—Drouet—Clermont—Varennes—Arrest of the royal family—Decree of the Assembly—Return—Clermont—St. Menehould—Châlons—Murder of M. de Dampierre—M. Cazotte—Epernay—Arrival of the three Commissaries of the National Assembly—The Dauphin and Barnave—La Ferté-sous-Jouarre—Meaux—Paris—M. Guilhermy—Expressions of the Dauphin—Reflections on the fatal issue of this journey.

THE question of the escape of the royal family had been already frequently discussed. The King had heretofore vehemently repelled the idea. Two historical recollections, ever present to his memory, had been his motives in this: James II., losing his crown for having quitted his palace; Charles I., led to the scaffold for having fought against the parliament. Persuaded then, that he should at all other hazards avoid two dangers, flight and civil war, he resolved to carry patience to its utmost limits, and to try to reign with the Constitution.

This essay, as we have seen, was protracted, painful, and terrible.

The anguish and trials of the King daily increased. At first he had no confidants at Paris in this idea of escape, so often discussed, and always repelled, but the Queen and Madame Elizabeth; and out of Paris, only the Marquis de

Bouillé, who had inspired him with a confidence, justified by the energy with which he had suppressed the insurrection of the garrison of Nancy, and restored discipline to his army.

Mirabeau, a few days before his death, had proposed a plan by which the King was to retire to a camp in a frontier town, and thence treat with the Assembly. This idea of Mirabeau, rejected at first like all similar projects, was ultimately adopted, when the King, out of patience, resolved to throw off a servitude become intolerable even for his conscience.

He had established a correspondence in cipher with the Marquis de Bouillé. This lieutenant-general commanded in person a considerable body of troops in Trois-Evêchés; he had under his orders the troops of Franche-Comté, Champagne, Alsace, and Lorraine, and thus protected our frontiers from Switzerland to the Moselle and Sambre.

But the breath of the revolution had tainted almost all the ranks of that army; and its chief could only rely on the monarchical fidelity of twenty battalions of German troops, and three or four regiments of cavalry.

A plan was concerted between the King and the general. Louis XVI. was to go to Montmédy, a fortress near the frontier.

M. de Bouillé had proposed that, to diminish the danger, they should divide it, by sending on the Queen first with the Dauphin; but the Queen had said, "If they wish to save us, it must be altogether, or not at all."

Louis XVI. then wrote to M. de Bouillé on the 29th April, that he had ordered expressly for his journey a berline large enough to contain all his family. The general urged him not to use a carriage, the form of which would draw attention, but rather to hire two small, light, English diligences, which were much in vogue at that period; unfortunately, the King did not follow this advice.

Before quitting Paris, the King, in order to save the responsibility of M. de Bouillé, wrote to him the letter of which we give a fac-simile, as also of the notification which the general made of it to M. de Mandel.*

The departure, first fixed for the night of the 19th, did not take place until that of the 20th, because of the necessity of concealing the preparations for it from a *femme-de-chambre* of the Queen, an ardent democrat, capable of denouncing the escape, and whose term of service expired only on the 19th.

It was of the utmost consequence to make haste. This project of escape already began to transpire, for by degrees it had been found necessary to initiate in the secret the assistants whose services were to be employed. These had gossiped in their circles, and the levity of the times and some incautious steps had doubled the number of the confidants. As a result, out of doors the news of the approaching escape of the royal family was disseminated in various well-informed circles, and at the Tuileries it had made its way even into the subordinate gossip of the domestics. It is thus that the rumour of the meditated flight of the royal family so agitated the public, on the days of the 19th and 20th June, that circumstantial relations of it were made to the police.† These rumours were naturally calculated to increase the surveillance, already so active and so scrupulous, to which the château was subjected. It must not, in fact, be forgotten that already at this period the Tuileries was a sort of prison, of which M. de Lafayette was the responsible keeper, the National Guard doing duty in the apartments. During the day, the officers in command of the different posts would receive the King, the Queen, and Madame Elizabeth, on alighting from their carriages, and escort them to their apartments, under the pretext of paying

* See Appendix, No. II.

† See the faithful relation of the flight of the King to Varennes, extracted from judicial and administrative documents, by M. Bimbenet, registrar of the royal court of Orleans.

them the homage due to their rank; but in reality to exercise a superintendence, which developed itself in proceedings of the most insulting nature: for at night when the King, the Queen, and Madame Elizabeth had retired to their rooms, the guards would place a mattress outside the door, so that the princes could not quit their apartments, without passing over the bodies of these strange defenders, thus become gaolers.* Flight, impossible by day, was extremely difficult by night.

The royal family, who knew the precautions with which they were surrounded by night, had some time past had secret doors made. So long back as January there had been formed in the panelling of Madame Elizabeth's apartment a door so artistically constructed that it was difficult to perceive its existence, unless upon the closest inspection. We quote this description from evidence given some time afterwards in a court of justice. This door opened upon a small staircase leading to a vaulted room which separated this apartment from that of the Queen. There had been constructed doors of this kind in the apartments of all the royal family; they were opened by means of folding keys which could be carried about without the smallest inconvenience, and they were so perfectly adapted to the panels of the woodwork and closed so hermetically, that no one would have discovered them without the greatest difficulty, even though they had not been hidden by tapestry. Lastly, they had provided for the possibility of passing through a door long since forgotten, and which had been carefully hidden behind a piece of furniture, which, opening on its two wings, concealed it without closing it up.

They could by this door go from one room to another, or from the interior of the château to the exterior. The inge-

* The authenticity of these details clearly results from the evidence given on the trial which followed the flight to Varennes, by Dubois, captain of the second company of the section du Roule, and by Mercier and François Chauveau, grenadiers of the sixth division.

nious foresight of these measures shows the rigour of the captivity of the royal family. Such art and fertility of invention belong only to prisoners.

On the morning of the 20th June, the Dauphin went out at ten o'clock in the morning to walk in his garden at the end of the Tuileries; at eleven, the Queen and the persons of her suite went to mass; on leaving the chapel, she ordered her coach to be ready by five o'clock that evening. "During the whole day of the 20th June," says Madame Royale, in the account she wrote of the journey to Varennes, "my father and mother seemed very much agitated, without my knowing the cause. At five o'clock, my mother went to take a walk with my brother and myself, Madame de Maillé, her lady in waiting, and Madame de Soucy, under governess of my brother, to Tivoli, at the end of the Chaussée d'Antin. During the walk my mother took me apart and told me that I must not be disquieted at anything I saw."

The King and his family, after taking supper at the usual hour, and giving audience, previous to retiring to bed, to the persons who habitually waited on them at that time, had retired after ten o'clock to their apartments. The customs of the château had thus been scrupulously observed; the Dauphin had retired to rest at nine o'clock, Madame Royale at ten, the Queen about half-past ten, and the King at about twenty minutes past eleven. All the orders had been given to the persons on duty for the morrow, the doors locked, the usual precautions had been taken, and in some places the sentinels doubled, especially at the door of Madame Elizabeth.

The domestics had scarcely withdrawn, when the King, the Queen, and Madame Elizabeth rose; in an instant they were ready for departure. The Queen proceeded to her daughter's chamber. Madame Royale first heard a slight noise at her door, and told her waiting-maid of it; the latter hesitated, but the Queen raised her voice; Madame Brunier thereupon hastened to open the door. As soon as the Queen had entered, she announced to Madame Brunier the project of flight, told her that she had appointed for her and Madame de Neuville to accompany her, and ordered her to dress Madame Royale and take her to the Dauphin. The frock destined for the young princess, had been ordered from a dress-maker who had been told to purchase the simplest materials; it was of brown calico, and cost four francs, ten sous.* They dressed the Dauphin as a little girl. In this costume he was charming. Awakened only at eleven o'clock, the child was heavy with sleep, and could not comprehend what was passing. His sister, who has given these details, asked him what he thought they were going to do. "I think," replied he with his eyes half shut, "that we are going to play a comedy, because we are disguised."

At the moment of departure, the Dauphin and Madame Royale were brought, by Mesdames de Neuville and Brunier, to the apartment of the Queen, where also was Madame de Tourzel. It was very nearly half-past eleven.

On quitting the closet of the Queen, and after having descended a staircase, they followed a corridor communicating with the door of the apartment of M. de Villequier. The Queen led her children by the hand; Madame de Tourzel and then Mesdames Brunier and de Neuville walked behind them. The door of the apartment took a long time to open, and Madame de Neuville, in order to keep the Dauphin, who was half asleep, quiet, sat down on the steps of the stairs, and supported the drowsy head of the child on her knees.

It was agreed that they should go out in separate groups, in order not to arouse the attention of the sentinels.

The Queen, continuing to advance, led to the coach, which stood in the Cour des Princes, the Dauphin, Madame Royale, and Madame de Tourzel. She made them get in, and returned to

* There still exists in the Registry office of the court of Orleans, a piece of this frock, which had been cut off on the return from Varennes, to be used in the examination of Madame Brunier.

the château. The driver of this carriage was the Count Axel de Fersen.*

The carriage left the Cour des Princes, and then to elude the vigilance of the keepers, it made several turns in the district, and returned to wait at the Petit Carrousel, as had been arranged. Whilst it was there, M. de Lafayette, who a few moments before had been at the chamber of the King, passed very near in his carriage, escorted by flambeaux, as usual with him. M. de Lafayette saw nothing, or recognised nothing. The Dauphin was at the bottom of the vehicle, covered by his governess's shawl. "At the expiration of an hour," says Madame Royale, "I saw a woman walk round the coach; I feared that we were discovered, but I recovered my composure on seeing the driver open the door and let in my aunt." On getting into the carriage, Madame Elizabeth inadvertently stepped on the Dauphin, who having been told that he must be quiet and not utter a word, did not let a complaint escape him.

The King and Queen delayed in coming, which disquieted Madame Elizabeth and Madame de Tourzel.

After waiting half an hour, the King appeared, accompanied by a Garde-du-Corps, disguised as a courier; it was M. de Maldent.

The Queen followed Louis XVI. at a short distance, but just as she was crossing the great court of the Carrousel, she saw

* A young and accomplished Swedish gentleman, who, admitted, in happier days, to the intimacy of Trianon, had vowed to the Queen a chivalrous adoration, which had become, in the days of misfortune, a passionate devotion. Arrived from Stockholm to offer his devoted services, this noble stranger, who was proprietary-colonel of the Royal Suédois in the service of France, was, with M. de Bouillé, the chief confidant and most important agent in the flight of the King. It was he who had arranged the construction of the coach for the journey. M. de Fersen was massacred on the 20th June, 1810, by the populace of Stockholm, because they suspected him, most unjustly, of having poisoned the Prince of Holstein-Augustemburg, who, a short time previously, had been elected Prince Royal of Sweden, and had died almost suddenly.

the carriage of General Lafayette approaching; and although she wore a bonnet which hid her face, she desired to avoid the meeting, and ran down the narrow streets which at that time covered the Place du Carrousel. Lost in this labyrinth, and not daring to ask the way of anyone, so near the Tuileries, it was only after a long time that she arrived at the appointed place, accompanied by a garde-du-corps disguised like the first.

Who knows what influence this delay of an hour was fated to exercise upon the destinies of the royal family of France, and of Europe?

They reached the new barrier of the Faubourg Saint-Martin, where they were to find the travelling carriage prepared by the care of M. de Fersen. It was there, drawn by five vigorous horses, and had been waiting two hours. Three men, one of whom was mounted on an English horse, had conducted it thither; these were MM. de Valory and de Moustier, both disguised in liveries, and lastly, the coachman of M. de Fersen, named Balthasar Sapel.*

This delay had given Balthasar occasion for reflection. Thinking he was with men of his own station, he said to them, "Who are your masters, comrades? They seem very rich." To which one of them replied: "Comrade, you will know by and by." Balthasar wanted to continue the conversation, but the laconic answers of his companions indicated their confirmed resolution of silence, and the conversation dropped. One of the two gardes-du-corps, M. de Valory, who was on horseback, went on to Bondy, where he was to arrange the change of horses. From this moment they continued to wait, without exchanging a syllable.

It was the shortest night of the year, that of the 20th June. The day began to dawn; it was past two o'clock in the morning, when a carriage arrived at a rapid rate. They brought the

* See the Notes and Documents, No. III.

two coaches alongside each other, and the persons whom this second coach contained, passed into the first. M. de Fersen closed both the doors; he left on one side of the road the carriage which had brought the royal family, and pushed one of the horses into the ditch, that it might not be able to stir Immediately afterwards, he mounted the box of the other vehicle by the side of M. de Moustier, who was already there, and said to his coachman, who was acting as postilion,—"Forward—courage! be quick!"

They set forth. The various parts were thus distributed.

Madame de Tourzel, under the name of *Baronne de Korff*, (a Russian lady of that name, who had made preparations to quit Paris with her family and a numerous suite, and had, at the request of the Comte de Fersen, placed her passport at the King's disposal.)*

This title of a Courland Baroness, and their destination of Frankfort, a town to which popular opinion assigned the richest and most extraordinary equipages, modified somewhat the unusual and suspicious features of the royal party.

I have mentioned Madame de Tourzel under the name of the *Baronne de Korff*.

Madame Royale and the Dauphin, as her daughters, under the names of *Amélie* and *Aglaé*.

Marie Antoinette, governess of her children, under the name of *Madame Rochet*.

Madame Elizabeth, lady's-maid, under the name of *Rosalie*.

Louis XVI., a valet-de-chambre, under the name of *Durand*.

The three gardes-du-corps.

M. de Maldent, servant, under the name of *Saint Jean*, sometimes sitting in the rumble, sometimes following on horseback.

M. de Moustier, servant, under the name of *Melchior*, seated on the box.

* See in Notes and Documents, No. IV., the *fac-simile* of this passport.

M. de Valory, courier, under the name of *Francois*.

The Queen wore a brown dress, in the form of a tunic; as a head-dress, a black hat *á la Chinoise*, with a long lace veil.

The King had on a dark green coat, with mother-of-pearl buttons; a waistcoat of white satin, embroidered; black silk pantaloons; white silk stockings; shoes, with oval silver buckles. His hair was confined in a bag of black taffeta.

M. de Fersen, at every instant, cracked a whip, crying out to the driver: "On, Balthasar! your horses are not well breathed; go at better speed. The horses will have plenty of rest with the regiment." The horses devoured space; but this speed seemed still too slow for the anxious impatience of M. de Fersen, who perceived the immense perils which pressed behind the royal family.

In half-an-hour they were at Bondy; they had rather flown than run. A relay of six post horses had been got ready by the care of M. de Valory, who had again set out to take the same precautions at Claye. It was at Bondy that M. de Fersen took leave of the King,—he returned to Paris, whence he departed the same day for Brussels.

At Claye, they met the ladies Neuville and Brunier, first femmes-de-chambre, the one of the Dauphin, the other of Madame Royale, and who had started a few hours before in a post-chaise. This post-chaise followed the berline, drawn by six horses. At this stage, the coach, although new, required several repairs. Oh! what blood and crimes did these lost minutes cost France! At Etoges, between Montmirail and Châlons, they were for awhile under some uneasiness. They thought they were recognised. The King, with his usual confidingness, showed himself too freely. He frequently descended from the vehicle, walked along the footpath, and even—according to some of the witnesses—entered into conversation with the villagers. At Châlons, where they arrived at four in the afternoon, they were perfectly recognised, both by the post-master, and by some persons who had seen the King at his coronation;

but these faithful and prudent subjects offered up in silence prayers for their escape,—they themselves assisted in harnessing the horses, and pressed the postilions to depart. They did not stop anywhere for their meals, which they ate in the carriage.

At the bridge of Somme-Vesle, the next stage after Châlons, a detachment of hussars was to have been ready to escort the carriage to Montmédy; but when the King arrived there, towards six o'clock, he found neither the troops nor MM. de Choiseul and Goguelat, who, in accordance with the orders of M. de Bouillé, should have arranged the escort. Unable to question any one on this subject, Louis XVI. was not made aware that these troops had presented themselves six hours previously, on the pretext of conveying a quantity of specie; that the presence of a detachment waiting for so long a period at the post-house had collected a great number of persons; that the municipality of Châlons had sent to inquire the meaning of the confusion, and that M. de Choiseul, fearful lest a single heedless word, however unimportant in itself, might arouse dangerous suspicions, had feigned to act upon the statement of a traveller that the diligence had that morning been unusually laden: "No doubt, it carried the expected treasure," said M. de Choiseul. "We have, then, nothing further to do here, we will go back." The hussars accordingly returned, and everything resumed its wonted tranquillity. Strange circumstance! At Paris, men had a presentiment of the King's flight; on the road, they had a presentiment of his passing. The hussars had departed scarcely an hour when the royal party arrived; the relay was furnished without difficulty.

Meanwhile, in the fear of exciting the same attention and the same movement at St. Menehould, M. de Choiseul had led his soldiers by cross-roads, in order to avoid the town; and in consequence, the King missed him on the highway. Arrived at St. Menehould, they were to have been joined by an escort of dragoons, but the officer in command of the detachment, Captain d'Andoins, had been obliged to go to the Hotel de Ville to explain this movement of troops, which had alarmed the disaffected population, and was, at this moment, almost a prisoner.

It was at this relay that, uneasy at the non-accomplishment of any of the measures which had been concerted, and frequently putting his head out at the window of the carriage, the King was perceived by Drouet, the post-master.* This man, though he had seen Louis XVI. at the federation of the preceding year, did not at first recognise him. But the presence of Captain d'Andoins and his dragoons aroused his suspicions; he took out an assignat, impressed with a very faithful likeness of the King, and compared the two faces. The Queen observed this movement, and was somewhat alarmed at it; but the carriage went on, and its progress dissipated her disquietude.

Drouet, however, had communicated his opinion to the municipal officers of St. Menehould; they assembled at the town-house, and all the inhabitants took arms. At this very moment—a quarter past seven in the evening—an express from the Directory of the department of Marne, arrived at Châlons, and brought the official announcement of the King's departure. It was at once decided that Drouet should proceed in pursuit of the fugitives, and have them arrested, should he overtake them.

He mounted on horseback and followed the carriages, accompanied by Guillaume, son of the landlord of the Grand Cerf, who had served for eight years in the regiment of the Dragons de la Reine; a man incapable of acting for himself, but who was impelled by the ascendancy of Drouet.

M. de Damas had proceeded to Clermont the evening before at the head of a detachment of dragoons. He had orders to get to horse at five o'clock in the afternoon of the

* Born 1763, and now consequently twenty-eight years old.

21st June, and, the royal carriage having passed through the town, to fall back on Varennes. He executed this order, and remained on horseback with his men until night; he then ordered them to unsaddle, and go into quarters It was now half-past nine, the carriages arrived precisely at that moment, and proceeded on. M. de Damas, who had seen them pass, sent his subaltern officers in search of their men. The town was aroused, the municipality put themselves in motion,—there was a discussion between them and the officers, which soon assumed the form of a sharp dispute. M. de Damas sounded to horse; the municipality beat the générale. Placed between the municipality and their officers, the dragoons disobeyed the latter. M. de Damas had scarcely time to effect his own escape.

The King's carriages had only just left Clermont, when Drouet reached it; he took a fresh horse and continued the pursuit. The King was on his way, his courier in front, his spy behind. M. Charles de Damas, the instant after Drouet's departure, sent a quarter-master in pursuit of him. This subaltern officer's name was Lagache; he afterwards emigrated and became a captain in the Choiseul Hussars,—in this detailed narrative it is my object to omit no name and no circumstance. Lagache had nearly come up with Drouet, when the latter dashed into a wood on the left of the highway, and disappeared, under favour of the night, in cross-roads with which he was acquainted, but which were quite unknown to his pursuer, and reached Varennes before the King, at a quarter past eleven at night.

The royal family arrived there at half-past eleven. There was no post-house at this little, isolated town; but the house at which the relay had been appointed, had been so clearly indicated to Louis XVI. that he at once recognised it. He knocked at the door himself, and asked for the horses; the people did not know what he meant. The fact was, that fresh misunderstandings and alarms had occasioned the relay to be transferred to an inn on the other side of the Aire, and the

King, from some inconceivable circumstance, had not been made acquainted with the change. The three gardes-du-corps went to all the houses where lights were visible, asking where it was likely the horses could be found ; but all their researcnes were futile. The Queen herself alighted, and walked about with the King, hoping that chance would send them some one who could supply the desired information ; but no such chance presented itself. These inquiries occupied much valuable time, which Drouet put to good account. The travellers getting once more into the berline, asked the postilions to proceed, but they said that their horses were weary, and could not travel any further. During this dispute, which lasted some time, the courier returned, bringing with him a man, who he said was in the secret. This man, who wore a night-cap and a dressing-gown, approached the King and Queen, and, while they were asking: " Well, where are our horses !" thrust himself almost entire into the carriage. "Your horses," he said ; " I don't know anything about them. I've got another secret, but I shan't tell it to you." " Do you know Madame de Korff?" asked Madame de Tourzel. "No; but I know something better,"—and so saying, he disappeared. At the pressing entreaties of the Queen, the postilions at length consented to proceed through the town. The travellers thought themselves saved; they attributed the occurrence merely to a misunderstanding, and already saw themselves, in hope, amongst the faithful troops of M. de Bouillé.

In order thoroughly to understand the events which are now about to take place, the reader must have an exact idea of the position of the little town of Varennes, which, since these events occurred, has undergone great alterations. Varennes en Argonne is built on a slope; there is, accordingly, an upper town and a lower town, or rather two districts, separated by the Aire, and united by a bridge. At that period, on coming to the town from Clermont, instead of traversing as now a fine square, you threaded a street which led to an archway, closed, at pleasure, by folding gates. This archway separated a belfry, —which still subsists,—from a church since pulled down, and against the belfry stood the little inn of the *Bras d'Or*, kept by a family of the name of Leblanc; the archway resembled the wicket of a fortified town, the inn the guard-house of the wicket. Outside the archway, was the bridge over the Aire. It was at this place that Drouet had placed the ambush which was to arrest the progress of the King. The landlord of the *Bras d'Or*, who was an officer of the National Guard, on being aroused by Drouet, hastened to M. Sauce, the procureur of the commune; then arming himself and his brother, and calling out a post of the National Guard, they placed themselves at the archway. Sauce, on his part, informed the municipal officer, representing the mayor, M. Georges, deputy of Clermontois in the National Assembly, and aroused all the other municipal officers. Messengers were sent communicating the intelligence to the surrounding communes. Georges, junior, a captain of grenadiers, took the command of the post, while Sauce's children ran about the town, by their father's orders, crying—Fire! Drouet, accompanied by the Sieur Regnier, a lawyer, took a loaded cart and placed it athwart the bridge, to close the passage. All these preparations were completed when the sound of the expected berline was heard. It had traversed, without obstacle, the upper town, where almost all the houses were closed and silent.

But at the moment it arrived beneath the sombre vault of the tower which rose at the entrance to the bridge, the horses, frightened by the overturned cart, and by other obstacles placed in their way, suddenly stopped, and immediately loud cries were heard on all sides : "*Halt! halt!*" cries raised by a dozen armed men, who, issuing from the darkness of the walls, rushed to the head of the horses, seized the postilions, ran up to the carriage doors and asked the travellers who they were. "Madame de Korff and her family." "Possibly," replied a voice; "but you must prove it."

At the first cry, at the first gleam of the muskets and sabres, the Gardes-du-Corps had risen from their seats, put their hands to their concealed weapons, and solicited, with a look, permission to employ them. Louis XVI. forbade them to use force. The muskets remained levelled at the carriage. Drouet took a lanthorn, put it to the King's face, and directed him, without naming him, to come to the office of the procureur and show his passports. Hoping that he might not be recognised, Louis XVI. alighted, and his family followed him.

At the moment the royal family were crossing the street, they saw some hussars. They were those whom M. de Choiseul had led by the cross roads from the bridge of Somme Vesle; M. de Goguelat appeared at the same moment. The National Guard, already numerous in the streets, and occupied in constructing barricades, did not permit them to pass until the National Gendarmerie had recognised them, and moreover, taken measures to keep them in check. The activity of Drouet had produced its effect; the tocsin sounded, the *générale* beat, the approaches were barred; already the adjacent villages were in movement, and the towns which the King had left behind him aroused at the news of his flight. All Varennes was on foot. The procureur's house, whither the royal family was conducted, consisted, on the first floor, of two rooms, arrived at by a winding staircase; the one of these looked into the street, the other into the garden. It was into the latter that Louis XVI. was conducted, but the two rooms communicated, and from the front he could see all that was passing in the street, and it was thus that, by the light of the lanthorns and torches, the royal family observed from the window, the crowd outside growing every minute larger and larger. Sauce, in the first instance, pretending to take for simple strangers the august travellers who were brought to him, had merely observed to them, that their horses being exhausted, they had better rest at his house, till a relay could be procured.

When, however, they considered that they had taken all

the precautions necessitated by the arrest of the King, the procureur of the commune and Drouet took upon themselves to address to the unhappy Louis XVI. cruel reproaches, for the intention which they imputed to him, of fleeing abroad, and exciting war against his people. The royal fugitive, still, for awhile, denied the identity of his person, and forcibly insisted upon his right to the liberty secured to all travellers; but Sauce and Detetz, one of the local judges, having declared that they perfectly recognised the Prince and his family, "Well," exclaimed the Queen, who had hitherto remained silent, "if you recognise him for your King, respect him as such." This observation recalled to the King that character of candour which he had had such difficulty in repressing; he avowed himself, and proceeded to explain fully the motives and aim of his journey; his projects, his ardent desire to ascertain the real wants of his people, the constant object of his affections, and to whose happiness he was ready to sacrifice everything; he protested against the idea that was imputed to him of desiring to repair amongst foreigners, and proposed to entrust himself to the National Guard of Varennes, who should conduct him to Montmédy, or any other town of the kingdom where his liberty would be secure. The paternal accent of Louis XVI., his words so impressed with kindliness and sincerity, imposed, for a moment, silence on that assembly of gazers and enemies, who could not listen to them without emotion. Sauce was giving way, and the King would have been saved had the matter depended on that man; but Drouet would not let go of his prey; he harangued, he stormed, he declared that their heads—his and those of all present—were in peril if the King were not sent back to Paris.

At this moment, there occurred a grave circumstance which decided the King's fate. A certain number of hussars, as we have seen, had penetrated into the town, and with them MM. de Choiseul, de Goguelat, and de Damas. These three officers, after much altercation and struggling, managed to get near the

King. The town was at this time under the military command of an old officer, M. de Signemont. M. d'Eslon, captain of a squadron of hussars, having learned at Dun, the situation of the King, had hastened at the head of his troops to Varennes, which he had himself been permitted to enter, but only on condition of leaving on the other side of the Aire, which was not fordable, the seventy-six horse under his command. We find from the contemporary documents, that when M. de Goguelat appeared before the King, his Majesty said to him :—"When shall we depart?" M. de Goguelat, consulting his zeal rather than his power, replied:—"I await your Majesty's orders." At the same moment, the major of the National Guard advanced to receive the King's orders for departure, and the King said, that he accepted as an escort, fifty or even a hundred men of the National Guard. But the municipality purposely kept up a confusion on the point. M. de Goguelat sought orders for the departure to Montmédy, the major of the National Guard for the departure to Paris. It was obvious that the moment approached when a collision must take place between these directions, and the problem stood thus: which should carry the day, the military direction or the municipal direction? The question soon became still more simple. M. d'Eslon, who had, with great difficulty, made his way to the King, requested his orders. "Will M. de Bouillé arrive in time?" asked the Queen in German. "To horse and let us charge!" cried M. de Damas in the same language. This was, in point of fact, the only course that would have been efficacious, had it been only possible. But it was not possible, as will presently be seen. M. de Goguelat had placed six hussars near a battery which commanded the approaches of the upper streets, and six others near a battery which defended the passage of the bridge and the adjacent streets. The commune thought it more expedient to place one of these cannon at the extremity of the street in which the King was, by which means, the first discharge would have swept away the whole detachment of cavalry. M. de Goguelat went to seek a reinforcement to prevent this proceeding: the major of the National Guard and five of his men arrested him as he was about to withdraw. This gave the signal for the collision which had been impending since daybreak. M. de Goguelat not only urged on his horse, so as to thrust aside the major, who received several kicks from the animal, but he drew his sword; the major thereupon fired a pistol at him, and wounded him in the shoulder, and at the same moment the horse stumbled and threw its rider. The hussars did not stir, all this while, so that it became clear they were not to be relied upon. M. de Goguelat, though his wound was slight, found it necessary to withdraw for a short time to his inn, and advantage was taken of his absence completely to gain over the hussars, who promised to obey the officer of the National Guard who was placed over them. The noise of this scene attracted to the window the King, the Queen, and Madame Elizabeth, who were saluted with cries of "*Vive le Roi! Vive la Nation! Vive Lauzun!*" Lauzun was the appellation of the regiment which had just deserted the King

All hope was lost; nothing but the arrival of M. de Bouille could change the face of things. The Queen had vainly essayed upon the heart of Madame Sauce the efforts which Louis XVI. had essayed on the mind of her husband. "You are a mother, Madame," she said to her, "you are a wife; you must feel all that I suffer; you might contribute to render us a great service. It is not the Queen, it is a wife, it is a mother who implores you to do so, with her prayers." The royal suppliant found only cold calculation in the trivial heart of the grocer's wife, and obtained merely this answer. "Madame, I will not compromise my husband; you think of your family, I of mine." The mother had solicited, the Queen became indignant. She rose precipitately, and, with Madame Elizabeth, rejoined her children, who, completely dressed, were sleeping profoundly on a bed in the back room with their femmes-de-chambre at their feet.

D*

The only hope at all conceivable, was from time and superior force. Night had passed away in progressive agitation: to the tocsin of Varennes, had responded the bells of the surrounding communes, whose National Guards had armed and hastened to assist those of Varennes. The crowd, which increased every half hour, overflowed the little town to which this fatal night has given an historical name. The pitiless will of Drouet was triumphant.

Between six and seven o'clock, Romeuf, aide-de-camp of Lafayette, arrived from Paris, the bearer of a decree of the Assembly, which, passed at the first intelligence of the flight, and after the reading of the royal declaration left at the King's departure, directed that the fugitive King, wherever found, should be brought back to Paris.

M. de Romeuf, alarmed at the mission which he had accepted, in order to shield his general, suspected of connivance, and involved in danger by the flight of the King, had overtaken, at Clermont, M. Bayon, an officer of the National Guard, dispatched four hours before him, on the same route, by Bailly, mayor of Paris, and they continued their journey together. M. Bayon entered by himself the back room in which the King was; his complexion, naturally sombre, had, from fatigue and excited feelings, assumed a still darker hue; his hair and clothes were in disorder, his features were agitated, and upon entering the room, he exclaimed, with a panting and broken voice: "Sire, you know . . . . perhaps, at Paris, they are cutting one another's throats—our wives, our children, are perhaps being slaughtered—you will not proceed —Sire, the interest of the state—Yes, Sire, our wives!—our children!"

At these words, the Queen seizing his hand with an energetic motion, and pointing to the Dauphin and Madame, who, exhausted with fatigue, were stretched sleeping on M. Sauce's bed, said: "Am I not a mother also?"

"What is it you require?" asked the King.

"Sire, a decree of the Assembly—"

"Where is it?"

"My companion has it."

And so saying, he half opened the door, and they perceived M. de Romeuf, leaning against the window of the front room, in the utmost disorder, and his face streaming with tears; he advanced with downcast eyes, holding a paper in his hand. The King snatched rather than received this paper, read it with rapid glance, and exclaimed: "There is no longer a King in France!" After the King, the Queen read it; then the King took it again, re-read it, and laid it on the bed where his children were lying; the Queen threw it thence with an impetuous gesture, exclaiming: "I will not have it sully my children." There arose hereupon a movement among the municipal officers and other inhabitants present, as though some sacred object had been profaned. M. de Choiseul hastened to pick up the decree and to place it on the table.

The children were awakened. The young Aglaé became once more the Dauphin, and was the object of special attention; some were in ecstacies at his beauty, others put questions to him, as to the departure from the Tuileries, which scarcely received an answer from the poor little child, still drowsy, whose eyes, as they opened, sought those of his mother, endeavouring to read there the explanation of all that was passing. "Oh, Charles," his sister whispered to him, "you were sadly mistaken; this is not a comedy." "I have perceived that long since," answered the Dauphin, in the same tone.

Meanwhile, the people, excited by Drouet, Bayon, and some of the municipal officers, urged the departure of the King with a rage, closely approximating to frenzy. The clamours increased every moment, intermingled with menaces; several of those furious men wished to force open the door of the house, and carry off the King by violence. "We'll drag him, if needs must, to his carriage," were words heard amid the clamours. The King presented himself at the window, to appease them, but in vain. Still the royal family disputed every minute, for every minute they gained, seemed to them a chance of deliverance. The fatal hour arrived. One of the femmes-de-chambre, in attendance upon the Queen, became ill; Marie Antoinette refused to depart without her. The royal family, like a drowning man, caught at every twig. They sent for a medical man, but when he had given the requisite assistance, the demands for their departure became more imperative than ever. The King, who had hitherto continued to speak of Montmédy, now saw that he could no longer combat an opposition which would evidently result in acts of physical violence; he requested to be left for a moment alone with his family, and after a brief and deeply painful conference with them, he yielded, and announced that he was ready to depart.

The royal mother took her son in her arms and herself carried him to the berline. It was now half-past seven in the morning; they departed.

Almost immediately afterwards, a considerable body of troops crowned the heights overlooking the town towards Verdun. Terror seized the people of Varennes; it was M. de Bouillé the younger, with the cavalry whom he had gone to bring from Dun. He sounded the river Aire, with the intention of fording it with his cavalry, and attacking in front the army of between five and six thousand men, who had taken charge of the King, and so to place them between his own troops and those of his father, who, informed of the imminence of the danger, was sure, ere long, to appear. There was no ford, however, and this last chance of safety vanished. General de Bouillé himself, advancing with all haste at the head of the Royal Allemand, learned from the hussars of Lauzun, before he reached Mouza, that the King had quitted Varennes, and that he was consequently too late. He accordingly turned back, heart-broken, with his regiment, just before full of hopeful courage, now so depressed and despairing.

The royal convoy was already far from Varennes. At the

moment of its quitting the town, the municipality had arrested MM. de Choiseul, de Damas, and even de Romeuf, though he was an aide-de-camp of M. de Lafayette, and bearer of the decree of the National Assembly. The King was captive with his family, in the carriage which was to have conveyed him to liberty. The coaches advanced leisurely, preceded by an excited populace, almost everywhere hostile, and often furious. They assailed with invectives all whom they supposed to be aristocrats, they maltreated all who were nobles; a poor village curé who had respectfully approached the berline, owed his escape from the popular vengeance only to the devotion of an officer of the National Guard. Impeded in its progress by the immense concourse of people, the berline was four hours accomplishing the distance between Varennes and Clermont. This town, in common with all those which the King had to pass through on his return to Paris, was filled with people; all the shops were closed, all the inhabitants in a state of furious excitement.

The most alarming rumours had in fact been disseminated with the greatest industry among the people.

In times of revolution, the absurd itself is a power, and nothing seems more probable to men's heated imaginations, than the impossible. It was announced in the rural districts, that the Austrians had entered France, and that they would spare neither women nor children. Excited by this intimation, the country people armed themselves with scythes, forks, hooks, and rushed on, they knew not whither, under the empire of absolute frenzy.

At Clermont, a detachment of the Dragons de Monsieur, joined the numerous train, which did not reach Menehould till three in the afternoon. This town owed much to Louis XVI., who had raised it from its ruins after a terrible conflagration. The mayor, M. de Furci, a worthy, excellent man, addressed the King in a short speech, to which the latter replied from the carriage window, that "his constant study had ever been the happiness of his people." The mayor invited the royal family to alight at the Hotel de Ville, where the municipal body received him in the council chamber. The King took his seat in one of the arm chairs that were placed for him and his family. The Queen remained standing, and took a jelly which one of the officers of the town presented to her in a silver cup. Louis XVI. intimated to the mayor of St. Menehould, as he had to the procureur of the commune of Varennes, the motives which had determined his departure. The King wished to rest for some hours at St. Menehould; the Prince Royal, worn out with a journey of seven hours, under a burning sun, had been seized with a violent attack of fever. But M. Bayon, who had constituted himself grand director of the journey, refused to comply with the request, and they were obliged to proceed. The dragoons were dismissed here, the distance now effected from the frontier rendering their escort needless; the National Guard of Varennes and that of Clermont also returned to their homes, replaced by that of St. Menehould, who in their turn were relieved by that of the next town.

The populace collected at every point of the route. In the proximity of the village of Han, near the Montagne de la Lune, rendered famous, in the subsequent year, by the encampment there of the King of Prussia, and especially by the battle of Valmy, the Marquis de Dampierre, seigneur of the village, came to pay his respects to the King. This prince conversed with him for a moment, then took leave of him in a most cordial manner. M. de Dampierre bowed, and kissed with respect the hand of his unhappy King. This testimony of respect was regarded as an act of factious servility by the populace. The faithful gentleman had scarcely quitted the carriage door, when the furious mob called on him to stop. Too confiding, he obeyed. They instantly rushed upon him, pulled him from his horse, and pitilessly massacred him under the very eyes of the royal family. His head, stuck on a pike, was for a moment carried as a trophy before the King's carriage.

While they were changing horses at the post-house of Orbeval, Drouet and Guillaume, the victors of the day, rode past on their way to Paris.

An eye-witness, bearing a name well known in royalist martyrology, Cazotte, commandant of the National Guard of Pierry, a little village standing a league from Epernay, has related, in his *Temoignage d'un Royaliste*, the arrival of the royal family in that town. His venerable father had told him to kneel; then, after giving him his blessing, he said to him: "Go, avail yourself of the uniform you wear, and heaven grant you may be able to give some consolation to our good master!" Thus in a few hearts, remaining pure and upright, amid the almost general perversion, the old French loyalty was preserved as a precious deposit. Young Cazotte departed at the head of his troop. As the National Guard of Epernay had been ordered to Châlons, which it was said the Austrians had entered and were subjecting to fire and sword, M. Leblanc, the president of the district, directed Cazotte and his troop to protect the approaches to the Rohan hotel, kept by M. Vallée, where the King was to alight. Cazotte administered a sort of oath to his men, and then ordered them to form a line and permit no one to pass it, other than the constituted authorities. These measures were only just completed, when the King's carriage, borne, as it were, on the waves of people, came up. The captives alighted, and a thousand expressions of abuse were directed against them, and more especially against the Queen.

"Despise this fury! God is above all," said in German, Cazotte, whose eyes had met those of the Queen. "Her Majesty," continues M. Cazotte, "looked at me attentively, and walked into the inn, followed by Madame Royal, Madame Elizabeth, and Madame de Tourzel, but mixed up with the populace, who had soon forced the line formed by the National Guards in the court-yard. The Dauphin, who was carried by a Garde-du-Corps, losing sight of his mother, asked for her with tears in his eyes, and it was to me he addressed himself; throwing his arms round my neck, my cheeks were wetted with his tears. We carried him into the chamber, whither the Queen had been conducted. She asked me if I could procure a workwoman to mend a portion of her dress, which some of the crowd had trodden upon and torn I went out and found in the house itself, the landlord's daughter, a young woman with most charming features. I took her to the Queen, and her respectful air, her eyes red with weeping, presented to her Majesty a touching contrast with the scenes which she had just witnessed. In an adjoining apartment, the municipal and law officers of the place surrounded the King. " Notwithstanding your faults," said one of these persons, "we will protect your return to the representatives of the people. Don't be afraid!" "Afraid," replied Louis, calmly, " amongst Frenchmen, I can never be afraid." A brief conversation ensued on the subject of his journey; the King repeated that his intention had not been to quit the kingdom, but that he could not remain at Paris, where his family was in danger. " Oh! yes, Sir, you'll find you can stay there;" replied one of the municipal officers, significantly. The King looked at him and said nothing further.

The truth of history is here taken from the very facts themselves, the living, moving, breathing facts. The confusion of ideas, the chaos of men's minds, the perversion of the passions, manifest themselves unveiled. As the Queen was re-entering her carriage, a woman said to her, " Ay, be off with you, my pretty dear; they'll soon show you what's what." This bird of ill omen, thus really predicted to the Queen the evil destiny which she merely wished for her.

Between Epernay and Dormans, the sad procession met the commissioners sent by the National Assembly to take possession of the King's person; Barnave, the Marquis de Latour-Maubourg, and Pétion. They had learned at Ferté-sous-Jouarre, that the King, arrested at Varennes, was approaching, and had thence addressed to the National Assembly the following letter, written by Barnave :—

"MONSIEUR LE PRESIDENT,

"We learn that the King and the persons accompanying him passed last night at Châlons, whither they were led and escorted by an army of National Guards, assembled from the contiguous departments, the moment the news of the King's presence at Varennes became known. We hope to join him this evening. We have given on our way the most precise orders for the security and tranquillity of his return, and we have been thoroughly supported by the favourable disposition of the citizens. Every where the feeling respecting the King's departure, is the same that prevails at Paris. The aspect of the people is serene and firm. We have throughout received from them manifestations of their confidence in and respect for the National Assembly.

"We have the honour, &c.

"BARNAVE, PETION, LATOUR-MAUBOURG

"La Ferté-sous-Jouarre, Thursday, 9 o'clock."

This letter and the arrival of Drouet, calmed the agitation of Paris, where there had been no previous news of the King's arrest.*

"Hotel-de-Ville, 22 June.

"We have, Sir, no news of the King's arrest. The general council, indeed, was informed that a courier had presented himself before the National Assembly, bringing intelligence to the effect that he was three hours' journey in advance of the official courier sent by the municipality of Lille to announce the fact, and offering to guarantee the truth of his statement on his head. Since that an officer of the National Guard has informed us that at the National Assembly the rumour is that the alleged courier had gone to the municipality. Both versions are equally false. The people, however, are persuaded of their truth, and the general council has accordingly entreated the deputies of sections who were at the Hotel-de-Ville to return to their quarters and to employ the promptest means for undeceiving the people.

"The Mayor of Paris, BAILLY."

The three deputies at first seated themselves in the royal carriage, but afterwards, to prevent the inconvenience and restraint resulting from this close packing, Pétion got out, saying: "I am like the nation, I feel the need to be free;" and with his colleague Latour-Maubourg entered the second carriage, leaving with the royal family Barnave, whose language and manners were soon found to present a most agreeable contrast with those of Pétion.

The accession of such companions had cast gloom over every countenance; the Queen had drawn her veil over her face, and until the exit of Pétion with Latour-Maubourg from the carriage, entire silence had prevailed. Each person having then resumed his original place, Barnave occupying that of the Dauphin over against the royal pair, Louis XVI. entered into conversation with the deputy, and explained once more, the object and ground of his journey. The young orator of Grenoble listened respectfully to the King, contesting, with deference, those points in which he did not concur, and, with emotion, sentiments which, despite himself, gradually gained upon him. The Queen, touched alike with his agitation, the decorum of his language, and the courtesy of his manners, soon joined in the conversation. A new light broke upon Barnave. The features under which the royal family were daily painted to the public, were wholly unlike those which he had now the means of observing for himself. He seated the Dauphin on his knees, and kept him there during a portion of the journey. When the conversation had subsided, he would seek to resume it by addressing the young prince on his knees, whose prompt responses, full of vivacity and amiability, greatly struck him. "Are you not very sorry to return to Paris?" "Oh, I am glad to be anywhere, so that it is with papa and mamma,—and my aunt, and my sister, and Madame de Tourzel," he added, as his eyes successively beamed on those three personages seated before him in the carriage. "It is indeed a very mournful journey for my children, Sir," said the King "How different from that to Cherbourg. Calumny at that period had not misled opinion, Now, how men's minds are prejudiced, how their heads are heated! They may misapprehend me, but they will not change me! The love of my people will remain the first necessity of my heart, as it is the first of my duties." The plaintive unction of these words deeply affected the Dauphin, who took his father's hand to kiss it. The King pressed him to his heart, calling him as of old: "My dear little Norman!" "Do not be sad, papa," said the child, the big tears rolling down his cheeks; "some other time we will go to Cherbourg."

At almost every change of horses, the two other commissioners came to see what was going on in the King's carriage: wondering to find the heir of the throne still, from stage to stage, on Barnave's knees, Pétion said to Latour-Maubourg, loud enough to be heard by the august travellers, "Decidedly Barnave is the right hand of future royalty."

The progress of the King encountered no impediment of any sort. The population, gloomy and silent, looked on with a sort of stupor. As this new escort of monarchy passed, no one thought of making an attempt in favour of his King. At Ferté sous-Jouarre, however, the royal family were consoled with a kindly reception. They stopped to dine at the house of M. Regnard; Madame Regnard before waiting upon them had the considerate attention to put on an apron, but the Queen, judging correctly, said to her: "You are, doubtless, Madame, the mistress of the house." "Before your Majesty entered it I was so," was the reply, which spoke the feelings and the heart of these generous hosts, who some time after paid a heavy price for the honour of having manifested their respect and attachment to royalty in its misfortunes.

On quitting Madame Regnard's house, the Queen said to the Dauphin—"My dear, do you also thank Madame for her attentions, and assure her that I shall not forget them." "Mamma thanks you for the kindness you have shown us," said the boy, "and I love you for having pleased mamma."

The other stages did not afford similar consolation to the august travellers. In some of the towns, revolutionary cries were even heard, and the Gardes-de-Corps seated on the box were insulted. On entering the suburbs of Meaux a great tumult arose, and a priest was on the point of perishing as M. de Dampierre had perished. The Queen, however, shrieked, and Barnave almost threw himself out of the carriage, as he exclaimed, "Frenchmen,—nation of brave souls!—will you become a nation of assassins?" Struck with admiration of Barnave, Madame Elizabeth held him by the coat, lest he should rush amid the furious mob, and himself become their victim. But the powerful voice of the commissioner had sufficed to snatch the ecclesiastic from death.

Pétion, on this, said to Latour-Maubourg: "It would appear that our colleague has a mission to defend not only royalty, but the clergy too."

After this action the Dauphin eagerly resumed his place on Barnave's knees, for in him he thought he saw a zealous partisan of his family, and the carriages entered slowly and quietly the town of Bossuet, where they remained for the night. The shade of the great mourner of royal misfortunes had perhaps risen to put its finger on the lips of revolt, that it might itself repeat to the powers of the earth the terrible warning, "Now, kings, learn! Instruct yourselves, arbiters of the world."

At eleven in the evening, while his colleagues were reposing after the long day's journey, Barnave sought the King's chamber, and had a long conversation with him, and with the Queen, as to their position. "Evidently," observed her Majesty, "we have been deceived as to the real state of the public mind in France." They both thanked Barnave for the grave counsels he gave them, solicited their continuance, and arranged to see him in private at the Tuileries. From that day forth, Barnave vowed to himself to live and die faithful to the throne, and devoted to liberty.

No other incident varied the remainder of the journey;

the King re-entered Paris on the 25th, at seven in the evening.

Pétion and Latour-Maubourg, at the last stage, had taken their seats in the royal berline, where nine persons were thus packed together under a burning sun.

On the preceding evening, numerous placards had been posted up, with this notice: *He who cheers the King shall be beaten ; he who insults him shall be hanged.* The police had not contented themselves merely with prescribing this disapproving silence on the passage of the royal captive. The National Guards were requested to receive him with their weapons reversed, and the people with their hats on. The mournful procession advanced along the Avenue des Champs-Elysées amidst two or three hundred thousand spectators. A thick cloud of dust, raised by this immense multitude, veiled, ever and anon, from the people the humiliation of their former masters, and from these the triumphant joy of their enemies. The forehead of the Dauphin streamed with perspiration; he could hardly breathe. His mother let down one of the windows, and seeking commiseration in the national militia who lined the road: "See, gentlemen," she said, "see in what a state are my poor children; they are half stifled." "We'll stifle you in another way," murmured some cruel voices from behind the ranks of the National Guards. The carriages entered the garden of the Tuileries by the Pont-Tournant, and had great difficulty in reaching the château, so great and so compact was the crowd that obstructed the gates. All heads were covered; such were the orders. One man alone, M. Guilhermy, a member of the National Assembly, took his hat off, and bowed with every indication of profound respect. The mob called upon him to put on his hat, but he threw it, instead, among them and remained uncovered, with brow erect and visage serene and firm.

The three Gardes-du-Corps alighted first from the box-seat of the front carriage; they were not bound, as was rumoured at the time, and as has been written since, but they had been exposed all the way to infinite insults, and now, furious men, drunk with rage and with wine, sought to inflict violence upon them, and it was with great difficulty that the National Guards could protect them. M. Hue, forcing his way through the crowd, reached the gate as the carriage came up, and put out his arms to receive the Dauphin. The royal child no sooner perceived this kindly companion of his walks, this gentle partner of his amusements, than his eyes filled with tears. Notwithstanding the effort of M. Hue to take the Dauphin in his arms, an officer of the National Guard got possession of him, carried him into the château, and placed him on the table in the council chamber. M. Hue reached the chamber at the same moment, and immediately afterwards the King, the Queen, and the Princesses entered it. His Majesty finding a group of deputies assembled, approached them, and said:

"I deemed it expedient to quit Paris, but I never had any intention of quitting France. I proposed to fix my residence for awhile in one of the frontier towns, and to become mediator in the dissensions which are daily multiplying in the Assembly. I desired, above all, to labour in perfect freedom, and with concentration of purpose, for the happiness of my people—the constant object of my care."

Overwhelmed with fatigue, covered with dust and perspiration, Louis XVI. then retired with his family to the interior of his apartments. An officer of the National Guard sought again to take possession of the Dauphin, but the King objected, and by his orders, M. Hue, raising the young prince in his arms, carried him to his apartment, and placed him under the charge of Madame de Tourzel.

Invested by the Assembly with the government of the château, and with the especial guard of the King and the royal family, M. de Lafayette had selected from the Parisian militia thirty-six officers, most of them personally devoted to their chief, and who were to relieve each other, by twelves, in the interior of the palace, every twenty-four hours. Two of these officers immediately installed themselves in the very chamber of the Dauphin. Madame de Tourzel, seeing that she was about to be arrested, and wishing to spare the prince the pain of witnessing the scene, withdrew into an apartment adjoining that in which he slept, having, by the medium of M. Hue, procured from Madame Elizabeth, a book which that princess had promised to lend her: *Pensées sur la Mort.* A few moments after she had taken possession of her new chamber, two other officers presented themselves in execution of the order they had received, not to lose sight of her. Madame de Tourzel, however, experienced the most considerate respect on the part of both these gentlemen, MM. Bance and Du Fays.

As soon as the Dauphin was in bed, he called M. Hue. "Tell me what all this is about," said he; "we had no sooner got to Varennes, than they sent us back again. Why was that? I can't tell at all; do you know?" The officers of the guard were at this time walking about the room, in conversation. M. Hue represented to the prince that it was absolutely necessary not to speak to anyone, or before anyone, of that journey. The recommendation—scrupulously observed—doubtless, aided materially to develope, in that young imagination, the grave reflection that engenders disquiet and fear. The child, despite his weariness, and wholly contrary to his wont, lay long sleepless that night, and on awaking next morning, said, in presence of his guards, and loud enough to be heard by all present, that he had had a frightful dream, in which he thought himself surrounded by wolves, tigers, and other ferocious beasts, that sought to devour him. M. Hue, from whom we derive these details, adds that, all in the apartment looked at each other, without venturing to say a word.

The King and his family were now evidently in a much more terrible situation than that from which they had endeavoured to escape. For all of them slavery had become more rigorous, their prison narrower, their humiliation deeper. The efforts they had made to break their bonds had only served to rivet them still closer. An inconceivable fatality, and, we must add, an extraordinary want of foresight, seems to have attended this unfortunate journey.

M. de Bouillé had urged the King to take the direct road from Paris to Montmédy through Reims, instead of that through Varennes, which, from Clermont to Montmédy, is only a second class road. Unprovided with post-houses, M. de Bouillé justly feared that suspicion would be awakened by the relays of post-horses which must, under such circumstances, be sent, under different pretexts; and also, by the presence of troops on a road they did not usually frequent.

The King, however, thinking he might be recognised at Reims, where he had been crowned, persisted in following his own plan.

This was a misfortune; it was not the only one. M. de Bouillé, feeling how essential it was for the royal family to have some trustworthy, firm, active, and energetic man with them, one who could meet the difficulties of the journey, and, if necessary, break through obstacles, had chosen for this important purpose the Marquis d'Agoult, a major of the Gardes Françaises, and proposed him to Louis XVI. The King promised at first to follow his advice; but the royal family being accustomed to have Madame de Tourzel constantly with the royal children, refused to part with her, and M. d'Agoult was therefore not taken.

Nor was this all. M. de Bouillé had begged the King to request the Emperor Leopold to operate on the frontier, towards Montmédy, a movement of troops, in appearance hostile, so as to justify, in the eyes of the alarmed population, the concentration of a corps of French cavalry about that town. Louis XVI. had answered, that his brother-in-law the Emperor would order a body of troops to march towards Longwy, and thus give a motive for the assemblage of French troops in that quarter. This movement, however, did not take place at the proper time, which greatly embarrassed the general, who feared if his detachments were too small, they would be insufficient to protect the King's flight, and if too large, they might impede it by exciting the vigilance and suspicion of the municipalities.

The consequences of the four-and-twenty hours' delay, also, were irreparable, disconcerting, as it did, all the arrangements as to time and place, and giving rise to inexplicable counter-orders, both as to the relays and the detachments, whose passage was now converted into a compromising halt, eminently calculated to arouse suspicions.

Lastly, a thousand mistakes in details were made,—so many, that we are disposed to believe in those as facts which still remain doubtful. Certain it is that presence of mind, promptitude of decision, rapidity of execution, ability and daring, were all on the side of the King's adversaries. Everything, indeed, was against him—the vices and passions of a great number, the illusions of all: the moral sovereignty had passed over to the Assembly, and with it the favour of public opinion, which now turned against royalty. As, at sea, almost everything depends upon the wind, so, in politics, the current of public opinion carries everything before it. Those who served the King acted as faithful but despairing servants, defending a lost cause, not in the hope of victory, but for the sake of honour. So extraordinary did this combination of unfortunate circumstances, incomprehensible blunders, and deplorable results appear, that some have thought,—and one grave historian* has written, that the journey to Varennes was, in reality, a plot, laid to ensnare the King and lead him to his ruin, into which he fell, with his most faithful followers.

Such was the issue of this fatal journey, so ill-concerted, so wretchedly executed. Everything seemed to conspire to render its success impossible: indecision in the measures, want of initiative in the characters, dangerous indiscretions, useless

* M. le Comte de Sèze, "*Histoire de l'Evenement de Varennes*"

preparations destructive of secrecy, a display of troops rather calculated to compromise than to secure the safety of the journey, while emigrants daily left the country who were not even asked for passports. Alas! everything was destined to be fatal to the unfortunate King,—excess of zeal and precaution alike with treason.

His life as king had, for the last two years, been a struggle. It seemed as though the monarch, at the first blow, had bowed before the inexorable fatality of his destiny, and that, like the Roman gladiator, he had seen the impassioned spectators give him the signal that it was time for him to die.

But let us speak more christianly of this most christian man: Louis XVI. born to misfortune, lived in it as though it had been his element. He saw calamity approach without amazement and without fear, as an austere friend, sent by religion. Ever ready to submit to God's will, he felt himself created to fall into those abysses, which nations, from time to time, dig in their days of anger and hallucination.

The King, accordingly, placed himself in the hands of the multitude he should have led, to become first its plaything, and afterwards its victim. Behold him now the sport of threatening doctrines, of severe utopias, of cruel popularity, which destroys as it caresses, and casts praises and stones together: fatally impelled towards his ruin, nothing could save him. The people awakened, full of malignant and sanguinary instincts; patriotism became hatred of authority. When such aberration takes possession of the heart and intelligence of a nation, the human flock soon devours its pastor. The implacable time of reparation was come; it must have its victim, and he who personified royalty was the victim promised for the expiation of ages, whose blood must atone for all the shame of courts, all the vices of princes, all the sufferings and all the errors of the people. Destined by Heaven to be a martyr, Louis XVI. had not the heroic energy that resists, but he had the heroic courage which knows how to die.

BOOK FOURTH.

THE DAY OF THE 20TH JUNE.

JUNE 26TH, 1791—JUNE 20TH, 1792.

Captivity of the Royal Family at the Tuileries—First promenade of the Dauphin—Situation of the Assembly in reference to the King—The Constitution decreed—The King accepts the Constitution—The Prince Royal—Fête in the Champ-de-Mars—Acclamations of the people—Happiness of the Dauphin—Confidingness of the King—Letter to his brothers—Anecdotes of the Dauphin—Dissolution of the Constituent Assembly—Accession of the Legislative Assembly—Its first proceedings—Reaction of opinion in favour of Louis XVI.—The Royal Family at the Italian Opera—Menacing attitude of Europe—Armed emigration—Decrees of the Assembly—Veto of Louis XVI.—Anger of the Revolution—Letter of the Queen—The Prince Royal's tutor—Day of the 20th June—Narrative of Madame Elizabeth—Remark by the Dauphin—Proceeding of M. de Lafayette—Reflections.

THE King and Queen were subjected to an inquiry, by the commissioners of the Legislative Assembly, as to the motives and circumstances of their flight. Although Barnave at the head of the moderate party, endeavoured to limit as narrowly as possible, the investigations relative to the event of the 21st June, all the parties charged as having been implicated in that unlucky attempt, shared the bondage and humiliations of the royal family. The three Gardes-du-Corps, after having spent the night, surrounded by sentinels, in a chamber near the King's apartment, were taken, with Mesdames de Neuville and Brunier to the Abbaye Saint Germain. MM. de Choiseul, De Damas, and De Floirac, arrested at Varennes, had been thrown into the prison of Verdun; a few days after, by a decree of the National Assembly, M. de Choiseul was trans ferred to the prison of Orleans, and MM. de Damas and Floirac to a prison in Paris. The two *femmes-de-chambre* were set at liberty in a few days, but the rest were not released until the King had accepted the Constitution and a general amnesty had been granted,

The Dauphin had frequently asked what had become of his *bonne*, so he called Madame de Neuville, his first *femme-de-chambre;* he was answered, that she had gone to visit her mother in the country. When she was restored to him, he said: "I have not seen you for a long time, but you have done right. In your place I think I should have stayed away much longer,"—and, throwing himself into his mother's arms, he covered her with kisses.

The King, whose mind was at times wavering, but whose soul was ever strong and noble, wished to incur the whole responsibility of the journey to Varennes himself. He framed all his answers to that effect, when Tronchet, Duport, and Andrè, deputed by the Constituent Assembly, came to receive his declaration, for so they called, in derisive respect, the interrogatory to which he was subjected. So fixed was this resolve, that the next day he sent to request the three commissioners would come to the Tuileries, to receive a supplemental declaration.* The object was clearly to establish that M. de Bouillé had acted under a formal command from the King, when he made arrangements to protect his journey from Châlons to Montmédy.

* "GENTLEMEN,

"Authorised by you, we waited upon the King. and having been introduced into his bed-chamber, were left alone with him,—he then said he had thought it right to send for us as he remembered he had omitted to mention in his declaration, that M. de Bouillé had acted under an order from him in protecting his journey from Châlons to Montmédy. When we observed to him that this order was already known, through the arrest of M * * *, the King declared himself ignorant of that fact, and added that, it was now unnecessary to make any addition to his declaration.

"TRONCHET."

For a few days, Barnave did not venture to come to the Tuileries; afterwards the most minute precautions were taken to ensure secrecy in his interviews with the King.

These interviews took place in a small room on the first floor. The royal couple often waited for hours together, holding the handle of the door, in order to open it without noise, the moment they should hear the footsteps of their secret protector, who had so fruitlessly accepted the difficult and perilous inheritance of Mirabeau. The men of late so powerful, by the revolution, against royalty, could now only bring to the support of royalty, against the revolution, the miserable wreck of a strength wasted in the work of social demolition, to which they had sacrificed all the freshness of their talents, and the ardour of their youth. On what depend the destinies of empires and the opinion of men! Had Barnave never been in contact with Louis XVI. and Marie Antoinette, he would have played a totally different part in the revolution. The journey from Varennes awoke his sensibilities to the detriment of his ambition, and won him over to monarchy; his policy, till then, had followed his imagination; it was now inspired only by his heart. Intercourse with the Bourbons has, in periods of discord, bound more than one enemy to their cause, won by the sole attraction of virtue and fallen greatness. That which made Barnave a royalist was the reading in the humid eyes of a beautiful queen, anxiety and entreaty; it was the having held on his lap the heir to the throne of so many kings, and played with the curls of his fair hair. Barnave did not possess the thundering eloquence of Mirabeau, but he had more elevation of sentiment. The man of genius had sold himself: the man of feeling gave himself.

The captivity of the royal family, and the insults heaped upon them, had for a moment mitigated the cruelty of their enemies, in whose eyes the King had become less the chief than the hostage of the nation, so that the word forfeiture which had been pronounced in the first effervescence, found no echo now. Several members of the Assembly even thought that they had gone too far, and felt the necessity of reconciling the King with the people. This it was that made Robespierre say, "My friends, all is lost, the King is saved."

Meanwhile, every measure was taken by Lafayette to prevent a second escape. The general, who had been so little watchful on the night of the 5th October 1789, now allowed himself no repose. At all hours of the day and night, the royal family were beset by his indefatigable activity; every movement was watched, every word observed. So rigid were the precautions, that mass was discontinued in the chapel of the chateâu, as being too far from the apartments. A room adjoining, where they erected a wooden altar, bearing an ebony crucifix and a few vases of flowers, became the chapel of the Most Christian King. The movements of the royal family were under continual constraint. Whenever the Queen, whose apartment was on the ground-floor, visited her son, she was accompanied by four officers of the National Guard, and went by a private staircase. She always found his door closed. One of the officers would knock, saying, "The Queen!" The two officers, constantly on guard, in Madame de Tourzel's rooms, then opened the door, and Marie Antoinette, taking her son, would conduct him to the King.

Ill-treatment could not mar the serenity of this august race, whose power might fail but not its heart, and which, in its decline, grew feeble indeed on the throne, but became great in misfortune. During this first captivity Louis XVI. read over the life of Charles I., which he had translated in his youth from Hume, thus initiating himself in the accomplishment of his own destiny; while Marie Antionette devoted a great part of the day to the education of her son and daughter, and of a young orphan (Ernestine Lambriquet), the daughter of one of the women attending on Madame Royale. In these hours of study, wherein each branch of instruction had its place, the royal instructress did not limit her lessons to cold precepts and barren advice; she sought to elevate the character, as well as to enrich the memory; to cultivate the heart as well as to enlighten the understanding. She taught her pupils to put aside every month a portion of the small sum appropriated to their amusements, in order to enjoy the far greater happiness of relieving the miserable. She presented herself as an example of the instability of human greatness, saying that we should never rely on the stability of fortune, but ever on the justice of God. The Queen had not waited till life had lost all charms for her, to do good; charity with her was an instinct necessary to her heart's happiness, and not the tardy fruit of misfortune. In the bright days of her power, she had founded an hospital at St. Cloud; every month she sent bountiful offerings to the curés of Paris, her agents with the poor. She formed part, not as an honorary patroness, not as a nominal president, but as an active and zealous member, of the *Société Maternelle*, so well known for its good works. Of the children of those attached to her service the little Ernestine was not the only one whom she had taken under her care. An officer of the King's chamber (M. Chaumont), and his wife had died within brief intervals, the one after the other, leaving three young daughters, without any fortune; the Queen adopted these orphans, placed the two eldest at school, and had the youngest brought up under her own observation. The infinite acts of charity of which she gave the example to her children, became, under the tenacious responsibility of Lafayette, the objects of minute surveillance. The Queen was no longer free to follow the precept of the Gospel, which directs us to conceal from the left hand the charity which the right hand giveth; an all-distrusting police sought conspiracy in all her acts, a stratagem in all her benefits. The King's movements were equally under constraint; he could not at once send for persons whom he wished to see; the names of these persons had first to be inscribed on a list, which the Duke de Brissac, captain of the Cent-Suisses, transmitted to the major-general of the National Guard, who then issued cards of admission for such of these persons as he thought fit to admit to the château. The servitude thus imposed within doors was efficiently supported without: if, in the evening of a hot summer's day, the royal family desired to breathe the fresh air, they could not present themselves at the windows of the palace without exposing themselves to the invectives of the lowest populace. The King was the prisoner of M. de Lafayette, a keeper all the more rigid that he himself had begun to be the prisoner of the revolution.

Meanwhile, the National Assembly, which, after the King's return from Varennes, had, by a decree, provisionally withdrawn from Louis XVI. the exercise of the royal power, was actively engaged in drawing up the new constitution. Public opinion was somewhat stilled. After a few weeks' captivity the Queen was at length permitted to walk with the Dauphin in the garden of the Tuileries. The chest of the young prince expanded with delight to receive the pure air. "Mamma," said he, bounding about, "how I pity the poor people who are always shut up." A number of birds, perched on the highest trees of the garden, had attracted his attention. In his eagerness to watch them as he walked, he stumbled and fell into a little hole covered with green leaves. His mamma and the attendants hastened to him: as he rose, he said: "Mamma, I am as heedless as the astrologer in La Fontaine," and he laughingly recited the first four lines of the fable:—

> Un astrologue un jour se laissa choir
> Au fond d'un puits. On lui dit: Pauvre bête,
> Tandis qu'à peine à tes yeux tu peux voir,
> Penses-tu lire au-dessus de ta tête?

His active and ever prompt mind delighted in applying to the little events of his day the lessons he had stored up. It was thus that, on two other occasions, our great fabulist furnished him with quotations exactly applicable to the purpose. His sister, speaking in his presence of some person who had, by adroit flatteries, extracted a pension from a minister, he said: "Poor minister! I don't think much of the crows who let go of their cheese in that way." Another time, after a long walk, in which he had taken active exercise in chasing butterflies, he returned with the double appetite of the child and the sportsman; the repast being delayed, Madame de Soucy reprimanded the attendant for this neglect. "Don't scold, pray, Madame, that won't enable me to eat any the sooner:

"Patience et longueur de temps
Font plus que force ni que rage."

The journey to Varennes had presented to all parties an opportunity to come forward; the republicans began to unfurl their standard. In fact, when an assembly is in a position to seize the King, to imprison him, to suspend him from his functions, there is no longer a monarchy; the republic exists, if not *de jure*, at all events *de facto*. The logical republicans of the minority opposed the constitutionalists, those inconsistent republicans of the majority, calling them aristocrats, the very name which the constitutionalists had applied just before to the royalists, by way of denouncing them to the public hatred. The same weapon was used; only it had changed hands, and was now turned against those whom it had enabled to conquer. Such is the eternal law of revolutions; the revolutionists of the first hour are devoured by those of the second.

Madame Elizabeth, who perfectly understood this law, wrote at this date (Sept. 1791): "Everything here is fearfully vague; no one knows how he stands. The Assembly is in a state of utter embarrassment; it cannot retrace its steps, because the republican party would then at once acquire the ascendancy."

The Assembly, the majority of whom was distinguished by

great talents—though these unfortunately were theoretical rather than practical—and even by the genuine virtue of many of its members, began to perceive the perils of its own situation. Strong against the King it was weak against the multitude. It accordingly expedited the completion of the constitution. There was belief at this period in the efficaciousness of those sovereign formulæ which, by the inconstancy of man's will, too closely resemble geometrical figures traced on the sand, as if destined to measure the world, but which a child effaces with his foot, as he passes over them in his sports. At length on 3rd September, 1791, was completed that act which deposed the royalty it affected to proclaim, and set up the republic under the forms of the monarchy.

The same day, M. de Lafayette waited on the King, in the council chamber. "Sire," said he, "the approaching presentation of the constitutional act enables me to withdraw the guards that have been placed about your person." "The Assembly placed them there," replied the King; "it is for the Assembly to withdraw them." Disconcerted by this unexpected answer, Lafayette retired without uttering another word. The King then sent for several of the officers, and expressed to them his appreciation of the consideration and respect which they and others of their body had throughout manifested towards him and his family. In the afternoon, the sentinels who had so insultingly converted the King into a hostage, and his palace into a prison, were withdrawn.

Next day, 4th September, 1791, a deputation came, with great solemnity, to bring the constitutional act to the King. Thouret, the chairman of the constitutional committee, presented it to his Majesty in these terms:—

"SIRE,

"The representatives of the nation offer to the acceptance of your Majesty the constitutional act; it consecrates the imprescriptible rights of the French people; it restores to the throne its true dignity, and organizes the government of the Empire."

The King replied to the deputies, that he would examine the constitution which the National Assembly had directed them to lay before him, and that he would communicate his determination respecting it, in the shortest delay compatible with the due examination of so important a document.

Thouret related the interview which had thus taken place to the Assembly, who received his report with loud cheers. The public hope manifested itself in all directions, deeming that it saw the termination of the storm in a compact unhappily ill-adapted for combining in harmony the vanquished authority of the monarchy, and the victorious authority of the Assembly, behind which latter revolution was getting itself ready.

On 13th September, after maturely consulting his reason and his conscience, the King addressed to the Assembly, by the medium of the minister of justice, a message prepared in concert with Barnave, and which accepted the constitutional act. The prince acted in perfect good faith; he saw, no doubt, that the charter presented to him contained the evil principles and dangerous or impracticable details inseparable from impromptu constitutions; but he was earnest to spare the state the new crises, and the people the new calamities that a rejection of the measure on his part would have occasioned. The diminution of his own power he accepted without regret; he had more faith in good than in evil. Undesirous of limitless and uncontrolled authority, he saw in power, less the enjoyments it procures than the obligations it imposes. As a man, he knew himself to be weak; as a Christian, he knew how to be humble, and he had learned from history, that we seldom do that which we ought, when we always do that which we will. He readily submitted, therefore, to the guarantees which the nation required against the ebullitions of the sovereign will; and the ancient power, which, according to his ideas and in his conscience, he derived from God himself, was ready, in his person, to contract a sincere alliance with modern liberty.

After setting forth the grounds on which his resolution proceeded, he nobly demanded that all processes and prosecutions connected with the events of the revolution, should be extinguished in a general reconciliation. In conclusion, he said: "I will swear to the constitution in the same place where it has been framed, and I will, for this purpose, repair to-morrow, at noon, to the National Assembly."

The general amnesty requested by the King was unanimously accorded, and a numerous deputation went to present the decree of indemnity to the King at the Tuileries. The royal family were assembled together. "Here are my wife and children," said Louis XVI; "they fully participate in my sentiments." The Queen advanced, and said in her turn: "Here are my children; we all participate in the sentiments of the King."

Next day, 14th September, the King at noon repaired, amid the roar of cannon and the joyous acclamations of the people, to the National Assembly. Having seated himself in the arm-chair placed for him, he said:—

"Gentlemen,

"I have come here, solemnly to consecrate my acceptance of the constitutional act; and thus I do so. I swear to be faithful to the nation and to the law; to employ all the power that is delegated to me, in maintaining the constitution decreed by the National Constituent Assembly, and in executing the laws.

"May this grand and memorable epoch be that of the re-establishment of peace and of union; may it become the source of the people's happiness, of the empire's prosperity!"

Universal applause, from the house and from the galleries, hailed this oath and the speech accompanying it.

While Thouret, as president, was replying to the King, the

Queen, with her son and daughter were perceived seated in a box. The acclamations just bestowed on the King were spontaneously renewed to the Queen, and to the heir of the constitutional throne. Cries of "*Vive le Prince Royal*" resounded from all parts of the chamber, as a public adhesion to the new charter, which abolished the designation of Dauphin, and conferred the title of Prince Royal on the heir to the throne.

The whole Assembly, with its president at its head, escorted the King to the Tuileries; the imposing procession could scarcely make its way through the floods of people, who were sending up to heaven their acclamations of joy.

Flourishes of trumpets and salvos of artillery, proclaimed to France the reconciliation of liberty with the throne, of the nation with the King.

France entered with phrenetic delight on the possession of her constitution, (18th September.) The proclamation of this solemn compact had all the characteristics of a fête; the Champ-de-Mars was covered with civic legions; thither pressed the municipality, with Bailly at its head, the departments, the public functionaries, the people—the party chiefly interested in the celebration—and there, from the altar of the country, was read the act of the constitution; one single cry responded to that reading, but it was a simultaneous cry raised by three hundred thousand voices, "*Vive la Nation!*" The citizens, without knowing each other, embraced as brothers, as members of the great regenerate family.

A splendid illumination prolonged the day; balloons, covered with patriotic inscriptions, rose aloft, as if bearing to the heavens evidence of the emancipation of a great people. At eleven o'clock in the evening, the King, the Queen, and their children, rode in their carriage, along the Avenue des Champs Elysées and the Avenue du Cours, glittering with garlands of lamps hanging from tree to tree, and extending from the Tuileries to the Porte de l'Etoile, and to Chaillot. Everywhere enthusiastic acclamations hailed them, converting into a path of triumph that same road which so recently they had traversed amid the imprecations and menaces of the multitude. *Vivats* were thundered forth for the King, for the nation, for the old name of Dauphin, for the new name of Prince Royal. The young Prince himself, forgetting the lateness of the hour, did not once think of sleep, and in his headlong joy, took his part in the fête, quite like a child of the people.

The remembrance of past sufferings, the anxiety of future calamities, were extinguished for a moment in the soul of Louis XVI. The shipwrecked man, amid the storm, grasps for safety at the frailest bark: the King trusted to the Constitution; he vowed to it, in his honest heart, honest fidelity, and followed the general impulse of public feeling. That same night Marie Antoinette, too, returned to the château with her full share in the universal delusions. "It is no longer the same people," said she, and taking her son in her arms, she showed him, with fond pride, to the crowd who thronged all the approaches to the palace.

A few days afterwards, the constitutional King gave a fête to the people of Paris; he began it, as his heart ever dictated, by care for the poor, to whom, that they might participate in the public joy, he gave abundant alms. A *Te Deum* was sung at Notre Dame, to bless the new era of happiness that men began to foreshadow for France.

Madame Elizabeth, who but slightly concurred in these hopes, wrote at this epoch to Madame de Raigecourt, with a slight shade of irony: "We have been to the opera; to-morrow we shall go to the play. Heavens, what pleasures! I am perfectly enraptured. To-day we had, during mass, a *Te Deum*. There was one at Notre Dame. The intruder wanted us to go there; but when one has them sung at home, one has no occasion to seek them elsewhere. You see we have been very quiet. This evening, we are to have another illumination; the garden will be superb,—all lamps,* and those glass machines

* *Lampions*, earthen pots filled with grease.

which, for the last two years, one cannot name without a shudder."*

During the fêtes given on the acceptance of the Constitution, the Revolution seemed to enjoy a lull. Louis XVI. secretly despatched M. de Fersen to the Emperor Leopold, entreating him not to awaken, by the clash of arms, the national spirit which was slumbering in its joy. He also sent the Baron de Viomesnil and the Chevalier de Coigny, to request his brothers and the Prince de Condé immediately to effect the disarming and the dispersion of the emigrants. No attention was paid to this order, which there was reason to suppose was signed by an enchained hand.

Louis XVI., as king, never desired intervention; in moments of discouragement he sometimes desired it as a man, a husband, and a father. The regency, which had been assigned, at Coblentz, to the Count de Provence, and which made all Europe regard Louis XVI. as a prince under tutelage, had deeply wounded the sensibilities of the Queen. The King himself felt also humiliated by it; but even had his thoughts ever turned to the possibility of an intervention, he would never have accepted a foreign power as master, or made other use of it than as an auxiliary. Never would this thoroughly French prince have betrayed and sold his country; his errors were those of his situation, his faults those of his fortune.

So soon as he discovered a gleam of hope on the road before him, he proceeded to advance, supplicating his friends to impede with no obstacle, the efforts he was making to satisfy the new ideas. It was to this purpose he wrote to Monsieur, and to the Count d'Artois, after the acceptance of the Constitution, the letter containing these words, so full of wisdom. "I have preferred peace to war, because peace has appeared to me at once more virtuous and more useful. The nation loves the

* Madame Elizabeth refers to the lamps—or, rather, to the lamp-posts—which the Revolution had converted into gallows.

Constitution, because that term only recalls to the lower classes of the people the independence they have enjoyed for the last two years; and to the class above them,—equality. They find fault with this or that particular decree, but this is not what they call the Constitution. The populace see that they are taken into account; the bourgeois, that he has attained a position, whence he can look freely about him, without a sense of inferiority; self-respect is satisfied, and this new enjoyment has superseded all others. They only awaited the completion of the Constitution to be perfectly happy; to retard that completion was in their eyes the greatest of crimes, because that was to bring with it all happiness. Time will show them how they have been mistaken; but their error, meantime, is none the less profound. If one were to seek now to overthrow it, they would only hug the idea of it more closely, as that of the means of the greatest happiness; and when the troops who had overthrown it should have quitted the kingdom, the perturbators might, with this chimera, keep up an incessant agitation, and the government would find itself involved in a system altogether counter to the public feeling, and without the means of keeping that public feeling in check."*

It is impossible to discern or to describe more clearly; the unhappy Louis XVI. was advancing, a devoted sacrifice, to the fatal goal, whither he was impelled at once by the malignant attacks of his enemies and the imprudent aid of his friends.

Some days after the oath to the Constitution, the King was requested to have painted for the National Constituent Assembly, in commemoration of the new era, a picture in which he should be represented exhibiting to his son the constitutional act. The events which soon after arose, prevented the execution of this project, by removing first the King, and then the Constitution.

The Constitution enacted (chap. ii., sec. iii., art. iv.) that a law should be framed for regulating the education of the heir

* Archives Nationales, serie historique, section des Rois, Carton K—163.

apparent and of the heir presumptive to the throne ; but this provision had no immediate effect, and when the captivity of the King had ceased, the Abbé Davaux resumed his functions about the Prince Royal. On the day when their studies recommenced: "If I remember right," said the Abbé to his pupil, "our last lesson had for its subject the three degrees of comparison: the positive, the comparative, and the superlative; but you have doubtless forgotten all about them." "You are mistaken there," replied the boy, "and for the proof, listen :—the positive is when I say, my Abbé is a good Abbé ; the comparative, when I say my Abbè is better than another Abbé ; the superlative," he continued, looking tenderly at his mother, "is when I say, mamma is the best and most beloved of all mammas." The Queen took her son in her arms, pressed him to her heart, and could not restrain her tears.

Some days afterwards, the Prince Royal visited, with his preceptor, the gallery of the Louvre, at the hour when the artists are admitted to copy the pictures of the great masters. The beauty of the boy, his graceful mien, the lively sallies of his intellect, excited the interest of the talented young men there assembled, who for a while suspended their labours, the better to see and hear him. The young prince, according to his custom, sought to explain, from his lessons in history and mythology, the subjects of the pictures that were in review before him. Pausing before one of the *chefs-d'œuvre* of the Italian school: "Can you tell me what that represents?" asked his preceptor. "I should imagine," replied the prince, "that it is Pyramus and Thisbe; there is the blood-stained veil,—but I see no lioness." "Gentlemen," said the celebrated Vien to the artists who surrounded the Prince Royal, "Monseigneur's observation is very just; more than one critic has already made the same remark."

M. Bertrand de Molleville relates, in his Memoirs,* the following anecdote :—

* "Memoires Secrets." London, 1797, Vol. II., p. 34.

" While the Queen was speaking to me, the little Dauphin, a boy beautiful as an angel, was singing and jumping about the room, with a little wooden sword in one hand, and a shield in the other. An attendant came to fetch him to supper, and in two bounds he was at the door. 'How, my dear!' said the Queen, 'are you going away without making a bow to M. Bertrand?' 'Oh, mamma!' replied the charming child as he skipped out, 'M. Bertrand is quite one of our friends. Good night, M. Bertrand.' 'Is he not a nice little fellow? said the Queen, when her son was gone. 'It is happy for him he is so young; he has not our griefs, and his gaiety is some consolation to us.' "

" This pleasing cheerfulness," adds M. Eckard, after quoting the above anecdote,* " did not exclude from the prince's mind either reflection, or discretion—that still rarer quality at so tender an age. He was passing the evening with some other young people in the apartment of Madame de Tourzel; all the games proposed by each of the children in turn had become exhausted. The Dauphin asked his tutor to suggest a fresh one; the Abbé Davaux formed a circle, and proposed that each of them should relate some short story. When it came to the prince's turn, he narrated a very singular incident, connected with the events of the revolution. 'Who told you that story?' asked Madame de Tourzel, altogether astonished. The Dauphin, noticing her surprise, cast a glance at his tutor, and judging from his grave and displeased air that the anecdote might compromise the person who had related it in his presence: 'Madame,' said he, 'M. l'Abbé arranged that each of us should tell a story; but it is not in the game that we should tell from whom we got our stories.' "

We do not like to see in children, generally, those precocious manifestations of the intellect which too often exhaust the sap, by raising it to the branches before the due season. **But**

* "Memoires Historiques sur Louis XVII." Paris, 1818, p. 28.

it seems, at times, that when an existence is destined to be brief, nature hastens to develope it, as those northern regions which, having but two months of summer, greedily avail themselves of the brief sun they have, and cover themselves, as by enchantment, with flowers, and fruits, and harvests. Let us, then, garner in, with respect, the little harvest of these two months of summer granted to the son of Louis XVI. If his spirit was vivacious, it was also artless and true. If he ceased at times to be a child, this was the fault of the revolution.

The Adventures of Telemachus was one of his favourite readings. In the fifth book, the son of Ulysses relates how the Cretans, having no longer a king to rule them, resolved to choose one who would preserve in their purity the established laws. To be worthy of this choice, the candidate must first signalize himself in the games of the circus, in wrestling, throwing the cestus, and charioteering; and then reply to three questions in the true sense of the laws of Minos. When the Abbé Davaux had, one day, read the second of these questions: "Who is the unhappiest of all men?" the Prince Royal interrupted him thus: "Let me, Monsieur l'Abbé, answer the question, as if I were Telemachus,—the most unhappy of all men is a king who has the affliction to see his subjects disobey the laws." Louis XVI., to whom these words were repeated, exclaimed: "The penetration of that child makes me uneasy for his heart." The King was needlessly uneasy; it was the heart of the son of Louis XVI. which had dictated this reply to the intellect of the pupil of the Abbé Davaux.

Another day, being in his mother's apartment previous to his lessons, he saw from the window the Abbé Davaux crossing the garden of the Tuileries on his way to the château. "Mamma," said he, "will you do me the favour to help me on with the cuirass, vambraces, and helmet, that I have received at various times as the reward of my application?" "For what purpose?" asked the Queen. "To surprise the Abbé when he comes in." The Queen complied with this fancy. "And now you are armed *cap-a-pié*," said she; "under what name shall I announce you?" "Mamma, I beg you to say that it is the Chevalier Bayard, on his return from Marignan."

M. Davaux entered; that which had been said was done; the Abbé complimented his pupil on his military mien and gesture, not less than on his chivalrous costume. "This would be," he said, "an excellent opportunity for having our new Francis I. knighted." He then asked the Prince why he had selected the name of Bayard. "It is," replied he, "because I would wish to be like him—without fear and without reproach."

A few days afterwards, having received a present of an exquisitely elaborated filagree lantern, he slighly lighted it, and, his last reading in history fresh upon him, feigned to be earnestly engaged in looking about for something. After a great many turnings to and fro he at last came up to the Abbé Davaux, and taking his hand, said: "I am more fortunate than Diogenes: *I have found a man*, and a good friend."

His desire for instruction, and his aptitude for it, were so great, that the hour for study never came soon enough for him, and it frequently happened that he solicited his preceptor, by way of reward, to prolong the duration of his lessons. Having often heard the Queen speak in Italian, he requested permission to learn that language, and he conceived such a liking for it, he applied himself to it with such ardour, that in a very short time he was able to read his *dear Telemachus* in Italian, and to converse in that language with his mother.

Meanwhile, this additional study did not make him neglect the other branches of instruction. His writing already began to acquire form, as may be seen from a fragment of one of his copies which we have re-produced; the earlier portions of arithmetic were familiar to him, and he had a tolerable idea of the first elements of geometry, and the first principles of astronomy, which he learned by means of an illuminated sphere of ingenious mechanism, invented by the Abbé Grenet, a celebrated professor of the university of Paris.

Handwriting of the Dauphin while a Pupil of the Abbé Davaux

Commissionnaireorganique

D

Demonstrationgeometrique

indicatif.

Présent

je suis.

tu es

il ou elle est.

nous somes.

vous etes.

ils ou elles sont.

I have given way to the pleasure of narrating these details; the eye reposes with a mournful charm on the last happy days of this life destined to be so brief.

When the constitutional act had been accepted by the King, the National Assembly substituted for the ostentatious name of Constituent, which it had adopted, the more modest designation of Legislative, and began to think of terminating its labours. Perceiving that it was losing its credit and its popularity, it hastened to convoke the primary assemblies. On the 30th September the King, in person, closed the Assembly; loud cries of "*Vive le Roi*" drowned, for a moment, his voice, and again saluted him on his departure.

The National Constituent Assembly thus resigned the responsibility of events, leaving, in presence of a feeble constitution, audacious tribunes, and an amnestied king, restored without force to his palace, and without authority to his power.

On the 1st October the new legislature assembled, and from its very outset announced the divisions which were to convulse its bosom, and the obstacles it was to interpose in the march ot the executive power.

The Constituent Assembly, either from pure abnegation, or from a feeling of jealousy against the leaders of the minority, whose party were likely to have the advantage in the elections, had resolved that none of its members should be eligible for re-election. This was an additional danger arrayed against royalty. To an assembly which owed to its very defects a commencement of experience, succeeded an assembly wholly experienced. The second revolutionary ban advanced hungering for destruction because it had not as yet destroyed. The level descended still lower, and the Girondists were soon to be the leaders of the majority. This revolutionary impulse burst forth at the first sitting. A letter from the King, announcing his intention of repairing to the Assembly to take the constitutional oath, having been read, violent clamours arose; a question was immediately put to the Assembly, whether it was worthy of the representatives of a free people, to employ, in addressing the King, the appellations, *Sire*, and *Majesty*, and the Assembly decreed that two arm-chairs exactly alike, should be placed in the chamber, and that the King should occupy the arm-chair on the left of the President. This was going too quick and too far. The bourgeoisie of Paris grew excited, the National Guard indignant, and the public clamours obliged the Assembly to withdraw the decree. This transitory reaction in favour of royalty may be readily explained; people were under the charm of the new constitution, which fanaticised common minds, accustomed to judge of things by words. That constitution reassured those timid men, who, satisfied with the diminution of royalty, had contributed to enervate it, but had no wish to destroy it. It inspired with blind confidence that well-disposed but unenlightened portion of the nation, who did not perceive that this constitution placed a king without authority, before a people without moderation, and that the feeble weapon which it had left in the hands of Louis XVI. could only serve to wound him. When these parties saw the Legislative Assembly assume, at its outset, so aggressive an attitude, they were alarmed, they were indignant against this Assembly which, at its first step, deranged, perhaps broke, that machinery which it had required so much labour to contrive in the mechanism of political institutions; and there was a vivid movement of reaction in favour of the constitutional throne. In seeking to impel opinion farther than it desired to go, the Legislative Assembly had repelled it towards royalty, which had, consequently, its day of popularity.

The traces of two years of outrage, the remembrance of Varennes, became, in that day, effaced; a last ray of hope glided into the hearts of the King and the Queen; a last breath of happiness seemed for a moment to purify the air, which, laden with storms, environed them. Reserving their cares and their anxieties to themselves, they desired to share their pleasures with their children, whom they took in the evening to the Italian Opera, happy in showing them to an enthusiastic people. The house repeatedly resounded with acclamations, amid which not a few sobs were heard, pity blending with admiration, sympathy with respect. The calm serenity impressed on the open features of Louis XVI., the majestic beauty of Marie Antoinette, and, above all, the artless, simple grace of the two children, produced an emotion which, at the moment, compensated the royal family for all the insults of the past.

The Prince Royal, seated on his mother's lap, attracted all eyes; his angelic features, vividly animated by the performance, were radiant with joy, and his charming little gestures imitated those of the actors, as he sought to explain to his mother the progress of the plot.

The crowd became gentle and compassionate as they looked on a king and queen so severely tried, yet so calm, so confiding, after having been so betrayed, and on a lovely boy, heedlessly laughing on the morrow of a storm, on the evening of a tempest.

There were, doubtless, on that evening many mothers among the auditory; since that boy seemed to have gained for his parents the hearts, the acclamations, and the tears of that auditory, to have compelled politics to become silent before nature.

The emotions of that evening soothed the King and the Queen, who were especially rejoiced with regard to their son. Hitherto, the young prince had scarcely seen the people, except in the dust of the tumultuous return from Varennes, and previously beneath the rags of revolt, through the pikes of the 6th October. To this child, whom they were bringing up to love the people, they gladly showed that people joyous and full of love. "All is tranquil here," wrote Madame Elizabeth at this date (12 Oct. 1791); "but who can say how long this will last? The King is at this moment the object of the public adoration. You cannot form an idea of the sensation he created on Saturday at the Opera. It remains to be seen how long this enthusiasm will last."

Meantime, Louis XVI., faithful to that constitution which had despoiled him, had again written to the powers, entreating them not to permit his brothers and the emigrants to assemble armed bodies within their territories; and to the latter, ordering them to return to France before the 15th January, under pain of being treated as enemies. The sincerity of these letters was held up to suspicion by the already avowed preachers of the Republican system: "Louis XVI.," said they, "detests the constitution; *he only embraces it that he may stifle it.* The journey to Varennes sufficiently indicates to the nation the faith it may place in him." The organizing society of the Metropolitan Jocobins, managed to have sent to it, from all the departments, addresses in which the affiliated societies, and even the local administrations, set forth their alarm at the equivocal conduct of the ministers, and at the collusion of a perjured prince with their enemies. In order the more easily to destroy, they degraded the King: insult and contumely were to precipitate his downfall. It was thus that the unhappy Louis XVI., constantly the object of betrayals, was himself constantly accused of betraying. The prosperity which had been promised to the people was expected in vain; they had been made to salute a bright dawn, whose day never rose. Money became scarcer and scarcer, the value of assignats became less and less; men's minds were in a whirl; there was disturbance in the public places. A word pregnant with crimes, the word treachery, began to circulate from mouth to mouth. "I have but one fear," exclaimed Brissot; "it is lest we should be betrayed."

Monarchical Europe looked on, agitated with what it had to fear, uncertain what it might venture to attempt. The Empress of Russia, who had joined the aggression of the powers against the revolution, marched her troops upon Poland, to stifle there the germs of the principles which it was desired to combat at Paris. The Emperor Leopold, that prince-philosopher, who brought to the imperial throne the ideas of a sage, prefaced war by his coronation at Frankfort This menacing attitude of the foreign powers gave exaltation, as was to be expected, to the national sentiment which was about to communicate so great a force to the revolution. Violence was everywhere in men's ideas; it soon manifested itself in their actions. Pétion was named Mayor of Paris (18th Nov. 1791) and Manuel, deputy syndic of the commune. The winter passed away in continual struggles between the Government and the Assembly; the spirit of disorder flew from province to province. The conspirators felt themselves powerful. They had seen that to save the ship from wreck, Louis XVI. had been compelled to throw overboard, piece after piece, the royal authority There only remained to throw over royalty itself.

To the boisterous seditions of the interior responded the echoes of Worms and Coblentz; 22,000 Frenchmen pressed, beyond our frontiers, around seven princes of the house of Bourbon; deaf to the counsels of its unhappy King, the emigration appealed to arms. Yet, let us not judge it by the ideas of modern patriotism. We now call treason that which was then called fidelity; desertion, that which was then honour. This military noblesse, bound by its oath to the throne, had never ceased to consider the throne as the living country. It had readily accepted, or generously offered the sacrifice of its personal titles, of its hereditary offices, of its social advantages; but it could not resign itself to the annihilation or servitude of the royal authority, which it was its duty to defend. It had, besides, abettors in every family. The women, with their sensitive imaginations, were on the side of the victims: the mothers and the sisters, exhorted the sons and the brothers to go and seek avengers for them. Those who did not so depart, were treated by them as cowards, and received a distaff, the symbol of weakness and pusillanimity.

This period no longer appertains to politics, it belongs to history, which should appreciate devotion, under all forms and under all flags. Who shall venture to scorn them? who can fail to pity them? All thought they were obeying a duty, that they were subserving the law of honour, that old religion of the French. Their King's orders were not heeded, for his constitutional words were, in their estimation, mere compulsory expressions, veiling a totally different thought. The emigration was a calamity and an error; but the Emperor Napoleon imagined he judged it accurately, when he said: "The emigrants, in quitting France, only obeyed the call of their captains-general, the princes who were out of France."

Assured of the powerlessness of Louis XVI. the Legislative Assembly resolved by menaces to remedy the sterility of the royal letter and proclamation addressed to the princes and emigrants. It passed a decree, requiring Louis-Stanislaus-Xavier, a French prince, to return within two months, into the kingdom, in default of which he should forfeit his eventual right to the regency. By another and more rigorous decree, it pronounced, in a state of conspiracy against the country, all Frenchmen, forming part of the assemblages out of the kingdom, and pronounced sentence of death against all who, before the 1st January 1792, should not have laid down their rebellious arms. The princes and the emigrants might be guilty of error and political imprudence, but not of cowardice. No one paid any attention to the menaces of the Assembly. The King by his veto stopped the decrees relative to emigrants and unsworn priests. The directory of the department of Paris, where the remains of a monarchical spirit still existed, had presented an address to him, entreating him not to give his sanction to the decrees issued against the clergy: "Since no religion is a law, let no religion be a crime." A remarkable letter in the same sense had been published by André Chénier. The petition of the directory had given rise to warm discussions in the Assembly. Legendre, the butcher,

Je ne peu resister au plaisir de vous embrasser, mon cher cœur, mais ce sera en courant, car l'occasion qui se presente est subite, mais elle est sure et elle jettera ce mot a la poste dans un gros paquet qui est pour vous; nous sommes surveillés comme des criminels, et en verité cette contrainte est horrible a supporter, avoir sans cesse a craindre pour les siens, ne pas s'approcher d'une fenetre sans etre abreuvée d'insultes, ne pouvoir conduire a l'air de pauvres enfants sans exposer ces chers innocentes aux vociferations, qu'elle position, mon cher cœur. encore si l'on avoit que ses propres peines, mais trembler pour le roi, pour tout ce qu'on a de plus cher au monde, pour les amies presents, pour les amies absentes, c'est un poid trop fort a —

endurer, mais, je vous l'ai deja dit vous autres ne sentiriez, adieu mon cher coeur, esperons en Dieu qui voit nos consciences et qui sait si nous ne sommes pas animé de l'amoure le plus vrai pour ce pays, je vous embrasse

Marie Antoinette

le 7 janvier

le roi entre et veut vous ajoutter un mot

je veux seulement vous dire, Madame la duchesse, que vous n'êtes point ici oublié, que l'on y regrette d'avoir si peu de vos lettres et que de près ou de loin vous et les vostres vous estes aimés

Louis

(*Translation.*)

Letter from the Queen to the Duchess de Polignac.

"I cannot resist the pleasure of embracing you, my dear, but it will be as I run, for the opportunity which presents itself is sudden, but sure. This will pass through the post in a large packet to your address. We are watched like criminals, and, indeed, it is horrible to be under such constraint; to be in incessant fear for one's family; to be deterred from approaching a window for fear of being loaded with insults; to be debarred from taking the poor children into the air without exposing those dear innocent creatures to vociferations. What a position, my dear heart! Still, if one had but one's own troubles—but to have to tremble for the King, for all that one holds dearest in the world, for friends present and friends absent—it is too much for endurance; but I have already told you so; you, and those who resemble you, support me. Adieu, my dear heart! Let us hope in God, who sees our consciences, and who knows whether we are or are not animated with the most sincere love of this country. I embrace you.

"MARIE ANTOINETTE.

"The 7th January.

"The King has just entered, and wishes to add a word or two.

"I only wish to say, Madame la Duchesse, that you are not forgotten here; that we regret to have so few of your letters, and that, near us or far away, you and yours have our love.

"LOUIS."

This letter is superscribed "For Madame la Duchesse."

pour Madame la Duchesse

now appeared, for the first time, at its bar, thundering against traitors and tyrants. Thus placed between the menaces of heaven and earthly threats, the King chose the right but most dangerous part; he exposed himself to the insurrection of the people sooner than act against the dictates of his conscience.

Although within the limits of the power conferred upon him by the Constitution, this refusal on the part of Louis XVI. to sanction two decrees, one of which wounded him in his affections, and the other in his religious faith, was looked upon as a blow aimed at the national sovereignty, and the acrimony of the opposition was much increased by it. Revolutionary manifestations were becoming daily more and more violent in front of the château; insults and menaces might be said to have placed the royal family in a state of siege. The annexed letter from the Queen at this time to the Duchess de Polignac, bears evidence of their situation.

Intrigues, calumnies, and pamphlets, had not, however, succeeded in stifling the feelings of affection the people still entertained for ancient royalty. On the 20th February the Queen went with her children to the Comédie-Française; they were received with acclamations. Some few who had ventured by murmurs to protest against the feelings of the majority, were forced to retreat, overpowered by thunders of applause. In a little piece, entitled "*Evénements Imprévus,*" the pit called four times for the repetition of a duet between the valet and lady's-maid, in which they speak of their affection for their master and mistress, and when this verse occurred—

"Il faut les rendre heureux,"

a great part of the audience rose, and cried—"Yes! yes!"

Madame Elizabeth, relating this circumstance in her correspondence, adds, "Can you understand our nation? We must admit its impulses are sometimes beautiful!" These impulses were unfortunately rare and of short duration. This was the last testimony of public sympathy the royal family ever received in France: I say in France, for on the throne of Sweden the most chivalrous devotion was manifested towards the house of Bourbon. But a pistol-shot soon struck down that Gustavus III., the liberal hero of the revolution, who died like Henry IV., whose vices he possessed, anxious to save expiring aristocracy, yet himself assassinated by the aristocracy.

The Prince Royal had now nearly completed his seventh year, and at this age, according to the traditions of the royal household, it was customary to place the sons of France under the care of a governor. The law announced by the Constitutional Assembly, which was to regulate the education of the heir presumptive to the crown, was not yet completed. The leaders of the Assembly wished to supply its absence, by controlling the list of candidates from which the King would have to select a governor for the Prince Royal. This list, at the head of which the Condorcets, Sieyes, and Pétions, were conspicuous, soon fell into disrepute by the addition of a certain number of obscure and worthless names. Although public opinion called upon the Assembly to encroach on the rights of the father by naming a governor for his son, yet the motion presented in the Assembly, for that purpose, was supported by ninety-two names only; it was received with universal laughter and the question adjourned. Louis XVI. profited by the ridicule thrown upon these overtures, to take the initiative himself in this affair, and on the 18th April, he announced through the medium of Duranthon, that he had chosen M. de Fleurieu, formerly minister of marine. This unexpected announcement greatly disconcerted the leaders of the Assembly, and if we are to believe the testimony of one of its members, deeply wounded a man who had been secretly authorised by the King to apply for this high appointment. Yes, Harmand (de la Meuse,) in a work published in 1814, asserts that, in order to paralyse, or at least to baffle the anarchical cabal, Louis XVI. had been induced to promise this place

Letter from Louis XVI *to the* Municipality.

le 23 May 1792

J'ai vu Messieurs une lettre que Mr le Maire a ecritte hier au soir au Commandant General de la Garde Nationale ou il le previent d'inquietudes sur mon depart pendant la Nuit, fondees dit-il sur des probabilites et des indices, il mesle cette nouvelle avec des bruits de mouvements ou d'emeute, et il lui ordonne de multiplier les patrouilles et de les rendre nombreuses. Pourquoi Mr le Maire sur de pareils bruits, donnet il des ordres a Mr le Commandant General et ne m'en fait-il rien dire, lui qui par la Constitution doit faire executer sous mes ordres les Loix pour le maintien de la tranquillité publique? A-t-il oublié la lettre que j'ai ecritte a la Municipalite au Mois de Fevrier. Vous reconnoitrez aisement Messieurs que ce bruit dans les circonstances presentes est une nouvelle et horrible calomnie, a l'aide de laquelle on espere soulever le Peuple et l'egarer sur la cause des mouvements actuels. Je suis informe de toutes les manoeuvres

qui on emploie et de celles qu'on prepare pour echauffer
les esprits, et pour m'obliger a m'eloigner de la Capitale
mais on le tentera vainement; lorsque la France à des
ennemis a combattre au dedans et au dehors, c'est dans
la Capitale que ma place est marquée, c'est la que j'espere
parvenir toujours a tromper l'esperance coupable des
factieux. je me fie sans reserve aux citoyens de Paris,
a cette Garde Nationale qui s'est toujours respectée, et
dont les detachements employés sur nos frontieres, viennent
de donner une nouvelle preuve de son excellent esprit.
elle sentira que son honneur et la tranquillité du
Royaume exige en ce moment qu'elle redouble de zele
et de vigilance. Secourue d'elle et fort de la pureté de
mes intentions, je serai toujours tranquille sur tous les
evenements, et quelque chose qu'on fasse rien n'alterera
ma ~~[illegible]~~ sollicitude et mes soins pour le bien du Royaume

Louis

Letter from Louis XVI. to the Municipality.

(*Translation.*)

The 23d May, 1792.

"I have seen, gentlemen, a letter written by the mayor, yesterday evening, to the commandant-general of the National Guard, in which he informs him of the disquietudes which prevail with respect to my departure during the night, founded, he says, on probabilities and certain indications, and he mixes up this news with reports of movements and riots, and orders him to increase the patrols, and render them individually stronger. Why does M. le Maire, upon such reports, give orders to the commandant-general without informing me? for, according to the constitution, his office is to see, in obedience to my orders, that the laws are executed, and public tranquillity maintained. Has he forgotten the letter I wrote to the municipality in the month of February? You will easily perceive, gentlemen, that this report, in the present circumstances, is a new and horrible calumny, employed to rouse the people and mislead them with respect to the cause of the present movements. I am informed of all the manœuvres now practised, and of those in preparation, to inflame the public mind, and oblige me to quit the capital; but the attempt will be vain. When France has to combat domestic or foreign enemies, it is in the capital that my place is marked: it is there that I hope to be always able to thwart the guilty hopes of the factious. I confide, without reserve, in the citizens of Paris, in that National Guard which has always respected itself, and from which detachments, employed on our frontiers, have just given a new proof of their excellent disposition. They will feel that their honour and the tranquillity of the kingdom require, under present circumstances, increased zeal and vigilance. Surrounded by them, and strong in the purity of my intentions, no events will disturb me; and, whatever anybody may do, nothing will change my solicitude, nor divert me from using my best efforts for the good of the kingdom."

to Robespierre! He gives very circumstantial details of the negociations commenced on the subject—details which have been repeated by other authors. We shall not here dispute an opinion which has met with no credit from serious, thinking people, but merely state that the nomination of Louis XVI. was not accepted; the only advantage resulting from it was the preventing the factions from interfering in the education of the young prince. M. de Fleurieu was not installed, and the King and Queen superintended, as before, the instruction of their son We shall hereafter see who had in reality been chosen by the revolutionary party as governor to the heir of Louis the Fourteenth's monarchy. The discontent excited by the King's *veto* soon broke out into insulting recriminations. Nothing now was spoken of but the intrigues of the court, the imprudences of the Queen, the King's treason, and the frequent couriers despatched to Coblentz and Vienna.

To these murmurs were added denunciations of pretended projects of flight attributed to the King. Louis XVI. had been sufficiently enlightened on the disposition of France, by the journey to Varennes, to entertain no ideas of flight; he felt that his leaving Paris would only give a motive to the Revolution, without obtaining any support for himself. These denunciations were therefore mere calumnies, destined to weaken his cause and open the way for striking at him in the end. He saw this. The letter written by him, dated May 23, of which we give a fac-simile, was intended to neutralise the effect of these injurious reports.

These popular accusaticns obliged Louis XVI. to make constant concessions. Devoted ministers had been succeeded by exacting ministers, and these again had been replaced by factious ministers. The constitutional guard of the King, organised on the 16th March, was disbanded on the 30th May, and the Duke de Brissac, who commanded it, sent before the high court of Orleans for some imaginary plots.

Deprived of the support of all good citizens, hunted down

by the perverted, Louis XVI. lost all power, his conscience alone remained unconquered; everything was obtained from him, except complicity, which was impossible. Isnard had demanded, amid the applause of the Assembly, that all unsworn priests—that is, all priests who had remained faithful to their vows of obedience to the Church, should be sent out of the kingdom, and if any well-founded complaints were made against them, should be punished by death. Whilst this man exclaimed "The law is my God! I have no other, and I will have no other," Louis XVI. continued to worship the God of heaven and earth.

By a fatality logically attending the existing situation of affairs, the danger of a contest abroad increased in proportion to the disturbances at home, and at home fury was excited by accounts of the preparations making against France abroad. Louis XVI. was at length brought by the force of circumstances, to propose to the Assembly that war should be declared against the King of Bohemia and Hungary. The Assembly received the proposition with formidable acclamations. All parties looked forward to this war: the royalists hoped it might bring forth a general who would control the revolution and save the monarchy; the constitutional party trusted Lafayette would be that general, and secure for them the empire over the revolution and the King; the Montagnards—for the most part, at least—hoped the tumult and over-excitement, caused by this conflict of arms, would sweep away both the monarchical and the constitutional party, and even royalty, leaving power to the boldest and most energetic.

The anniversary of the journey to Varennes was also that of the oath taken by the Tiers Etat at the *Jeu de Paume* at Versailles; the return of this double anniversary, the recollection of both events seemed a propitious occasion to rouse popular fever, and to punish the refractory monarch for the veto which neither prayers, or threats had induced him to withdraw. On the 20th June, early in the morning, mobs were formed, com posed at first of the sans-culottes of the Faubourgs Saint Antoine and Saint Marceau, but they were increased in their progress by crowds in rags, armed with guns and pikes, as hideous a mob as that which appeared at Versailles at the opening of the revolution: men, women, and children, to the number of thirty thousand, led by Santerre, a brewer, who from the beginning of the disorders, had acquired a dangerous ascendency over the populace of his quarter; they were divided into three bands, and were four hours marching through the Rue Saint Honoré, from which they made an irruption into the very bosom of the Legislative Assembly; and there insisted on reading the petition they were taking to the Tuileries, in order to obtain the sanction of the decrees.

Three municipal officers came to inform the King that the Assembly was impeded by the influx of the multitude, and that the passages were so crowded that the doors might be forced. At their request the King consented to allow this army of petitioners to defile along the terrace of the Feuillants, and go out by the door of the riding-school.

Madame Elizabeth, who witnessed and very nearly became a victim to these fearful scenes, has described them in a letter (July 3rd, 1792), written at a time when she might be said to have them still before her eyes. "A short time after," she writes, "in spite of given orders, the other garden doors were opened, and the garden soon filled. The pikemen began to defile in order under the terrace, in front of the chateau, where three ranks of National Guards were stationed; they went out by the door of the Pont-Royal, and appeared to cross the Carrousel to return to the Faubourg Saint-Antoine. At three o'clock they seemed disposed to force the door of the great courtyard. It was opened by two municipal officers; and the National Guards, who had not succeeded in obtaining any orders since morning, had the mortification to see them cross the courtyard without being able to stop them. The Department haa given orders to repel force by force; but the municipalit had taken no account of this. We were at this time standing at the King's window; the few people who were in his valet's room joined us, and the doors were shut. An instant after we heard a knocking: it was Aclocque, with a few grenadiers and volunteers who had been induced to come with him; he requested the King to show himself alone. The King stepped into his first ante-chamber, whither he was followed by M. d'Hervilly and a few more grenadiers he had brought with him. The Queen was forced into her son's room by her friends, at the moment the King was going into the ante-chamber. I was more fortunate,—no one attempted to separate me from the King. The Queen had scarcely left, when the door was broken open by the pikemen. The King mounted on some coffers which were in the windows, and was immediately surrounded by Marshal de Mailly, MM. d'Hervilly, Aclocque, and a dozen grenadiers. I remained close to the panelling, surrounded by the ministers and a few National Guards. The pikemen burst like thunder into the room, seeking the King; one, especially, using the most dreadful language,—a grenadier put his weapon aside, saying, 'Wretch, it is your King!' the rest of the pikemen responded mechanically to this cry. In less time than I take to relate it, the room was filled with persons calling for the sanction and the dismissal of the ministers. This cry was repeated during four hours. A short time after some members of the Assembly came. MM. Vergniaud and Isnard addressed the mob, telling them they were wrong to demand the King's sanction in this manner, and persuading them to retire; but it was as if they had said nothing. They were long before they could obtain a hearing, and then scarcely uttered a word before the cries commenced again. At length Pétion arrived with some members of the municipality; the former harangued the people, and after praising the *dignity* and *order* of their march, persuaded them to retire with the same tranquillity, that they might not be accused of having been guilty of any excess during a civic fête. The mob at last began to move off. I forgot to say that, shortly after the entrance of the mob, some grenadiers had forced their way through, and separated them from the King. Let us now return to the Queen, who was dragged, against her will, to my nephew's room. He had been so quickly carried off to the other end of the apartment, that she did not see him as she entered, and you may imagine her state of despair; M. Hue and M. de V., an officer, were with him; he was brought back. She did all she could to return to the King, but was prevented by the people about her. A moment later we heard the doors broken open; some, however, the people could not find: and, misinformed by one of my nephew's attendants, who told them the Queen was at the Assembly, they dispersed in the apartments. During this time the grenadiers entered the council chamber, and placed her, with her children, behind the council table; the grenadiers and other faithful servants surrounded her while the people filed off before her. A woman placed a red cap on her head, and on that of my nephew. The King had had one from the first moment Santerre, who led the mob, came and harangued the Queen saying that she was surrounded by people who deceived her by telling her the people did not love her; that she was beloved· and assured her she had nothing to fear. 'What should one fear with honest people?' she said, at the same time extending her hand to the grenadiers, who all eagerly seized it. This was very affecting.

"The deputies who had come, had come of their own accord. Now a real deputation arrived, and urged the King to return to his own apartments. As I was told this, and did not wish to remain alone with the crowd, I left about an hour before him, and returned to the Queen; you may conceive my happiness at once more embracing her,—yet I was ignorant of the danger she had been exposed to. When the King returned to his chamber, nothing could be more affecting than the moment when the Queen and her children threw their arms round him;—the deputies present shed tears. The deputations succeeded each other every half-hour, till perfect tranquillity was restored. At ten o'clock the castle was vacated, and all retired to their separate apartments."

This account,—full of dramatic simplicity, and in which the confusion of the scenes it relates is somewhat reflected,—brings the mechanism of the 20th June clearly home to us. The castle was betrayed by the municipality, that is to say, by Pétion—betrayed in two ways: first, the doors were opened by the municipal officers, and, secondly, no orders were given by the municipality to the National Guard, who could have defended the entrance. It must be remarked that the enemies of royalty dared everything against it, while its defenders dared nothing against the revolution. In this contrast, the issue of the struggle was written; on the 20th June France was foretold the misfortunes which were to follow. "In Heaven's name," wrote Gerbert, nearly nine centuries before, "prevent insurrection against your master and Christ: the reign of the mob is the ruin of all kingdoms."

Instead of preventing, the Assembly allowed everything to take place; the official deputation did not arrive till all was over. The castle invaded, all became a scene of unutterable confusion; here the King, there Madame Elizabeth, and, after some time, farther off, the Queen, surrounded by a handful of devoted men, forming groups which seemed like islets lost in a revolutionary sea. It is only necessary to add a few details to those already given by Madame Elizabeth; her angelic modesty made her pass over some in silence, because they were to her honour; others escaped her, for this drama was made up of episodes, and the members of the royal family saw only that point of the struggle in which they themselves were engaged. At the moment when Madame Elizabeth was separated from the King, and driven by the crowd against the panel of a window, some pikemen—so she said—mistook her for Marie Antoinette. "Ah! here is the Austrian!" cried they, "we will have the Austrian's head," and immediately lowered their pikes. "What are you doing?" exclaimed M. de Saint-Pardoux, equerry to Madame Elizabeth; "it is not the Queen." "Why undeceive them?" said Madame Elizabeth to him; "their mistake may save the Queen." And turning aside with her hand a bayonet which nearly touched her breast: "Take care, Sir," said she gently, "you might wound some one, and I am sure you would be sorry to do so."

Weapons were blunted and hatred appeased by words so unexpected. The furious mob now prepared to read their petition. "This is no time to propose or grant anything," said the King in a firm voice. A young man, two-and-twenty years of age, of a mild and pleasing countenance, now exclaimed that the royal family must all be put to death.* Another, still younger, vociferously seconded the motion of the elder.† A third, of a most hideous aspect, wearing a pasteboard cap with the inscription DEATH, uttered no threat;—but, silent and livid, looked at Louis with blood-inflamed eyes, and followed all his movements with frightful contortions. A fourth, the favourite of Legendre the butcher, who appeared by his side during this scene of horrors, placed a red cap on the monarch's head. A fifth, bustling about in the crowd, and brandishing a stick armed with a long spike, cried out, "Where is he, that I may kill him?" A National Guard seized this madman, and, throwing him down at the feet of Louis XVI. forced him to cry "*Vive le Roi!*"‡ A sixth presented a bottle and glass to Louis XVI., and asked him if he would drink to the nation. "The nation," answered he, "cannot doubt my love, after all I have done for it; most heartily do I drink to its prosperity." And in spite of apprehensions and protestations, Louis XVI., as confiding as Alexander, raised the dubious beverage to his lips.

Outside, the picture is as gloomy as it is within. The riotous mob, which the castle could not receive or contain, were all agitation in the courtyard, and sanguinary cries rose at

* His name was Clément. † He was named Bourgoing.

‡ This National Guard's name was Cannolle.

intervals, "When are you going to send the King's head, and the Queen's?"

The Queen hearing these cries from the more distant apartments, where she had tried to shelter her children, could no longer resist the wish to share the dangers which these cries announced to her. She was in vain reminded* that she was a mother as well as a wife, in vain entreated to listen to prudence, and not compromise her safety uselessly, since there was not the slightest hope of assisting the King, but rather the certainty of exposing him to still greater danger. "I will not be kept from going to my post," she cried; "no one shall prevent me:—" and she rushed towards the King's apartment; when, suddenly hearing the tumult increase, she returned to the door of the room she was leaving, crying out: "Save my son!" then hastened off again, followed by Mesdames de Lamballe and De Tarente. M. Hue took the Prince Royal, and carried him to his sister's room, where the noise was scarcely heard; but the poor child's uneasiness was not diminished. Fully understanding the perils which surrounded his family, he inquired, sobbing, what his father and mother were doing. No one could answer—no one dared to comfort him. The Princess of Tarente came to say that, not being able to reach the King (all issues having been closed), the Queen had retired to her son's apartment. M. Hue took the young prince to her. The child had scarcely passed from his arms to those of Madame de Tourzel, and from hers to his mother's,—had scarcely received her embraces, when repeated blows were heard at the door of an adjoining room. M. Hue, on hearing this noise,

* These are the names of those who were with the Queen and remained by her throughout the awful day: the Princess de Lamballe, the Princess de Tarente, the Duchesses de Duras, De Luynes, and De Maillé, the Marchioness de la Roche Aymon, the Baroness de Mackau, the Marchioness de Soucy, the Countess de Ginestoux, the Duke de Choiseul, the Counts d'Haussonville and De Montmorin, the Viscount de St. Priest, the Marquis de Champcenets, and Baron de Wittinghoff, lieutenant-general in the French service.

rushed into a passage which led from the room they were in to the King's bedroom,—he opened it; and the Queen, with her child and the persons who accompanied her, entered precipitately. Most artistically cut in the wood-work, the door of this passage was perfectly imperceptible. The mob penetrated to this very spot, and a panel close to the door was struck down by a hatchet, yet, although the wall was laid bare the door was not discovered, and this last refuge of the Queen and the heir to the throne was concealed. A profound silence reigned in the hiding place, where, stifling his cries and restraining his tears, the royal infant pressed his poor mother in his arms as if to protect her. She trembled, not for herself, but for her husband and children. A long time was thus spent without Marie Antoinette or Louis XVI. being able to learn anything of each other's situation. One of the King's valets (Bligny) had contrived to escape from the apartments to seek for help. This succour he found in the devotion of the battalion of the Filles Saint Thomas, whose fidelity remained unshaken. The grenadiers of this battalion, headed by M. Boscary de Villeplaine, flew to defend the royal family; they took possession of the council chamber, and at length subdued the seditious horde. The people then asked to see the Queen: Marie Antoinette appeared at the end of the room; she was surrounded by a few grenadiers, who pushed before her the council table, to serve as a barrier against the crowd. Santerre, who, till then, had remained in the court-yard, now came up, followed by a frantic group; the castle resounded with shouts of "*Vive Santerre!*" "*Vive le Faubourg Saint Antoine!*" "*Vive les Sans-culottes!*" The popular brewer entered the room where the Queen was with her children, and the crowd precipitated themselves after him. Marie Antoinette was standing, holding by the hand her daughter, fourteen years of age. The Prince Royal was seated on the table by the side of the Queen, more astonished than frightened; he turned constantly towards his mother, to read in her eyes if he had to confide or to fear. In this attitude the royal family was found by the mob. At the head of the triumphant crowd was a yelling, drunken woman, who, throwing a red cap on the table, demanded in the most insulting and abusive manner, that it should be placed on the head of Marie Antoinette. M. de Wittinghoft ok up the cap, and, at the command of the Queen, placed it for a moment on her head, his hand trembling with indignation: then he withdrew it and placed it on the table. Cries now arose: "The red cap on the Prince Royal! Tri-coloured ribands on little *Véto!*" The ribands were thrown on the table, beside the red cap. "If thou art so fond of the nation," cried the Faubourgians, "place the red cap on thy son's head." The Queen, ever calm, ordered M. Hue to gratify the multitude; the red cap glared on the boy's fair hair, and the tri-coloured ribands were tied around his neck and to his button-holes. The child, who did not comprehend whether this was in sport or in insult, smiled with an air of amazement. But, an instant afterwards, M. de Montjourdain* and several officers and National Guards pointing out that the heavy wool covering was, in that excessive heat, insupportable by so young a head, M. Hue removed the cap.

Some of the men applauded the Queen; but the women—more pitiless towards a woman—incessantly abused her. Obscene expressions, derived from the lowest market-places, sounded, for the first time, beneath the ceilings of the chateau, struck, for the first time, on the ears of the royal children, These did not heed words they did not understand; ignorance preserved them from shame. Marie Antoinette blushed, but it was not for herself, it was for the people, for her children The pride of the Queen was supported by the indignation of the woman. "How full of hatred and haughtiness the Austrian is!" cried a girl of decent appearance, and mild face. Struck

* M. de Montjourdain was one of the forty-eight *commandants de bataillon* of the Parisian Guard. Condemned to death under the tyranny of Robespierre, he composed, ere he marched to the guillotine, a song full of elevated courage and feeling.

with the contrast between this girl's gentle countenance and her violent language, the Queen spoke to her: "Why should I hate you? You hate me. Have I unconsciously done you any harm, in any way offended you?" "Not me," replied the girl; "but the nation." "Poor child!" tenderly rejoined the Queen, "they have told you so, and you believe it. What interest could I have in doing injury to the nation? You call me the *Austrian;* but I am the wife of the King of France, I am the mother of the Dauphin; I am a Frenchwoman in all my sentiments as a wife and a mother. Never again shall I see the country of my birth. I can be happy or unhappy only in France. I was happy when you loved me." Affected by the gentle reproach, the girl said, weeping as she spoke: "Pardon me; I did not know you. I see now that you are not wicked"

Santerre himself, at sight of the princess whose head he had perhaps wished to strike off, was awe-struck. The hall was crowded to suffocation; he was requested to turn out the mob, upon which, violently striking the table which stood between him and the Queen, he exclaimed, "Oh! fear nothing, Madame, no harm will be done you; but remember that you are ill-advised, and it is dangerous to deceive the people. In their name I tell you so." It was at this moment that the Queen exhibited the touching movement related by Madame Elizabeth; the National Guards were deeply moved, the mob even ceased to murmur,—some wept. "How brave the Austrian is!" cried one. "How beautiful the young prince is!" said another. For the mob, like a capricious child, is credulous, inquisitive, and blustering, carried away by the slightest noise, flying at the least display of authority; a breath may render it cruel, and a word excite its generosity; childlike in the mobility of its sentiments and ideas under every fresh impulse, but unfortunately possessed of man's strength to do harm. Santerre, though brutal, was easily moved. He had drawn closer to Marie Antoinette, resting his hand upon the table, and bending towards her: "You have very injudicious friends, Madame," said he in a low tone, "I know some would serve you better." Then rising all at once, with an imperious movement, he commanded a retreat; and the appeased multitude passed before the Queen, contenting themselves with addressing a few insults to her. The aspect of this march was at once grotesque and terrible; it seemed a masquerade steeped in blood. Several bands were distinguished by small banners bearing emblems and inscriptions; one bore these words: "*Sanction or Death;*" another, "*Tremble, tyrant, thine hour is come.*" One man carried an instrument made of wood, in the shape of a gallows, from which the effigy of a woman was suspended, with this device: "*Beware of the lantern!*" Another bore about a guillotine, with these words at the bottom: "*National justice for tyrants; down with Véto and his wife.*" A third, carried a heart smeared with blood, on which were these words: "*Heart of aristocrats and tyrants.*"

The principal conspirators had shown themselves; Pétion alone, going to and fro in the courts, had not yet appeared in the apartments; he came at last: "Sire," said he, "I have this instant learned what was going on." "I am astonished at that," answered Louis; "as it has now been going on for more than three hours." Mounted on a stool, the Mayor added: "You have nothing to fear, Sire." "To fear!" answered the King, "an upright man whose conscience is at rest, knows no fear. Here," continued he, taking the hand of a grenadier* who was at his side; "place your hand on my heart, and tell

* This grenadier, whose name was Robert, came, says M. Hue, from Burgundy; the King had him transferred from the National Guard to a regiment of the line. Another grenadier named Lalanne, has claimed this honour, and his pretensions seem justified by the sentence of the 12th Messidor, in the year 2, which condemns to death one Jean Lalanne, the tailor, for having manifested, on the 20th June, 1792, sentiments of a mean valet of the tyrant, by boasting, in presence of several citizens, that Capet had taken his hand, and placing it on his heart, said to him: "Feel, my friend, if it palpitates."

that man how quietly it beats!" It was then that Pétion turned towards the people and delivered his extraordinary harangue, of which the following is another reading, modifying a little the text given by Madame Elizabeth: "Citizens, you have commenced this day with wisdom and dignity; you have proved yourselves free: conclude in the same dignified manner, and follow my example;—go home to your beds."

The crowd continued to disperse, and Madame Elizabeth was now able to make her way, as she relates, to the room where the Queen was, and throw herself into her arms: "All is well! all is well!" said she, "the King is saved!"

Exhausted with fatigue and the excessive heat, Louis was brought back to the council chamber by the National Guard and the deputation of the Assembly. From this room he passed into his own bed-room, where his family immediately joined him. His wife, children, and sister fell upon his neck; the officers, deputies, and all present were moved to tears. Some endeavoured to reconcile the King to the events of the day, by complimenting him on the courage he had displayed. "I have done no more than my duty," answered the unhappy prince. Just then, a new deputy familiarly accosted the Queen, saying in a jocular tone: "You were famously frightened, Madame; own it." "No, Sir, I was not frightened; but I suffered greatly at being separated from the King, at a time when his life was in danger. My only consolation was the being with my children, and fulfilling thus, one at least of my duties." "Without wishing to excuse all," continued this deputy, "you must own, Madame, that the people proved themselves very good." "Sir, the King and I have never doubted the goodness of the people; they are wicked only when misled." "How old is this young lady?" continued the deputy, pointing to Madame Royal, and still addressing the Queen. "My daughter, Sir, is of an age already to feel but too deeply the horrors of such scenes." Other deputies surrounded the Prince Royal, and curious to judge for themselves of the compass of his intellect, and the extent of his information, they put a number of questions to him upon the history of France, and on geography. One among them, recalling a fatal recollection, had mentioned the massacre of Saint Bartholomew, when one of his comrades, feeling the offensive awkwardness of the speech, immediately said, "Why speak of that? We have here no Charles IX." "And no Catherine de Medicis," replied the young prince. This answer was immensely admired. The crowd about him increased, and questions having been put to him on the new division of the French territory into departments and districts, he answered them all with so much memory and precision that his auditors were amazed.

The apartment was now entered by an officer of the National Guard, who had displayed the greatest zeal in defending the life of the King, at whose side he had been honourably wounded. He was greeted on his entrance by the greater part of his comrades with the praises due to his conduct. The Dauphin said to M. Hue: "What is the name of the soldier who has so nobly defended my father?" "I do not know, your highness; I would advise you to ask him yourself. It will give him pleasure." The prince ran immediately to ask the officer; who, however, in the most respectful terms refused to satisfy him, and the prince, in spite of entreaties, could obtain nothing. M. Hue then accosted this generous citizen, and asked his name. "I dare not tell it you," answered he with tears in his eyes; "I have begged his highness to allow me to conceal it. My name is unfortunately the same as that of a most execrable man." (His name was Drouet.)

The deputations were renewed every half hour, until tranquillity was completely restored; Louis XVI. received them with his quiet benevolence. They approached the royal family with proper respect. They were shown the broken doors, and other traces of violence which the riotous mob had left on their passage; locks wrenched, hinges torn off, panels of wainscoting shivered, spikes, stumps of swords, even cannon, loaded with grape-shot, all strewed about the floor. A remark was made which must not be omitted here: the mob had uttered a thousand insults in the Queen's room, a thousand jeers in the blacksmith's workshop of the King, groans and hisses as they passed through the throne-room; but on entering the Dauphin's study they became calm, soothed by the sight of the books, maps, and other implements of study belonging to a child. At ten o'clock the castle was cleared, and the approaches to it tranquil; the little prince was so peacefully asleep, you might have fancied he had been lulled by the recollections of some delightful day.

The next day, June 21st, 1792, the agitators were early on foot, trying to influence the populace, as they had done on the eve. "This," said they, "is the anniversary of Véto's flight; he must be made to expiate that desertion." The roll-call was beaten in all parts of the city, and crowds were already forming in the courts of the Tuileries. The Queen went to her son, who, upon seeing her, said innocently, "Mamma, is it still yesterday?" Alas! yes, it was still yesterday; the 20th June continued, and was to continue till the 21st January. The sacrifice of Louis XVI. commenced on the 20th June. On that day the Christ of royalty took the painful path on which he clearly saw his Calvary.

Some minutes later, Marshal the Duke de Noailles Mouchy presented himself at the Queen's apartment. Although in the evening the King had given formal orders to his faithful followers to retire, the old marshal, trusting that his age would be a dispensation from obedience, had not left the King's person, and had been fortunate enough to give proof of his devotion in danger. "Marshal," said the Queen to him, "the King has told me how bravely you defended him yesterday; I fully share his gratitude." "Madame, I did little in comparison with the wrongs I wished to repair; they were not mine, but they touched me so nearly! * The Queen wishing to turn the

* These details are related by M. Hue.

conversation, said: "My son, repeat to the marshal the prayer you addressed to God this morning for the King." The child knelt, joined his hands and raising his eyes towards heaven, like the infant Samuel in Sir Joshua Reynolds's picture, sang with the deepest feeling these words from the opera of Peter the Great:

Ciel, entends la prière
Qu'ici je fais;
Conserve un si bon père
A ses sujets!

M. de Malesherbes soon followed the Marshal de Mouchy; the ex-president, wearing, against his custom, his sword. "It is a long time since you wore a sword," said some one to him. "It is true," answered the excellent old man; "this dress is not familiar to me, but who would not wear a sword when the King's life is in danger?" Then looking at the Prince Royal, he said to the Queen: "I trust, Madame, at least that our children may enjoy brighter days; the storm is too violent to last long."

Louis XVI. did not share the hopes and illusions of his former minister. After having denounced to France in a proclamation, the threats and outrages which had assailed him in his own palace, he wrote to the superior of the Eudist fraternity,* conveying his apprehensions in these words: "Come and see me to-day; I have done with men, and only now look to heaven."

Pétion soon appeared at the chateau; he endeavoured to exonerate the municipality from the excesses of the evening; he spoke with much arrogance. Louis XVI. replied with firmness; and when the factious Mayor, while protesting on the part of the populace, great respect for the royal person, dared

* The Eudists were a congregation of secular priests, devoted to the work of missions and to the direction of schools. The superior at this time was Hebert, one of the King's confessors; he perished in the massacre of the Carmelites of the Rue de Vaugirard, with the Archbishop of Arles, the Bishop of Beauvais, Saintes, &c.

by his look and gesture to exclude the Queen from this public sentiment, the King desired the insolent visitor to be silent, told him that his duty was to watch over the tranquillity of Paris, and that he had better return to his functions. He had scarcely left the room, when the Prince Royal, who had been closely following the conversation and watching Pétion's movements, threw himself into his mother's arms, exclaiming: "Mamma, that person is very wicked, but he is also very unfortunate, for he does not know you. Why did they make him Mayor of Paris?"

The affronts committed and the crimes projected on the 20th June, and the royal proclamation which had denounced them to France, had once more elicited the symptoms of a favourable reaction. Louis XVI., for a moment, again had the advantage of his enemies. Some days after, the department of Paris, which had ordered an inquiry into the disorders of that day, suspended provisionally from their functions, the Mayor and the Attorney-General of the Commune. Pétion, however, derived new strength from this momentary disgrace, which naturally rendered him dearer to the populace, and disposed in his favour the society of the Jacobins and the Legislative Assembly itself.

On the news of the proceedings of the 20th June, General Lafayette, whose name had still a certain degree of influence upon public opinion, brought to the bar of the Assembly the complaints of his army (28th June, 1792), who, he said, shared the indignation and alarm felt by all good citizens at the acts of violence committed at the Tuileries. He entreated the Assembly to have the instigators and chief actors of these outrages prosecuted and punished as guilty of treason to the nation; to destroy a faction which was invading the national sovereignty, tyrannizing over the citizens, and whose public discussions left no doubt as to the atrocity of the projects of those who were at its head. He conjured it, lastly, to adopt efficacious measures for making the constituted authorities respected, and to give to the army the assurance that the constitution should receive no detriment in the interior, while brave Frenchmen were spilling their blood in its defence on the frontiers.

Lafayette, had he required that the Assembly, before it rose, should decide upon the proposition which he thus presented, and which was received with loud cheers, might have obtained a favourable vote; but there was not in his character sufficient resolution to strike a decisive blow. He did not sufficiently understand that dykes are as necessary for society as for the ocean, and that the government of a people can as little dispense with force as with justice. Endowed with unquestionable virtue and probity, with an earnest love of mankind, Lafayette constantly left to their enemies full time for effecting their projects. Provided with all the means of preventing, he never prevented; always more disposed to regularise revolt than to restrain it, he, to a certain extent, merited the reproach made against him at the time, that all he did, when he came forward, was to introduce somewhat of *order* into *disorder*. The King, on his part, had no materials wherewith to supply Lafayette's want of energy; the initiative for which the general ever waited, the King could not give. Both of them faithful to the constitution, and resolute to attempt nothing beyond its limits, the latter would not seek a *coup-d'état* which might seem to trench upon his oath, the former would have feared to second a movement that might place the monarch too loftily upon his throne. Louis XVI. did not like Lafayette, to whom, in part, he attributed his misfortunes; Pétion did not like Louis XVI., his jealous susceptibilities still rankling with the scornful indifference which the monarch had displayed towards him on the return from Varennes, in contrast with the marked attention which he had bestowed on Barnave. One is sometimes disposed to think, that with the aid of these two men, the one of whom led the army, the other the people, the King might have spared his country and his own family, the fearful catastrophe which overwhelmed both ; but on maturer reflection, it becomes clear that if MM. Lafayette and Pétion had been exempt, the former from the defects, the latter from the vices which prevented them from acting a great part, they would not have obtained the popular favour which had placed them on the stage where that great part was to be played; for it is the very defects, and the very vices of popular idols, which especially earn for them their popularity. The historian of the revolution, in common with his readers, is tempted to think, at every point, that had men acted otherwise, they would not have perished; whereas, the truer proposition would be, that had they acted otherwise, they would merely have perished otherwise. These three men, who had followed such various paths, since the outset of the revolution, were, all alike, marching to their destruction: the King to the scaffold of the 21st January; Lafayette to the Austrian prison of Olmutz; Pétion to the dark wood, where his body was to serve as food for wolves and birds of prey.

BOOK FIFTH.

THE DAY OF THE 10TH AUGUST.

21ST JUNE—13TH AUGUST, 1792.

Remark of the Duchess de Maillé—The Dauphin in the period between the 20th June and the 10th August—Observations of the Prince on the 14th July—Ambition of Pétion—Relations of the chateau with Danton—Guadet at the Dauphin's bed—Last visit of the Dauphin to his garden—Address for deposition—Preparations for the 10th August—Last night of the Royal Family at the Tuileries—Review of the Troops—Rœderer—The Royal Family repair to the Assembly—The King's Speech—Vergniaud's reply—The Reporter's box—The Assembly suspends the King from his functions—The Royal Family pass the night at the Feuillants—They attend, next day, the sitting of the Assembly—The Temple is assigned as their residence—They repair thither on the 13th—Popular manifestations—The King's words to the Dauphin—Arrival at the Temple.

IN the evening of the 20th June, the Duchess de Maillé had said, at the Marchioness de Tourzel's, amidst a circle of friends alarmed at the events they had witnessed: "Alas! the first of these visits will assuredly be the last!"* This ebullition of grief was a prophecy.

It may be said that, from the commencement of the revolution, royalty had resembled a great tree being felled by successive strokes. After the blow struck on the 20th June, the roots only remained to be separated from the earth.

The interval between the 20th June and the 10th August was occupied by the sort of gentle melancholy which ever succeeds great catastrophes, and by the preparations for the final crisis which was to overwhelm the monarchy.

* Cazotte, *Temoignage d'un Royaliste.*

In fact, the malady was stronger than the remedies. The revolutionary fever returned in more terrible strength than ever after its momentary prostration, and monarchy grew feebler and feebler till its final fall. "Royal majesty," says Montaigne, "falls with greater difficulty from the summit to the middle than it precipitates itself from the middle to the bottom."

The young Dauphin, inseparably mixed up with these terrible events, became initiated in humiliation and sorrow, by the spectacle of the sorrow and humiliation of his family. It seemed as though God willed to teach him thus early patience, in its most christian aspect, by the daily example of those whom children are most especially called upon to imitate, a beloved father and mother, in order to dispose this young soul for its painful destiny.

We have given various anecdotes and remarks which prove that the heart of the child was open to these lessons. Several of these were already known. There are others which it is my happiness to be the first to publish. Among these, I should not omit two circumstances which belong to this period.

In the earlier days of July, 1792, the royal family were reading a pamphlet directed against them, and especially against the Queen. "I wish I knew the men who hate me," said the Queen, "so that I might essay to punish them by doing them good." The young Prince, who had hitherto been apparently paying no attention to what was passing, here raised his head, ran and threw himself into his mother's arms, and said to her, with humid eyes and swelling heart: "Be sure, mamma, that everybody loves you."

The anniversary of the federation arrived. Pétion availed himself of it to annul the proceedings which had been adopted against him. The federates of Marseilles and Finistere added their suffrages to the ovation decreed him by the populace. On returning from the ceremony of the Champ-de-Mars, the last at which they were destined to appear, the royal family passed on, amid cries of "Down with the King! Down with Veto! Hurrah for Pétion!" vociferations which, like continuous thunder, overpowered the few *vivats* uttered in favour of the monarch. Louis Charles, unable to restrain his generous indignation and his filial anger, exclaimed all at once: "Oh! it is M. Pétion, then, who is king to-day." But when his parents looked at him, with an affectionate and mournful gaze, the child took his father's hand, and kissing it, said: "No, papa, it is still you who are King, for it is you who are just and clement."

The young Prince was attired that day in the uniform of the National Guard; his mother had so directed, as a testimony to that guard of her good will. The circumstance was remarked by many persons, and, in particular, by some declared partisans of Pétion, who pointed it out to the observation of their chief. "He must accustom himself to wear our colours," said the popular mayor. If, before this period, Pétion had meditated the annihilation of the royal power, it is certain that now he desired, under the pretext of public utility, to collect its ruins, in order to construct on them the edifice of his own grandeur. The intoxication of triumph so excited the fever of his ambition on this memorable day, that he deemed himself destined to rule France. The vulgar only appreciate persons of their own stamp. I scarcely know any idol of the people, who was really a great man. Popularity is, for the most part, denied to virtue and genius, marching with head erect and eye heavenwards; it is given to mediocrity, which stoops to receive it, and humbles itself to preserve it. The populace called Pétion, *King Pétion*, so long as he humoured their excesses. Nothing appeared more simple to this man than to dethrone Louis XVI., and, retaining for his son the title of king, to establish a council of regency of which he himself was to be president and ruler The visit of the Marseillais and Breton federates had thoroughly perverted the minds of the Parisian populace; the clubs resounded with propositions of the most extravagant anarchism. Pétion shut his eyes to these proceedings, doing nothing to suppress them, and ready to legalize them should they prove victorious. The factions were entirely agreed as to the necessity of disorganizing the state, of overthrowing legitimate authority, of taking possession of the high offices and of the great properties; but they did not seem at all disposed to come to an understanding as to the form of the future government. The monarchical system, however, was so decried and so damaged, that it had become difficult to reconstruct it in favour of M. Pétion.

Meanwhile, a number of well-meaning people, who had, from enthusiasm, rushed onwards to revolution, were disposed, from reflection, to return towards monarchy. They had combatted the King, all powerful, but they desired not to have the King prostrate and miserable; they would not believe, that in the interior of the palace, where he was under constant surveillance, the King was conspiring with the enemies of the country. They desired to stay the car of revolution; but they were to learn that, while it is easy to unchain a people, it is not easy to curb it. Since the dissolution of the Constituent Assembly, Barnave had no other arena than the club of the Feuillants, composed of the remnants of the constitutional party. Barnave had not quitted Paris, and had secret conferences with the King; but the brilliant orator, like the benevolent King, was a fallen authority. His counsels, as those of Mirabeau, came to the King at the precise time when they were of no value; other men, revolutionists only from ambition, were disposed to negociate with royalty, if they could do it to their own advantage; but they would not give to the civil list the equivocal aid of their popularity, without an equivalent. Of these was Danton Less eloquent than Mirabeau, as venal, and more immoral, he secretly accepted the part which the latter had meditated, and maintained with the court an understanding, for which he received from the court rich rewards. A demagogue at the club of the Cordeliers, where his violence veiled his relations with the court—moderate and almost a royalist with the court, to which his ingenuity ever presented a ready and plausible explanation of the language he held elsewhere, he betrayed at once both allies, emphatically describing his double position in the terrible words: "*I will save the King, or kill him.*"

Danton was not the only influential enemy whom the court essayed to gain over. Propositions were secretly made to Guadet, whose ascendancy was especially dreaded. Gold, however, had no attraction for the austere Girondist—he refused everything, except a private interview with Louis XVI. and the Queen. That interview took place at night. Guadet brought to it the cool reserve required by his position—the Queen her noble attributes, and her disquiet heart—Louis XVI. his confiding goodness. It was less as king, than as husband and father, that the unhappy Prince depicted to the deputy for Bordeaux the anguish of his position. Commencing coldly, the conversation became pathetic; republican inflexibility became less inflexible, royalty had shed tears. As Guadet was about to withdraw, the Queen asked him whether he would not like to see the Dauphin, and herself taking a candle, she led him into the contiguous chamber, which was that of the young prince. "How tranquilly he sleeps," said the Girondist, in a melancholy tone, while the Queen, leaning over the Dauphin's bed murmured: "Poor child! he alone in the chateau sleeps thus." Marie Antoinette's accents touched the Girondist's heart—he took the child's hand, and without awakening him, kissed it with an air of emotion; then turning to the Queen, he said: "Madame, educate him for liberty—'tis the condition of his life." "The condition of his life! Alas, the conditions of life are very uncertain, for him as for all of us! God alone knows our destiny!"

Such are all the particulars we have been able to collect of that nocturnal interview in which revolution gave a last counsel to expiring royalty, a last kiss to sleeping innocence. This strange interview had no other result than to manifest all the mockery of fate, all the vicissitudes of human weakness. In vain had the Queen of France aroused the sensibilities of a foe, by showing herself to him with her heart-sprung tears, with the profound humiliation of the diadem, with the touching grace of her child. The evanescent emotion which the deputy had felt, rapidly evaporated in the hot air of the street, in the shuddering contact of the opinion of the clubs; and the lips that had kissed the hand of the child were destined ere long to pronounce the doom of the father. "God only knows what fate he has reserved for each of us." Guadet, perhaps, recalled to memory these words when proscribed. After the triumph of the Terrorists over the Girondists, he was outlawed, wandering from town to town disguised as a working carpetmaker, and at last, having embarked in Brittany for Bordeaux, where no one durst give him an asylum, he arrived at his father's house, at Libourne, was there arrested, taken to Bordeaux, condemned, and executed on the 20th July, 1794. On mounting the scaffold he wished to address the people, whom, by his eloquent and beloved voice, he still hoped to raise in his favour. Vain effort! A mysterious analogy manifested itself between the execution of the King and that of his judge. By one of those providential agencies which moral law sometimes brings to pass, as if to present to itself and to the world the evidence of its justice, the drummers who had been on the place on the 21st January, were at the foot of the scaffold of Gaudet.

The Prince Royal had been constrained to part with his garden, after a last effort made towards the end of the month of July, and which was very near having a disastrous issue. It was on a Tuesday; the Queen had gone to walk with her son in his little garden; she was insulted by some federates. "Four officers pierced the throng which surrounded her," wrote to his family a young Swiss officer, who was fated to perish on the day of the 10th August; "they placed her in the midst of them with the Dauphin, and two grenadiers cleared a passage. When we reached the house his Majesty thanked us in the most touching and expressive manner. That poor family, how they are isolated."

The formerly sacred enclosure of the royal residence was now approached only by hatred and insult. A long tricoloured riband separated from the rest of the garden the terrace of the Feuillants, adjacent to the hall of the National Assembly, and at intervals, there was this inscription nailed on the trees, adjoining the terrace, "Citizens, respect yourselves; give to this feeble barrier the force of bayonets." The terrace of the Feuillants was called the *Terre de Liberté*, the rest the *Terre de Coblentz*. Two inscriptions announced to passers-by this new topography, and whoever ventured on the *Terre de Coblentz* was pursued with yells and hootings, and insulted as an aristocrat.

Relegated to the corner of the proscribed ground, the farthest from the throng, the little garden of Louis Charles was only approached by a few visitors whose affection was not shaken by the fear of sarcasm and insult. The aspect of this little deserted plot, of this parched and yellow grass, of those neglected flowers, burnt up by the sun, revealed to them the but too protracted absence of the youthful proprietor. He, meanwhile, his face sometimes fixed against the window of his room, followed, with an envious eye, those solitary strollers, who, more free than himself, could at least breathe the air of heaven in the garden of his ancestors. Once only they found means to procure him a moment's diversion, by taking him to the house of the Marquise de Leyde; it was in a retired garden, at the end of a faubourg of Paris, that the Prince Royal was enabled to play, for the last time, with a child of his own age.

Pétion had not yet lost his illusions. Although revolt was preached in all the crossways, although seditious songs were sung in all the cafés and hawked through all the streets, although the riotous mob daily grew more numerous and more insulting under the very windows of the Tuileries, and the most unbounded license reigned from one end of the city to the other, without being repressed, the ambitious mayor flattered himself that, at the appointed time, his credit would be stronger than all those movements, and that his powerful voice would be able, like the god of the fable, to appease the winds and to rule the tempests. Petitions arrived from all quarters, demanding from the National Assembly, some the suspension of the King, others, his deposition, some his impeachment. The almost entire unanimity of the sections of Paris (forty-six out of forty-eight), roused by this signal, and yielding to the instigations of the conspirators, produced an address tending to an immediate resolution on the question of the deposition incurred by the King. Pétion had the melancholy courage to become the reporter and advocate of this address. On the 3rd August, at the head of a deputation of the Commune, he presented himself at the bar of the Assembly, and read in the name of the people and the municipality of Paris, a long speech which commenced with a recapitulation of all the crimes imputed to the King for the last three years, and finished with the following demand :—

"The head of the executive power is then the first link of the counter-revolutionary chain. His name is in daily struggle with the nation ; it is the signal of discord between the people and their magistrates, between the soldiers and their generals. The King has separated his interests from those of the nation ; we, on our part, also separate them. Far from having opposed himself, by any formal act, to the enemies within and without, his conduct is a formal and continuous act of disobedience to the Constitution. So long as we have such a King, liberty can never gain strength ; but it is our will to be free. By an act of indulgence, we could have wished to have been able to demand from you the suspension of Louis XVI., so long as the country remains in peril ; but the Constitution forbids such a course ; we invoke it in our turn, and we demand his deposition. This grand measure once carried, as it is very much to be doubted whether the nation can place confidence in the present dynasty, we demand that thoroughly responsible ministers, appointed by the National Assembly, but taken apart from its own members, according to the law of the Constitution, denominated by ballot, by free men, shall exercise provisionally the executive power, until the will of the French people, our sovereign and yours, shall be legally pronounced in a national convention, as soon as the safety of the state shall justify such a step."

The orator received the congratulations of part of the Assembly, and the applause of part of the galleries. The debate on the deposition was fixed for Thursday, the 9th August, But already anticipating, in hope, the vote of the Assembly. Pétion, intoxicated by so many suffrages, said, openly, in the very hall: "I see clearly that the regency has devolved upon me—I cannot escape it!"

It was easy to move the sensibility of Louis XVI., but not to provoke his resentment. On hearing of the conduct of the Mayor of Paris, he contented himself with saying quietly: "If my person is disagreeable to them, I am willing to abdicate." There is no doubt that had he thought by this means to secure to his country calmer and more prosperous days, the unfortunate Prince would have joyfully performed the sacrifice, which would have protected him from all insult and from all servitude; but he saw that, for the time being, there was no room, in the ancient monarchy of France, even for the throne of an infant, and he feared to compromise, by abdication, the future rights and perhaps the life, of his son. His conscience as a king and as a father, ordered him to reserve for himself all perils; and his inspirations as a Christian, resigned him to the eventuality of martyrdom. He drew, as all the unhappy do, similitudes between the misfortunes of dethroned princes and his own; he had in his closet a portrait of Charles I., and on his table a history of that unfortunate monarch.

For a long time past the conspirators had promised to take

their revenge for the day of the 20th June, which they considered a failure. The orators had roused the people in the streets and in the clubs. "Citizens," said Marat, in one of his pamphlets, "watch around this palace, the inviolable asylum of all plots against the nation. There a perverse queen fanaticises an imbecile king; there she is bringing up the young wolves of tyranny; there refractory priests bless the arms of insurrection against the people; there they are preparing another St. Bartholomew for the patriots."

Their plan arranged, the conspirators fixed its execution, at first, for the 29th July, and afterwards, and definitively, for the 10th August. The King was informed of these arrangements. In the critical position in which he found himself, two projects of escape were offered to him; he rejected them. The Queen participated in his views: "'Tis as well," said she, "to die here, as to suffer the fate of King James." The difficulties of escape were immense, the danger as imminent as that of a protracted struggle. There was, besides, the experience of Varennes, and the sort of shame that attached to the word *flight*. At length, amidst a fermentation ever on the increase, arrived the moment for discussing the question of deposition. In order to ensure its success, the republican party distributed in the sections non-active citizens, that is to say, those excluded by law as not possessing any property, and admitted them, and also many foreigners, to deliberate and vote in these assemblies. The most violent agitation reigned in the greater portion of these meetings, where the innovating spirit of the club was reinforced by all the passions of the street. Three sections* declared that they no longer considered Louis XVI. as king of the French people, nor would recognise either National Assembly or municipality. "It is now time," said they, "for the people to rise in a mass and govern themselves."

* The sections of the Quinze Vingts, of Mauconseil, and of La Fontaine de Grenelle.

The section of the *Theatre Français** improved on these manifestations; sitting day and night permanently, under the presidency of Danton, it declared, of its own authority, that its members were inviolate, and that it was in a state of insurrection. It decreed that, if, on the evening of the 9th, the legislature had not pronounced the deposition on the stroke of midnight, the générale should be beaten, and that to the sound of the tocsin and of cannon, they would proceed armed to the château of the Tuileries; that this decree should be immediately communicated to the other forty-seven sections of Paris, and also to the federates, with an invitation to adopt it. France resembled a diseased man whose vital functions are unhinged, and who becomes imbecile on the approach of the last agony.

However, to be just, the revolution, before commencing the attack, prudently disorganised the defence. The Assembly had decreed in the last fortnight of July that two Swiss battalions and several regiments of the line should depart for the frontier, and a Swiss officer† wrote to his friends at the end of July, 1792: "They have quietly managed to send all the armed force out of Paris. Here are the five regiments of the line and two-thirds of the regiment of Swiss guards, that they so feared, put out of the way of harming the factious. We shall soon see the tragedy begin."

This loyal soldier was right; the fatal day arrived. Louis XVI. counted on some means of defence; M. Mandat, an ex-captain of the French guards, who had embraced the cause of the revolution, and had become chief of one of the six legions of the National Guard,‡ had, in accordance with an order, extracted with difficulty from Pétion, taken measures for opposing force to force. At eleven o'clock in the evening,

* Previously called the section of the Cordeliers.

† M. de Forestier, above mentioned, who was killed some few days after, on the 10th August.

‡ The National Guard, since its formation, was composed of six legions, each of which had a commander. These six chiefs performed in turns the duties of commander-in-chief. It was, at this time, the turn of Mandat.

he had ranged in battle array on the Place du Carrousél, in the courts of the château, in the garden, and about the wickets, the troops, on which he thought he could depend. But Danton, Collot d'Herbois, Billaud-Varennes, and Tallien had installed themselves in the Hotel de Ville, and, in the name of the law and municipal authority, which they had usurped, they summoned Mandat to their bar. The latter was deaf to this injunction, believing it to be his duty not to desert the constitutional King in a critical moment; but on a second summons, Mandat allowed himself to be persuaded that he ought to obey the civil power, and presented himself before the commune. He entered, and found, to his utter astonishment, the municipal council entirely changed. Accused of forming a project for cutting off the column of the people, and of detaining the mayor a hostage in the château, he became confused, defended himself ill, or rather not at all. The council ordered him to be taken to the Abbaye; it was the signal for his death. He had scarcely passed out of the hall, when he was killed by a pistol shot, and his body was thrown into the Seine. The order of resistance extracted from Pétion was annulled, and this murder, facilitating the success of the conspirators, disconcerted the measures taken for the defence of the palace, and spread consternation among the already wavering troops.

All the royal family, after supper, had retired to the council chamber; the ministers and some persons of the court had assembled there to pass the night. Solely occupied with the King and her children, Marie Antoinette forgot her personal danger, she went from one person to the other, trying to inspire the courage which she had, and the hope which she had not. In embracing her son, whom they were about to take to bed, her tears betrayed her: "Mamma," said the child, "why do you weep now, when you bid me good night?—I wish I might not leave you this evening; every one is sad; do not let me go to bed." "Be easy, my child, I shall be near you." She reassured him, embraced him once more, and sent him to his rest. That Queen who had seen her means of safety disappear, day by day, now saw them vanish minute by minute; but her eye remained steadily fixed on the increasing immensity of the perils; she felt that disarmed royalty was nothing more than the hostage of the ancient rule in the hands of revolution. Fall is honourable and glorious, when one falls in one's belief. Monarchical faith had its martyrs.

The menacing hour, indicated by the anger of the sections, was come, and the decree for the King's deposition had not been past. Midnight struck. Immediately the tocsin was heard at the Cordeliers, and found its echoes throughout Paris. The générale was beaten in all the quarters, and cannon shots mingled at intervals with the roll of the drum. The sections rose, the agitators ran to arms. Each hour, each minute, brought more and more alarming news. The insurgents, in close columns, approached with their artillery. Already bands, armed with pikes, had profited by the confusion to glide into the ranks of the faithful troops, whom they disorganised. Day dawned. Marie Antoinette, foreseeing an approaching catastrophe, and fearful that the sword of the Marseillais would surprise her children in their beds, had them dressed immediately; and from that moment kept them near her person. Louis XVI. and herself embraced them with that redoubled tenderness inspired by the fear and the presentiment of separation. The Prince Royal opened his eyes wide, unable to understand why he was disturbed at such an unusual hour, the meaning of those military preparations, that general disorder, and that tumultuous confusion which reigned in the apartments, in the courts, in the garden. However, despite the simplicity of his age, he saw that a struggle was in prospect, and that some great danger threatened his father. "Mamma," said the poor child, kissing his mother's hands, "why should they do any injury to my father? he is so good!" His words, his looks, his caresses, added a charm and a grief to the uneasiness of his family. The King saw the necessity of visiting all the posts of the château, of showing himself to the Swiss guards, to the grenadiers, to the gendarmerie, to the gentlemen, to the bourgeoisie, to the volunteers of all ranks, assembled in the apartments, on the staircases, in the posts, and in the courts. The Queen, her children, her sister, and Madame de Lamballe, accompanied him. The attitude of the King, calm, but in no degree military; his words, more paternal than emphatic in so critical a moment, made no great impression on the minds of the soldiery; but the presence of those three women, and of those two lovely children, coming silently to make a last appeal to the generous sentiments of their friends, produced on the last defenders of monarchy, a sort of moral electricity. In the grand gallery of the castle a vivid enthusiasm manifested itself as they passed along. Emotion swelled every bosom; tears filled every eye. Amidst the excesses of modern ideas, appeared a scene of the middle age, where the old spirit of chivalry for a while resumed its empire. About two hundred gentlemen hastened to the Tuileries, on the first report of the King's danger; they had no uniforms, and they carried their arms under their clothes, which procured for them the name of the *Knights of the Poniard.* The courageous and desperate protest of emigration, they had come to die rather than to fight, resigned victims of the old French honour. There was not a man there who did not thrill with respect and admiration for the Queen, not one who would not have given his life for her. Some begged her to touch their weapons, in order to render them victorious; others requested permission to kiss her hand, in order that death might seem sweeter to them. A thousand transports of love and hope burst forth at once: "Long live the King of our fathers!" cried the young men; "Long live the King of our children!" cried the old men. And the Dauphin of France was lifted in their arms above their heads, like a living standard, for which they vowed to die.

One cry of fidelity and devotion accompanied and received the royal family at all the interior posts of the château; but Louis XVI. did not choose to expose them to the doubtful reception of the outposts. Arrived at the vestibule of the grand staircase, he made the Queen, her children, her sister, and Madame de Lamballe return to their apartments. His presentiments had not deceived him. Soon the cries of "*Vive le Roi!*" were mingled with sinister clamours. Arrived at the end of the Via Dolorosa that he had traversed, the King was agitated, not by his own imminent danger, but by the cruel necessity of accepting the effusion of blood. The fatality which was precipitating monarchy towards the abyss (if we may use the heathen word *fatality* to express the logical connection of causes and consequences), presided over the defence of the Tuileries with the same mockery as over the flight to Varennes; royal imprudence, unskilful auxiliaries, ill-fortune, all conspired, in both cases, to assure the triumph of insurrection.

Returned to the château, perspiration on his forehead, and despair in his soul, Louis assembled a council, and was alreade deliberating as to the means of defence, when the assailants debouched from all sides on the Carrousel in close columns, bringing with them cannon and ammunition. An immense crowd filled the square and the approaches to the château, sending forth, with unanimous voice, those cries which shook like thunder the palace of Catherine de Medici and Louis XIV.: "Deposition! Deposition or death! Death!" "You hear, the people will have deposition," said a municipal officer, abruptly opening the door of the council chamber. "Well," replied the minister of justice, "let the Assembly pronounce that sentence!" "But, after that act," said the Queen, "what will follow?" The municipal bowed, and was silent.

"Your last day is come," said a chef de legion* entering;

* M. de la Chenaye. He was massacred on the 2nd September following, in one of the prisons of Paris.

"Madame, the people are the strongest: what carnage is about to take place!" "Sir," cried Marie Antoinette, "save the King, save my children." And weeping, she extended her hand towards Louis XVI., as if to protect him, then embraced her children with a painful despair.

At this moment the procureur-general appeared precipitately at the head of the directory of the department, girt with his scarf. "Sire," said he, in utter fear, "the danger is beyond all expression; resistance is impossible. Of the National Guard, there are but a few on whom we can rely; the rest, intimidated or corrupted, will, at the first shock, join the assailants. Already the cannoniers, on the mere recommendation to remain on the defensive, have discharged their pieces. The King has not a minute to lose; there is no safety for him but in the middle of the Assembly,—there is no sure shelter for his family but among the representatives of the people." This idea entered the château with Rœderer; it entered there, borne by the wind which blew from the street,—it entered with the sudden flash of revolutionary lightning. There are those fatal moments in the life of kings and of nations in which reflection is impossible,—those moments when the echo of revolt, rising from the plain, has attained all the heights. Louis XVI. remained speechless; but the Queen, proudly raising her head: "How say you, Sir," cried she; "you propose to us to seek refuge among our most cruel persecutors? Never! never! They shall nail me to these walls before I consent to quit them! But say, Sir, are we utterly abandoned?" "Madame, I repeat it, resistance is impossible. Will you cause the massacre of the King, of your children, of your servants?" "God forbid! may I be the only victim!" "Another minute," pursued Rœderer, "a second perhaps, and it will be impossible to answer for the life of the King, for your own, for that of your children!" "My children," said she, pressing them to her arms; "no, no; I will not give them up to the knife." And approaching the King and his ministers: "Well, it is the last sacrifice; but you see the object. Monsieur Rœderer,' added she, raising her voice, as if to take to witness everything around, "you answer for the person of the King, for that of my son!" "Madame, we answer for dying at your side; that is all we can guarantee."

Some military arrangements were rapidly made to cover the departure of the royal family. The members of the Department formed a circle, in the centre of which they were placed. As they traversed the halls, a shudder shook every soul that surrounded them. "No excitement," cried Rœderer. "You may occasion the death of the King!"

"Remain," said Louis XVI. "We shall return soon," added the Queen. All was over. Dying royalty had quitted the palace of the throne to expire under the very eyes of its enemies. It was a quarter past six in the morning. Louis XVI. had Madame Elizabeth's arm, Marie Antoinette gave her hand to her two children; but at the door of the château, a grenadier seized the Prince Royal, and carried him in his arms. There, upon the very threshold of his abode, the King learned that a portion of the National Guard had withdrawn to protect their houses and their families; others, as is ever the case, had already declared against royalty which they saw feeble, in favour of the revolution which they saw victorious. In fact, from the tumultuous throng, which scarcely made way for the ancient race of kings to pass, they heard nothing but insults and threats. Some members of the Assembly, who came to meet the monarch, could not pierce the thick waves of the crowd. On the terrace of the Feuillants, the cry of "Down with the tyrant! Death! death!" was repeated more loudly than ever. "Do not be afraid," said the grenadier, who was carrying the little Prince, "they will do you no harm." "Not to me, perhaps," said the Dauphin, "but to my father!" and the tears of affection rolled down his cheeks. So long as the life of his father was not menaced, there was a luminous circle of joy playing on the forehead of that child; but then he trembled and was afraid. The unhappy father, himself, felt for a moment tears in his eyes. "What, then, have I done to my people?" said the Christ of royalty, as he went on his way to Pontius Pilate. It took half-an-hour to traverse, amid a storm of invectives and insult, that short distance which separates the palace from the asylum to which Rœderer was conducting the royal family. In the annexed plan the reader will be able to follow the mournful procession from the château to the riding-school, where the National Assembly was sitting, and to understand the aspect of those localities, where, at that period, stood the convent of the Feuillants and the temporary hall of the Assembly, of which there are now no traces, the Quartier-Rivoli having utterly effaced them. Never had a king of France, never had a king of any people, never had a man, since the passage of the Man-God to Calvary, made so dolorous a journey.

At the gates of the riding-school the cries redoubled. The procureur-general harangued the populace, and succeeded in quieting them; but in the narrow passage, blocked up by the crowd, an irresistible movement separated for an instant the royal family. The mother trembled for her son; but the grenadier, who had taken possession of the child, raised him in his arms above the crowd, and clearing the way with his elbows, entered the hall behind the King, and deposited in the Assembly his precious burthen amid the applause of the galleries. The King took his place beside the president, and the Queen and her suite on the ministerial benches. Scarcely was the Dauphin left to himself, when he hastened to return to his mother. A voice immediately exclaimed: "Take him to the King, beside the president, he belongs to the nation. The Austrian is unworthy of the confidence of the people!" An usher came to take the child; but the latter, his arms extended towards his mother, and with fright depicted on his countenance, wept; and his tears drew from the galleries an expression of interest which made the usher desist from his

The procession to the Assembly.

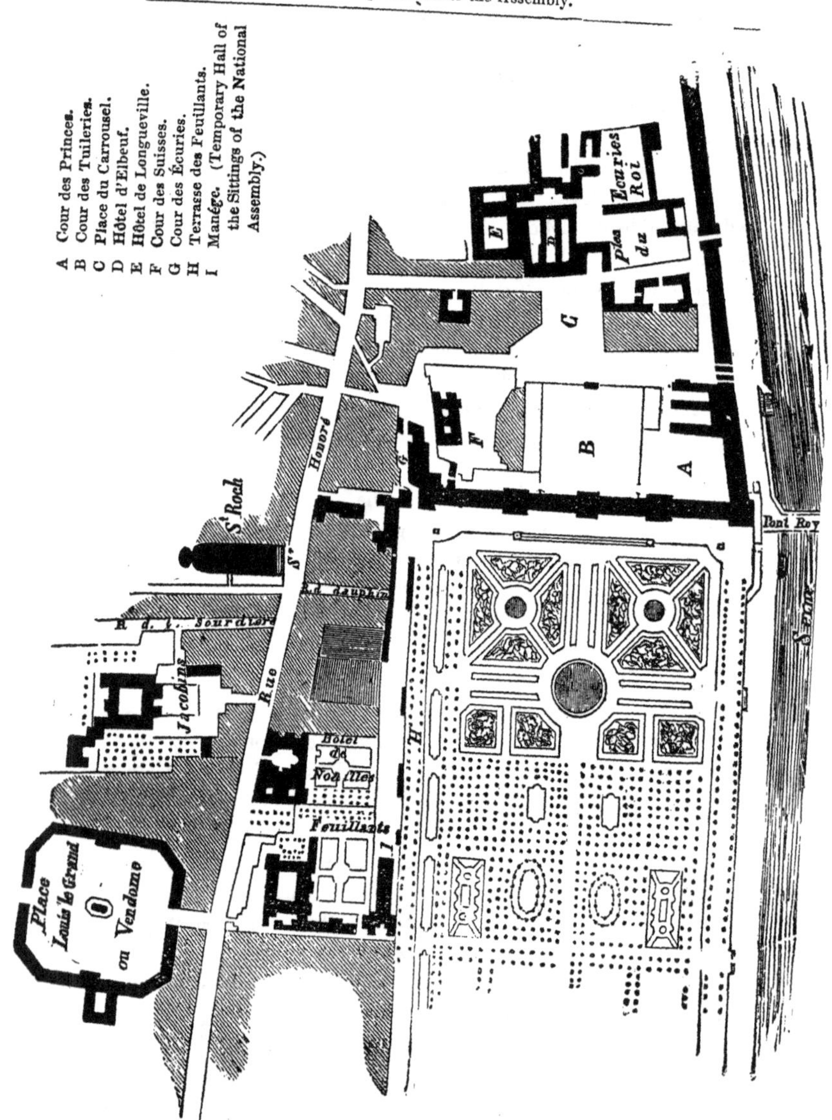

purpose. At this moment, some gentlemen made their way, sword-in-hand, into the very hall of the legislative body: "You compromise the King's safety!" exclaimed some of the deputies, greatly alarmed; and the armed men withdrew. Quiet was restored and the King spoke:

"I have come here to avoid the commission of a great crime; and I think I could not be more secure than amidst the representatives of the people." "Sire," replied Vergniaud, "you may rely on the firmness of the National Assembly. It knows its duties; its members have sworn to die in support of the rights of the people and of the constituted authorities."

The King seated himself; the Assembly was sad; hatred became modified by the spectacle of so many sorrows. Men's eyes turned with a sort of respectful stupour, but without com miseration, on the humiliation of so much greatness.

The discussion commenced; but some of the members, observing that the constitution did not allow the legislative body to deliberate in the presence of the sovereign, it was resolved, under this mockery of a pretext, that the King and his family should retire to the box where the reporters of the journal called the *Logographe* sat. Placed on a level with the lowest ranks of the Assembly, behind the seats of the president and the clerks, the place was so small, that it would scarcely hold the reporters, and so low that they could not stand upright in it. Thither they conducted the royal family. Louis XVI. seated himself in the front of the box, Marie Antoinette in a corner, where her noble head sought a little relief from so much opprobrium; the children and their governess, placed themselves with Madame Elizabeth and the Princess de Lamballe on a bench, behind which stood several gentlemen, the generous courtiers of misfortune, who had hoped to fight at the Tuileries, and who, at least, were resolved not to shun death, if they could not achieve a battle.

Meanwhile, battle and death awaited their companions who had remained at the château; but the fight there only presented the defence of an empty palace, and the devotion of a useless death. These attendants on royalty had hoped for more, had desired more; they had followed the King to make for him a rampart with their bodies, and to fall dead at his feet. They had not this consolation, and, less happy than the National Guards, than the Swiss, than the gentlemen slain at the Tuileries, they were compelled to be present at the degradation of their sovereign for whom they would have willingly died.

It is no part of our subject to relate the individual murders which were committed in the court-yard of the riding-house, the general massacre which filled the Tuileries and the environs of the château with blood; the tumult, the pillage, the assassinations, the *auto-da-fé*, which marked this fatal day, and the horrible night which followed it. At the first cannonade the King exclaimed: "I have given orders not to fire." A second order was despatched; the King enjoined the Swiss to evacuate the château, and their officers to come to him; a courier departed in all haste to meet a division that was marching from Courbevoie, and gave it the order to return. It was too late or too soon: too late, for blood had flowed; too soon, for it was giving an advantage to the insurrection. Already driven back and broken in more than one point, it abandoned the field of battle of the Carrousel to the defenders of the throne, who, although few in number,—200 volunteers, 250 National Guards, and 900 Swiss,—had yet compelled the immense concourse of the assailants to give way, when this fatal order arrived! Murder reigned all around the legislative hall, in the interior of which, despite the noise of the Assembly, the conversations of the deputies, and the motions of the orators, were heard the vociferations of the assassins, the cries of their victims, and even the echo of the blows which inflicted death. The hall and the galleries were thronged with people, coming and going every minute; the agitation was extreme, the heat excessive; and the place wherein the royal family were packed, the white walls of which reflected the ardent rays of the sun, had become simply a furnace, where all the burning vapours and the sounds of the carnage were concentrated. Perspiration flowed from every forehead; violent emotions swelled every breast. The Dauphin, who during the first hour had never ceased to question his father, inquiring the name of each deputy who passed or who spoke, had lost his speech; panting and almost suffocated, he sought life and quiet in his mother's eyes, and found them not. The frightful spectacle displayed before him overwhelmed all his ideas, and increased his uneasiness; he saw men covered with blood, bring in succession, and deposit on the table of the president, silver dishes, rouleaus of gold, portfolios, and diamonds, which had been found in the apartments of his family. He was astonished to see the spoils of the Tuileries saluted as trophies—he was at a loss to know why acts of vandalism and pillage were applauded as acts of honour and probity. He watched by turns in the faces of his father, of his mother, of his aunt, of his sister, the effect produced by the sudden apparition of petitioners, whose ferocious gestures and horrible mien were more intelligible to him than their threatening words; but the King's face remained calm and serene, that of the Queen preserved its proud dignity; Madame Elizabeth bowed her head in submission to the will of God, and the young Marie Thérèse was bathed in tears. The perplexity of the child was very great. At length a petitioner so emphasized his words as to efface from the depth of that youthful soul all happy doubt. This man revealed all the horror of the situation—he was a cannonier of the National Guard, who, with blasphemy in his mouth, showed the Assembly his bare and blood stained arm: "I offer," said he, "to take the King's life if it be necessary." The poor child threw himself into his father's arms, but finding him, as usual, calm and unmoved, he turned, and, weeping, placed his head on his mother's knees, which trembled at the words of the artilleryman, who stood but fifteen paces from the King.

Hitherto the inactive but not apathetic spectator of all that passed, the Legislative Assembly was divided between the fear of supporting the throne and the fear of being crushed under its fall. Several deputations had already appeared before it, demanding the deposition of Louis XVI. The first was that of the Thermes de Julien. The names of its members, set forth in the Report (most of them workmen, mechanics, and students), are a curious monument for history; they show how, under such circumstances, and for such a motion, a section of Paris was represented.

A deputation from the new Commune, improvised by revolt, soon arrived—"Pronounce the deposition of the King," said the deputies. "To-morrow we will bring you the Report of this memorable day; Pétion, Manuel, Danton, are still your colleagues; Santerre is at the head of the armed force." Another deputation expressed itself in still more imperious terms—"For a long time past the people have demanded from you the deposition of the King, and you have not even pronounced his suspension. Know that fire has been set to the Tuileries, and that we will not arrest its progress until the vengeance of the people has been satisfied. We are once more charged, in the name of that people, to demand from you the deposition of the King."

The will of the people, declared by the roar of cannon and the glare of conflagration, was obeyed. Vergniaud quitted the presidential chair, which, during that terrible sitting, was in turn occupied by him, Guadet, Gensonné, and Muraire; the deputy of the Gironde hastily drew up, in the committee, and under the influence of his faction, the act of provisional suspension of royalty. Sad, pale, and bent down by the weight of fatality, he mounted the tribune, and read, amid profound silence, that decree, which was not discussed, and which the King heard without surprise, and saw adopted without regret.

"I come, in the name of the extraordinary commission, to propose to you a rigorous measure; but, the grief with which you are filled will, I am persuaded, convince you how much the public safety is concerned in its immediate adoption.

"The National Assembly, considering that the dangers of the country have attained their crisis, that the evils under-which the Empire groans are chiefly attributable to the distrusts inspired by the chiefs of the executive power, in a war under taken in its name against the constitution and the national independence; that these distrusts have provoked from all parts of the Empire, the desire for the revocation of the authority entrusted to Louis XVI.

"Considering nevertheless, that the legislative body has no wish to augment, by any usurpation, its own authority, and that it can only fulfil its oath to the Constitution, and its firm resolution to save liberty, by making an appeal to the sovereignty of the people, decrees as follows:

"The French people are invited to form a national convention.

"The chief of the executive power is provisionally suspended from his functions; a decree will be proposed in the course of the day as to the nomination of a governor to the Prince Royal.

"The payment of the civil list is suspended.

"The King and his family shall reside with the legislative body until quiet is re-established in Paris; the department will cause the Luxembourg to be prepared for him, under the guard of the citizens."

It may be readily imagined that under the impression of the events of the day this decree was carried unanimously. By this measure, the enemies of the King deprived him of his crown, and his friends thought that his life was saved. The announced appointment of Condorcet, as governor of the Prince Royal, seemed also to resolve, in favour of monarchy, the question left in suspense of the form of the future government.

Many pacific spirits, little acquainted with the course of events, embraced this hope; but they were far from having sounded the depth of the abyss when they accepted this plank of safety from wreck that was thrown to them. There are always, in all revolutions, a mass of men in the rear of those ideas which guide the van. Political hypocrisy always secures an accomplice, in critical junctures, in that systematic imbecility which finds it more convenient to believe than to resist. In many families, while weeping over the virtuous man, who, as King, was immolated to the exigencies of the revolution, prayers were offered up for the young Prince, whose reign the announced national convention would no doubt inaugurate, aiding him with a council of regency adapted to the circumstances. For the first time, the name of Louis XVII. was mentioned; the revolution treated as simpletons the ingenuous individuals who pronounced it. In accordance with its usual custom, it had not told every one what it meant to do.

The tumult and massacre lasted all night; fires were lighted to consume the dead bodies. The Assembly, by the light of the funereal flames fed by murder, continued its sitting till two o'clock in the morning. The royal family remained up to that time in the box of the *Logographe*, spectators of their own fall, struck and wounded, under the eye of their enemies, in the innermost fibres of human sensibility. Louis XVI. alone, since the preceding evening, had taken some refreshment; his children had only touched some fruit, and the rest of his family had tasted nothing but a few drops of currant water, which they owed to the pity of the inspectors. Moral suffering absorbed the feeling of physical suffering; the children themselves, in their deep emotion, and in the burning air which nearly stifled them, had forgotten hunger; the Dauphin, broken down with fatigue and covered with perspiration, had at last fallen asleep on his mother's lap. Towards two o'clock, some commissaries of the Assembly and the inspectors of the hall came to take the royal family and conduct them to the apartments which, after the promulgation of the decree of deposition, had been hastily prepared for them in the upper floor of the old convent of the Feuillants, above the corridor, where the committees of the Assembly were held. This lodging consisted of four rooms—I should rather say, of four cells—paved with brick, and uninhabited since the destruction of the monastic orders. The holy men whom the tempest had driven from this cloister, little imagined the same storm would bring thither, a short time after, the King and Queen of France, driven from their palace! Each of the four cells opened by a small and similar door on the same corridor. The architect of the Assembly had had the greater part of his own furniture carried to these small apartments, the instant he was informed of their destination

Supper also had been served there; no one touched it but the children. The recollection of his favourite dog came across the mind of the Prince Royal. He asked about it; no one could give him any information. The poor animal had, no doubt, wished to follow his master on their departure from the Tuileries. Had it been crushed under the feet of the roaring mob; had it been carried off by faithless hands? They never saw it again; they sought for it, but in vain. To comfort the Prince, they told him that it would return one day; but he was persuaded that it had been crushed to death by the mob, and he was greatly grieved at the loss. Madame Elizabeth said to him with melancholy gentleness, "Dear child, console yourself: there are sorrows more cruel; continue to love God that he may preserve you from them."

In the first room, which served as an ante-chamber, the last servants of fallen royalty kept their virgils;* in the second, the

* MM. d'Aubier, de Briges, Goguelat, the Duke de Choiseul, the Prince de Poix.—Misfortune brings devotion. By the next morning, that ancient part of the convent contained the true friends of royalty, those whom it retains in the time of its misfortunes. There were to be seen the Duke de Rohan-Chabot, the Marquises de Tourzel and Nantouillet, MM. de

King slept half dressed; in the third, the Queen and her children; and in the fourth, Madame Elizabeth, Madame de Tourzel, and the Princess de Lamballe, who had come in the evening to claim a share in the royal misfortunes. These three holy women prayed and wept all night at the door of the chamber where Marie Antoinette in vain invoked sleep beside her slumbering children.

Despite the long and painful watching which had exhausted her strength, it was only on the approach of morning that the unfortunate Queen closed her eyes in sleep. Wishing to prolong this unexpected repose of her sister, Madame Elizabeth had silently removed the children to dress them. The Assembly required that the royal family should take the same place as on the preceding evening, and the hour of the sitting approached. Soon awakened from her feverish sleep by the voices and caresses of her children, whom Madame Elizabeth brought to her: "Poor things," cried the Queen, embracing them, "how cruel is it to have promised them so fair a heritage, and to say: This is all we have to leave them; all ends with us!"

The Queen rose in haste, and immediately admitted into her room some of her women, who, since the dawn, had successively come to offer her their services. Marie-Antoinette sobbed, and extending her arms towards these women, whom misfortune rendered friends: "Come," said she to them; "come, unhappy women, and behold a woman still more unhappy than yourselves; for it is she who is the cause of all your misery." And when the little Dauphin, seeing his mother and every one around him weeping, began himself also

Fresnes and de Saint Pardoux, Chanterène, inspector of the wardrobe; Hue, who had miraculously escaped the massacres of the preceding evening: there arrived in succession, Mesdames Thibaud, Campan, Auguié, Navarre, de Mervey, Schlick, Basire, Saint Brice, all in the service of the Princesses; Thierry and Chamilly, father and son, first valets-de-chambre to the King; Bligny and Gourdain, valets-de-chambre; Levasseur, employed in the wardrobe, &c., &c.

to weep: "My child," said his mother, embracing him, "I have also consolations; the friends that misfortune has made me lose, are not so valuable as those it has given me."

At ten o'clock the royal family was reconducted to the Assembly, to pass there the whole day. The horrors of the previous day were renewed; the action of the drama became still more gloomy and terrible,—the words were more menacing, the petitions more sanguinary. A savage horde demanded, in loud tones, the heads of the Swiss who were prisoners in the barracks of the Feuillants. "Great God! what cannibals!" exclaimed Vergniaud, himself moved to indignation by these vociferations. The intervention of Danton saved the Swiss until the 2nd September.

The success of the insurrection had just inaugurated a power superior to the National Assembly—that of the Commune of Paris; from that day, it controlled and annulled all such legislative acts as had not its approval. The palace of the Luxembourg, intended as the residence of the royal family, seemed to it, no doubt, too sumptuous a dwelling for fallen royalty. It disapproved of the selection of this residence, seeing that the Luxembourg *offered means of escape by its subterranean passages.** The Assembly, which now began to grow weary of the humiliations with which the King was overwhelmed before its eyes, was quite willing to remove to a distance this troublesome spectacle until the day of the last sacrifice. It decreed that the Hôtel de la Chancellerie, in the Place Vendôme, should be immediately prepared for his reception; but the dominant Commune annulled this decree, and, after thinking, for an instant, of the Abbaye Saint-Antoine, it demanded, by the medium of Manuel, the tower of the Temple as the residence of the King, whom the nation kept as a hostage. "Nothing remains to Louis XVI.," said he, "but the right of justifying himself before the sovereign. The Temple will

* Sitting of the Council General of the Commune of the 10th August, 1792. (Records of the Hôtel de Ville.)

serve him and his family as a residence; he will there be guarded by twenty-four men, supplied by the sections; they will intercept all communications with him and his family, for their friends are only traitors. The streets they traverse on their way will be lined with all the soldiers of the revolution, who will make them blush at their folly in having thought that there were among them slaves ready to support despotism; and it will be their greatest punishment to hear the cry of 'Long live the nation!'"

The proposition of Manuel was carried in the Assembly, and his prediction was about to be accomplished in the street. The Commune triumphed,—the Assembly had suspended royalty, the Commune degraded it. All persons, except those connected with the domestic service of the King, received orders to depart. "It is only now," said the Queen to them, "that we begin to feel all the horror of our situation. You had so soothed it by your solicitude and devotion, that we have not perceived it hitherto." "I am a prisoner, then!" said Louis XVI. on his part, to the inspectors, with a mournful accent; "Charles I. was happier than I; they left him his friends up to the scaffold." Royalty degraded is no longer royalty. All its wealth passed into the rapacious hands of the revolution, and men asked one another if ever the hand of God would raise up again that race once the most powerful on earth, and now fallen so low. The royal family came to the Assembly without money and without linen; the faithful servitors, whose names we record, well knew this. Five of them, who had not yet obeyed the injunction to retire, laid on the table the gold and assignats they had about them. The Queen, perceiving this, said: "Gentlemen, keep your pocket-books; you have more need of them than we. You have, I hope, longer to live."

At this moment, the guard came up to execute the order that had been given to arrest the five persons who had delayed obedience. Four of them separated so as to avoid recognition.

and escaped by a private staircase. M. de Rohan-Chabot was not so fortunate; he had passed the preceding night as a National Guard, near the person of the King. Suspected, arrested, thrown into the dungeon of the Abbaye, he was there massacred in the days of September. Once the eye of royalty, cast on a criminal led to execution, saved him; now the contact of royalty was death to virtue.

The decision of the Assembly had warned Louis XVI. to take measures with reference to the persons whom he desired to retain about him, for his service and that of his family. He directed M. Hue to write out a list of those persons, among whom figured Madame de Saint Brice, and M. Hue himself, both of them designed for the service of the Dauphin.* This list was addressed to the council of the Commune.

The château having been given up to pillage, and the seals having been set on all that escaped the grasping hand of anarchy, linen, clothes, articles of the toilette, everything was wanting to the royal family. M. Pascal, officer of the hundred Swiss, offered some clothes for the use of the King, and the Duchess de Gramont some body linen for that of the Queen. It

* "The Paper, as I sent it to the Mayor of Paris," says M. Hue, "that he might deliberate about it with the Council of the Commune, set forth:

FOR THE SERVICE OF THE KING.

M. de Fresnes, equerry; M. Lorimier de Chamilly, first *valet-de-chambre;* M. Bligny, *valet-de-chambre;* and Testard, chamber page.

FOR THE SERVICE OF THE QUEEN AND MADAME ROYALE.

Madame Thibaud, head lady's-maid; Mesdames Auguié and Basire, ordinary women of the chamber.

FOR THE SERVICE OF THE DAUPHIN.

Madame Saint Brice and M. Hue.

FOR THE SERVICE OF MADAME ELIZABETH.

M. de Saint Pardoux, equerry; and Madame Navarre, first lady of the chamber.

To these the King added the Princess de Lamballe, the Marquise de Tourzel, and her daughter. (Last years of the reign and life of Louis XVI. Second edition, pages 316 and 317.)

was through the pity of a foreigner the child of kings escaped the disgrace of being left in a state of utter destitution; Lady Sutherland, Ambassadress from England, who had a son of the same age as the Dauphin, promptly sent for the use of the young Prince the necessary articles of dress. Marks of touching interest displayed themselves through every obstacle, even to this unfortunate family.

Three days had thus slowly passed with them between the box of the *Logographe* and the cell of the Feuillants; but it was neither the tribulations under the gaze of the Assembly, nor the painful restraints of the convent cells that they had most to dread. A still more painful trial awaited them morning and evening; it was the journey they had to make, amid the yells of the people, between the two asylums which had been meted out to them avariciously for their use by day and by night. The first time they left the Assembly to reach their night residence (it was, as we before said, nearly two o'clock in the morning), they were obliged to cross the garden amidst a body of pikes still reeking with blood; they were lighted by candles placed in the barrels of muskets; ferocious cries added to the horror of the scene. "On seeing these murderers covered with blood," says M. d'Aubier,* "press on our footsteps, the Queen feared, like myself, lest the Prince should be struck in my arms. She was too tender a mother to leave to her servant the honour of shielding with his body that of her child: forgetting that she was the person most menaced, she ordered me to give her the Prince; in whom fear had created an almost convulsive agitation, and she whispered a few words in his ear. At that happy age, the mind is easily quieted. Scarcely were we on the staircase, than he began to leap with joy, exclaiming: "Mamma has promised to let me sleep in her room, because I have been very good before those wicked men."

* Letter of M. d'Aubier de la Montille, gentleman in ordinary of the chamber to Louis XVI., to M. Mallet-Dupan.—December, 1794.

The next day fresh insults awaited the royal family on their way. A young man, well dressed, approached the Queen, and putting his fist under her nose: "Infamous Antoinette," said he to her, "you would bathe the Austrians in our blood—you shall pay for it with your head." The Queen remained calm and silent.

At length, after three days and three nights thus passed between constraint and insult, the departure for the Temple was announced to take place on Monday, 13th August. The Mayor of Paris, accompanied by Manuel, the attorney-general of the Commune, by Michel, Simon and Laignelot, municipal officers, presented himself before the King to intimate that the council of the Commune had decided that none of the persons proposed as his attendants could follow the royal family to their new abode.* Louis XVI., however, by dint of remonstrance, obtained a concession in favour of MM. Hue and de Chamilly, and Mesdames Thibaud, Basire, Navarre and Saint-Brice, who were excepted from the prohibition.

The moment of departure arrived. It was five o'clock in the afternoon. A compact crowd filled the inner corridor and the Cour des Feuillants. The royal family and suite made their way slowly and with difficulty through the moving mass, to the vehicles destined for their conveyance to the Temple: these were two great carriages, drawn each by two horses only. Into the first ascended the King, the Queen, their children, Madame Elizabeth, the Princess de Lamballe, the Marquise de Tourzel, and her daughter. The Mayor of Paris, the Attorney-General, and Michel, the municipal officer took their

* "The council decrees, that the King shall only be surrounded by persons whose civism is unsuspected." (Sitting of the General Council of the Commune, August 12, 1792).

"Decreed. That all the persons who have been heretofore in the service of the King and his family, shall be dismissed, and that this family shall be attended only by such persons as shall be selected by MM. the Mayor and the Attorney-General of the Commune." (Sitting of the General Council of the Commune, August 13, 1792.)

places in the same carriage, all wearing their hats. In the second carriage, two other municipal officers installed themselves with the King's suite. A number of National Guards on foot, and with their arms reversed, escorted these over-laden carriages, around which roared an innumerable multitude, armed with all sorts of weapons, but unanimous in their yells of menace and imprecation. The troops who formed the line took no steps to suppress the tumult, or to silence these vociferations. Thus, that which the Attorney-General of the Commune had announced, was realized beyond his hopes; a populace, mad with fury and impious joy, assailed at every step of this new Via Dolorosa, with indescribable insults, the fallen royalty whom it was thus conducting to ultimate death. The carriages were stopped for a few instants in the Place Vendôme, in order that the fallen descendant of powerful potentates might have leisure to witness the equestrian statue of Louis the Great, hurled from its pedestal, and trodden under foot by the populace, whose thousands of voices shouted with one cry: "'Tis thus we treat tyrants." "How wicked they are,' said the Prince Royal, as he sat on his father's knees, looking up to his eyes for approbation of what he thus said. "No, my dear," replied the King, with gentle commiseration, "they are not wicked, they are misled."

This humiliating and mournful march lasted for two hours. Never was there a King a more honest man, or who had been overwhelmed with insults so monstrous; never were children more innocent, nor subjected to hear blasphemy more fearful; and as to the Queen, so noble, so lofty, never was abandoned woman driven from her den with more insolence, with more cruelty.

They reached the Temple at seven in the evening. Santerre was the first person who presented himself in the court-yard where the carriages stopped; he signed to the coachmen to draw up at the door, but the municipal officers countermanded the direction, and made the royal family alight in the middle of the court-yard, and walk thence to the entrance. All present kept on their hats, and gave the King no other title than Sir. One man, in particular, with a long beard, made a great point of repeating the *Monsieur* at every sentence. The crowd who had accompanied, or who had met the procession, unable to make their way into the court-yard, remained in a compact mass outside, vehemently vociferating "*Vive la nation!*" Lamps suspended from the projections of the walls, and from the battlements of the great tower, lit up the savage joy of the multitude, which seemed only to regret that the thick walls of the Temple shut them out from the sight of the immense affliction within.

THE TOWER OF THE TEMPLE.

BOOK SIXTH.

THE TEMPLE.

13TH AUGUST—3RD SEPTEMBER, 1792.

Historical reminiscences—Enclosure of the Temple—The palace of the Grand Prior—The towers of the Temple—The royal family temporarily installed in the little tower—Prescribed works—The patriot Palloy—The persons who had accompanied the royal family are separated from them—Sojourn of the royal family at the Temple—Prayer of the Dauphin—The King continues to educate his son—Hue, creditor of the King—Vexations—They take away the King's sword—Threats—The public criers—Suspicions of the municipal officers—Cléry enters the Temple—The King's present to M. Hue—Prayer of Madame Elizabeth—Massacres of the 2nd September—Hue removed from the Temple—The Princess de Lamballe—Her corpse is dragged to the Temple—Her head is exhibited at the windows of the Tower—Her heart is devoured—Fear and horror of the royal family.

WE here come to the Temple. The memory of the Temple is so strongly bound up with that of the Dauphin, the son of Louis XVI., and the memory of the latter is so inevitably attached to the edifice where he spent the last years of his life, that one cannot think of the Temple without recalling to mind the young prisoner,—and on the other hand, the image of the prisoner calls up before the mind the image of the prison. There it was that he lived, that he suffered, that he reigned,—if we can, without irony, give the appellation of reign to that painful agony which continued from the death of the father to the death of the son. Louis XVII. is not called in history the child of Versailles, the child of the Tuileries,—he is called the child of the Temple.

It is, then, necessary to give some account of the theatre,

before we relate the drama which was there enacted; and the more so, that the ancient edifice, the witness of those great sorrows, disappeared at the commencement of this century. We have even been so vividly struck with the close tie which exists between these two names, Louis XVII. and the Temple, that we had at one time the idea of writing the history of the monument, before we wrote that of the destinies which the most illustrious guests it ever sheltered found within its walls. But this thought yielded to the fear of diminishing the interest by dividing it. We will content ourselves, then, with summarily relating the origin and historic outlines of the Temple; but we will give, with the greatest possible precision, the topography of that edifice, at the time it received the royal prisoners within its walls. It is a desire one often feels, and which is rarely satisfied, in history, to know exactly the spots where the events, both happy and terrible, took place, of which we read the narrative. Topography assists us in understanding events; there are even facts, which one could scarcely understand exactly, without having a clear notion of the places wherein they were performed. Besides, one is much more strongly moved when one can replace in our thoughts the drama on its scene,—we know the deep impression produced upon the Crusaders by the sight of those holy places where the great mystery of the Redemption had been accomplished, and where every step recalled the majestic reminiscences of the Bible, and the touching recollections of the Gospel.

The ancient edifice of which we are about to speak, disappeared at the commencement of the present century. Built in an age of faith, it was demolished in an age of impiety. It held an important place among the historical monuments of Paris. With its name, for the past six centuries, were associated, from age to age, recollections, which already deserved perpetuation when the French revolution came to give it a solemn consecration, by making it the witness of a great and prolonged martyrdom. One might, before that time, have set one's self down at the cradle of the Temple and interrogate its infancy as to the destinies of its founders, the knights, and the Temple would have recounted their bravery, their power, their wealth, the persecutions they underwent, their frightful death, and the end of that illustrious order which had filled Christendom with its services, and the world with its renown. Interrogated as to its youth and its maturity, it would have told of the ascendancy of the kings, and the names of its new masters, armed, like the first, for the defence of Christ; then, later, and nearer our own times, the elegance and the smiles of beautiful and high-born dames, the toasts of the topers and the songs of the poets, when the gay muse of Chaulieu startled with its mundane accents the echoes which had responded to the austere psalms of David, wherein the soul of the penitent laments in the presence of its sins and of the terrible justice of God.

Now all these recollections have given place to a still grander recollection. The very destruction of the order of the Templars, and that pile, which Jacques Molay ascended with Guy, Dauphin of Auvergne, after a trial which is still before the justice seat of history,—so difficult is it to discern at this distance the truth from error, justice from iniquity,—have been effaced by the darkest drama that has ever disgraced human annals; the burning of the Grand Master is henceforth, in history, masked by the scaffold of the King.

The Temple owes its name to the Templars, the first of all the military and religious orders, founded at Jerusalem in the year 1118, before the divine tomb which it was called upon to protect. The Templars, who came to Paris at a period which is not exactly identified, but which some chroniclers place about the year 1128, settled in the environs of that town in the midst of marshes, the pestilential vapours from which brought on, from time to time, epidemic diseases. The labours of these indefatigable men transformed these marshes into fertile plains, smiling gardens, and agreeable dwellings. Reed and weed gave place to useful trees, to shady hornbeams; a vast tract of land, fertilized by that most potent of all labour, the labour of prayer, was thus created to the north-east of Paris,—it was called the Culture du Temple. Enclosed like the citadels of old, by high walls, furnished with battlements, and supported, at intervals, by turrets, it extended as far as the Montagne de Belleville, where the knights possessed some pleasure houses, then called Courtilles. The name still remains to the place, whither the people resort every Sunday to divert themselves after the labours of the week.

In the centre of the circuit of the Temple was erected, it is said by brother Hubert, treasurer of the order, who died in 1212, an edifice remarkable for its massiveness and solidity; it was composed of a large square tower, the height of which exceeded one hundred and fifty feet, without including the roof, and the walls of which were, on the average, nine feet thick. It was, at its four angles, flanked by four round towers, and on the north side it was accompanied by a tower of smaller dimensions, surmounted by two low turrets; a broad ditch completed the defences of the fortress, environed the building on all sides, and separated it from the gardens.

The large tower was intended to receive the treasure and arms of the order, and of the four angular towers, three were destined to serve as prisons for those knights who had infringed the monastic or military discipline; the last contained the staircase. This place became the chief residence of the order. The church, of clumsy architecture, had been built, it is said, on the model of Saint John at Jerusalem. In this church took place the admission of the Templars, and, in later times, that of the knights of Malta. Notwithstanding the buildings and cultivated lands within the precincts of the Temple, the esplanade was large enough to allow four hundred men, armed with their cross-bows and their halberts, to exercise there freely. In recompense for the gigantic labours they had performed, and the new means of defence with which they had provided the great city, King Philip III. granted to the Templars of Paris the privilege of extensive and independent juridical rights. Their court of justice was held on the place which now adjoins the Rue du Temple, and the Rue des Vieilles-Haudriettes; this was the limit of the jurisdiction of the commander of the Temple. The royal charter, dated August, 1279, *accords the right of middle and low justice from the gate Barbette, reserving to himself high justice, as far as the gate of the Temple; and in respect of places without the town, gives them middle, high, and low justice, from the aforesaid gate Barbette, along the road of the Courtille towards the gate of the Temple, with power to permit their men to carry arms and other things necessary to the execution of justice.*

In 1792, the Temple by no means preserved the extent i had at this early time. The city of Paris, in advancing north-east, had, century after century, curtailed its limits, and ulti mately surrounded it on all sides; but it still formed a sort of small town by itself, whence it was sometimes called La Ville Neuve du Temple, and its gates were closed every evening Its narrow streets were crowded with a numerous population, composed generally of workmen and families of debtors, who concentrated on that point, made the Temple a close and dismal quarter. However, since the greater part of the place had been sold (1779), the new administration had undertaken the sanitary improvement of this quarter. Some wretched barracks pulled down, some useless walls demolished, had given passage to the air and sun. The Rotunda, a large oval house, had been erected in 1781, and already the space situated between it and the Rue du Temple was gradually widening, to make room for the market for old linen, now to be seen there. Singular depôts, built (1809) in parallel lines; old clothes shops, where the poor man comes to dress himself as in the golden age, where the refuse of the most opulent wardrobe passes to the shoulders of the poorest purchaser; an amazing bazaar, serving as a boudoir for the toilette of penury.

The precints of the Temple, properly so called, now scarcely occupied two hundred yards in its greatest length, and as much in its greatest breadth; the rest lay hid beneath the pavements and houses of the great city, with its barracks, its gardens, and its cemetery. Only a few years ago in making a new sewer in the Rue des Enfants Rouges, there was discovered a coffin, containing the body of a man clothed in the ancient garb of the Templars. The rich clasp which adorned the mantle of this knight, made it probable that the remains discovered were those of a commander of the order of the Temple.

In one of the angles of this enclosure was the hotel, which had received the appellation of Le Palais du Grand Prieur, an ostentatious denomination to be applied to a small and low-built house, which, although placed between a court and a garden, had nothing about it worthy of a prince or a lord.

Above the shapeless mass of buildings contiguous to this, rose a lofty tower, of a square form, and flanked with turrets. This tower it was which the Commune of Paris destined as the prison of Louis XVI. and his family. For the first time the people regretted that they had demolished the Bastille.

We have seen that Louis XVI. arrived at the Temple at seven o'clock in the evening. The King persuaded himself that the palace of the Temple was to be his future abode; he visited all its rooms, and pleased his fancy by allocating the various apartments. Whilst giving way to this illusion, Santerre placed sentinels in the courts-yards, gates, and out-buildings of the Temple; and the servants prepared, in accordance with the order of the municipal officers, the bed-rooms of the royal family in the small tower. It was only after supper, which they took at ten o'clock, that Manuel informed the King of these arrangements, and offered to conduct him and his family to the apartments which were temporarily destined for them, until the great tower was ready to receive them. "Meanwhile," said he, "you can live in the palace in the day-time, and be with your family." Louis made no reply. With a calm and apparently indifferent air, he repeated to the Queen what he had just heard; and by the light of lanthorns carried by the municipal guards, the prisoners were led to the little tower, to the apartments previously occupied by the keeper of the records of the order of Malta, M. Berthélemy—apartments that we shall fully explain, by a plan and detailed description.

The little tower stood against the great one, but without any interior communication; and it formed a long square flanked by two turrets. Reached by four external steps, the entrance door, narrow and low, opened on a stairhead, and this, at a certain distance, to a winding staircase. This door, considered too slight, was, next morning, strengthened by strong cross bars and furnished with a thick bolt, brought from the prisons of the Châtelet. To the left, on entering, was the lodge of two Cerberi, with human faces, charged by the Commune with the custody and keeping of the door,—one was called Risbey, the other Rocher.

On the ground-floor there was only a large room, which served as a repository for the archives, and a kitchen which was not used. The building was four stories high.

The first consisted of an antechamber and a dining-room, which communicated with a closet in the turret, where was a library of twelve or fifteen hundred volumes. This room served as a bedchamber for Mesdames Thibaud, Basire, and Navarre, during the few days they remained at the Temple.

The staircase wound round as it rose. Wide from the commencement up to the first floor, it narrowed as it mounted to the second.

On the second story, you entered a very dark antechamber, where the Princess de Lamballe lay. On the left, the Queen and her daughter occupied a room which looked out on the garden; in this room, less gloomy than the rest, the royal family generally passed nearly the whole day. To the right, the Prince Royal, Madame de Tourzel, and Madame Saint Brice, slept in the same chamber. It was necessary to cross this room to get into the cabinet in the turret which served as a closet for the whole building, and which was common to the royal family, the municipal officers, and the soldiers.

The decree passed in the National Assembly, on the proposition of the commune, to make the Temple the residence

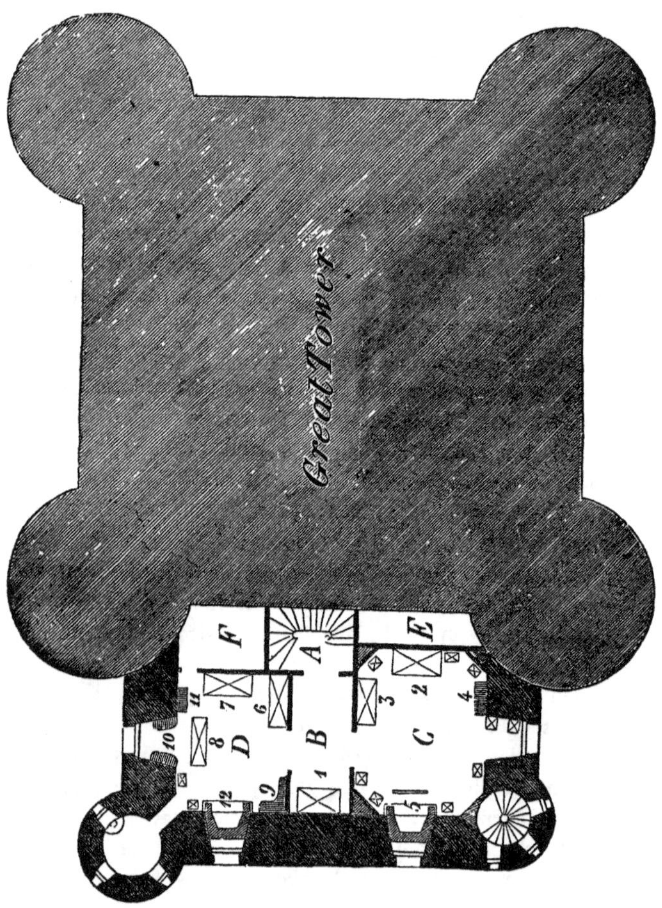

of Louis XVI. and his family, had been so unexpected, that nothing had been got ready for their reception. Several rooms were totally devoid of furniture, particularly, as M. Hue tells us, that intended for the King. It was not till some days afterwards that they distributed in more equal proportions the furniture of M. Berthélemy. We can, from a note written with his own hand, give an exact list of the articles that were placed at the disposition of the royal family.

We are on the second floor.

LITTLE TOWER.—SECOND STORY.—*THE QUEEN.*

A. Staircase.
B. Antechamber.
  1. Bed of the Princess de Lamballe.
C. The Queen's room, formerly M. Berthélemy's saloon.
  2. The Queen's bed; worked stuff, white ground, with flowers.
  3. Bed of Madame Royale, behind the Dauphin.
  4. A backgammon board, with the boxes and pieces of ivory and ebony.
  5. A chimney-piece with a screen of white taffeta, and a fire-place gilt with ormolu, representing a lion.
  Three mahogany corner pieces.
  Four arm chairs, called *à la Reine*, in white and blue silk.
  Two stools of the same material.
  Two lounging and another chair, of striped stuff. The curtains of this room are of blue taffeta.
D. Madame de Tourzel's room.
  6. Madame de Tourzel's bed.
  7. The Dauphin's bed, afterwards that of Madame Royale.
  8. Tressel-bed for Madame Saint Brice.
  9. A canopy of circular form.
  10. Two ottomans of blue and white Utrecht velvet.
  11. A chiffonier with five or six drawers.
  12. Fire-place.
  Three arm-chairs of white and blue Utrecht velvet.
  Two chairs of green taffeta.
E. Boudoir.
F. Closet.

The third story was a repetition of the second. In the antechamber, above the room of the Princess de Lamballe, there was, behind a partition, a narrow place, admitting no light but by a small window in the roof. This was the lodging of Hue and Chamilly. After the first few days the window disappeared under a cover of masonry, on the pretence that the "tyrant's" valet communicated by it with the sentinel on duty on the terrace, a sentinel whose legs he could scarcely see, and who was relieved every hour.

To the right of the antechamber was the King's room, lighted by a window which looked out on the Rotunda of the Temple. To the right, on entering, was a little alcove. A

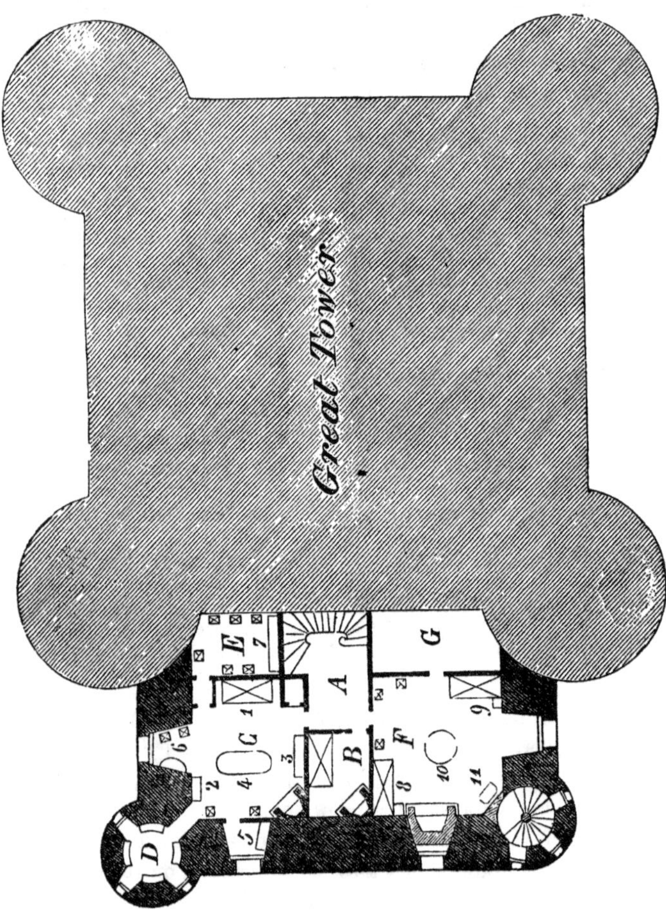

few engravings, the subjects of which were not the most decent, hung from the walls of the chamber. The King, on arriving, took them down himself, saying, "I do not wish my daughter to see them." The little room in the turret served the King as a reading room.

On the other side of the antechamber, opposite the King's apartment, was a room intended for a kitchen, and which contained all the necessary utensils. Two trestle-beds were made up here for Madame Elizabeth and Mdlle. de Tourzel.

The subjoined plan of this part of the mansion will, how ever, give a clearer notion of it.

LITTLE TOWER.—Third Story.—*THE KING.*

A. Staircase and landing.
B. Room and beds for MM. Hue and De Chamilly.
C. The King's room.
1. Double bed of the King, with top of red and yellow camlet.
2. Chest of drawers, of inlaid work, with marble top.
3. A large canopy of crimson velvet.
4. A large dining table.
5. A sideboard with four doors.
6. A small table with top of white marble.
Four arm-chairs, in crimson Utrecht velvet.
Six straw chairs.
D. The King's reading room, with circular benches of lilac taffetas, with fringed drapery and tassels.
E. Boudoir.
7. Cupboard filled with prints.
F. An old kitchen, the room of Madame Elizabeth.
8. Madame Elizabeth's bed.
9. Bed of Mdlle. Pauline de Tourzel.
10. Table.
11. A chair of red, lilac, and white cotton.
Three chairs.
G. Closet.

Such was the place which served as the residence of the King from the 13th August to the 29th September, and of the royal family from the 13th August to the 26th October. With the assistance of these plans we can follow the domestic life of the prisoners.

Arriving at the place which the revolution assigned them over night, it was not till the next morning, the 14th August, that they could examine the arrangements of the building. They traversed all the interior of the great and little towers, and were informed that the Council of the Commune, which, from the first, had assumed to itself the right of exclusive jurisdiction in all matters relating to the guard and management of the Temple, had just ordered considerable works for isolating and fortifying this house of detention. A commission was appointed to survey these works, and to regulate their expense.

On the same day the patriot Palloy, accompanied by Sautot, his colleague, and MM. Poyet and Paris, architect and surveyor of works of the Commune, came to examine the localities. This ambitious mason, already celebrated as having demolished the Bastille, that citadel of tyranny, had sought the glory of constructing the prison of the tyrant. His workmen took possession of the place. The walls and buildings attached to the main towers were pulled down, so as to separate the main building on all sides. The tenants of these buildings were dislodged forthwith, with the promise of an indemnification. The trees next to the tower were cut down. The ground was turned up; but a sort of indecision prevailed over the commencement of the works. In accordance with a resolution of the Commune, a large and deep ditch was first ordered to be dug round the building; but it was filled up before it was completed. The outer walls were raised to double their former height; several windows looking on the part of the enclosure called the Rotunda, the nearest inhabited part, were blocked up.

These various operations caused no little outlay; but the revolution became generous when it was a question of securing the captivity of the King. The royal family found persons working each day at their prison.

They had arrived at the Temple entirely destitute even of necessaries. They were obliged, therefore, to have external communication, sometimes for one thing, sometimes for another, and these communications, impeded by a thousand obstacles, after a while became matters of suspicion. Those who had the touching privilege of following them in their misfortunes, were denounced to the Commune, which in its sitting of the 17th August, ordered them to be removed from the tower. The notification of this decree was transmitted, on the morrow, to the Temple by two municipal officers. It was the hour of dinner, two o'clock; the royal family were, according to their usual custom, at table in the King's room. "Gentlemen," answered the King, "it is by virtue of an order of the mayor that these persons have followed me and my family." "No matter," replied the commissaries, "the new order which we bear annuls the first; the Commune will select other persons to wait on you." (It appears that it was the intention to surround the royal family with the wives and relations of municipal officers.) "Gentlemen," said the King, "if they persist in removing the servants we have here, I declare that my family and myself will wait on ourselves. Let them not, therefore, present any persons whatever to me." "We will," replied the envoys of the Commune, "inform the council-general of the result of our mission;" and they withdrew. Manuel came to the Temple about five o'clock; he was affected by the grief manifested by the King and the Queen, at the idea of losing persons so attached to them, promised to use his best efforts to obtain a revocation of the order, which had just been issued, and departed to confer with the Council of the Commune on the point. Late in the evening, two municipal envoys presented themselves in the tower, took down in writing the names of the Princess de Lamballe, of Madame and Mdlle. de Tourzel, and of all the persons in the service of the royal family, and then, without explaining the object of their proceeding, withdrew. On the night of the 19th, these two municipal officers again presented themselves, commissioned to bring away *all persons who were not members of the Capet family.* The Queen in vain opposed the departure of Madame de Lamballe, declaring that she was her relation, and that the decree of the Commune could not affect her. Their parting was heartrending. The two children, awakened by the noise, mingled their tears and caresses in this scene of sorrow, which the municipals could only put an end to by violently dragging away Madame de Lamballe and Mesdames de Tourzel, assuring them that they would be allowed to return after they had been examined. Hue and Chamilly, the ladies Saint Brice, Navarre, Basire, and Thibaud, were, with these three captives, led by torch-light across the garden. Reaching the gate of the Temple, they entered hackney coaches, without knowing whither they were going, and were taken first to the bar of the Commune, and thence to the Hôtel de la Force.

On the morrow, the 20th August, 1792, M. Hue, alone, was taken back to the Temple; he knew not the fate of his companions, yet his return inspired the hope that they, like himself, would be restored to the tower.* That hope was never to be realised In the afternoon, towards six o'clock, Manuel presented himself; he told the King that he had not succeeded in his efforts, and that he regretted to tell him, on the part of the Commune, that Madame de Lamballe, Madame and Mdlle. de Tourzel, Chamilly, and the ladies of the chamber, would not return to the Temple. "What has become of them?" asked Louis. "They are prisoners in the Hotel de la Force," replied Manuel. "What will they do," resumed the King, looking at M. Hue, "with the last servant that remains to me?" "The Commune will leave him with you," said Manuel; "and, as he would not be sufficient for your service, they will send other persons to assist him." "I want none · if he be not enough, we will ourselves do whatever he

* The municipal officer who led him back to the tower belonged to the moderate party. Questioned on the way by M. Hue, as to the fate of the persons arrested with him, and taken, like himself, to the Hotel de Ville. "My colleagues," replied the municipal officer, "have passed several nights without sleep; they are gone to take some rest; but this evening the Assembly will be complete, and will determine the fate of these persons; their examination is finished. I presume they will be sent back to their duties." This man's name was Michel.

cannot perform, God forbid we should give to devoted servants they have taken from us the pain of finding themselves replaced by others!"

The joy of the Prince Royal at the return of Hue had been ardent; his disappointment was great on seeing the Queen and Madame Elizabeth prepare for the new prisoners of La Force the articles they absolutely required. Manuel was surprised to see these two Princesses make up packets of linen, with cordial eagerness and a natural simplicity. He saw that, as the King had said, the race which had commanded the world was able to serve itself. As to the little Prince, saddened by these preparations which foreboded a long absence, he exclaimed with chagrin: "But why do they prevent Madame de Tourzel from coming back?" His little bed, on the night before, had been placed in his mother's room, and on the 21st, after the distressing news brought by Manuel, Madame Elizabeth quitted her apartment, on the second story, which was, as we have said, an old kitchen, and installed herself in the deserted room of the Dauphin, and Madame Royale, who had hitherto passed the night in her mother's room, established herself in her aunt's apartment.

The day was passed in the royal colony, amid regrets for the past and apprehensions for the future, in the following manner:

Louis XVI. rose between six and seven o'clock; he shaved and dressed himself, and immediately passed into the cabinet of the turret, adjoining his chamber, said his prayers, and read till the breakfast-hour. This room being very small, the municipal guard remained in the bed-chamber with the door partially open, so as always to have his eyes on the King. The pious monarch prayed on his knees for five or six minutes, and then read till nine o'clock.

Meantime, Hue got ready the chamber, prepared the breakfast table, and then descended to the Queen's room.

Marie Antoinette rose still earlier than the King, dressed her son, and heard him say his prayers. It was the only moment of freedom of which she could dispose. She did not open the door till M. Hue came, so as to prevent the municipals from entering her chamber. It was about eight o'clock when M. Hue, having arranged the King's room, came, eager to perform the services which the necessity of circumstances required of his zeal, and to present himself to the Queen; with him entered, for the rest of the day, the commissaries appointed by the Commune to guard them. These official spies passed the whole day in the room of the Queen, and the night in the room serving as an antechamber, which separated Marie Antoinette's apartment from that of Madame Elizabeth. At nine o'clock, the Queen, her children, and Madame Elizabeth went up to the King's room to breakfast. After having served them, Hue arranged the rooms of the Queen and the Princesses.

At ten o'clock, the whole family descended to the Queen's room, and there passed the day. Louis XVI. gave his son lessons in the French language, in the Latin language, in history and geography; Marie Antoinette occupied herself with the education of her daughter, and Madame Elizabeth taught her drawing and arithmetic.

At one o'clock, if the weather was fine, and if Santerre was present, the royal family descended to the garden, accompanied by four municipal officers and the chief of the National Guard. During the walk, the young Prince played at foot ball, quoits, running, and various other games. Bad weather, or the absence of Santerre, sometimes prevented this diversion—a privation which was only distressing to the royal family on their son's account, who had need of air and exercise.

At two o'clock, they again went up to the King's room to dine.

After dinner they re-descended to the Queen's apartment; it was the hour of recreation; the amusements of the children threw some rays of gaiety into this sombre interior. Sometimes the King went into the library, and selected some books; more generally the Queen and Madame Elizabeth proposed a game of picquet or backgammon, in order to divert him from reading and labour, into which he was ever ready to plunge.

Sometimes, towards four o'clock, the King took, in his arm chair, a few moments' repose. Ranged around him, the Princesses opened a book or worked at their tapestry; silence reigned throughout; the Dauphin studied his lessons. When his father awoke, he repeated them, and turned to his arithmetic and his copy-books. Hue looked over his work; the task done, he took him to Madame Elizabeth's room, and played with him at ball or shuttlecock.

Towards seven o'clock, all the family ranged themselves round the table; the Queen and Madame Elizabeth, relieving each other, read aloud some book of history, or other select work, adapted to instruct and amuse youth, but in which striking and unforeseen analogies with their own situation would often present themselves, and excite very painful thoughts. These applications especially occurred in reading Madame d'Arblay's *Cécilia.*

At eight o'clock, M. Hue prepared, in Madame Elizabeth's room, the supper of the Prince Royal; the Queen superintended it; Louis XVI. also, to amuse at that hour his little family circle, would sometimes propose some charades, extracted from a collection of *Mercures de France*, which he had found in the library.

The horizon of the family cleared up for awhile, in the radiant smiles of the children. After supper, the young Prince undressed himself and said his prayers. He said one in particular for the Princess de Lamballe, then another for his family and his governess; it was this:—

"Almighty God, who hast created and redeemed me, I adore thee.

"Preserve the life of the King, my father, and those of my family.

"Protect us from our enemies! Give Madame de Tourzel strength enough to support the weight of the misfortunes which she endures for our sakes."

Marie Antoinette herself heard him repeat these two prayers when the municipals were too remote to hear; but when they were near, the child had the precaution to say them in an under tone. Adversity and captivity are rude but useful teachers, inculcating prudence to the heedless, and giving experience to children.

Hue then put the little Prince to bed; the Queen and Madame Elizabeth remained in turns with him. Upon serving the family supper, Hue carried hers to the Princess, thus occupied. The King, on leaving the table, returned to his son. In a few moments, he took gently the hand of his wife and sister, bade them adieu, received the caresses of his children, and went up again to his room, and thence into the turret, which he only left about midnight, to retire to rest.

The Princesses also stayed some time together, their tapestry in their hands. They often availed themselves of this quiet hour to mend the clothes of the family; then, after a tender farewell, they parted to seek their repose. One of the two municipal officers on guard in the tower, remained in the little room which separated their chambers, the other had followed the King, These commissaries were relieved at eleven o'clock in the morning, at five o'clock in the evening, and at midnight. Louis XVI. waited till the new municipal relieved his predecessor, and then retired to rest; and if he had not seen the man before, he would direct M. Hue to ask him his name.

This sort of existence lasted all the time that the King remained in the little tower (up to the 29th September). The days succeeded each other in sorrow, in captivity, in agitation, and insult.

Then the night enveloped the old donjon of the Temple in its dark shade, bringing to the just a sleep as tranquil as their conscience.

Yet at times one woman watched there during a part of the night; the King and the Dauphin, having each but one garmènt, often Madame Elizabeth, secretly, unknown to all except Hue, who was necessarily her confidant, passed long hours in repairing and altering those clothes which he brought to her at midnight. More than once the municipals searched a garment which was brought from the room of Madame Elizabeth at six in the morning. Undeniable evidence has confirmed to me these minute details which I have deemed sufficiently touching not to be puerile. God ordained that this great family of the Bourbons should exhaust all kinds of suffering, from anguish of the deepest grief to that displeasing guest,—the sting of poverty,—in order to afford to all a consolation and a lesson.

Such was at the Temple the distribution of the hours of the day, which, as we see, was divided between prayer, reading, the instruction of the children, work, and sometimes walking (when it was allowed), and occasional conversation with the commissaries when they were inclined to be civil. Punctual in every respect, Louis XVI. had himself regulated the occupations of the day. One of his greatest consolations was to employ his time in the education of his son.

In this child of seven years and a half old, there was a combination of force and grace, rare even in the most endowed natures. Sometimes, the seriousness of his thought gave his conversation a character full of nobleness; sometimes, on the contrary, the frank playfulness of his years shone forth without regrets and without desires. Already he thought no more of past greatness; he was happy to live, and he was only turned to grief by the tears which sometimes stole down his mother's cheeks. He never spoke of his games and walks of former days; he never uttered the name of Versailles, or that of the Tuileries; he seemed to regret nothing. He seemed to forget his playthings—his infantine tastes. His precocious intellect perfectly corresponded to the anxious solicitude of the King. His memory, already stocked with La Fontaine's most amusing fables, became enriched with choice passages from Corneille and

Racine. His father, as he recited them, accompanied them with interesting explanations He was in the habit of making him read the History of France, and dictated to him fragments from the *Esprit de la Ligue*, to which, when he read them over in his copy-book, he would add an instructive commentary, while correcting the orthographical errors. It was at once a lesson in writing and a lesson in history. We are happy to be able to place before our readers a page of this copy-book; they will find there a specimen of the Dauphin's handwriting at this period of his life.

The method which the King adopted for instructing him in geography was, to mark on a sheet of vellum paper an outline of the coasts of the continents, the position of the mountains, the course of the rivers; then, the frontier points of kingdoms and provinces. To this framework, thus prepared, the Prince adapted the names, his memory rarely failing him, particularly when France was in question, of which he not only knew the provincial capitals, but the chief towns of the departments and even of the districts; for it was the new geography of France that his father taught him. By the mere frontier lines the child recognised the countries, and distributed the towns in their right places. He learnt also to wash the maps, and it gave him great amusement to mark the countries with different colours.

It was thus that, in prison, Louis XVI. once more renewed in the eyes of Europe the spectacle which an Emperor of Rome had afforded to his court in educating his own children, and, more fortunate than Augustus, he saw his care crowned with far fairer success.

On her part, Marie Antoinette, entirely absorbed in maternal cares, shared by Madame Elizabeth, instructed the youthful Marie Thérèse in the austere principles which make the good Christian and the virtuous woman, relieving these graver studies with lessons in music and drawing. One day, when the brother and sister met after their studies, and came

Writing Lesson of the Dauphin.
Corrected by Louis XVI.

A peine Luther eut-il fait connoître sa doctrine
que l'amour de la nouveauté lui attacha des parti=
=sans dans le Royaume. Calvin n'eut point de
peine ensuite à s'insinuer dans des esprits déja
prévenus, et à supplanter même bientôt les autres
réformateurs, par l'attrait d'un dogme moins char=
=gé de mystères, et dégagé de plusieurs rites, qu'il
comme inutile et onéreux
eut l'adresse de faire envisager long-temps son
troupeau foible, exposé à la sévérité des Edits
et aux recherches rigoureuses des magistrats, ne se con=
=serva que par le silence et la dissimulation.

to their father, holding each other by the hand, the King said: "Yes, my children, be ever industrious, and ever united; labour will be to you a consolation, your mutual tenderness a support, and prayer almost a hope. Labour, love, and prayer, my children; therein is life!"

In his picture of life, the King did not mention the word sacrifice; he would have fain confined to his own silent heart all sufferings, so as to keep them from his family; but all were fated to follow him in the path of sorrow which he was about to pursue.

There was no privation to which the Commune did not subject him; clothes, body-linen, bed and table-linen, covers, napkins, in a word, all the most necessary articles of use, were so scantily provided, that they did not suffice for their daily requirements On some nights, Hue was obliged make the bed of the Prince Royal with sheets torn in several places. The communications which this faithful servant had, in the course of his duties, with the commissaries of the Commune, became daily more painful, and the requests which he made were often left unanswered. The five hundred thousand livres, destined for the annual expenses of the King, had been voted by the National Assembly before it saw the real projects of the chiefs of the Commune, or, at least, before it had dared to connect itself with them. Hue had already written several times to the Mayor of Paris, to demand, in the King's name, payments on account of this sum, and the Mayor had sent no reply. Louis XVI. was the more sensitive to this annoyance, that, foreseeing the fate which awaited him, his rigid probity was afflicted at not paying, from week to week, the advances made by the purveyor. On coming to the Temple, he had a very small sum with him. Hue having given to Manuel a list of various articles which the King required, Manuel had bought them, and sent them to the Tower with a bill amounting to 526 livres. At the sight of this account, which Manuel himself had signed: "I am not in a position," said Louis XVI to his servant, "to pay out of my purse such a debt." "I beg the King," replied Hue, "to discharge this bill; I have still six hundred livres, and I hope that his Majesty will prefer the giving me great pleasure, to the contracting with Manuel a pecuniary obligation."

To the stings of poverty were added vexations of all sorts. The royal family could not descend into the garden without being exposed to insult. Rocher and Risbey, with their pipes in their mouths, made them pass the wicket between two clouds of smoke. The soldiers on guard outside the tower took marked care to put their hats on and sit down as soon as they saw them, and to rise and take off their hats when they had passed. As there were a great number of workmen within the Temple employed in pulling down the houses and in building new walls, they only allowed the prisoners to walk in a portion of the chestnut avenue. The Prince Royal found there a little exercise and recreation, a precious advantage which his unfortunate parents bought so dearly for him. They were obliged to witness the spectacle of the building up of their own prison; they saw the walls rise, the ditches hollowed out; they saw the workmen furnish with bars of iron the casements of their future dwelling; they saw them mask the windows with the shutters called *soufflets*, by means of which prisoners receive the light and air only through a vertical opening, and cannot see from their room what is passing without. The most strict orders were given, in that strange style which began to prevail at this period.* Louis XVI. had modified the rigours of the gaols for the unfortunates whom crime brings thither, considering that prisons should be only secure places of detention, and not of premature torments. Yet it was for him and his family that men now calculated, to avaricious

* Order of the 24th August, 1792, in the fourth year of Liberty and the first of Equality.

"In consequence of the decree of the general council, the commander-in-chief orders that the garden of the Temple shall be closed to all persons whatever, with the exception of the adjutant and the officers on guard in the interior, and about the King's person."

nicety, the portion of air and light that their prison should admit. More than one cruel reflection passed through their hearts during these sad promenades; but always worthy of themselves, and resigned, no look betrayed the agony of their souls, no word the bitterness of their feelings. Once, and once only, the King said to the commissaries who surrounded him: "Why, gentlemen, what expenses, what precautions! I have not, I assure you, any idea of escaping."

The restraint of the interior corresponded with the gloomy sadness without. Most of the municipals, on entering the Temple, seemed to have for their mission the aggravation of captivity by insult.

The Queen, by entering into conversation with them, essayed in vain to awaken in their hearts some emotions of humanity. "Where do you live?" inquired she of one of the men who were attending at dinner. "*In my country!*" replied he, with stupid emphasis. "Your country!" repeated Marie Antoinette, with inexpressible sweetness; "ah! that is France."

One morning, as Louis XVI. was dressing himself, one of these commissaries, called Lemeunié, approached him and proceeded to search him. Without testifying the least impatience, the King took out the contents of his pockets, and placed them on the chimney-piece. The municipal examined everything with attention; then, returning them to M. Hue: "I have done," said he, "what I have been ordered to do." After this scene the King directed his valet henceforth to give him his clothes with the pockets turned inside out. Consequently every evening, when his master had retired to rest, Hue took care to empty his pockets.

On another occasion, on the 24th August, between midnight and one o'clock in the morning, several municipals entered the chamber of the King. Awakened by the noise, Hue rose hastily, and rushed to his master's bed, which was already surrounded by the commissaries. "In execution of a decree of the Commune," said one of them, "we have come to examine your room, and to take away all the arms that may be there." "I have none," said Louis. They searched the room, nevertheless, and having found nothing: "That's not enough," resumed they; "on entering the Temple you had a sword,—give it up." Constrained to endure every mortification, Louis ordered his *valet-de-chambre* to bring the sword.

On rising next morning, the 25th August, the King spoke of the deep pain which this insult had occasioned him. He begged Hue to write to the Mayor of Paris, and inform him of what had passed during the night, and to request him to lay down some fixed rule as to the mode in which the decrees of the Commune should, for the future, be made known to him. Pêtion sent no answer.

In the evening there was a new alarm. A municipal, called Venineux, of lofty stature, robust frame, and dark visage, with a knotty stick in his hand, suddenly entered the King's room. The King had just stepped into bed. "I am here," said this fellow, "to make a special examination. We don't know what may happen, so I wish to make sure that Monsieur (speaking of the King), has no means of escape." "Your colleagues made that visitation last night," said Hue, "and the King gave his consent to it." "Gave his consent! that's very good," replied Venineux; "he could not help it. If he had resisted, I wonder who would have had the best of it." Taking alarm as to the intentions of this new-comer, Hue resolved not to lose sight of him for a moment. "I shall not go to bed," said he; "I shall remain with you." The King, hearing these words, insisted. "Go to bed," said he; "tired as you are I command you." Without giving any reply to this command, Hue retired; but as the door was so situated that the King, from his bed, could not see that of his servant, Hue, without undressing, threw himself upon his mattress, keeping his eye on their ferocious visitor, and ready, upon the slightest suspicious movement, to fly to his master's assistance. His fears, however, proved groundless. This officer, who had intruded upon them so like a wild beast, slept soundly till morning. "That man gave you serious alarm," said Louis, when he arose, to his valet; "your anxiety touched me, for I also felt no slight apprehension of danger; but in the condition they have reduced me to, I am prepared for everything."

Notwithstanding repeated applications, Louis had never been able to obtain the perusal of any newspapers, except those which, either purposely or from neglect, were left by some of the municipals on the table of the ante-chamber. One day there appeared written in pencil on one of these sheets, the following words: "Tremble, tyrant, the guillotine is permanent." Similar threats generally covered the walls; they were even written on the door of the King's room; and though Hue took special care to efface them, they did not always escape the attention of the royal family. The same devotion led him to suggest a means of supplying the absence of the public press. Every evening, hawkers were in the habit of crying beneath the Temple walls, the news contained in the journals they were selling. At that hour, Hue would ascend the turret, and there climbing a window, three parts blocked up, he would cling to it till he had succeeded in catching the most interesting intelligence, after which he immediately repaired to the Queen's apartment; Madame Elizabeth, rising at his appearance, would step into her own room, and thither, under some pretext or other, Hue would follow her and impart to her all the information he had thus been enabled to gather. Elizabeth then hastened to place herself at the balcony of the only window in the Temple that had not been condemned so entirely as not to leave a wide aperture; Louis could venture to this window, without giving cause of suspicion to the guards, for the purpose of breathing the fresh air, and his sister seizing this opportunity, would communicate to him all that Hue had learnt. By such means alone did the heir of a line of powerful monarchs learn, by dint of stratagem and caution, a portion of the great events which were agitating his empire.

Thus was he made aware of the entrance of the allied troops on the French territory, of the reduction of Longwy and Verdun, of the desertion of Lafayette with his staff, of the death of M. de Laporte, intendant of the civil list, and of De Durosoi, editor of the *Gazette de Paris.*

But it too frequently happened that among the news published daily by these hawkers, exaggerated statements, false occurrences, and lying announcements were made. "Here you have," cried they, on one occasion, "here you have the decree ordering the separation of the King from his family." Marie Antoinette, who was at that moment so placed that she could distinctly hear these words, fainted away, and with difficulty recovered, but never afterwards could get rid of the impression of terror they had given her. It was, however, for the most part, friends from without, who took pains to send criers in whom they had faith. Sometimes, they even revealed their attachment to the captives, by teaching hurdy-gurdy players a few of the airs popular among royalists of the day. "*Pauvre Jacques!—Henri, bon Henri, ton fils est prisonnier dans Paris!*" These burdens occasionally reached the ear of the royal princes, and anon they died away in the distance, resembling the vain and fleeting hopes they had called forth.

It was not only upon the least detail of the service in the tower, that the municipal control was exercised; it encroached even upon the more private rights of the education of the Prince Royal. Louis, despoiled of his privileges as a King, of his liberty as a man, saw himself on the verge of being deprived of his prerogatives as a father. The copies which had habitually been set for his son to write from, had been by his desire chiefly taken from the works of Montesquieu and d'Anquetil. On one occasion a municipal guard named Leclerc, who was present at the lesson, thought some of the reflections from *l'Esprit des Lois* very impertinent. He with much rudeness interrupted the exercise, and began to hold forth on the republican principles which it now became the Prince to receive in his education. He wanted to substitute for these readings, those of revolutionary works. "The youngster," said he "must now be taught to live for the times as they are, and not as they were."

Again, while taking his Latin lesson, the Dauphin was wrong in the pronunciation of some difficult word, and the royal preceptor did not correct his son, upon which the municipal guard bluntly said: "You should teach that child to pronounce better, for in these times he may have to address the public more than once." "You are right, Sir," calmly answered Louis; "your remark is just, but my son is yet but an infant, and I think it best to wait until time and habit shall have unloosened his tongue."

The lessons of arithmetic were soon put a stop to. A municipal guard named Godard, observing that the royal pupil was being taught the multiplication table, thought proper to infer that they were teaching him how to communicate his thoughts in cypher. A small treatise on arithmetic, which Hue placed every night on the Prince's pillow, that he might learn in the morning the task set him by his father, was accordingly metamorphosed by the suspicious Godard into hieroglyphical letters, invented to facilitate the correspondence of the royal family. From that moment the general council of the Commune, on the denunciation of this member, prohibited the study of cyphering.

Another proof of their extreme sagacity was shown on the same day by another of these guards, whose name remains unknown to me. Hue had been commissioned to obtain from the drawing master of the young Princess, Marie Thérèse, some models of heads for her to copy; M. Van Blarenberg—so the master was called—immediately forwarded a certain number of them Their delivery excited against the Queen the animosity of this intelligent commissary, who insisted on seeing in these heads—which were copies of antiques—the likenesses of the principal sovereigns then allied against France. His brilliant appreciation nearly deprived the Princess of her models, and Hue and Van Blarenberg of their liberty. Again, this same blunder occurred with respect to some tapestry which the Queen and the Princesses occupied their time in working. The Queen, having completed some chair-covers, gave orders that they should be sent to the Duchesse de Sérent. The municipals, imagining that they saw in the designs of this tapestry an emblematical language, issued a protest prohibiting the works of the Princesses from being conveyed out of the Temple.

We will cite one more of these ridiculous vexations, occasioned by a municipal officer at a time when the royal family were all assembled. Marie Antoinette was reading to her children a passage in the History of France, where the Constable de Bourbon takes up arms against France. She was rudely interrupted by this guard, who moodily exclaimed, that he supposed she selected such sentences to inspire her son with feelings of revenge against his own country.

It must be allowed, however, that the municipals were not all of the same stamp. All were, certainly, recommended by their civism to the public suffrage; but their position, character, and education, established a vast dissimilarity among them. Hue was once commissioned by one of these to present a memorial to the King, soliciting the post of tutor to the Prince Royal. "I presented the same memorial," said he, "to Count Alexander Beauharnais, at the period when that deputy presided over the Constituent Assembly. I entreat you to remit this to the King, and to speak to him in my favour." "It is out of my power to be of any service to you," said Hue; "I never speak to his Majesty but when he condescends to address me, and in the present state of things I do not see how your memorial could be received." Just then Louis appeared. Thomas,—the municipal guard,—warmly assured him of his fidelity, testifying the utmost indignation at the insults his colleagues daily offered to the King. "It would only lower me," said Louis, "did I show myself sensible of the treatment I meet with at their hands. Should it please God to restore to me the reins of government, they shall learn that I can forgive." Upon this, Thomas proffered his petition; but the King merely replied: "For the present, I myself suffice for my son's education."

This task occupied much of the King's time. Therein he found duties which consoled him, and fatigues which amounted to relaxation. What gave him most concern was, that the whole weight of the service in the tower fell upon his faithful valet; and he justly feared lest, in the end, his physical strength should succumb under the zeal of his devotion. For the purpose of obtaining relief for him, Louis applied to the council for a man who could undertake to do the laborious duties in the Temple. The mayor selected for that employment an ex-keeper of the Barriers, named Tison, a man of a hard and suspicious disposition, and imbued, like most of his class, with strong prejudices against the King.

This man took up his quarters in the tower with his wife, who seemed a gentle and compassionate woman. It will shortly be seen what was the nature of the services required from the zeal of these creatures, and that the royal family found in them spies rather than servants. Be this as it may, Hue contrived to obtain great assistance from their co-operation, and had only occasion to speak in terms of approval of both the one and the other.

A few days after Tison's instalment, Pétion wrote thus to the King, 26th August, 1792:—

"Sire,

"The valet who has been attached to the person of the Prince Royal ever since his infancy, has requested to continue to attend upon him; as I have reason to believe this proposal will be acceptable to you, I have acceded to his wishes," &c.

Louis, upon handing over this letter to Hue, said to him: "Read this, and tell the Mayor in answer, that I consent to it; add, however, that it is not without much displeasure that I find the municipality leave my demands unanswered, and more particularly my request to have my children's own physician to attend upon them."

On that same day, 26th August, at eight o'clock in the evening, a municipal officer introduced Cléry into the Temple. He was searched; advice as to how he was to conduct himself was given to him, and he was then admitted to the tower.

It will be a matter of surprise, no doubt, that after depriving the royal family of those servants who were most attached to them, the Commune should now consent to give them back Cléry, who passed for being no less devoted to their interests; still more so, perhaps, that this concession should follow the arrival of Tison and his wife, who had been considered sufficient to fulfil, with the help of Hue, all the duties required in the tower; but I should be loth to infer from this measure that any one could impute motives compromising to the honour and respect awarded to the character of Cléry. The Duchesse d'Angoulême, it is true, always retained suspicions of the disposition of Cléry, on his return to them in the Temple. She remained persuaded that he was from the first a tool of the revolutionary party. Her respect for the venerated will of the martyr king, prevented her from publicly avowing her sentiments relative to Cléry; but her opinion, in general so justly formed, both upon men and circumstances, never changed on this subject. It is in obedience to my conscience as a faithful narrator, that I have mentioned this Princess's suspicions of the motives which brought back Cléry to their service; but it is also my duty to add, in justice to him, that however that may have been, at all events the spectacle of the virtues and sufferings which he now beheld had the effect of completely converting the agent of the Commune. Marie Thérèse has, in her writings, spoken of him in terms which clearly prove all former prejudices to have been removed.* He himself thus relates his entrance into the tower.† "It is out of my power to describe the impression I received from the sight of this august and unfortunate family. The Queen was the first to address me, and after a few words full of grace and kindness, she concluded by saying: 'You will wait upon my son, and you will concert with Monsieur Hue as to all that concerns us.' I was so overcome on beholding so much suffering and virtue, that I could scarcely find words to reply."

As he was chiefly engaged with the Prince Royal, Cléry's attendance on the King was limited to the occupation of dressing his hair in the morning and rolling it up at night; it was still Hue only, who was charged with fetching and receiving all the necessaries for the royal family. As the confidant of proscribed royalty, and as minister to an imprisoned prince, on him devolved the painful duty of claiming the daily food for his master from a committee which was renewed every day by envoys of the municipality. This task was for ever giving rise to the most painful and hazardous discussions. The kitchen being detached, and at a great distance from the tower, Hue, in order to reach it, was obliged to pass several posts of guards, and obstacle upon obstacle, question upon question, and insult upon insult, followed in succession. The municipals, who always accompanied him everywhere, for the most part encouraged these outrages by applause, and frequently provoked them by their own instigations. In the palace of the Temple these Arguses of the Commune had an assembly-room, which they termed the Hall of Council · here the linen and other articles. which were transmitted to and fro, underwent a rigorous examination.

* See "*Récit des Evènements arrivés au Temple.*" (Recital of the events which occurred in the Temple). Page 22.—*Audot*, *Paris*, 1823.

† "*Journal de ce qui s'est passe à la tour du Temple pendant la captivité de Louis XVI., Roi de France. Par M. Cléry, valet-de-chambre du Roi. Edited by the Countess of Schomberg.*" (Journal of what took place in the tower of the Temple during the captivity of Louis XVI., King of France. —*London*, *Baylis*, *Greville Street*, 1798.

When anything had to be brought in or taken out, Hue was summoned by one of the officers, and guarded all the way to or from this hall. Every article of food for the royal family was subject to this visitation; not only by the council, but by others in authority, who would cut in two the loaves and any other of the eatables that had a doubtful appearance. In short, not a single article was ever allowed to pass into the tower or out of it without being first rigorously visited; the inquisition existed everywhere, and sarcasms were on everybody's lips. On one occasion the King overheard the invectives which were heaped on the head of his generous servant. That very night, after the curtains of his bed had been drawn about him, he seized the only occasion when he could venture to speak, without fearing that every word he spoke would be stored up by the officer on guard, and addressing Hue, said: "You have had many hardships to endure this day; continue, for the love of me, to bear them, and do not answer a word." The Christian resignation emanating from the soul of his master had already taken root in the heart of the servant. At another time, whilst Hue was fastening to the King's bed-curtains a watch hook, which he had contrived to make out of a hair-pin, the King slipped into his hand a small packet. "It is a lock of my hair," said he; "I have nothing else to present you with at this moment." The unhappy prince had a presentiment that this honest man in whom he had found a friend would soon be snatched away from him. This thought haunted him. In the room where Hue slept were three doors, one led into the King's chamber, the opposite one into the former kitchen, and the third opened upon the staircase. Through the latter the municipal officers were in the habit of frequently entering on a sudden, to ascertain if they could, whether this man who would work so zealously all day, did not also spend the night in plotting conspiracies and in carrying on secret correspondence. One night the King, who had frequently been disturbed by the noise this nocturnal intrusion occasioned, was more than usually anxious in consequence, and as soon as it was day he arose, and gently opened the door of communication. Hue being startled, became alarmed at seeing the King so attired: "Sire," said he, "is your Majesty in want of any thing?" "No; nothing. But as I heard some commotion in the night, I began to fear lest you had been taken away. I only wished to satisfy myself that you were still near me."

The Queen and the Princess Elizabeth were subjected to the same constraint. Surrounded as they were by municipal gaolers, they could only by stealth contrive to confide their wishes and sorrows to Hue.

On entering one day to perform his accustomed duties, he found the Princess in her room engaged in earnest prayer; his first impulse was to retire. "Remain," said she, "attend to your occupations; they will not disturb me."

I here insert the prayer of this spiritual-minded woman; Hue obtained a copy, and has preserved it for our benefit:

"What may befall me this day, oh, my God! I know not; but this I know, that nothing can happen which Thou hast not ordained eternally. It is enough, Oh, God! and I am calm. I adore Thy eternal decrees; I submit to them with my whole heart; I desire all, I accept all; I resign all to Thee, desiring to add this sacrifice to the sacrifice of Thy dear Son, and entreating Thee, by His holiness and through His divine merits, to grant us patience under our afflictions, and that perfect submission to Thee, which we are bound to have in those trials, which are either ordained or permitted by Thee."

This prayer being concluded: "Not so much for the unhappy King," added she, "as for his wandering people, are my prayers offered up to Heaven. Oh! that God, touched with compassion, would deign to behold France with pity." Observing how deep an impression her words were producing, she turned to Hue, saying: "Come, come, be of good courage, God never sends us heavier burthens than we can bear." How great must have been her courage in His sight, who thought fit to afflict her so heavily!

Ever since the arrival of Tison and his wife, and Cléry, Hue had been much relieved in his duties at the Temple; but his bodily fatigues were as nothing compared with the bitter sorrow of heart that lay in store for him. He had already noticed that the marks of kindness with which he was honoured, gave rise to much ill-will on the part of some of the municipal guards, and from day to day he apprehended he should be discharged from the tower. This presentiment was too justly grounded, yet, for all this, the King maintained his usual serenity. His oppressors saw, even in this profound tranquillity, as in everything that related to him, a subject of anxious suspicion. Beholding him so calm in his prison, they said among themselves: "It is doubtless because he is expecting a speedy deliverance, and his hopes are entertained through the relations he has contrived to preserve with his brother princes, and with foreign monarchs. He must have gained information of the movements in his favour about to be set on foot by all the absolute powers of Europe!" His very patience thus became a crime in the eyes of his persecutors, who interpreted the forbearance with which he submitted to everything, as the result only of hope in the termination of his sufferings.

The Commune were employed, day and night, in endeavouring to detect correspondences, which had existed, but had long been dropped. The plans of the allied powers they represented in the most alarming colours; the journalists attributed to them projects of a far more alarming nature than any of those which had been revealed by the violent manifesto of the Duke of Brunswick. They said that the enemy would neglect fortified places in order to march directly to Paris, which would first be reduced by famine; that the city once taken, the inhabitants would be removed into the open country, and all the revolutionists put to death. France was agitated by a thousand fears, the actors of the 10th August trembled at the thought of royalist vengeance, the remains of the regiment of Flanders and of the French Guards trembled at the civic spirit of the National Guard, and the National Guard trembled at the fanaticism of the federates of Brittany and Marseilles. All the authorities mistrusted each other, and all parties feared each other; the most alarming rumours were circulated. The deputies proposed that the Assembly should retire to Saumur; but the man who had said · "Boldness is required, boldness still, boldness ever!" cried in his thundering voice: "They tell you to do this thing, and that thing; I tell you but one thing—the royalists must be terrified" This was the announcement of the days of September.*

A great stir took place about the Temple on the 2nd September. But as yet all was tranquil within; and as it was Sunday and the weather very fine, the King and his family went down again after dinner to walk in the garden. In the morning Cléry had remarked that the municipals looked uneasy; walking behind them, following the King, he heard one of them now say to his colleagues: "We have done wrong in consenting to take them out this afternoon." It was near

* We cannot assert that Danton imagined and ordered the massacres of September, but we do say that he foresaw them. He was forewarned, yet permitted them to take place, and afterwards represented that, which was the impious work of murderers, as the official policy of the committee of public safety. The truth of this is proved by the famous circular addressed by the committee of inspection of the Commune, on the 3rd September, to all the municipalities of France:—

"The members of the Commune of Paris hasten to inform their brethren in all the departments of France, that a part of the ferocious conspirators confined in the prisons have been put to death by the people; an act of justice which they deemed indispensable to terrify and keep in check the legions of traitors concealed within its walls, and at the moment they were about to march to the enemy: the entire nation will, no doubt, after the series of treasons which have brought it to the brink of the precipice, eagerly adopt means so necessary to public safety, and all Frenchmen will exclaim like the Parisians: 'We go to meet the enemy, but we will not leave brigands behind to butcher our wives and children.'"

This circular, signed by

PANIS, SERGENT, MARAT, DE FORGAS, LECLERC, CELLY,
J. DUPLAIN, L'ENFANT, JOURDEUIL, ET DU FORTRE,

was sent into the provinces, with the counter-signature of the minister of justice, DANTON.

five o'clock. The *générale* is suddenly heard. The commissaries hurry Louis XVI. and his family in,—two other commissaries coming out of the palace of the Temple, rush after them; they are scarcely assembled in the Queen's room before one of them, named Mathieu, addressing the King, said: "You know not, Sir, what is going on, the *générale* is beating in all quarters, the alarm gun has been fired, the people are furious and call for revenge It was not enough to have assassinated our brethren on the 10th August, and to have used jagged bullets against them, thousands of which were found in the Tuileries; you are now bringing upon us a ferocious enemy who threatens to slaughter us and our wives and children. The King of Prussia is marching on Chalons. They have sworn our death,—we know it; but before we meet it, you and your family shall perish by the hands of the municipal officers who guard you. It is, however, still time; and if you will, you can——" "I have done all for the happiness of my people," answered the King; "nothing remains now for me to do."

During the commissary's address, Hue had hastened to his master's side. The King had scarcely done speaking when Mathieu continued: "I arrest you." "Who, me?" said Louis XVI. "No, your valet." "What has he done? He is attached to me; that is his only crime. Do not attempt his life." "By what authority do you arrest me?" asked M. Hue; "and where do you propose taking me?" "I have no account to give thee,"* answered Mathieu; "I have my orders." M. Hue wished to go up into his room; Mathieu seized him by the arm, saying: "You are not allowed to go there without me; you are in my custody." They went up together a few minutes after. Hue wanted to take some linen and razors with him: "No razors," said the municipal; "you will be shaved where I am taking you; I can even promise

* It should be remarked that the word *thee* (*te* in French) is here employed as an insult.

that there will be no lack of barbers." Hue was silent, fully persuaded that he was about to be taken to the scaffold. Seals were immediately put upon the closet he occupied. On his return to the Queen's room with the permission of the municipals, he delivered some papers to the King, which concerned him. "Unhappy man," said Louis XVI., "the little money you had, you have advanced for my use, and now you are going, totally without resources." "Sire, I need nothing." From each member of the royal family he received assurances of sympathy. Fearing its fatal effects, Hue, by an effort, put an end to a scene so affecting. "I am ready to follow you," he said to his conductors. When going away, Mathieu said to Cléry: "Beware how you conduct yourself, or the same fate awaits you."

At the foot of the tower, two gendarmes joined Mathieu and stepped with him and M. Hue into a hackney carriage. What a fearful sight struck their prisoner while driving through the streets! The passengers were fleeing in affright; men were closing with haste their doors, windows, and shops, and taking refuge in the remotest parts of their dwellings. There was heard the roar of the assassins, the cries of the victims; monsters covered with blood, armed with pikes and cutlasses, rushed along the streets, parading in triumph, at the end of their pikes, the mangled limbs of human beings. The carriage stopped on arriving at the Place de Grève; it had become impossible to make way through a compact multitude, agitated like the sea, and brandishing in the air pikes, swords, and guns. The prisoner was desired to alight, and they conducted him to the Hôtel de Ville, through a crowd, furious with rage, whence issued, with fearful imprecations, these words: "Here's game for the guillotine; it is the *valet-de-chambre* of the tyrant!"

Hue was calm: a devoted heart is ever brave; he offered up the sacrifice of his life, and he was prepared to accomplish it with honour. Entering the Salle de la Commune, he was placed near the president. At a short distance was Santerre. This commander of the Paris militia was listening with infinite gravity and attention to the plans which a number of half drunken men were developing to him, for stopping the hostile armies. Some, with an air of immense science, were explaining the various machinery of their strategic operations, and others, taking the straight line, simply proposed a general rising of the people to march against the foe. In the Parquet, the wonted place of the procureur of the Commune, Billaud-Varennes, one of the substitutes, was in vehement motion, and near him, Robespierre, calling about, giving orders, and seemingly much agitated.

In this hall, and the adjoining apartments, the tumult was very great. Amid the disorder the president interrogated the accused. Before he had time to reply, voices were heard on all sides, shouting,—"To the Abbey! to La Force!" At this moment the prisoners were being massacred there.

Silence was effected and the interrogatory began. It was full of matter, mostly imaginary. "You passed into the tower of the Temple," said one of the municipals, "a trunk filled with tri-coloured ribands and various disguises. This was to facilitate the escape of the royal family" Another cried, "I heard the King say *forty-five*, to him, and the Queen *fifty-two* These two numbers were to designate the Prince de Poix, and the traitor Bouillé." A third pretended that Hue had ordered a waistcoat and trousers of the Savoyard colours, a certain proof that he held communications with the King of Sardinia.* A fourth clamoured about secret correspondence, carried on by means of hieroglyphics, of which we have already spoken. Others accused him of having sung in the tower the song, "*O Richard! ô mon roi! l'univers t'abandonne!*" which was untrue, M. Hue never sang; and lastly, of having attached to himself, on the part of the royal family, an interest which they displayed towards him, while they would scarcely speak to the commissaries of the Commune;

* M. Hue had indeed signed an order for such a dress for Tison. And this order had received the sanction of the commissary on guard.

which was true. At this last reproach, the accused was dumb. The clamour renewed: "To the Abbey! to la Force!" At last, the fury against the prisoner attained its height. Billaud-Varennes exclaimed: "This valet, sent back once to the Temple, has betrayed the confidence of the people. He deserves exemplary punishment." A municipal rose and said: "Citizens, this man holds the thread of the conspiracy hatching in the tower; to secure his person, confine him close, and obtain from him all the information he can give, would be far wiser and more useful than to send him to the Abbey or La Force." Whatever was the motive of the municipal, his words saved the life of M. Hue. It was decided that the prisoner should be confined in one of the dungeons of the Hôtel de Ville, and placed under the care of a gaoler. He was conducted to the cell destined for him.

As soon as M. Hue had departed from the tower, Louis XVI. called Cléry and placed in his hands the papers which had been given him, and which contained an account of the condition of the clothes, and certain private expenses of the King. The unfortunate Prince had in vain endeavoured to discover of what crime his faithful attendant was accused. His anxious thought found only this answer, "He was attached to me and that is a great crime." The silence, the caution, the important manner of the municipals, the uproar of the people round the Temple, agitated his heart cruelly. After he had gone to bed, he told Cléry to stay with him all night; and Cléry placed his bed by the side of the King's.

On Monday, 3rd September, whilst dressing himself, the King asked Cléry, the only person left to wait upon the whole royal family, if he had heard anything of M. Hue, or of what was passing in Paris. Cléry, during the night, had heard that the people had directed their steps to the prisons. He knew no more, but proposed to go and procure intelligence. "Take care you do not expose yourself to danger," said Louis, "for then no one would remain to us, and I fear it is their intention to place strangers about us." At eleven o'clock, the whole of the royal family being assembled in the chamber of the Queen, a municipal told Cléry to ascend to that of the King; where he found Manuel and other members of the Commune. Manuel asked him what the King said about the removal of M. Hue. "It makes him very anxious," answered Cléry. "Nothing will happen to Hue," said Manuel; "but I am ordered to inform your master that he will not return hither; and that the council will send a substitute. You can make this known to him." "I pray you to excuse me from doing so," replied Cléry, "and the more so that the King wishes to see you with respect to various articles of which his family are in the greatest need." It was with difficulty Manuel made up his mind to consent; but on seeing the King, he communicated to him the decree of the general council with respect to M. Hue and of the approaching arrival of another attendant. "I thank you," said the King; "I will make use of the *valet-de-chambre* of my son, and if the council will not sanction this, I will wait upon myself; on this I am determined." The King then spoke of the requirements of his family, who had not sufficient linen or other clothes; Manuel answered, he would report the matter to the council, and retired. Whilst conducting him out, Cléry inquired if the excitement still continued? Manuel, by his answers, made him fear that the people would come to the Temple. He added, "You have undertaken a difficult service; you will need all your courage."

The procureur-syndic of the Commune pronounced these words with an anxious tone. He knew that the massacres, begun the day before at half-past two in the prisons of Paris, were still going on. Without doubt, not having been able to prevent them, he feared that part of the responsibility of these odious transactions might be attributed to him—transactions which historians will explain in various ways, but which they can have but one voice to denounce.

It does not belong to us to describe them. Let us inquire only what became, during these dreadful days, of the persons attached to the royal family, and who were torn from them at the Temple on the 19th August, to be conducted to La Force.

The register of the Petit Force, preserved in the archives of the Prefecture of Police, informs us that this prison, at the time of these events, contained one hundred and ten women, most of them altogether unconnected with political affairs. Amongst them were many loose girls, and miserable creatures of every age, accused of having stolen linen, china, &c., from the Château of the Tuileries during the day of the 10th August and the night of the 11th. Amongst these one hundred and ten females there were only nine confined on political grounds. Here is an extract from the gaoler's book:

19th August.

Madame de Navarre, first *femme-de-chambre* of Madame Elizabeth. . . Madame Bazire, *femme-de-chambre* of Madame Royale. . . . . Madame Thibault, first *femme-de-chambre* of the Queen. . . . . Madame Sainte-Brice, *femme-de-chambre* of the Prince Royal. . . . . . Madame Tourzel, *gouvernante* of the King's children. . . . . Mademoiselle Pauline Tourzel, do. . . Marie Thérèse Louise de SAVOIE de BOURBON-LAMBALLE.	By order of M. Pétion, Mayor, and of MM. the commissaries of the forty-eight sections.

30th August.

Angélique-Euphrasie Peignon, wife of M. de Septeuil, native of Paris, aged twenty-one years and a half; sent to this prison to be there confined till further orders; by the order of MM. the administrators of police

2nd September.

Madame Mackau, sent to this prison with Mdlle. Adélaide Rotin, her *femme-de-chambre*, voluntary prisoner with her mistress, by order of MM. the administrators of police, members of the commission of surveillance and the public safety

Madame Sainte-Brice and Mademoiselle Pauline de Tourzel were set at liberty on the 2nd September, by the order of Messrs. Truchon and Duval-Destaines, commissaries of the Commune.

Mesdames de Navarre, Bazire, Thibault, de Tourzel and de Septeuil, were released on the 3rd, by the popular tribunal which was installed at La Force. It was the same with Madame de Mackau and her *femme-de-chambre*, who had entered the prison the evening before at the moment when the massacres were commencing. Some say they were liberated without trial, as well as the hundred and one other women of whom we have already spoken.

As regards Madame de Lamballe, on examining her description in the gaoler's book, it is obvious that a special fate awaited this unfortunate princess. The absence of any profession, the words De Savoie and De Bourbon-Lamballe emphatically written in large characters, manifest that an exceptional destiny was reserved for her. History has not clearly told why she was assassinated, or who were her judges and executioners. The same hand that in the register in question has traced the description of Madame de Lamballe merely added to her name, these words, which were a sentence of death: "Conducted, the 3rd September, to the great Hôtel de La Force."

Maton de la Varenne states that Dangé, Michonis, Laiguillon, and Monneuse, members of the general council of the Commune, decorated with the title of Grands Juges du Peuple, composed the sanguinary tribunal installed at La Force. Roch Marcandier* says that Madame de Lamballe was interrogated by Fieffé, registrar of La Force; that the impromptu tribunal was composed only of some private individuals; Peltier relates that it was Hébert himself who presided at this tribunal when Madame Lamballe was conducted before it, the 3rd September,

* In his "*Histoire des Oiseaux de Proie.*" (History of Birds of Prey.)

at seven o'clock in the morning. This alleged interrogatory appears to me very doubtful. Contemporaries have recounted that, conducted very early in the morning to the gate of the prison, the Princess there found her assassins; these having questioned her about the Queen, she only answered, "I have nothing to say to you; to die a little sooner or later has become indifferent to me; I am prepared:" and that then, dragged through the courts over many dead bodies, she was slaughtered. Others assert that, conducted to the bar, Madame de Lamballe fainted, and could not speak a word, and that a person wearing a tri-coloured scarf, cried out almost immediately: "Let Madame go!" a form of words under which was hidden the sentence of death; that the Princess was then dragged to that part of the Rue des Ballets which separated, up to a few years since, La Force from the Rue St. Antoine, and which was in 1792 an *impasse*,* called the Cul de Sac des Pretres, and that there one stroke from a sabre struck her on the back of the neck, and laid her on a heap of corses.†

We are certain, however, as to the atrocities which followed this assassination. After having killed this friend of the Queen with pikes and sabre thrusts, they exposed her fair body for hours to the lascivious gaze of the spectators, and exposed it to brutalities at which cannibals would have blushed. Death itself became an insufficient guardian of modesty. Then, cutting off her breasts, her head, and other parts of her body, each of these bleeding remains was placed on a pike. Her left side was opened; a man plunged his hand in and drew forth the bleeding heart, which was also stuck on a pike, to be, in like manner with the rest, paraded through the streets. Civilization, which separated itself from God, thus surpassed, at one bound, the fury of savages; and the eighteenth century, so proud of its intelligence and humanity, finished by cannibalism.

The approaches to La Force, as well as those to all the

* An alley or court through which there is no thoroughfare.

† See Document No. V.

prisons on that day, were crowded by a populace, composed in a great measure of women and children in rags. The spectacle that was to be presented wanted not its spectators. It was noon when the pikes were raised in the air; cries and shoutings saluted the bleeding trophies, and the hideous procession set forward. A woman who had experienced the gentle nature of Madame de Lamballe, and felt a grateful affection for her,—Madame Lebel, the wife of a celebrated painter,—was trying, at this moment, to approach her prison, in the hope of obtaining some news of her. Observing the great commotion in the crowd, she asked what was passing. The reply was: "The head of La Lamballe, that they are parading through Paris." Seized with grief and fright, Madame Lebel hastily retraced her steps and took refuge in the Place de la Bastille, at the house of a hair-dresser whom she had known as *valet-de-chambre* in a great family, and of whose loyalty she was sure. She had not time to rest herself before the multitude arrived at the same place; they stopped, and the principal actors in the drama ordered the hair-dresser to arrange the head of Madame de Lamballe. At this sight, Madame Lebel fainted; having fallen between the shop and the partition behind she escaped observation, thanks to the coolness of the hair-dresser, who, placing himself before her, pushed her into the room, while he, talking with his horrible customers, washed, combed, and powdered the fair hair covered with blood. "At all events, now, Antoinette will recognise it," said the bearer, raising the pike, at the end of which he had replaced the head of his victim, and the procession again proceeded on.

We have said that Manuel had left the Temple. His visit and certain rumours had caused uneasiness there.

At one o'clock, the family did not as usual walk in the garden. The municipals would not allow it. During dinner, the beating of drums was heard, and a rumbling noise in the distance. That sound drew nearer, and soon an immense crowd came within sight of the Temple, covered with dust, their clothes torn, their hair disordered, and their hands stained with blood. This refuse of humanity, having at their head an old man and a child, whose violent antics made them appear more like furies, formed a horrible army, which approached roaring like wild beasts. Some of their leaders brandished hatchets, some swords, others clubs and pikes. It was a demoniacal picture, requiring for its painter, Milton—that painter of the abyss.

Dispersed groups assembled from all parts, and formed a compact mass of many elements. Drunken women sung, children in rags danced, ragged men shouted forth a thousand clamours. And amongst all these confused cries, one name was heard above the rest, pronounced by women, children, and men: "La Lamballe! La Lamballe!"

Increasing as it went, dragging with it all it met on its passage, that avalanche stopped from time to time before the public-houses, and with thundering voices demanded drink; then they again set forward, with such ardour that those who were at the head of the procession, impelled by the ranks behind, felt as though they were borne onward by mighty waves.

The noise and tumult increased; the air resounded with clamours, shoutings, blasphemies, and ravings of triumph.

Arrived before the Temple, at the order to halt, the mass stopped; the chiefs of the rioters took up their position before the gates: and, still more noisy in their halt than in their march, the hideous battalions saluted the sombre edifice with a deafening clamour that acted as a summons to all the furies of the district.

Their ranks then opened, and a body, without a head and mutilated, was seen, men and children disputing among themselves for the horrible honour of dragging it by a rope in the gutter.

The municipals on duty had sent in great haste to the Rue Phélippeaux for tri-coloured ribands, to make a barrier at the gate of the palace, in order to impose respect on this multitude and stay its progress. To these ribands was fastened this inscription: "Citizens, you who know how to unite with a just vengeance the love of order, respect this barrier, necessary for our guard and responsibility."

The populace, meanwhile, with roarings similar to tnose of wild beasts, had taken the disfigured body of the princess, now covered only with a chemise, like itself stained with blood and dirt, and bathed it in the fountain of the Temple, on the left of the great door.

Before the threshold of this door, were on guard, throughout the day, two men, taken from the dregs of the populace, a sort of watchmen, whose occupation was indicated by the name given them at the Temple—the searchers. One of these wore a large sabre in a tri-coloured belt; he was a robust man, in the prime of life, with a vulgar expression of countenance, long red moustaches, a brown great coat, and a scarlet cap. This man hesitated for awhile between his orders and his feelings; but the latter prevailed, and he was about to admit the populace that they might present the horrible spectacle to the royal family. Happily, the municipal officers interfered, and kept back the crowd. Three men, however, advanced from the mob to the door; one of them held in his hand the heart of the Princess: he begged, with this bleeding passport, entrance into the first court. "Pass alone," said the searcher. On entering, he saw Meunier, whom the man with the shoulder belt designated as the cook. He cried out, extending his ensanguined hand: "Here, take and cook this, that I may eat it."

Meunier, who, during the tumult outside, had changed his official dress, fearing, doubtless, that the victorious mob entering by force into the Temple, would treat him as one of the King's servants, replied, "The fires are out; what you ask is impossible." "Re-light them, I am hungry;" said the cannibal. But, being ejected by the municipals, he mixed with the ever yelling crowd, whose increasing waves the tri-coloured ribands could no longer check. At their head were twenty patriots, who declaimed incessantly against Marie Antoinette, asserting that there would be no safety for France till the last royalist was guillotined; and, waving in the air the head of the Princess, "We want," said they, "a pendant for La Lamballe; give us the Austrian;" and the filthy herd repeated: "The Austrian! the Austrian!" The soldiers had taken up arms, but the requisite reinforcements did not arrive. The rioters opposed a violent resistance, insisting upon carrying into the tower the naked corpse of Madame de Lamballe, and on returning with that of Marie Antoinette in addition. The municipals tried to calm them; one of them, named Daujon, got on a chair, the seat of one of the searchers, and harangued them in these terms: "The head of Antoinette does not belong to you alone; the departments have also their right to it. The head of the King will answer for the dangers or the reverses of the nation. France has confided the guardianship of these great criminals to the city of Paris. It is to you w must look to aid us in keeping them, until national justice shall avenge the people."

Refused admittance at the gate of the palace, but still raging and roaring, the populace marched round the tower to the rotunda. The man that carried the head of the Princess mounted on the ruins of the houses pulled down to isolate the tower; others followed him with vociferations, and, amongst them, the horrible possessor of the heart of the victim, which he elevated in the air on the point of his sword, jealous of the other trophy, which he could not reach.

Meanwhile the royal family had risen from table, and were assembled in the Queen's room. Cléry had gone down to dine with Tison and his wife; suddenly the latter uttered a scream; she had just seen at the window the head of Madame de Lamballe. The assassins outside thought they recognised the voice of the Queen, and they welcomed with hideous laughter the cry of fear that issued from the tower. Imagining that the Queen was still at dinner, they had, from the top of the rubbish, put forward the head of their victim in such a manner that she could not avoid seeing it. Though blood-stained and pallid, the face was not disfigured; the fair hair, which had lately been dressed in horrible mockery, floated round the pike.

Cléry ascended hastily, in the hope of informing, in a low tone, either the King or Madame Elizabeth. His countenance was so dejected that the Queen perceived it, and said: "What is the matter with you, and why do you not go to dinner?" "Madame, I do not feel well," said Cléry. The two municipals of the guard were at their post; a third entered at this moment: "The enemy is at Verdun," said he, addressing the King; "we shall all perish; but you shall perish the first." The King heard him tranquilly; the Prince Royal ran into another room, and burst into tears: his mother recalled him, his sister brought him back, but both together could scarcely console him Another municipal officer came in, and talked mysteriously with his colleagues. The King asked if his family was in danger. "A report is circulated," said they, "that you and your family are no longer in the tower; they demand that you shall appear at the window; but we will not allow it,—the people should have confidence in their magistrates." "Yes," answered the first municipal officer; "but if the enemy approaches, the royal family will perish." And seeing the despair of the young Prince, he added: "The Dauphin inspires pity; but, being the son of the tyrant, he will perish also." Meantime the cries outside increased; insults addressed to the Queen were distinctly heard. Another municipal entered, followed by four men, deputed by the populace to ascertain whether the Capet family was in the tower; one of them, in the uniform of the National Guard, wearing two epaulettes and trailing a great sabre, insisted upon the prisoners showing themselves at the window. The municipals objected. One of them, named Mennessier, said: "Oh, no! for pity's sake, no!" opposing the King's progress; "do not approach, do not look!—how horrible!" On observing the charitable resistance of the commissaries, the National Guard at the head of the deputation said, with a satanic voice: "They want to hide from you the head of La Lamballe, which we were bringing, to show you how the people revenge themselves on their tyrants. I advise you to appear, if you would not have the people come up."

The Queen fell, fainting; Cléry flew to her assistance. Madame Elizabeth assisted to place her in an arm-chair; her children melted into tears, and essayed to restore her by their caresses. The man did not retire; the King said to him, with energy: "We are prepared for everything, Sir; but you might have spared the Queen the knowledge of this calamity." The man then departed with his comrades; their object was accomplished. Marie Antoinette, restored to consciousness, mingled her tears with those of her children, and retired with the royal family into the chamber of Madame Elizabeth, where the clamour of the people was less distinctly heard. These cries of rage and death, celebrating the murder already committed and coveting another, these scenes of cruelty and blood endured till night. Reinforcements, demanded by the municipals from the Commune, were in vain expected during six hours: during six hours it was uncertain whether the royal family would not be massacred: during six hours tumultuous hordes rolled to and fro in the vicinity of the Temple, the tower of which rose like a rock amid a sea agitated by the tempest.

Ere they were recovered by the pious care of the Duke de Penthièvre, the body and head of the Princess de Lamballe had yet to divert the filthy populace; as to her heart, the horrible cannibal who possessed it went, about three o'clock, to the wine-shop opposite the gate of the Temple, where finding a cook less scrupulous than Meunier, he had it cooked, and, with a companion whom he had invited to the festival, devoured it with avidity. The names of these two men have escaped the execration of the world. What matters it? They themselves will not have escaped the justice of God.

Towards eight o'clock matters assumed a calmer aspect in the neighbourhood of the Temple. Cléry obtained all the information he could relative to the events of the day, and the municipal guard from whom he obtained it, made a demand of forty-five sous, which he had laid out in the purchase of the tri-coloured ribbon.*

While undressing the King, Cléry took occasion to report to him all the details he had learned. Louis inquired of him which of the municipals outside had shown most courage in defending the lives of his family. Cléry mentioned Daujon, who had addressed the mob, and succeeded in curbing their fury. This man happening to be on duty at the tower four months after, the King remembered his conduct, and thanked him. As to the commissary who had prevented the royal family from witnessing the abominable spectacle brought under their very windows, Louis XVI. had not waited till night to ascertain his name; he had asked it of the man himself, and in the last hours of his life he expressed, with tears in his eyes, to M. de Malesherbes, how deeply he had been touched by the proceeding. "Having no other way," added he, "I begged him to give me his name and address." "Did you make the same request to him who wished to force you to the window?" "Oh, as to him," answered Louis XVI., "I had no desire to know."

Let these words, which do honour to humanity, close a day which will ever be a disgrace to history.

* Note of expenses incurred by Cléry for the service of the King, in the month of September, 1792.

BOOK SEVENTH.

THE REPUBLIC PROCLAIMED BEFORE THE TEMPLE.

4th September—27th October, 1792.

Penury of the King—The Prince Royal's toys—The commissaries of the Temple—Simon—The turnkeys of the tower—Some consolation—Interview between Hue and Chaumette—Accession of the Convention—Abolition of royalty—Serenity of Louis XVI.—Discovery of the iron closet—Sayings of the Dauphin—The royal family deprived of the means of writing—Louis XVI. removed to the great tower—Turgy, Marchand, and Chrêtien—Cléry suspected—The King is deprived of his insignia — The Dauphin provided with clothes — Arrest of Cléry—He is reinstated at the Temple—The Queen, her children, and sister removed to the great tower—The Dauphin separated from his mother and placed with his father—Words spoken by this child to Mercereau the mason.

Tuesday, September 4th, the massacres continued systematically in the prisons of Paris. The bloodthirsty populace, who had rushed to murder, had not yet satisfied the thirst for gore which inflamed them. The tranquillity which had been restored in the neighbourhood of the Temple, and the silence of the municipals, kept the royal family in ignorance of the full extent of the horrors committed during these fatal days; but what they did know gave them the idea and suspicion of what they did not. Still absorbed in the heart-rendering remembrance of what they had witnessed over-night, they resumed the uniform life they had adopted the first day of their captivity. Cléry replaced Hue; like him, valet to the King and Dauphin, and the purveyor of all news, whether from private confidants or from the public voice, he was, moreover, hairdresser to the whole family. After having completed the toilet of the King and the Dauphin, he dressed the Queen's hair, and afterwards performed the same duty for Madame Royale and Madame Elizabeth. During the time of this toilet he gave the Princesses all the information he had obtained. A signal had been arranged by which they knew he had something to tell them, and one of them then contrived to engage the attention of the municipal by conversation. Tison and his wife, excluded from any closer attendance, only assisted Cléry in the service of the apartments; they had, therefore, plenty of leisure to bestow on the more important duty they had to fulfil—that of seeing and hearing everything, and more especially that which they perceived it was desired to conceal. In the Temple they were the eyes and ears of the Revolution.

On the 4th September the King received, for the first and also the last time, a small sum on account of the five hundred thousand livres* the National Assembly had voted for his annual expenses. Pétion's secretary brought him the sum of two thousand livres in assignats, and asked him for a receipt. Tormented by the recollection of the debt he owed to his most attached and faithful servant, the King begged Pétion's messenger to remit to M. Hue the sum of five hundred and twenty-six livres, which he had advanced for his use; the secretary and commissaries promised to do so. Louis XVI. then dictated in these terms the receipt, which was written on a stamp, and signed it with his own hand:—

"The King acknowledges to have received from M. Pétion the sum of two thousand five hundred and twenty-six livres, including five hundred and twenty-six livres which the commissaries of the municipality have engaged to remit to M. Hue, who has advanced that sum for the King's use.

"Paris, September 3rd, 1792. "LOUIS."

It was published in several newspapers at this time that the King, in his distress, had accepted a loan from the mayor

* Livres of Tours, equivalent in value to the present French franc.

of Paris. This was a fact, as is proved by a document which states that Pétion was afterwards repaid this sum out of the five hundred thousand livres granted to the King by the decree of the 12th August, 1792.*

The advance made by the mayor of Paris to despoiled royalty came very opportunely. The Prince Royal and his sister had not a sheet of paper for their lessons; the Queen was indebted to Bréguet for a repeater, which she had ordered through the medium of M. Coutelle, a municipal officer, the day after she arrived at the Temple. This debt weighed upon Marie Antoinette's mind; the King insisted that the watch-maker should be instantly paid. Some toys had for a long time been promised the Prince Royal, as a reward for his studies; he looked for them with impatience: Louis XVI. was at length enabled to do for the heir to the kingdom of France what the meanest citizen can do for his child. On Thursday, the 6th September, the Dauphin received from Vangeois's toy shop (the Singe-Vert—the Green Ape), a cup and ball, a solitaire, a beautiful draft-board, and two bastard senna-trees.

On the same day, Madame Elizabeth collected a few trifles belonging to Madame de Lamballe. Left at the Temple by this unfortunate Princess when she was carried off, these things

* This is the document: we have preserved under the date of the 4th, mentioned by Cléry, the fact to which it relates.

"I request the commissaries of the national treasury to pay to citizen Pétion the sum of 2,526 livres; that is, 2,000 to repay himself for an advance to that amount made to the *ci-devant* King, and 526 livres to be paid into the hands of M. Hue, if such sum be due to him, or into the coffers of the municipality, if the advance was made out of them. All according to the acknowledgment of the 3rd September, signed Louis, examined by the municipal officers on duty at the Temple, and now annexed to the decree of the council-general of the Commune of the 5th instant, deposited in my offices; which sum of 2,526 livres will be included in the distribution of the 26th November to the 1st December next, and the order immediately sent to the national treasury.

(Signed) "ROLAND.

"Paris, 28th November, 1792."

ever and anon drew tears from the Queen and her daughter. Madame Elizabeth gave them to Cléry, with orders to send them, with a letter, in a packet, to Madame de Lamballe's first lady's-maid. He afterwards learned that neither letter nor parcel had reached its destination.

We have recorded a few facts from the recollections of Hue, relative to the municipal officers chosen to inspect the Temple. Some anecdotes from Cléry's journal will complete the picture of the character of these men, who had most of them taken a part in the Revolution of the 10th August, and some of them in the massacres of the 2nd and 3rd September.

A municipal guard, named James, a teacher of English, insisted on following the King into his reading closet, and sat down beside him. The King mildly observed to him that his colleagues had allowed him to be alone, and that, the door being open, he could not lose sight of him, but that the room was too small for two. James insisted in the coarsest and rudest manner on remaining; the King, obliged to yield, gave up reading that day and returned to his room, where this commissary continued to oppress him by the most tyrannical watching.

One day the King, on rising, fancied the commissary then on guard was the same who had been there on the previous evening, and expressed his regret that they had forgotten to relieve him. To this amiable remark, the municipal answered: "I am here to examine your conduct, and not for you to trouble yourself about mine;" and approaching the King with his hat on, "no one, and you less than any one, has a right to interfere with that." This man's name was Lemeunié; it was he who, being on guard on the 19th August, wished to search the King,*

Among the six commissaries charged to inspect the works

* Lemeunié was the son of a hairdresser. He had the imprudence to mount a horse from the stables of the Louvre; the animal ran away with him, and, as he passed the Quai de Gèvres, a sentinel cried out to him:

and expenses at the Temple, was one named Simon, a shoemaker and a municipal officer, who alone, under pretence of doing his duty, remained constantly at the tower. This man never approached the royal family without giving utterance to some offensive speech. Often would he say to Cléry, within hearing of the King: "Cléry, ask Capet if he wants anything, that I may not be troubled to come up again." Cléry's answer was always, "He wants nothing."

At a later period we shall frequently have to mention this odious name of Simon. Insolent to the father, inhuman towards the son, it was this man's destiny to oppress two royal generations. His was the envious hate of the alley to the palace. Some of the commissaries never spoke of the King, of his son, or of the Princesses, without adding some insulting epithet to their names. One of them, whose name was Turlot, said once, before Cléry: "If the executioner does not behead this cursed family, I will behead them myself."

More than once the National Guards made themselves a party to these insulting proceedings of the commissaries When the royal family went out to walk they had to pass a number of sentinels, several of whom, even at this time, were placed in the interior of the little tower. These sentries always presented arms to the municipal and other officers, but when the King approached them, they either stood at ease or reversed their muskets in a marked manner. One sentry in the interior wrote one day on the door of the King's room, and on the inside: "The guillotine is permanent, and awaits the tyrant Louis XVI." Cléry was about to efface these words, but the King prevented his doing so.

"*Qui vive* (who goes there)?" He was unable to stop, and the sentinel fired at and killed him. The Commune of the 10th August, to which he belonged, decreed him the honours of a civic funeral on the ruins of the Bastille, took his widow under its protection, and ordered the scarf worn by this citizen, who died in the discharge of his duties, "to be suspended in the hall of the council-general."

If, at times, the National Guard happened to be better constituted, it was insulted in its turn by the turnkeys, who pretended, as purer revolutionists, to have the right of inspecting them. One of the turnkeys, named Moustache, was thus himself made the subject of a report addressed to Roland, minister of the interior.

Encouraged by the applause and laughter of the guards, the two porters at the tower, especially Rocher, strove daily to invent fresh insults to heap upon fallen greatness. Others had overthrown royalty; these took a pleasure in trampling its ruins under their feet. Remarkable for his hideous countenance, dressed as a sapper, with long moustaches, a bearskin cap on his head, a sabre at his side, and a belt from which hung a bunch of large keys, Rocher appeared at the door whenever the royal family wished to go out, but never opened it till the King was close to him, when (under pretext of choosing among the great number of keys, which he shook with a frightful noise), after having kept the royal family waiting, he would draw the bolts with a crash. Then hurrying down, he placed himself at the outer door with a long pipe in his mouth, from which he would puff smoke into the face of each member of the royal family, more particularly into those of the Princesses. Attracted by this insolence, which amused them, some of the National Guards would collect round Rocher, greet every puff of smoke with shouts of laughter, and indulge in the coarsest expressions; some, in order to enjoy the sight more at their ease, even brought chairs and seated themselves so as to obstruct the passage, which was already very narrow. During the walk, the cannoniers would assemble and dance to revolutionary songs. The labourers who worked in the garden joined in these insults. One of them boasted before the King, that he should like to strike the Queen's head off with the tool he held in his hand.* When the prisoners

* "Account of the Captivity in the Temple," by Madame Royale.

returned to their prison, they had to endure the same outrages. Revolution formed a line to insult royalty as it passed.

The walls were covered with insulting sentences, in such large characters that they could not escape observation. "Madame Veto shall dance! We shall know how to diet the fat pig! Down with the cordon-rouge! Down with the Austrian she-wolf! The little cubs must be strangled!" A gibbet was sometimes drawn, to which a figure was suspended, and under it the words: "Louis taking an air bath." Sometimes it was a guillotine, with the words: "Louis spitting in the sack," &c. Thus did they contrive to make a torture of the short time allowed the prisoners for exercise. The King and Queen might have avoided this; but as we have said, the father and mother daily endured outrage without complaining, in order that their children might enjoy a breath of air and a ray of sunshine, so necessary to their health, and which could only be purchased by them at so heavy a price.

One night, between nine and ten o'clock, the patrols found themselves in an embarrassing position, owing to the neglect of the chiefs, in not having agreed upon the watchword: all within the Temple were upon the alert, the cry was raised, "To arms!" Municipal officers, soldiers, and turnkeys, imagined that the foreign armies had arrived. The stupidity of human nature, which is always fearfully aggravated in times of revolution, now increased the perils of the royal family. The most implacable terrorists are always those who themselves are under the influence of fear. Cries of alarm and fury were everywhere heard. Armed as usual, Rocher rushed up stairs, entered the room where the King and his family were at supper, and, rage flashing from his eyes, and extending his clenched fist towards Louis XVI., he exclaimed: "If they come, I kill thee."

Let us hasten to contrast these expressions of rage and hatred with evidences of sympathy and compassion. A municipal, on guard for the first time, entered at the moment the King was giving his son a lesson in geography. When asked where Lunéville was, the Prince Royal answered, "In Asia." "How, in Asia!" said the municipal smiling; "are you not better acquainted with the place where your ancestors have reigned?" The manner in which the commissary corrected the child's mistake pleased the King and Queen greatly. Marie Antoinette entered into conversation with him in an under-tone, and concluded by saying: "Our sufferings would be much more endurable to us, if your colleagues resembled you."

A National Guard was on duty at the door of the Queen's room; he was from the suburbs, and dressed in a peasant's attire, but very clean. Seeing Cléry alone, and reading, in the farther chamber, this sentry contemplated him attentively, and with apparent emotion. Cléry passed him; the National Guard, presenting arms, said, in a tremulous voice: "You cannot go out." "Why not?" "My orders are to keep you in sight." "You are mistaken," said Cléry. "What! Sir, are you not the King?" "You do not know him, then." "I have never seen him, Sir, and would gladly see him anywhere but here." "Speak lower. I am going into that room. I will leave the door ajar, and you can then see the King; he is with his children, seated near the window with a book in his hand." Cléry communicated the sentry's wish to the Queen, and she told the King, who was good enough to walk from one room to the other, in order to pass before him. When Cléry again approached him he exclaimed, greatly moved: "Oh! Sir, how good the King is, and how dearly he loves his children! No," continued he, striking his breast, "I cannot believe that he has done us so much harm." Cléry, fearing least this man should compromise himself by his agitation, left him.

Another sentry, posted at the end of the Allée de Marronniers, a young man of interesting countenance, expressed by looks his wish to make some communication to the royal family. Madame Elizabeth, as she walked round again, approached him, to see if he would speak to her, but, whether from respect or fear, he did not; yet tears started to his eyes, and he indicated by a sign that he had deposited a paper in the rubbish close by. Cléry looked for this paper, pretending to be choosing stones for the Prince Royal to play at quoits with. The municipals, however, desired him to retire, and never again to approach the sentinels. The intentions of this young man still remain a mystery.

This hour's walk was the source of other emotions to the royal family. A great number of royalists profited by it daily to observe them from the windows of the houses which overlooked the garden of the Temple; it was impossible to be mistaken as to their sentiments and their views. Cléry thought once that he recognised Madame de Tourzel, in the person of a woman who followed every movement of the Prince Royal with the greatest attention, whenever he moved away from his parents. He mentioned this to Madame Elizabeth. On hearing the name of Madame de Tourzel, this Princess, who believed her to have been one of the victims of the 2nd September, burst into tears, saying: "Is it possible she still lives?" Cléry was mistaken; he learned the next day that Madame de Tourzel was at one of her estates. He also ascertained that the Princess de Tarente and the Marquis de la Roche-Aimon, who were at the Tuileries at the time of the attack of the 10th August, had escaped death. It was a great consolation to the royal family, who had wept over them as lost, to know that these devoted friends still lived. It was for them like the resurrection of loved ones; but they were soon overwhelmed with grief, at hearing of the massacre of the prisoners of the high court of Orleans. The Duke de Brissac and M. de Lessart were among the number of the King's friends who were not tried, but assassinated, at Versailles, on the 9th September, 1792. M. de Brissac's head was stuck on one of the spikes of the gate of the Château. M. de Brissac could never be prevailed upon to leave the King from the beginning of the Revolution. After the disbanding of his regiment, he might have fled, and the King urged him to do so; but the heart of this faithful and devoted subject had been deaf to the entreaties of his unhappy king. "Sire," he had answered, "if I fly they will call me guilty, and you will be thought an accomplice; my flight will be an accusation against you, and I would rather die." He died.

Among those who came daily to the neighbourhood of the Temple, to watch for the moment when they might see the royal family, we must not omit M. Hue, who, after having spent nearly a fortnight in the dungeons of the Commune, suffering all the agonies of death, had just been restored to liberty. The idea of the King's captivity was ever present to his mind, and left this faithful servant no repose; the only solace to his grief was bending his steps towards the Temple. Tormented night and day by the desire once more to enter the tower, he took steps to address Pétion; and finding he had gone over to the National Convention as a representative, he determined to see Chaumette, who was now attorney-general of the Commune, in place of Manuel, who had also been named deputy in the Convention. By him he was received much better than he expected; Chaumette wished to converse confidentially with him, and desired his door to be closed to any one else. He first spoke to him of his obscure origin, his laborious youth, and the harshness he had experienced from the government, He then made important disclosures of the infidelity of several persons in the King's service, who were receiving daily, as the price of their information, one or more louis, stipulated to be paid in gold. M. Hue, in his work, "*Dernieres Années du Regne et de la Vie de Louis XVI.*" (Last years of the reign and life of Louis XVI.), has been generously silent respecting the treachery of these wretches, not deeming it right, as he says, to divulge their names when his virtuous master had chosen to conceal them, and in his immortal will, had entreated his son to remember nothing but their misfortunes: so thoroughly had the heart of this worthy servant been imbued with his master's sentiments of ineffable mercy and forgiveness.

Then, speaking of the royal family, Chaumette appeared interested in the Dauphin. "I wish," said he, "to give him some education. I will separate him from his family that he may lose all thoughts of his rank; as to the King, he must perish. The King loves you——" At these words, M. Hue could no longer restrain his tears. "Do not control your grief," continued Chaumette; "did you for one moment cease to regret your master, I myself should despise you." Notwithstanding this confidential reception, M. Hue's application was not successful

About this time the Legislative Assembly was replaced by the National Convention. The revolutionary drama was drawing to a close; the catastrophe was approaching. The Legislative Assembly, which had possessed neither the courage of virtue nor the energy of crime, had brought the victim to the Temple, and the Convention was to immolate him. It bore on its brow the brand of its odious origin. Framed under the auspices of the massacres of September and during these massacres, it may be said to have been conceived in blood and murder. The greater number of the electors had been prevented from attending the election by fear or violence. One million five hundred thousand only had taken part in the ballot, and all the favourites of the Revolution had been triumphant; the workmen were well fitted for the bloody task that awaited them.

At the first sitting of the Convention, 21st September, 1792, on the motion of Collot d'Herbois, and almost without discussion, royalty, already suppressed in fact, was formally abolished, and the republic proclaimed. The King, indeed, had been, for upwards of a year, nothing more than a crowned mockery.

On the same day, at four o'clock in the afternoon, a municipal officer, named Lubin, surrounded by mounted gendarmes and an immense concourse of people, came to read a proclamation in front of the tower. The trumpets sounded, and a profound silence followed. Lubin possessed a stentorian voice; the royal family could distinctly hear the proclamation.

"Royalty is abolished in France. All public acts will be dated from the first year of the Republic. The state seal will bear the words *République de France*, as its legend. The national seal will represent a woman seated on a sheaf of arms, and holding a pike surmounted with the cap of liberty."

Hébert, so well known under the name of Père Duchêne, and Destournelles, afterwards minister of taxes, were on guard about the royal family; seated close to the door, they endeavoured to read in the countenances of the captives the secret emotions of their hearts. The King discerned their intention in their expressive smile, and continued reading a book he held, without betraying the slightest change of countenance. Like him, the Queen maintained her calmness and dignity; there was not a word, not a movement, which could add to the pleasure of their observers. When the proclamation was finished, the trumpets again sounded. Cléry went to the window: the eyes of the populace were instantly upon him,—he was mistaken for Louis XVI. and overwhelmed with insults. The gendarmes threatened him with their swords, and he was obliged to retire, to put an end to the tumult.

That same evening Cléry told the King that his son wanted blankets and curtains for his bed, as the weather was growing cold The King told him to make the request in writing, and signed it. Cléry worded it as he had hitherto done: "The King requests for his son," &c. "You are very bold," said Destournelles to him, "to make use of a title which you have just heard has been abolished by the will of the people." "I heard a proclamation," answered Cléry, "but I do not know what its object was." "It was the abolition of royalty," said the member of the Commune; "and you may tell *Monsieur*," pointing to Louis XVI., "to cease the assumption of a title no longer recognised by the people." "I cannot," said Cléry, "now alter this note, which is already signed, as Louis would inquire into the cause of it, and it is not for me to inform him." "You can do as you please." replied the commissary; "but I shall not certify your demand." The next day, Madame Elizabeth recommended Cléry for the future to write in the following manner when he had any request to make: "*Required, for the use of Louis XVI.—of Marie Antoinette—of Louis Charles—of Marie Thérèse—of Marie Elizabeth,*" &c.

Cléry was obliged to renew these demands frequently. The small quantity of linen in the possession of the royal family had been lent them by Lady Sutherland, during their stay at the Feuillants; and the Prince Royal had, for several days, no other coat than that of the son of this distinguished foreigner, a child of the same age as himself. Cléry at last obtained some fresh linen for him. The workwomen having marked it with crowned letters, the municipals ordered the Princesses to remove the crowns, which was done.

The anger of the people against the King now increased. This unhappy prince, having seen his palace more than once invaded and violated, desired to put his most important papers into a place of security. In the recess of a door, which separated his room from that of his son, he had himself, before the 10th August, made, by the aid of a gimlet—the only instrument he could use without noise,—an aperture of twenty-two inches high and sixteen wide, and made in the wall, without being perceived, a hole of eight or nine inches deep. He removed each day the piece he had detached from the wainscot, and when his day's work was done fastened it in again with four screws. This done, he had, with his own hands, arranged four brackets, upon which he had placed a double row of wooden shelves; here he deposited his papers. He was obliged to have a locksmith to line the piece of wainscot which covered this aperture with a sheet of iron. The workman, named Gamin, who was thus honoured by his confidence, and whom he had loaded with benefits, had the ingratitude to inform Roland, the minister of the interior, of the affair. The National Convention was immediately apprised of it. The hidden aperture was eventually designated the "iron closet," and became a source of inexhaustible accusations. The news of this discovery, which, according to the report of Roland, afforded the clue to a vast conspiracy (and caused the death of several innocent persons), came to the ears of the Prince Royal, whose acute observation allowed nothing to escape him. One day there was a cake upon the table that he much wished for. "Mamma," said he, "look, what a delicious cake! I know of a closet here into which, if you think proper, I will put it. It will be in the greatest safety; nobody, I assure you, can take it out." They looked at each other; they surveyed every corner of the room, without, however, being able to discover any cupboard. The commissaries of the Commune already began to harbour terrible suspicions, and were, doubtless, preparing another denunciation. "My son," said the Queen, "I do not see the cupboard you speak of." "Mamma," replied the child, pointing to his mouth with his finger; "here it is." This sally, with its combination of ideas and of infantine sportiveness, brought a smile to the lips of the royal family. Poor child, whose innocence found a subject for pleasantry in an event which was about to furnish pretexts for those who were plotting his father's death!

On Wednesday, the 26th September, Cléry was informed by a municipal that it was proposed to separate the King from his family, the apartment which was intended for him in the great tower being nearly ready. Cléry announced with great caution this cruel news to his master, expressing how much it pained him to give him this affliction. "You cannot give me a stronger proof of your attachment," said the King; "I demand from your zeal to hide nothing from me,—I expect everything. Try to learn the day of this painful separation, and let me know it."

On the 27th, the municipal commissaries composing the council of the Temple declared, in a report addressed to the council-general of the Commune, that nocturnal assemblies of three or four hundred men collected outside the tower; that they there played various airs on the flageolet, made signals, and that cries of "Long live the King!" had even been heard. "We have taken measures," added they, "to frustrate these schemes." They further proposed to the council-general to deprive Louis XVI. of the embroidered star, the red riband, and all the other insignia of feudalism that he wore.*

On the 28th, Santerre complained to the Commune of the slow progress of the works at the Temple, and of the impediments occasioned, by the pulling down and building up, to the proper guard of the posts, which were almost destitute of defence. The commandant proposed to expend on the prompt execution of the plans adopted, the 500,000 livres destined for the civil list of the King, and to suppress the post above the King's apartment. The suggestion of Santerre was received. A great impulse was given to the works, and, as to the post referred to, it was easily dispensed with, the measure taken next day rendering its continuance needless.

On the 29th, at ten o'clock in the morning, five or six municipals entered the Queen's apartment, where her family was assembled. One of them, named Charbonnier, read a decree of the council of the Commune, ordering them to remove paper, ink, pens, pencils, and even written papers, both from the persons of the prisoners and from their rooms, and also from the *valet-de-chambre* and other persons employed in the tower; not to leave them any weapon whatever, offensive or defensive: in a word, to take all necessary precautions for preventing any communication on the part of Louis the *Last* with any other persons than the municipal officers. The commissary added, in a loud tone, addressing himself to the King: "When you require anything, Cléry will go down and write your

* "*Histoire du Dernier Règne de la Monarchie.*" Vol. I., page 126.

demand on a register, which will be kept in the council hall." Louis XVI. and his family, who made no observation, were searched, and gave up their papers, pencils, &c. The municipals then examined the rooms and the cupboards, and took away all the articles indicated by the decree. Cléry was apprised by one of them that the King would be transferred to the great tower that evening; he found means to inform the King of this through Madame Elizabeth.

In fact, after supper, as the King was leaving the chamber of Marie Antoinette to return to his own, a municipal desired him to wait, the council having something to communicate to him. In the course of a quarter of an hour the six commissaries who, in the morning, had taken away the papers, came and read to Louis XVI. a second decree, ordering his separation from his family. Never had the edicts of the Commune assumed so harsh a form.*

Although prepared for this event, the King was deeply affected by it. His disconsolate family sought to read in the municipals' eyes how far their projects would proceed; the King received their adieus, leaving them all in the most intense

* Commune of Paris,—29th September, 1792, fourth year of Liberty, the first of Equality, and the first of the French Republic.

Extract from the register of the deliberations of the council-general:—

"The custody of the prisoners of the Temple becoming every day more difficult, by their concert and the measures they may take among themselves, the responsible position of the council-general of the Commune renders it absolutely necessary to prevent the abuses which may tend to facilitate the escape of these traitors; it has passed the following decree:

"1. That Louis and Antoinette be separated.

"2. That each prisoner have a separate cell.

"3. That the *valet-de-chambre* be put under arrest.

"4. That citizen Hébert be added to the five commissaries already appointed.

"5. That they have authority to put into execution the decree of this evening forthwith, and even deprive the prisoners of plate, and eating utensils; in a word, the council-general gives full power to its commissaries to do anything that their prudence may dictate for the security of these hostages.

alarm. Marie Antoinette and Madame Elizabeth shed hot tears Louis took their hands and pressed them with an ardour which seemed to say, "Let us be resigned." The moment of this parting, which preluded so many other misfortunes, was one of the saddest this unfortunate family had yet passed in the Temple. They learned every day that the bounds of a misfortune they already believed boundless, could be extended still farther; the Revolution hurried them down an abyss of sorrows hitherto unequalled, and which, it is to be hoped, God will spare to the future.

Cléry followed the King to his new prison.

The apartment of Louis XVI. in the great tower was not yet completed ; there was only one bed ; no other furniture had as yet been placed there ; the painters and paper-hangers were still at work, causing an intolerable smell. They prepared for Cléry a chamber remote from the King's ; but he passed the first night in a chair beside his master, and the next day the King obtained, not without some difficulty, permission for his servant to occupy a room next to his own.

After the King had risen, Cléry wished to go to the little tower, to dress the young Prince ; the municipals refused to allow him. "You will have no further communication with the prisoners," said one of them (Veron) to him; "nor will your master see his children again."

At nine o'clock the King requested to be conducted to his family. "We have no orders to that effect," said the commissaries. Louis made some remonstrances, to which they gave no reply.

Half an hour afterwards two municipals entered, followed by a servant lad, who brought the King a piece of bread and a bottle of lemonade for his breakfast. The King expressed his desire to dine with his family; they answered that they should seek the orders of the Commune. "But," added Louis, "my *valet-de-chambre* can go down ; it is he who has the care of my son, and there is nothing to prevent his still waiting on him." "That does not depend on us," said the commissaries, and they withdrew.

Cléry was in a corner of the room, absorbed in the most gloomy reflections; on the one hand, he saw the sufferings of his master: on the other, he pictured to himself the young Prince abandoned, perhaps, to other hands. There had already been mention made of separating him from his parents, and what fresh agony would this not cause the Queen! Cléry was engaged in these painful thoughts when the King drew near him, holding in his hand the bread they had brought him, and, offering him half of it, "It seems they have forgotten your breakfast," said he; "take this, I have enough without it." Cléry refused; but Louis insisted. Cléry could not suppress his tears; the King perceived them, and himself began to weep.

At ten o'clock other municipals brought operatives to proceed with the works in the apartment. One of these commissaries told Louis that he had just been present at the breakfast of his family, and that they were all well. "I thank you," replied the King; "I will beg of you also to give them news of me, and to say that I am in good health. Could I not have," added he, "some books that I left in the Queen's room? You would oblige me greatly by sending them to me, for I have nothing to read." Louis XVI. named the books he desired. The municipal acceded to his request; but, himself unable to read, he proposed to Cléry to accompany him. Cléry congratulated himself on the ignorance of this man, and at once went down with him. He found the Queen in her room, surrounded by her children and Madame Elizabeth; they were all weeping, and their grief increased on seeing him: they asked him a thousand questions about the King, to which he was obliged to answer with reserve. Marie Antoinette, addressing the municipals who had entered with Cléry, earnestly repeated her wish to be with the King, at least during a short period of the day, and at meals. Hers were no longer merely complaints or tears, they were outcries of grief. "Well," said a municipal, "they shall dine together to-day; but, as we act under the orders of the Commune, to-morrow we must do what the council shall command." At these words a feeling, almost amounting to joy, soothed those sad hearts. The Queen, pressing her children to her arms, Madame Elizabeth, with her hands raised towards heaven, thanked God for this unexpected favour. Some of the commissaries could not repress their tears,—Simon himself was moved, and said aloud: "I do believe that these devils of women will make me cry." Then, addressing Marie Antoinette, he added: "When you were assassinating the people, on the 10th August, you did not weep." "The people are much deceived as to our sentiments," replied the Queen sorrowfully.

Cléry took the books the King had asked for, and brought them to him. The municipals entered with him, and announced to Louis XVI. that he should see his family. "I can then, doubtless, continue to wait on the young Prince and the Princesses?" said Cléry to the commissaries. The latter did not object, and Cléry thus found an opportunity of informing the Queen of what had passed.

They served up dinner in the King's room at the usual hour, and brought his family to him. By the transports of joy which they exhibited, the fears they had felt were manifested. They heard no more of the decree of the Commune, and the royal family continued to take their meals and their walks together.

After dinner the Queen and Madame Elizabeth were permitted to visit the apartment preparing for them above that of the King; they begged the workmen to make haste, but the work was not finished for three weeks. During this interval, Cléry divided his time between all the prisoners, waiting on them, keeping an account of their expenses, and finding means to maintain some sort of communication among them. The attention of the King to the education of his son received no interruption; but this residence of the royal family in two separate towers, by rendering the *surveillance* of the municipals more difficult, rendered it also more tenacious. The number of the commissaries was augmented, and their distrust left little opportunity for learning what was going on without. All correspondence was interdicted, even for religious purposes; and the curate of Fontenai-sur-Bois having written to Madame Elizabeth, his letter was sent to the Commune.* However, under pretext of bringing linen and other necessaries, Cléry obtained permission for his wife to come to the Temple once a week. She was always accompanied by a friend, who passed as a relation, and was devoted, like herself, to the royal family. On their arrival, Cléry came down to the council chamber, now no longer in the palace of the Temple, but on the ground-floor of the great tower. He could only speak to them in the presence of the municipals, so that the first few visits were not successful in their object. He then made the two female visitors understand that they must only come at one o'clock in the afternoon; this was the hour for the promenade, during which most of the commissaries were with the royal family, one only remaining in the council hall: and he, when he happened to be a good-natured man, would give them liberty to talk, without, however, losing sight of them. Cléry, by this means, received information as to those persons in whom the royal family were interested, and of what was passing in the Convention. An old cook, named Turgy, who, from affection to his former masters, had managed to

* Extract from the register of the deliberations of the council-general, of the 19th October, 1792 :—

"The council-general appoints citizen Léger one of its members, whom it orders to go to the Temple forthwith, for the purpose of taking thence a letter addressed to Madame Elizabeth by the curate of Fontenai-sur-Bois, and to bring it to the council.

(Signed) "DARNAUDERIE, Vice-President.
COULOMBEAU, Registrar pro tem."
(National Records.)

obtain employment in the Temple, with two of his companions, Marchand and Chrétien, was also in a position to give valuable information. Going out twice or thrice a week, and running about the city to buy provisions, he always collected some important news; but the difficulty lay in communicating it to Cléry, who alone came in close contact with the royal family All the *employés* were forbidden to speak to the *valet-de chambre*, except in the course of their duties, and in the presence of the municipals. When Turgy had something especial to impart to his honest accomplice, he notified it by a sign, previously agreed on. Cléry then endeavoured to converse with him under various pretexts; sometimes he would beg to dress his hair: Madame Elizabeth, who was in the secret, would then converse with the municipals, and draw off their attention. At other times he would supply him with an occasion to enter his chamber, and Turgy would seize this moment to throw under the bed the journals or other papers he had to give him.

When the King or the Queen desired some immediate information, and it was not Madame Cléry's day for coming, Turgy was entrusted with the mission. If it was not his day for going out, Cléry feigned to want something for the royal family. "It will do another day," Turgy would say aloud. "Well," replied Cléry, carelessly; "the King will wait." This affected indifference was intended, and sometimes with effect, to induce the municipals to give Turgy permission to go out. When he received it, the same evening or the next morning he would communicate the desired news. It was by these circuitous ways that these two ingenious conspirators often attained their ends, taking care never to use the same means a second time with the same municipals.

Cléry, as closely watched as Hue had been, could only, as we have said, speak to the King while undressing him, and a few instants before, while the commissaries were being relieved. Sometimes, however, he succeeded in saying a word to him in the morning, before his keepers were ready to make their appearance. Cléry would affect an unwillingness to enter without them, but, at the same time, giving them to understand that Louis wanted him. If the municipals allowed him to enter alone, he immediately drew back the bed-curtains, and while he was putting on his master's stockings, he would converse with him, unseen and unheard. Generally speaking, this attempt did not succeed, and Cléry, frustrated in his hopes, was obliged to wait till the toilet of his keepers was finished, and they were ready to go with him into the King's room. Several of them treated him even with harshness, some making him take away their trestle-beds in the morning and bring them back at night; others were incessantly insulting him; but Cléry, by opposing to their rudeness, gentleness and complaisance, charmed them in spite of themselves, divested them by insensible degrees of their suspicions, and, pacifying their hatred, often succeeded in learning from themselves what he wished to know. Thus he was pursuing with care the plan traced out by his predecessor, when an event, as singular as it was unexpected, made him fear that he himself, like Hue, would be separated from the royal family.

One evening, that of Wednesday, 5th October, 1792, towards six o'clock, after having accompanied the Queen to her apartment, he was going up again to the King, with two municipals, when the sentinel placed at the door of the *corps-de-garde*, on the first-floor of the great tower, taking hold of his arm, said: "Cléry, how are you?" and lowering his voice, "I want to have a talk with you," added he, with a mysterious air. "Speak out," replied Cléry; "I am not allowed to converse in an under-tone with any one." "They told me," replied the sentinel, "that the King had been in a dungeon for several days past, and that you were with him." "You see that such is not the case," replied Cléry, walking on. One of the municipals preceded him, the other followed; the former had heard the whole of this colloquy. The next morning two municipals awaited him at the door of the Queen's apartment;

they conducted him to the hall of council, and the commissaries there assembled interrogated him. The accused repeated the conversation precisely as it was held. The commissary who had heard it confirmed his account; the other declared that the sentinel had given the accused a paper, of which he had heard the rustling, and that it was a letter for the King. Cléry denied the fact, inviting the municipals to search him and to make inquiries. Cléry was confronted with the sentinel, and the latter, a hasty young man,* was, for having spoken while on duty, condemned to twenty-four hours' imprisonment.

Nevertheless, Cléry's fidelity underwent grave suspicion on account of this affair, especially when it was ascertained that he had not yet taken the oath required, on the 14th August, by the National Assembly. He took it during the sitting,† in the presence of the commissaries, and then returned to his duties, thinking to hear no more of the matter, and little imagining that it would be revived afterwards, as we shall soon see.

* His name was Alexandre François Breton.

† Commune of Paris.—Safety of the Temple.

Extract from the register of the deliberations of the council of the municipal officers on duty at the Temple since the 6th October, 1792, the year 1 of the French Republic :—

"It appears that the citizen Jean-Baptiste Cant-Hanet Cléry, attached to the service of the late king, came to the council for the purpose of taking the oath prescribed by the National Assembly on the 14th August last, not being able to leave the Temple to take it in his section; the council has received his oath to be faithful to the Commune, to maintain to the utmost of his power equality and liberty, and to respect, and cause to be respected, persons and property, and has signed J. B. C. Hanet Cléry.

"This present extract of the above oath has been delivered to him to serve in case of need.

"Done at the Temple, the day and year aforesaid, and signed by the commissaries on duty, Thouvenot, Lebois, and Leclerc, municipal officers.

"We hereby certify that the above extract from the original, delivered the 4th November, in the above-named year, is correct.

"MENNESSIER, Commissary in the service of the Temple.

"THOMAS, Commissary in the service of the Temple.

"DESTOURNELLES, Commissary of the Commune, on duty at the Temple.

"ROCHE, Municipal Officer."

On Sunday, the 7th October, at six in the evening, Cléry was summoned to the council hall, where he was surprised and uneasy at seeing Manuel, who, since his appointment to the National Assembly, had not made his appearance at the Temple. Manuel was surrounded by twenty municipals, over whom he presided with austere gravity. He ordered Cléry to remove that evening from the King's coat the orders with which it was still decorated, such as those of St. Louis and the Golden Fleece.* Cléry represented that it was not his business to signify to Louis XVI. the decrees of the council. The commissaries at first refused to go up to the King's room, but they consented when Manuel offered to accompany them. They found Louis XVI. seated, and reading a volume of Tacitus. "How are you?" asked Manuel; "have you everything you require?" "I content myself with what I have," replied Louis XVI. "You have, doubtless, heard of the victories of our armies, of the capture of Spires and Nice, and the conquest of Savoy?" "I heard some mention of them a few days ago, from one of these gentlemen, who was reading the evening paper." "How! have you not the papers, which are now so interesting?" "I receive none." "You must," said Manuel to the municipals, "give *Monsieur* all the journals; it is important that he should know of our successes." Then, again addressing Louis XVI.: "The principles of democracy are spreading far and wide; you know that the people have abolished royalty and adopted the republican form of government." "I have heard so; and I pray that the French may find the happiness which it was always my wish to procure for them." "You know, also, that the National Assembly has suppressed

* Louis XVI. had not for some time worn the order of the Holy Ghost. The Assembly, which, in the month of July, 1791, had suppressed orders of chivalry and marks of distinction, had decreed that the King and the Prince Royal should be the only persons allowed to wear the blue riband of the Holy Ghost. The King said, in reply, that this decoration had no other value in his eyes than the power of granting it to others, and that he was determined to lay it aside.

all the orders of chivalry; the officers should have told you to lay aside their insignia: having become one of the citizens, you must be treated as such. As to other matters, ask for anything you think necessary, it shall be procured for you." "I thank you," said the King, "I want nothing." He immediately resumed his reading.

Had Manuel sought to detect regrets or impatience? I think not; at all events, he only found an unalterable serenity. The deputies withdrew. Cléry, on the order of a municipal, followed them to the council hall, where they again directed him to remove Louis's decorations. "You will do well," added Manuel, "to send to the Convention the crosses and the ribands."

The next day, 8th October, in presenting to the King his clothes, destitute of all ornaments, Cléry told him that he had kept and locked up the crosses and the ribands, though Manuel had told him that he had better send them to the Convention. "You have done well," said Louis XVI.

On the 9th October, they brought Louis the journal of the debates of the Convention, and, the following days, four more journals were remitted to the Temple, with this address upon them: "*To the Valet-de-chambre of Louis XVI., at the Tower of the Temple.*" Cléry could never ascertain whether he owed these to some official order, or whether they were the testimony of a secret devotion, which had paid for them. However that might be, the favour did not last long. A municipal,—Michel, whom we named before,—called upon Cléry to state by what order he caused these journals to be sent to his address. "I have neither received nor given any order in the matter," replied Cléry; "and I have been no less surprised than you to see these papers come in my name." They required him to write to the editors of the journals for an explanation; but their replies, if any, were not communicated to him, and Michel procured a decree, prohibiting, henceforth, the admis sion of newspapers into the tower. We have every reason to believe that the transmission of the journals, so unaccountable to Cléry, proceeded from a generous feeling on the part of Manuel, who, affected by the touching spectacle of so much greatness depressed and resigned, moved by the calmness of the King, the firmness of the Queen, and the gentleness of their children, had, for some time past, been using his best efforts to render their captivity less galling. His mind insensibly tended to kindness. A municipal having denounced to the council-general one of his colleagues, who had been guilty of having taken off his hat to Marie Antoinette and her sister-in-law, Manuel essayed, if not to justify, at least to extenuate, the crime of this commissary.

Though the newspapers were not allowed to be introduced into the Temple, yet the eager malignity of certain municipals made exceptions to the rule. They kept back, indeed, all the public journals relating the sanguinary calamities of France, the political pamphlets which were perverting the conscience of the people; but insult, threats, or calumny, directly addressed to the Capets, served the journals as passports to the political and moral lazaretto where royalty was prolonging its mournful quarantine, and which nothing was permitted to enter but what might add to the torments of the present the apprehensions of a still darker future. These odious papers were placed on the mantel-piece or drawers of the King or Queen. Louis XVI. read in one of them the demand of a cannonier for "*the head of the tyrant Louis XVI., wherewith to load his gun, and send it to the enemy.*" Another newspaper, pouring insults on Madame Elizabeth, essayed to destroy the admiration which her virtues and sisterly devotion inspired in the public mind. A third declared that it was necessary to stifle those two young wolf-cubs in the little tower—meaning the royal children. Very few of these articles escaped the King, but he only seemed affected by them with reference to the honour of the nation: "The French," said he, "are most unfortunate in being thus deceived."

On Monday, the 15th October, the King desired Cléry to

demand a second coat for his son. The Queen wished to avail herself of the opportunity to send to Lady Sutherland the linen and other articles belonging to her; and, being at this time destitute of pen and ink, she begged Cléry to write to the ambassadress, to thank her. The municipals authorised the King's demand;* but they rejected that of the Queen, and kept the linen and effects.

There is not in humanity a position so deplorable but that a certain amount of self-love enters into it; jealous of the confidence which Marie Antoinette seemed, to his own exclusion, to repose in Cléry, Tison represented to the Queen that, on this last occasion, he would have been at least as eligible an agent as his colleague. A sort of conflict as to functions which arose between these two servants, so different in heart and pretensions, combined with the habit which each member of the royal family had individually adopted, of addressing itself for any service to the commissary who seemed best disposed towards it, occasioned the passing of a decree at the council of the Temple, determining the manner in which the royal family should henceforth convey their requests to the council. The municipal James, who was Tison's patron, said to him, in communicating to him the result of the deliberation of the council: "Be content; the ministry is formed: you are entrusted with the female department." The seeds of the complete separation of the royal family were contained in this

* "Louis Capet demands for his son a cloth frock coat, and a morning one of Florence taffeta.

"This 15th October, 1792, year 1 of the French Republic.

"CLERY, on duty at the Temple."

"Having considered the above, we, members of the council-general of the Commune, on duty at the Temple, give authority for the purchase of the articles in question.

"This 15th October, 1792, year 1 of the French Republic.

"VINCENT. DESTOURNELLES."

decree.* Three days after, Wednesday, the 26th October, while the royal family were dining, a municipal entered, accompanied by a registrar and an usher, both *en costume*, and followed by six gendarmes, sword in hand.

Thinking they were come for the King, the royal family, full of terror, rose. Louis XVI. asked what they wanted with him, but the municipal, without answering the question, called Cléry into another room ; the gendarmes followed, and the registrar having read a decree for Cléry's arrest, they took him into custody, in order to lead him before the tribunal. "A month ago," said the usher, "I was ordered to arrest you; then the Commune suspended its decision: but now I am directed to carry their order into execution." "Permit me to inform Louis XVI. of the circumstance," said Cléry. "From this moment," returned the commissary, "you are not permitted to speak with him; just take a shirt with you: *your affair will soon be settled.*" Cléry followed him without further observation, passing, on his way, the King and the royal family, who were all standing, and in utter consternation at the manner in

* Extracts from the register of the deliberations of the council acting at the Temple, dated the 23rd and 27th instant.

"The council, after having deliberated, has resolved that, to reform all the abuses that might result from the various demands of the captive family, no attention shall be paid from the said day (the 23rd October), henceforth, to the demands of Louis Capet, unless made through citizen Cléry, and so with respect to those of his son.

"That citizen Tison shall present all those made on behalf of the women,—mother, aunt, and daughter Capet.

"All which requests shall only be received by the council when previously entered in the registers.

"Resolved, moreover, that this determination be made known to the prisoners, and to citizens Cléry and Tison.

(Signed) "DAUNAY, JOURNAY, BARILLON, and JAMES,
and afterwards, on the 27th October, aforesaid, COCHOIS, ROCHE.

"Extract, copied conformably with the said resolutions, delivered to citizen Cléry, to be by him obeyed.

"27th October, 1792, year 1 of the French Republic.

"ROCHE, Municipal Commissary, President of the Council-board at the Temple. COCHOIS, Secretary."

which their servant was being thus taken away. The populace, assembled in the outer court of the Temple, assailed the prisoner with insults, and loudly demanded his head. An officer of the National Guard, however, pointed out that it was necessary to preserve his life until he had revealed certain secrets, of which he was the sole depository. At this period, in order to prolong the lives of the victims, it was sometimes necessary to assert the superior claims of the scaffold, as the proper instrument of vengeance. On reaching the Palais de Justice, Cléry was placed in a dungeon, where he remained for six hours, occupied in the futile endeavour to account for his arrest; he could only recollect that, on the morning of the 10th August, during the attack at the Palace of the Tuileries, some persons had entreated him to conceal, in a chest of drawers that belonged to him, various papers and valuable effects; he imagined that these papers and effects had been seized, and were about to occasion his destruction.

At eight o'clock, he appeared before judges whose faces were altogether unknown to him, composing a revolutionary tribunal, established on the 17th August, to do the executioner's work on those who had escaped the fury of the populace. Great was his astonishment when he perceived, on the prisoners' bench, the same young man who had been suspected, three weeks before, of giving him a letter (Alexandre-François Breton); and, in his accuser, the municipal officer who had denounced him to the council of the Temple. Cléry was interrogated; witnesses were heard. The commissary renewed his charge; Cléry replied, that since he had heard the rustling of paper, and had thought that he saw a letter pass, he should have had the guilty person searched on the spot, instead of waiting to denounce him, ten hours afterwards, to the council of the Temple. Breton enlarged on the same point. The proofs were wholly deficient; the judges consulted together, and, upon their finding, the two prisoners were acquitted. The president directed four of the municipal officers in waiting to reconduct Cléry to the Temple: it was now midnight. Cléry arrived just as the King was going to bed, and he was permitted to announce his return. The royal family had taken a vivid interest in his fate, and it is from this epoch that Marie Thérèse dates the genuine services of Cléry; she relates that, on his return to the tower, he declared himself truly loyal, stating that the exhortations of Madame Elizabeth, the grief of the Queen, and the goodness of Louis XVI., had deeply affected him, and that, thenceforth, he was not only faithful but devoted.

A great change had taken place at the Temple during this same day (Friday, 26th October). The official presence of the magistrates and of the armed force had not merely the arrest of Cléry for its object; it had also to superintend the installation of the Queen, her children, and her sister, in the great tower. This moment, so earnestly desired by the prisoners, and which seemed to promise them some consolation, was marked, on the part of the municipals, with a new feature of hostility against Marie Antoinette. The council of the Temple, consisting of Roché, Jérosme, Massé, and Cochois, passed, on the motion of one of their members, a personal enemy to the Queen, a decree which, under the pretext of propriety, withdrew the young Louis Charles from the charge of his mother, and transferred him to that of his father.* Without notifying this decision to Marie Antoinette, on the very evening of her

* Commune of Paris.—Security of the Temple. Year 1 of the French Republic, 27th October, 1792.

Extract from the register of the deliberations of the council, on duty at the Temple, 26th October.

"Upon the observation, made by one of the members on service at the Temple, that the son of Louis Capet was, day and night, under the direction of women, his mother and aunt, and considering that the boy is at an age when he ought to be under the direction of men, the council, having deliberated on the subject, has decreed and decrees that the son of Louis Capet shall forthwith be removed from the charge of women, to be placed and remain with his father, day and night, except that, after dinner, he shall go up to his mother's room while his father is reposing, and come taking possession of her new apartment, her son was removed from her. Her grief was excessive; ever since her arrival in the Temple she had consecrated her existence to the care of this child, and found some alleviation of her misery in his gratitude and his caresses. He was the last joy of her sad life,—the last ray that lighted up the night of her thoughts, dark as the grave. She indulged in the hope that, next morning, more completely settled in her new abode, they would restore the boy to her prayers and her tears; but, next morning, she was informed of the decree of the council, and a copy of the decree was given to Cléry. The municipality at once ratified the decree.* The poor child was himself so afflicted at being separated from his mother, that he availed himself of the first opportunity of manifesting his resentment. There was a mason, named Mercereau, who sauntered about the Temple instead of working; he addressed every one in the most familiar manner, and, by his extreme demagogism, had acquired a reputation well calculated shortly to give him a seat in the council-general of the Commune. As the young Prince

down again between four and five o'clock in the afternoon, being all the while under the charge and conduct of one of the commissaries on duty.

"Done at the council, sitting at the Temple, the aforesaid day and year.

(Signed) "MASSE, JEROSME, ROCHE, COCHOIS.

"A true copy.

"ROCHE, { Municipal Commissary, on duty and presiding at the Temple.

"COCHOIS, Secretary.

"Delivered to citizen Cléry, on duty with Louis and his family."

* Commune of Paris.

Extract from the register of the deliberations of the council-general, 26th October, 1792.

"The council-general approves of the decrees framed by the commissaries at the Temple, relative to the transference of the women to the third floor of the great tower, and to that of the son of the ex-king to his father.

"Authorizes them to place any (*sic*) wickets they may think necessary within the said tower.

(Signed) "BOUCHER RENE, President, in the absence of the Mayor.

"COULOMBEAU, Secretary-Registrar, ad interim."

Repartee of the Dauphin.

did not exhibit towards him the respect to which the future dignitary of the Revolution aspired: "Dost thou not know," said he one day to the Dauphin, "dost thou not know that liberty as rendered us free, and that we are all equal?" "Equal, if you please," replied the boy; "but it is not in this place," added he, casting a glance at his father, "you will persuade us that liberty has rendered us free."

BOOK EIGHTH.

THE GREAT TOWER OF THE TEMPLE.

27TH OCTOBER—2ND DECEMBER, 1792.

Description of the interior of the great tower—The gaolers and attendants—The guard—External appearance of the Temple—Life of the King in the great tower—Marie Antoinette—Madame Elizabeth—The Dauphin—Madame Royale—Visit of the commissaries of the Convention—The municipal officers—Wanton insults—The manner in which news was conveyed to the Temple—The King's illness—That of the Dauphin, of the Queen, of Madame Royale, and of Madame Elizabeth—Cléry tended, in his illness, by the royal family—Attention of the Dauphin to his mother—Anecdotes.

THE events of which we shall have henceforward to write, having passed in a different locality from that of which we have given the plan and the description, it is expedient, in like manner, to describe here the new habitation of the royal family.

We have mentioned that the altitude of the great tower exceeded one hundred and fifty feet, and that the average thickness of its walls was nine feet.

The building consisted of four stories, all vaulted, and supported in the centre by a great pillar, extending from the basement to the fourth floor. The interior was between thirty four and thirty-six feet square.

GROUND FLOOR.

The ground floor underwent no change; it remained with its old bare walls, recalling, however, despite its bareness, past times and past events, still reflected in the open work of its ceilings, in the elegant capitals of its pillars, and even in the four beds, with their twisted columns, ranged along the four walls of its vast hall. It was in this apartment, of grand and austere architecture, that, from the 8th December, as will be seen, the municipal officers not on duty at the doors of the King and Queen were to deliberate, eat, drink, and sleep. They designated it the Council Chamber, in order to indicate, by a lofty appellation, the most distinguished of the various uses to which it was applied. Of the three turrets on the ground floor, one served as a cupboard and closet for the commissaries, the second as a wood-cellar, and the third as a wardrobe. The fourth contained the staircase which, as we have already mentioned, led to the battlements, and up which wickets had been erected, at intervals, to the number of seven. Each floor was entered from the staircase through two doors, the first of very thick oak, studded with nails, the other of iron.

FIRST FLOOR.

The first floor, which also remained exempt from the operations of the workmen and the arrangements of the gaolers, preserved its original aspect, and served as a guard-room. It was a repetition of the ground floor, with the exception of the beds. Against two of the walls were placed planks of wood, slightly inclined, which, with some mattresses, formed a bed for the guard. In the centre of the hall, around the pillar, the soldiers' arms were piled. Two of the turrets served as closets for the officers, and the third as a wardrobe. This guard-room, next to that of the Château du Temple, was the most important post in the place.

SECOND FLOOR.

The second floor was designed as the King's lodging. Being, like all the other floors, a single room, it had been divided into four chambers by planks, with linen ceilings. The first room was an antechamber, whence three separate doors led to the three other rooms. Opposite the entrance door was the chamber of Louis XVI., in which was also placed a bed for his son. On the left were Cléry's room and the dining-room, separated merely by a glazed partition from the antechamber. The King's room had a chimney; the others were heated by a large stove that stood in the antechamber. Each room was lighted by a window; but the great iron bars and the blinds prevented the free circulation of air. The embrasures of the windows were nine feet deep; all the partitions were covered with coloured paper,—that of the antechamber represented large stones, placed the one on the other, like a scene in a play, representing a dungeon. On the wall, to the left as you entered, was placarded the "*Déclaration des Droits de l'Homme et du Citoyen*" (Declaration of the Rights of Man and of the Citizen), written in very large characters, and framed within a broad tri-coloured border, on which was inscribed: "Year 1 of the Republic."

On opening the King's door, you saw the chimney in front, facing the window; to the right hand, the turret; to the left, the bed of Louis XVI., and, at its foot, the little couch of the Prince Royal. A yellow glazed paper, decorated with white flowers, covered the walls of the King's room. On the mantel-piece you read, "*Liberty, equality, property, safety.*"

On the chimney-slab was a clock, with these words engraved on its dial: "*Lepaute, clockmaker to the King;*" but, on the installation of Louis in the great tower, the commissaries on duty had stuck a wafer over the word "*King,*" and not very long afterwards the clock was taken away and another one substituted.

The turret which adjoined the chamber served the King as an oratory and reading-room; its plastered walls were painted grey. A small stove was placed in this closet, where this unfortunate prince passed so many hours in study, prayer, and meditation. In the corner of the chamber, to the right of the Dauphin's bed, a door opened on a lobby leading on the left to

Cléry's room, and à little further on, inclining towards the right, to the closet in the second turret. Cléry's bed, parallel with the King's, was merely separated from it by a partition. The turret which communicated with the dining-room served as a wood-house.

We give here a descriptive plan of this floor.

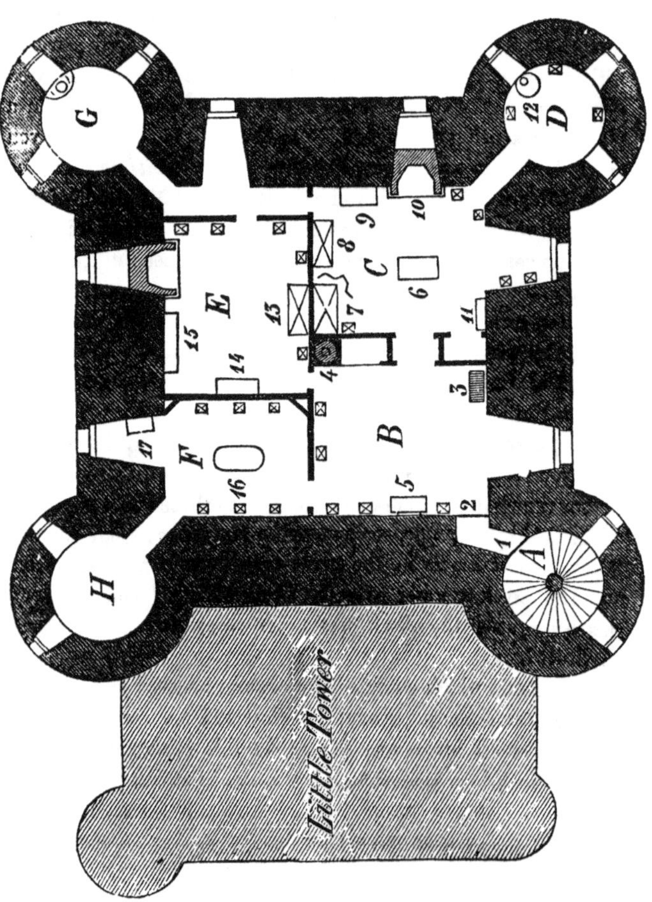

Details.

GREAT TOWER.—SECOND FLOOR.—*THE KING.*

A. The staircase.
  1. Oak door.
  2. Iron door.

B. Antechamber.
  3. A card table and chesnut backgammon board.
  4. Stove.
  5. Writing-table, with a drawer, above which was fastened to the wall the declaration of the rights of man.
  Five crimson velvet chairs.

C. Chamber of the King.
  6. Table covered with green morocco.
  7. The King's bed, with four pillars painted white, with furniture of green damask, a hair mattress or palliass, three mattresses, and a bolster
  8. The Dauphin's trestle-bed, with two mattresses, two blankets, and a bolster.
  9. Mahogany chest of drawers, with a white marble top and three drawers.
  10. Chimney, with a glass, 48in. by 38in., in a white frame. On the chimney-piece, a striking clock, with the name "Chevalier Dutertre, of Paris," in ormolu, on a grey marble stand.
  11. Scrutoire veneered with rose-wood, and having four drawers.
  Two little straw stools.
  An arm-chair, with cushions of green damask.
  Two arm chairs, covered with green damask.
  Plated candlesticks. Two gilt barometers.
  A screen, covered with cloth of a green ground, and having six folds, breast high.

D. The King's oratory.
  12. Small stove.
  A cane chair, a straw chair, a horsehair stool.

E. Cléry's chamber.
  13. A four-post bedstead, with green, red, and yellow furniture, a horsehair palliass, two mattresses, a bolster, a feather bed, and two blankets.
  14. A chest of drawers, veneered with rose-wood, with white-veined marble top and three large drawers.
  15. An oak cupboard, with folding doors.
  A padded arm-chair, covered with orange-coloured linen.
  Four chairs, in green and white Utrecht velvet.

F. Dining-room.
  16. Mahogany dining-table, 4ft. by 2ft.
  17. Small table.
  Chairs.

G. Wardrobe.

H. Wood-house.

THIRD FLOOR.

The third floor, destined for the Queen's lodging, was arranged much the same as the preceding. The antechamber, preceded by two doors, the one of oak, and the other of iron, was of the same size; but the paper was different, representing, instead of prison walls, yellow marble with red veins.

Details.

The chamber of Marie Antoinette and her daughter was above that of the King, of which it was an exact repetition in all except the lobby. It was in the corner over this lobby that the bed of Madame Royale was placed. The Queen's bed occupied the same relative position with that of the King. A

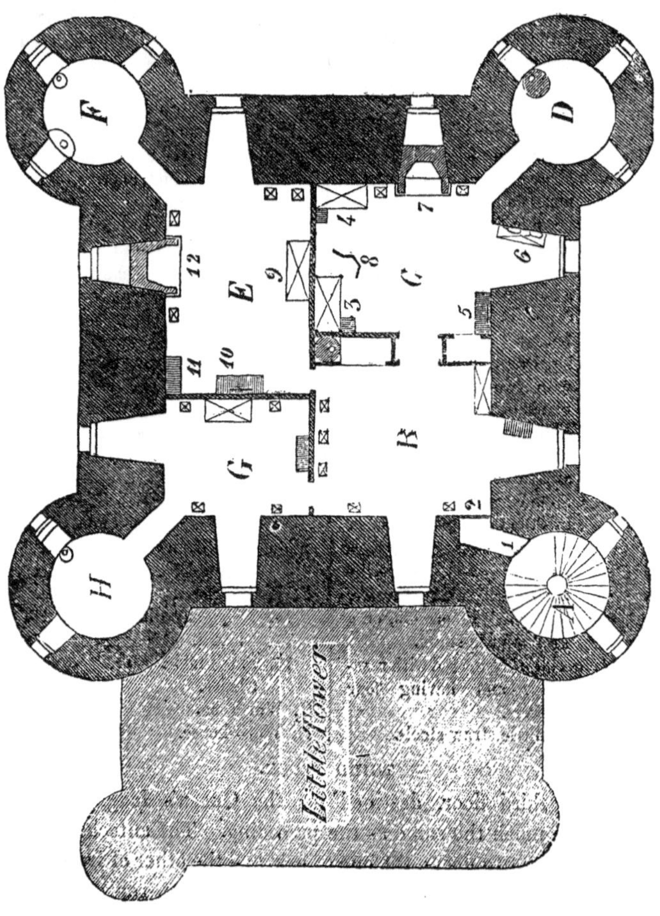

clock, representing Fortune and her wheel,— a singular mockery of these great fortunes, so overthrown,—adorned the chimney. The room was covered with a paper representing blue and green zones, of an extremely delicate colour. The turret which served the Queen and her daughter as a closet had the same paper. The two other rooms were covered with a yellow paper.

The following plan will give an exact idea of this third floor and its furniture:

GREAT TOWER.—THIRD FLOOR.—*THE QUEEN.*

A. Staircase.
 1. Oak door.
 2. Iron door.
B. Antechamber.
 Table, couch, and chairs.
C. The Queen's chamber.
 3. The Queen's four-post bed, with furniture of green damask, a hair palliass, two mattresses, a bolster, and a Marseilles quilt.
 4. Madame Royale's bed, with palliass, three mattresses, a hair palliass, bolster, and two cotton quilts.
 5. Mahogany chest of drawers, with marble top, and looking-glass.
 6. Sofa, with two pillows.
 7. Chimney, with the clock already described, and a glass, 45in. by 36in.
 8. A wooden screen, painted in imitation of mahogany.
 Two *tables de nuit.*
D. The Queen's cabinet.
E. Madame Elizabeth's room.
 9. Iron bedstead, with green furniture, a hair palliass, two mattresses, a feather bed, a bolster, and a Marseilles quilt.
 10. Chest of drawers, with marble top.
 11. A walnut table.
 12. A chimney, with glass, 45in. by 32in.
 Two chairs.
 Two arm-chairs.
 Plated candlesticks.
F. Wardrobe.
G. Tison's room.
 Bed, chest of drawers with marble top, a dressing glass, a clock by Lepaute on the drawers, several chairs (two of them cane), plated candlesticks.
H. Closet in which Tison was shut up, September, 1793.

All the details of furniture contained in these two plans are derived from two inventories, made, the first on the 25th October, 1792, when the royal family entered the great tower; the other, on the 19th January, 1793.*

* National Archives, E, No. 6, 206.

FOURTH FLOOR.

The fourth floor, not being destined for occupation, remained in all its original simplicity. It seemed larger than the other stories, on account of its loftier ceiling, and of the absence of the central pillar, which did not ascend above the third story. Some old furniture and a quantity of planking were stowed away in this apartment.

Between the battlements and the roof of the great tower ran a gallery, sometimes used as a promenade. The openings between the battlements were afterwards boarded up, so that no person walking there could see or be seen outside.

Such was the last palace of the Kings of France, fitted up by the trowel of revolutions.

Now that we have sketched the interior arrangements of this edifice, let us endeavour to convey a general idea of its external aspect, an outline of the establishment placed within it, and of the precautions adopted by the republican authorities.

At the grand entrance from the Rue du Temple was a porter named Darque, formerly beadle of the Grand Priory, a simple-hearted, kind man, who set up no pretensions to a descent from the glorious virgin of Orleans, though the coincidence of names frequently involved him in coarse jokes on the subject. Darque was even, in all probability, totally ignorant that Jean d'Arc had ever existed. A sexagenarian servant of the Hôtel de Conti, the Revolution had come upon him in the harmony of his peaceful functions, and disturbed the serenity of his latter days. He did not, however, very clearly comprehend what it was that was passing around him, and his ignorance was to him a great mercy from heaven. The vicissitudes that were hurrying on men and things, had left him an asylum beneath the roof under which he had grown old, and this was all he desired; he regarded himself as an intrinsic portion of the Temple.

In Darque's lodge was a bell-pull, communicating with the

interior of the council hall, which was placed in the interior of the palace of the Temple on the first day of the King's detention, but from the 8th December in the ground floor of the great tower. A number of strokes, previously agreed on, indicated to the municipal officers stationed at the guard-house of the Temple the nature of the messages, or the importance of the visitors. A prolonged peal announced the arrival of a superior authority. On this summons, the municipals would come to meet the great personages, and introduce them, if there was occasion. These members of the Commune, at first eight in number, were day and night on duty in the interior of the Temple, one with Louis XVI., and one with Marie Antoinette; the six others constituted the council of the guard of the Temple. Two slept in the ante-chamber of the King, two in that of the Queen, the four others in the council chamber. These eight commissaries, whose term of duty was forty-eight hours, were relieved every day, four by four, selected by lot in the council of the Commune. When on duty with the prisoners, they were bound only to reply to vague and unimportant questions, and that as laconically as possible.

To the right and left, in the court-yard, rose several buildings applied to different purposes; to the right, was the apartment of Jubaud, the old door-keeper of the palace; the new steward, named Coru, occupied a part of this lodging.

In the building to the left, facing the house of Coru, dwelt the old porter of the château of the Temple, named Gachet, a dependent of M. le Comte d'Artois, an old relic, like Darque, of that ancient régime, under which they drank and sang without foreseeing the terrible visitors that were to come and break the glasses, and put a stop to the songs. The storms of the times had somewhat dulled the jovial humour of old Gachet; but they had not made him discontinue his old habit of selling drink to his neighbours. Since 1784 his little business had been carried on by an old bachelor of the name of Lefèvre, who paid little attention to the great drama that was being acted under his very eyes. Lefèvre only saw, in the arrival at the Temple of the municipal officers and the armed force, a good addition to his trade, and, without any ill-will to the royal family, whose bounties he had received, he willingly accepted a state of things that brought custom to his wine-shop. Such is poor humanity, when not sustained by a nobler sentiment; one judges general history from the point of view of one's own particular history. Guests met at the house of father Lefèvre to learn all that was passing, to converse on the affairs of the day: it was the resort of the quid-nuncs of the neighbourhood.

Also to the left, and under the same roof with the *buvette du Père Lefèvre*,—for so they called this establishment,—were the kitchens, which supplied, not only the prisoners, but the commissaries of the Commune, the officers, the entire armed force in the Temple, and all the *employés* bound by their duty not to leave the Temple.*

* The following is the list of all the persons employed in the Temple, during the first period of the captivity of the royal family, with their salaries:—

Gagnié, head cook (formerly employed by the King at the Tuileries)	4,000	fr. per an.
Remy, head butler	3,000	,,
Maçon, second butler	2,400	,,
Nivet, pastrycook	2,400	,,
Meunier, roaster (formerly at the Tuileries)	2,400	,,
Mauduit, assistant in the pantry	2,400	,,
Penaut, kitchen assistant	1,500	,,
Marchand, servant (formerly at the Tuileries)	1,500	,,
Turgy, ditto ditto	1,500	,,
Chrétien ditto ditto	1,500	,,
Guillot, pantry assistant	1,200	,,
Adrien, washer	1,200	,,
Fontaine, lackey	600	,,
Tison, in the service of Antoinette, of Elizabeth, and of the daughter of Antoinette	6,000	,,
The wife of Tison (Anne Victoire Baudet)	3,000	,,
Mathey, porter of the tower	8,000	,,
Rocher, doorkeeper	6,000	,,
Risbey, ditto	6,000	,,

The palace, or château, faced the entrance-gate, and occupied in its greatest width the first court. In the château was the grand post of the Temple. It appears from the diaries of the château at this period, that the guard of the Temple consisted of 1 commandant, 1 colonel, 1 sub-adjutant-general, 1 adjutant-major, 1 standard-bearer, and 20 artillerymen, with 2 cannons, forming, with the National Guards, including officers and sub-officers, an effective force of 267 men. This guard was furnished, from day to day, by the eight divisions of the National

Richard Fontaine, keeper of the door between the château and the tower	3,000	fr. per an.
Mancel, at first sweeper, and afterwards the colleague of Richard Fontaine	1,000	"
Le Baron, porter	2,000	"
Le Baron, house-porter and keeper of objects under seal	1,200	"
Jérome, key-keeper	1,200	"
Gourlet, ditto	1,200	"
Angot, woodcutter	1,000	"
Vincent-Petit Ruffon, cutter and carrier of wood	1,200	"
Herse, ditto	1,000	"
Jean Quenel, messenger	1,000	"
Danjout, haircutter	600	"
Roekenstroh, superintendent of the linen	1,000	"
Roekenstroh, steward's clerk (15½ years old)	1,000	"
Darque, porter at the grand gate	1,500	"
Picquet, doorkeeper at the stable	600	"

This numerous train was successively modified and diminished; the expenses, which were at first on the basis of 500,000 livres, decreed on the 12th August, 1792, for the use of the King and his family, were reduced; the abuses which had crept into the first organization were redressed by authority; several servants were dismissed, others replaced. Thus it was that, on 12th December, 1792, Rocher and Risbey were dismissed; that Guillot, Adrien, and Fontaine were replaced by Caron, Lermuzeaux, and Vandebourg; that afterwards, on the 13th October, 1793, Turgy, Chrétien, and Marchand were discharged; that Coru, the steward, who had succeeded Jubaud, was in his turn succeeded by Lelièvre; and that the latter, being denounced, lost it for a while, resumed it, and then again gave it up to Liénard. It was under this man, in Fructidor, of the year 2, that the great reforms were effected. Liénard himself set the example, by proposing to limit his own salary to 3,000 francs. Gagnié was thanked, and replaced by Meunier.

Guard of Paris, in turns. After the King's death this force was reduced to 208 men, including 14 cannoniers.

The entrance to the garden was by the interior of the château; it was to obviate this inconvenience that, upon the jealous suggestion of the Commune, and under its stern surveillance, the patriot Palloy,—he was never mentioned without this prefix,—erected a high, thick wall, which thus formed a new court-yard between the château and the garden.

This new wall had two gates, one of them for carriages, closed in by a strong oak door, furnished with iron bars and bolts, and which could be only opened by two porters, each the possessor of a different key.

The second gate, to the left side of the first, consisted of a narrow wicket; two keys were also necessary for the opening of this door. These keys were in the hands of two men, whose lodges were situated beside these two gates, one inside, the other without. An iron wire and a double bell connected these two dwellings through the wall. The two door-keepers there passed day and night without any intermission, disturbed every moment, depending on each other, and condemned, like Sisyphus, to perpetual action. One of these unfortunates was named Richard, the other Mancel.

When you had passed these gates, all the buildings contiguous to the tower having been pulled down, the gloomy edifice, the depository of the wreck of royalty, appeared in its sad segregation, shut in, with a few clumps of trees, between four bare walls. Its complete isolation gave it an aspect at once solemn and redoubtable. At its angles, four round turrets sent forth their pointed roofs, the equally pointed gable of the great square tower dominating the rest by its imposing mass. The eye discerned in them no traces of armorial bearings; there was nothing above the castle gate to indicate the feudalism of the ages of faith,—the Templars were not commemorated there,—the escutcheons of the grand masters were no longer displayed over the portal. The whole monument as sombre and strongly impressed with the physiognomy of the chivalric ages; but without anything epic or romantic in its simple and severe architecture, and destitute of those beautiful fantasies and those capricious images which the middle age cut in stone.

Since then, deserted by its noble guests, deprived of its arsenal and its trophies, it had, in silence, served as a repository for dusty records; a dark melancholy seemed to hover over it, and to announce that it was one day to be a prison. Men felt, as they gazed on the exterior, that gaiety could not inhabit it, and that the hand of adversity alone could bring inmates to such a dwelling. A theatre, perfectly adapted for the terrible tragedy that was about to be performed there, the architect, in making it so gloomy, seemed to have predestined it for the funereal purpose to which it was to be applied.

The assembling of the royal family in the great tower made little change in their habits. The meals, the lessons, the walks, the education of the children, all were regulated as before. On rising, Louis XVI. entered the turret, and read the service of the Knights of the Holy Ghost. As they had prohibited the celebration of mass in the Temple, even on festival days, he had requested Cléry to buy him the breviary used in the diocese of Paris. Always in pursuit of knowledge, and feeling now more than ever the necessity of prayer, this prince was in spirit a Benedictine, and in his heart a holy recluse of the Thebaid. He devoted four hours each day to the perusal of Latin authors, and making comments on them in pencil; then came books of travels; then, by turns, Montesquieu and Buffon; Pluche's "*Spectacle de la Nature;*" Hume's "History of England," in English; "Tasso," in Italian; and then, last and always, "The Imitation of Jesus Christ," in Latin. It was thence he derived the virtues which astonish us, that superhuman patience, which could only be realised by the perpetual contemplation of the Divine patience.

More excitable than her royal consort, Marie Antoinette

said short prayers morning and evening; her mind, in a state of incessant agitation, only devoted to prayer those moments in which she felt herself perfectly absorbed with God. As to Madame Elizabeth, the wickedness of man no longer made any impression on her. Often in the course of the day, amid the oaths and blasphemies which surrounded her, she would kneel beside her bed, and would pray with imperturbable calmness, isolating herself in meditation and angelic fervour. Meanwhile, like two fawns amidst their family, surrounded by the hunters, two fair infantile heads would rise, awakened by the bayings of the revolutionary hounds, and the fatal cry which already announced the death whoop.

At nine o'clock, Louis XVI. and his son were summoned to breakfast. Cléry accompanied them; he arranged the hair of the three Princesses, and, by the Queen's orders, taught Marie Thérèse how to dress her hair. Meantime the King played at chess or draughts, sometimes with the Queen, sometimes with Madame Elizabeth. The hours of study for the young Prince and his sister were not altered, nor that of the walk; all the family descended together into the garden. After dinner the children played in the antechamber at shuttlecock or other games. Madame Elizabeth, always present, took a book, and sat down at a table; Cléry remained in the room, and, by the Princess's order, sat down also, book in hand. The captive family, thus dispersed, often disquieted the two municipals on guard, who wished neither to leave the King nor the Queen alone, nor to quit each other's company, so mutually distrustful were they—at the same time watchers and watched. This was the moment of which Madame Elizabeth availed herself to enter into conversation with Cléry, who listened, and replied to her, without taking his eyes from his book, so as not to be surprised by the commissaries. The Prince Royal and his sister, in concert with their aunt, facilitated their conversations by their noisy games, and would intimate by signs, the entrance of the municipals. The captives had most to distrust Tison, who was feared by the commissaries themselves, because he had more than once denounced them. It was in vain that Louis XVI. and Marie Antoinette treated this man with kindness, nothing could subdue his natural malignity.

In the evening, the municipals placed their beds in the antechamber of the King, and in that of the Queen, so as to blockade the room occupied by the august prisoners. They took care also to close the doors of communication between the chamber of Louis XVI. and that of Cléry, and to remove the keys. If the King called his valet during the night, the valet was obliged to undergo the ill-humour of the commissaries, and to wait until they chose to rise to let him pass, and accompany him.

The animosity of most of the commissaries became aggravated; the influence of the journals and other sanguinary writings had much to do with the conduct of these men, who, theretofore, had not been so harsh or so distrustful. Every circumstance, even the most insignificant, was a source of suspicion; every suspicion, a ground for vexation and tyranny. One day, Sunday, the 28th October, after dinner, Cléry having written an account of expenses in the council hall, he put it into a desk, of which they had given him the key. Scarcely had he gone out when a municipal, named Marinot, said to his colleagues, although he was not on duty, that they must open the desk and examine the contents: "I know him well," added he, "and I know he is in correspondence with the enemies of the people." Then, accusing his colleagues of over-gentleness, he loaded them with insults, threatened to denounce them to the council of the Commune, and proceeded to execute his design. A list of all the papers contained in the desk, was then made out and sent to the Commune, where the angry commissary had already made his denunciation. Two days afterwards a draught-board was brought to Cléry, of which, with the permission of the municipals, he had had the squares mended. Marinot, now on duty, affirmed that the board contained a hidden correspondence: he took it entirely to pieces, and, not finding anything, he had the squares glued on again in his presence.

Other commissaries showed their vexatious and insulting hatred by childish and ridiculous acts. This broke open a macaroon cake, to see if there were not some letters concealed in it. That, under the same apprehension, had the peaches cut open before him, and the kernels broken. Another compelled Cléry to taste the shaving soap brought for the King, affecting to fear that it was poison. At the end of each meal Madame Elizabeth gave Cléry a small gold-bladed knife, to wipe it; more than once, the municipals snatched it from his hands, to see if he had not slipped some paper into the handle. Madame Elizabeth had begged him to return a prayer-book to the Duchess de Sérent; the commissaries cut the margin of the book, fearing that they had written something on it with sympathetic ink. One of them forbade Cléry one day to go up to Marie Antoinette's room to dress her hair: she was obliged to descend to the King's room, and to bring everything necessary for her toilette with her. Another persisted in following her when, according to custom, she entered, at noon, the room of Madame Elizabeth, to take off her morning gown. Cléry represented to this man the impropriety of such a proceeding, but he persisted; the Queen then left the room, and would not dress herself at all. When Cléry received the clean linen, the municipals made him unfold it, piece by piece, and examined it in the light; the washing book, and every paper, serving as an envelope, was held to the fire, to make sure that there was no secret writing on the pages; the linen which the prisoners put aside was also examined. Such were the insults to which the royal captives were daily subjected.

Shut up for two months and a half in the tower, the royal family had seen no one but the envoys of the Commune, when, on the 1st November, there was announced to them a deputation from the National Convention,* consisting of J. B.

* See Document No. VI.

Drouet, François Chabot, and Duprat; this deputation reached the Temple at ten o'clock in the morning. It declared its powers, installed itself in the Château, interrogated the municipal officers and the commandant of the armed force; and, having obtained from them all the requisite information, ordered the commissaries to open to them the gates of the tower.

Accompanied by Santerre and some members of the council of the Temple, the deputies ascended to the second floor, where they found the royal family assembled together. They examined the apartment in detail, and returned to the King's room, where Drouet seated himself beside Marie Antoinette; following his example, Chabot and Duprat took each a chair. On beholding the post-master of St. Menehould, the Queen could not suppress a gesture of horror. Drouet saw it not, or at least affected not to see it. "We come," said he, addressing himself more particularly to Louis XVI., "to ask you if you are in good health, if you want anything, if you have any complaints to make?" "I complain of nothing," replied the King, "I have no desire to complain, when I am with my family." Some questions were then put to him about the convenience of the apartment, and about his food. "I have said I have nothing to complain of; I only desire to be allowed the satisfaction of living with my family." Cléry, who was standing near the door, with the municipals on duty, observed respectfully, that the authorities did not pay the tradespeople, who supplied the Temple with necessaries. Chabot replied: "The nation is not particular about a crown or two." "Yes, gentlemen," said Louis XVI., "that is a point to which it is my duty to call your attention. I request also the commission to give to my valet, or leave in the hands of the council of the Temple, a sum of two thousand livres, for current expenses, and to provide us with linen and other garments, of which we stand in the greatest need." The commission promised to comply with this triple request.

The third floor was inspected with the same care, and all

the out-buildings of the Temple, and particularly the kitchens and works in course of construction. The patriot Palloy assured them that the works would be completed in a month; but he complained of the delay of the architects of the Commune, in not examining his accounts. "This must," said he, "be seen to to-morrow, so that my workmen may be paid on Saturday." This demand was not made in vain,* but the three demands of the King resulted in nothing. The mason had long since possessed greater authority than the King.

The envoys of the Convention passed the day at the Temple. After dinner they paid a second visit to the prisoners. Drouet seemed embarrassed: the instrument of the royal misfortunes, was his conscience wounded with all the evil he had done—did the sight of that unfortunate family awaken in his breast some passing remorse? I know not, but it is certain that, before leaving the Temple, he again ascended to the third story of the great tower. He was pale; his voice was hesitating; he asked the Queen, in a melancholy tone, whether she had any complaints to make. The Queen made no reply. He repeated twice the same question: "It is very important to know whether you have reason to complain of anything or anybody." The Queen regarded him with a haughty look, and, without uttering a single word in reply, proceeded to seat herself, with her daughter on her sofa. Drouet, opening and stretching out his arms like a disappointed man, but one who perhaps feels rather regret than anger, bowed and withdrew. Seeing her mother's emotion, Marie Thérèse pressed her in her arms, and kissed her hands, when she heard her address these words to Madame Elizabeth: "Why, my sister, did the man of Varennes come up again? Is it because to-morrow will be *Le jour des Morts?*" (All Souls—literally, the Day of the Dead.)

In the sitting of Saturday, the 3rd November, a question

* A few days later, citizen Lemarchand, contractor for the carpenter's work at the Temple, signed an engagement to terminate his work on the 28th November. National Archives, Case E, No. 6,207.

was raised in the council-general, as to the annual allowance to be made to the *valet-de-chambre* of Louis XVI., *but, considering that the trial of the ex-King was about to take place*, the council limited itself to granting a provisional allowance of five hundred livres a month. This was the first time that the Commune had thought of rewarding devotion, of paying fidelity.

On Tuesday, 6th November, after dinner, the royal family heard a great noise outside; they listened at the windows; it was an immense mob, making the precincts of the Temple resound with shouts, and demanding the heads of Louis XVI. and Marie Antoinette.

On the 8th, Cléry's wife came to the tower with a friend. Cléry was allowed to see them as usual in the council hall; the royal family, who were walking in the garden, saw them through the windows. The Queen and Madame Elizabeth nodded to them; this motion, of mere interest, was remarked by a municipal, and sufficed as a ground for his arresting the two visitors, as they were leaving the council hall. They were interrogated separately. Madame Cléry, when asked who the lady, her companion, was, replied: "She is my sister." Questioned on the same subject, the other said, she was her cousin

This contradiction occasioned a long report, and the gravest suspicions. A commissary pretended that this lady was a page of the Queen's in disguise. At length, after an examination of three hours, the two women were liberated. The municipal, the instigator of this insulting inquiry, was no other than Marinot. A few days after, on the 14th November, illness began to visit the royal family. Louis XVI., first of all, had a severe cold and face ache, which greatly incommoded him. The royal family immediately requested that M. Dubois-Foucou, his dentist, might be sent for; the council of the Temple, after a long discussion, rejected the request.

On the 22nd November, fever came on; the Commune, informed of this, was alarmed, and permitted M. Le Monnier, first physician to the King, to enter the tower, accompanied by

M. Robert, surgeon, and sent every day for a bulletin of the invalid's health. Cléry again solicited fresh clothes for his master, and obtained them.* He availed himself of the more favourable disposition now manifested to re-produce a list of classical authors, which Louis XVI. had dictated to him a month ago, and the demand for which had not then been complied with by the commission of the Temple. The commissioners transmitted the petition to the council-general of the Commune, which consented, though not without discussion, to the purchase of the desired books.† The royal prisoner learned this decision with the more pleasure, that the Temple library afforded a very slender source of instruction for his son, and of solid reading for himself.

The grief of M. Le Monnier had been very great on seeing his master again, to whom he had vowed the deepest affection. He gave him the most earnest attention ; he came to the tower twice a-day. He was searched each time before his visits, to which he was escorted by several municipals : he was ordered to speak in a loud tone ; even his prescriptions were obliged to be countersigned by them.‡ Marie Antoinette, her sister, and her

* "The citizen Bosquet, tailor, shall make for Louis Capet, at the Temple, a frock coat of Marseilles quilting, a cloth one for the day, and two pairs of black cloth breeches.—At the council of the Temple, this 21st November, 1792 ; 1st year of the French Republic.

"CLÉRY, in the service of Louis Capet and his son, at the tower."

"The Council authorises citizen Bosquet to make the aforesaid articles.

"JOLLY BERTHAULT, commissary on duty.

"MAILLET, officer on duty at the Temple."

† See Document VII.

‡ "We have found the invalid with a slight fever, the pulse full and high, the heat rather above the natural, the veins are red. These symptoms induce us to believe that the bile is beginning to flow back towards the liver. We hope that these irregularities will disappear on the application of some light purgatives, &c.

"At Paris, this 18th November, 1792.

"LE MONNIER, d. m. p."

"RIOTTOT, commissary. TOULAN, commissary. GRENIE, commissary.

"BELLUET. LAMIER. MICHONIS.

"ROCHE, municipal officer, acting as secretary."

children, always near the King during the day, served him tenderly, and even envied Cléry the pleasure of making the bed of the beloved invalid.

One day, M. Le Monnier requested permission to remain at the Temple a few hours, to see the effect of a medicine he had prepared for the King; and as he stood, while several commissaries present were seated, with their hats on their heads, Louis XVI. pressed him also to be seated. The excellent old man having refused to take, in the prison and in the presence of misfortune, any other attitude than that which he had always observed in the palace and in the presence of power, the municipals treated him as a courtier and an aristocrat. He only replied by the silence of contempt. The indisposition of the King lasted ten days; he suffered less from his illness than from his inaction; he bore with greater patience his own pain than the impossibility of being useful to his children. Marie Antoinette had requested that, during the King's illness, she might be permitted to have her son in her own room, but this had been refused. Three days after, the royal infant fell ill of a severe hooping-cough, accompanied with fever. His mother demanded, with the most earnest entreaties, to be allowed to pass the night with her child: "You refused him the favour of coming up to me, grant me that of going down to him." Her prayer was fruitless; she was only allowed to bestow her cares on her son during the day: the Revolution no longer persecuted the Queen, it persecuted the mother. Marie Antoinette soon caught the disease she sought to cure. The malady also attacked her daughter and her sister. M. Le Monnier was permitted to

On a slip of paper annexed to this is the following prescription, in the hand-writing of M. Le Monnier.

"Take a pint of clarified whey in several doses in the morning. for three successive days, lukewarm. "LE MONNIER.

"A light infusion of saffron, diluted with milk, for Madame.

"LE MONNIER.

"This 15th November, 1792.

"BELLUET. RIOTTOT. TOULAN."

continue his visits. The gaolers and the physicians often met. Illness had entered the prison, that no description of suffering might be wanting to the martyrdom.

Cléry fell ill in his turn; his room, without a chimney, and all but inaccessible to the air, intercepted as it was by the blind, was damp and gloomy. Fever, and an acute pain in the side, compelled him to keep his bed. On the first day he wished to rise and dress his master; but Louis, seeing in what state he was, refused his services, ordered him to lie down, and dressed his son himself. The little Prince, restored to health, scarcely left Cléry's bed during this first day; he himself brought him his diet-drink. In the evening, Louis XVI. profited by a moment when he was less strictly watched to enter the room of his servant; he gave him his drink, and said to him, with a kindness of manner which touched him to the soul: "I would fain myself attend upon you, but you know how strictly we are observed; take courage, to-morrow you will see my physician." When the hour of supper came, the royal family went to Cléry's room, and Madame Elizabeth, without the municipals perceiving it, gave him a phial containing an eclegm—a thick, soft, pectoral medicament—of which the Princess, who was under the influence of a severe cold, deprived herself for his sake. He would have refused, but she insisted. After supper, Marie Antoinette undressed her son and put him to bed, and Madame Elizabeth rolled the King's hair.

The next morning Le Monnier arrived, and ordered Cléry to be bled; but the consent of the Commune was necessary before a surgeon could be admitted. They talked of transferring the invalid to the Château of the Commune; he, however, fearing lest, if he once left the tower, he should never return to it, would not be bled. In the evening, the commissaries arrived, and the question of removal was not revived. Turgy requested to be allowed to pass the night with Cléry, and was permitted to do so; as also were his colleagues, Chrétien and Marchand, who each, in his turn, rendered this service to the patient. Cléry remained six days in bed, and each day the royal family came to pay him a visit. Madame Elizabeth brought him drugs, which she had obtained as if for herself; the invalid recovered a portion of his strength, less from the efficacy of the remedies, than from appreciation of the interest which was manifested towards him. It was, indeed, a touching spectacle, to behold that ancient race of kings, forgetting their own misfortunes to occupy themselves in allaying the sufferings of one of their servants; and renewing, at his bed-side, the tradition of the example of Saint Louis, whose royal hands loved to serve, in the persons of the infirm and the diseased, the members of Christ suffering.

Nurtured in the school of virtue and calamity, the heart of the Dauphin was open to all tender and generous feelings. One evening, after having put the royal child to bed, Cléry retired to make way for the Queen, who, with the Princesses, came to embrace her son, and bid him good night in his bed. Madame Elizabeth, whom the vigilance of the municipals had prevented from speaking to Cléry, seized this moment to give the child a small box of ipecacuanha, telling him to hand it to the valet when he came back. The Princesses returned to their room; Louis XVI. passed into his turret; Cléry went to supper, and did not return till about eleven o'clock to prepare his master's bed. When he was alone there in the room, the King having remained in his closet, the young Prince called to him in an undertone. Cléry was very much surprised at not finding him asleep, and, fearing he was uncomfortable, asked him why he did not yet slumber. "Because my aunt gave me a little box for you," said he, "and I would not go to sleep until I had given it to you; you just came in time, for my eyes have already shut several times." "Mine were filled with tears," adds Cléry, in his recital of the anecdote we have just related; "the Dauphin perceived it, embraced me, and in two minutes was fast asleep."

The young Prince combined with the kindly feeling of which we have spoken the graces and amiability of his age. Young enough to smile and play, but reasonable enough to comprehend the tears and sorrows of his family, he was still the joyous child who diffused gaiety through the Palace of Versailles; but now, less boisterous and more obedient, he appreciated why he should pay more care and attention to his parents; he perceived their cruel situation, which sometimes made them forget his little drolleries; he, himself, felt that he was a prisoner. There is a feeling which the instinct of danger inspires at every age. This gay and thoughtless child became reserved in his conduct, guarded in his conversation; not a single word escaped his lips that might awaken in his mother's heart an afflicting thought, a sad regret; but, did a municipal arrive whom he knew to be gentler than his colleagues, he would run to the Queen and eagerly announce him, saying, with an expression of the most radiant joy: "Mamma! it is Monsieur so-and-so to-day!" Noble and royal child! It was the same sentiment that, in the days of his short prosperity, inspired him, ere the Queen awoke, to place on her toilet table a bouquet of flowers, gathered from his garden at Versailles! He now contented his ambition with being the first to utter a name less disagreeable to her ears—in announcing to her a more humane gaoler.

"Why do you stare at me so?" inquired a commissary of him, one day, on whom he was fixing his eyes. "Because I know you well!" replied the Prince, without reflection. "And where have you seen me?" The child still looked at him, but made no reply. To this question, several times repeated, he refused to reply. "You do not know him," said Marie Thérèse; but he, bending down to his sister's ear, said—"Hush! before Mamma. It was on our journey to Varennes."

The following anecdote offers a fresh proof of his filial tenderness:—

A mason was occupied in making holes at the door of the

King's antechamber, to admit some enormous bolts. The young Prince, whilst this workman was at breakfast, amused himself with his tools. Louis XVI. took from his son's hands the mallet and chisel, to show him how to handle them. He used them for a few instants: the mason, astonished at the King's thus working—"When you leave this place," said he to him, "you will be able to say that you worked at your own prison." "Ah!" replied the King, "when, and how, shall I leave it?" Scarcely had he uttered these words when the Dauphin, in deep emotion, threw himself into his arms weeping bitterly. His father let fall the mallet and chisel, and, returning to his room, walked about with hasty steps.

BOOK NINTH.

THE KING'S TRIAL.

2ND DECEMBER, 1792—20TH JANUARY, 1793

Situation of parties—Cause of the King's trial—New municipality—Redoubled persecutions—The King learns that his trial is about to take place—Decree of the Commune—Searches made at the Temple—Rocher and Risbey discharged—Measures of security adopted by Roland—The executive council, the department of Paris, and the Commune sitting permanently—The Dauphin taken from the King—The King before the Convention—Agony of the Queen and Madame Elizabeth—The King is not permitted to see his family—The King chooses his counsel; Malesherbes, Tronchet, and Desèze—The King foresees his condemnation—Commission of the Convention sent to the Temple—Louis XVI. allowed to see his children, on condition that they shall not see their mother—He refuses—The indictment and other official documents connected with the trial communicated to the King—Conferences of Louis XVI. with his counsel—M. Edgeworth de Firmont—Secret communication between the two floors of the Tower—Anniversary of the birth of Madame Royale—Conversations with Malesherbes—Desèze reads his plea to the King—The King's will—The King again at the bar of the Convention—His defence—His speech—The 1st January, 1793—The journals—Manifestation of opinion at the theatres—Illness of Madame Royale—The *Ami des Lois* read at the Temple—The King declared guilty—The nominal appeal—New message to M. Edgeworth de Firmont—Condemnation of the King—His speech—Appeal to the nation—The King's farewell to M. Malesherbes—Inventory drawn up at the Temple.

DURING the imprisonment of the royal family at the Temple, we have not narrated the events which succeeded each other out of doors, except where their echo penetrated this gloomy abode. To keep within the limits of our subject, we could only touch on the general history of the Revolution when it was closely connected with the description of the misfortunes and captivity of the royal family. It is from this point of view that we shall here say a few words respecting the movement which was hurrying on the Convention. Louis XVI. and that Assembly were about to face each other. We must explain the causes which led to this encounter of royalty and the Revolution, and what combination of circumstances determined the Assembly to summon the King to their bar, and constitute themselves his judges.

The Convention, as is known, was elected in a fit of revolutionary fever. All events tended to extremes, and over-excited passions produced a sort of furious madness, of which those who have not lived in times of social crises can form no idea. Since the breaking out of the Revolution, there had been but one mode of government—it was that passion which had been roused in all minds and hearts against the Monarchy. The Constituent Assembly, which came first, had assailed the institution: it had weakened and enervated royalty, and deeply humiliated the King. The Legislative Assembly, which succeeded it, had continued to heat that terrible locomotive called revolutionary passion; it had pushed matters further, because it had received them in a more advanced state; and, on retiring from action, had left royalty virtually abolished, and the King a prisoner, with his family, in the Temple. Fate had decreed that, in the progression of events, the Convention should come, and kill the King.

It was the only thing the Assemblies, its predecessors, had left it to do. From Versailles they might lead Louis XVI. to the Tuileries, more or less transformed into a prison; from the Tuileries they might take him to the Temple; but, from the Temple they could only lead him to the scaffold. It was a fated progress. The Convention,—which, like the Constituent and Legislative Assemblies, and more than these two predecessors, was compelled to live on the revolutionary passion,—had only this last and terrible aliment to give it. Everything impelled it on to the goal; the outward situation,—that within,

—its own position. The outward situation was one full of the raging fury and terrible distrusts of war. The situation within was full of sufferings, suspicions, and that inextinguishable rage which fires the blood, and drinks deep of it without quenching its thirst,—water stanches and appeases the thirst for water; blood inflames the thirst for blood. There was wanting a crime, atrocious, unheard of, to this revolutionary population, whom the last days of the Legislative Assembly and the first months of the Convention had lured to murder and crime. After the commission of so many atrocities, regicide alone remained, for mankind pursues perfection in evil as well as in good. It was, therefore, written that regicide should be perpetrated. The internal state of the Convention contributed to force it to this dire consummation; it was divided into three parties—the Girondists, the Mountain, the Plain; the two first were contending for the direction of the Revolution and of the Assembly; the Plain, composed of timid and vacillating spirits, who preferred the Girondists, but feared the Mountain—it was not the majority, but it gave the majority. Therefore, as at bottom the Plain obeyed its fears rather than its taste, victory, and the conduct of the Revolution, was in the long run, to fall to the party which should get possession of the violent and impassioned populace of Paris, the domininator of all events, of all the constituted bodies,—of the executive, as of the legislative power,—and which might well be called the living army of the Revolution. This phrenetic population willed that the king should be killed. Passionate, it belonged to the most impassioned: violent, to the most violent. Woe to him that did not advance before this formidable pack! He was overtaken and devoured. Its hoarse barkings expressed but one sound: March! March! This is why the two rival factions precipitated themselves towards revolutionary extremes. Thence, between the Girondists and the Mountain, that emulation in regicide. Ambition mingled the ardour of its desires with the excitement of fear—that detestable counsellor. The Mountain desired first to reign, then to live; the Girondists desired first to live, and then to reign: this is why it was necessary that Louis XVI. should die.

To the Commune of the 10th August succeeded, on Sunday the 2nd December, 1792, a new municipality; a great number of the members were re-elected. The management of the prison did not derive any improvement from this change. On the same day, at ten o'clock in the evening, the new commissaries came to inspect Louis XVI. and his family, and to take possession of the tower. Heretofore, there had only been one municipal with the King and one with the Queen; the new municipality required that there should be two. It is also from this time we must date the arrangement for installing, in the ground-floor of the tower, the council, which had before sat in one of the halls of the Château of the Temple. The number of the municipals increased their emulation, and emulation increased tyranny; the surveillance became so close that the prisoners lost all hope of learning for the future any news; each day brought fresh decrees, which rendered the chains of servitude more galling. The severity, the harshness towards Cléry were redoubled; and Turgy, Marchand, and Chrétien, who had obtained a licence from the other commissaries, were expressly forbidden by the new comers to converse with him. Everything seemed to announce new evils.

Struck by this fatal presage, Marie Antoinette and Madame Elizabeth eagerly watched Cléry's looks and words; but his looks, frozen by doubt, his words, fettered by fear, only increased their sad presentiments. At last, on Thursday, the 6th December, Madame Cléry arrived with her friend. They made her husband come down to the council. She affected to speak to him in a loud tone, to remove the suspicions of the new inquisitors; and whilst she was giving him a detailed account of his domestic affairs, "Next Tuesday," said her friend, in an undertone, "they lead the King to the Convention: the trial will begin; the King will be allowed to choose counsel—all this is certain."

In the evening, while undressing Louis XVI., Cléry contrived to tell him all he had thus learned; he even gave him the presentiment that it was intended to separate him from the Queen and his family during his trial; and he added, that only four days remained for concerting with the Queen some means of correspondence. The arrival of the two municipals on guard put an end to the confidential communications of Cléry and the expressions of his devotion. Next morning, he could not find means to utter a single word. The King and his son went up to breakfast with the Princesses; after breakfast, he talked for a few moments with the Queen, from whose look, so full of sorrow, Cléry comprehended that the conversation had reference to what he had told the King on the preceding night.

Some precursory proceedings already seemed to confirm the sad news of the trial. The King had scarcely returned to his apartment with his son when a municipal, at the head of a deputation from the Commune, came to read to him a decree, which ordered *the removal from about the prisoners in the Temple, as also from those about them, and from their servants, all kinds of cutting instruments, or other arms, offensive or defensive,—in a word, all which other prisoners, presumed criminals, are deprived of.* During the reading of this decree the municipal's voice was broken; it was easy to see the violence he was doing to his own feelings. Louis XVI., without testifying the least anger, took from his pockets a knife and a little case of red morocco, from which he took a penknife and a pair of scissors; and, giving these things to the commissaries with his own hands, he merely said, shrugging his shoulders: "They need fear nothing from me." The whole apartment was searched; the razors, the curling-irons, the toothpicks, and other articles in steel, gold, and silver, were removed; then, having searched Cléry, and examined his apartment, the commissaries ascended to the third story. There they read the same decree. "If that be all," said Marie Antoinette, with marked anger, "you had better take our needles, for they prick very sharply." She would have said more, had not Madame Elizabeth touched her with her elbow, to invite her to be silent. The Queen and the Princesses gave up their scissors. The municipals took away even their working materials. "That is not all," said one of them; "we have orders to remove Cléry and Tison, and to taste all the dishes that are served up to you."

Having descended into the council chamber, the commissaries called Cléry, and asked him if he knew what things remained in the case which Louis had replaced in his pocket. "You must take that case this evening," said one of them, named Sermaise. "It is not for me," replied Cléry, "to search his pockets." "Cléry is right," said another municipal; "it was for you, citizen Sermaise, to make the search."

They drew up a list of all the things taken from the royal family, and made up the articles themselves into packets, which they sealed.* They then ordered Cléry to put his signature to a decree which enjoined him to inform the council, should he find, in future, any *edged instruments* on Louis, on the Princesses, or in their apartments; these various papers were then sent to the Commune. Sermaise next told Cléry to follow him into Louis's chamber. The King was seated near the chimney-piece, his hair-tongs in his hand. "The council has charged me," said Sermaise, "to examine the remaining contents of your case." The King, without making any reply, took the case from his pocket, and opened it; there was nothing in it, but a screw-driver, a worm (used to unload pistols), and a small steel. Sermaise took possession of them. "These tongs that I hold in my hand," said the King, turning his back, "are they not also edged instruments?" The municipal withdrew, and Cléry had thus an opportunity of telling his master all that had passed in the council hall.

The hour of dinner arrived. The commissaries saw great

* See Document No. VIII.

impropriety in the royal family's making use of knives and forks; some consented to leave the forks. The dispute lasted for a while, but at last the more amiable views prevailed, and it was decided that no change should be made, but that, after each repast, the knives and forks should be taken away.

The privation of the little articles taken from the Princesses, was the more sensibly felt by them, that they were obliged to give up various occupations, which hitherto had contributed to divert the tedium of captivity. One day, Madame Elizabeth, while mending the King's clothes, having no scissors, was forced to break the thread with her teeth. "What a contrast!" said Louis XVI. to her, fixing on her a look of sorrow: "you wanted nothing in your house at Montreuil!" "Ah! my brother," replied she, "can I feel any regret, while I share your sorrows?"

The approach of the trial increased every minute the distrust and the precautions; the municipals scarcely exchanged a word with the King; they no longer replied to Cléry's questions. The latter, under various pretexts, had in vain essayed to get down to the council hall, in the hope of procuring some information to communicate to his master, when, on Saturday, the 8th December, a commission arrived at the Temple, to audit the expenses of the royal family. Cléry was summoned before them to give explanations, and this circumstance enabled him to learn from a well-disposed municipal, that the separation of the King from his family, proposed by the Commune, had not been ratified by the National Assembly.

Shortly afterwards, Turgy was able to hand him a journal, which announced that Louis Capet would be brought before the bar of the Convention: to this journal was annexed a memoir, by Necker, on the King's trial. Cléry had no other way of delivering these two papers to the royal family, than by hiding them under an old piece of furniture in the closet, and informing the King and the Princesses where they were to be found.

It was in consequence of the visit of these two commissions, —the one directed to remove *all defensive and offensive arms*, the other, to regulate the expenses,—and on their report, that the council-general adopted some new measures, and modified others previously taken. From this day the council of the Temple was transferred from the palace to the ground-floor of the tower; this new arrangement did not affect the position of Mathey who remained porter, but it rendered the services of Risbey and Rocher no longer necessary; these two door-keepers were accordingly paid, and discharged forthwith.*

As to the two municipal officers on guard over the persons of the prisoners on each floor, they had anticipated the formal order they received, to remain both of them during the night in the antechamber of their prisoners; already, since the 2nd of the same month, they had, in this respect, complied with the verbal request of the Commune. The assistant-cooks, Turgy, Chrétien, and Marchand, were forbidden, thenceforth, to quit the Temple.

These measures of precaution exercised within the prison,

* These are the terms in which the decree of the Commune was framed.

"1. The council-general decrees, that the citizen Cléry, *valet-de-chambre* to the prisoners, shall lodge and sleep in the tower, on the left side, looking towards the dining hall, not sleeping elsewhere on any pretext.

"2. That the council of the Temple shall be installed in the tower.

"3. That the citizen Mathey, porter, shall have the care of the said tower, and shall not leave it under any pretext whatever.

"4. That the present door-keepers being, under the new arrangement, of no use, shall be discharged forthwith, after receiving their dûe.

"5. That the kitchen shall be placed in the tower, and that the subaltern officials, shall not leave it.

"6. During the night, two municipal officers shall guard the prisoners on each floor.

"7. And finally, the same kitchen shall serve for the commissaries of the Temple."

Note. Art. 1. had been observed for some time back; every evening the municipals took care to shut the door of Cléry's room, which opened to the lobby leading to the King's room, and to take away the key. Art. 5 was not put into execution; it was physically impossible to put the kitchen in the tower.

corresponded with the most severe police regulations without. On the eve of the day fixed for that great trial,—*by which the offences committed against the sovereignty of the people would be judged, and sentence, passed on their author,*—Roland, the minister of the interior, intimated to the administrators of the department of Paris, "*that it was their duty to hold a permanent sitting.*" He informed them, "*that the executive council would hold extraordinary sittings every day, morning and evening; that, immediately on the receipt of this letter, they must send to him, at the Tuileries, a deputation, for the purpose of concerting all measures necessary for the maintenance of the public tranquillity; that it was also incumbent on them to declare themselves immediately in permanent session, and that they must be perpetually on the alert; that they must request the municipality to observe the same permanence, and to maintain with them, and with the commandant of the public force, an uninterrupted correspondence.*"

On Tuesday, the 11th December, a great uproar awoke all Paris; the *générale* sounded in every direction, and, at five o'clock in the morning, a body of cavalry, with cannon, entered the court of the Temple. This noise and this display would have really alarmed the royal family, had they not known its cause; they, however, feigned ignorance, and demanded some explanation from the commissaries on duty, who refused to answer. At nine o'clock, according to custom, the King and the Dauphin went up to take breakfast in the apartment of the Princesses. The royal family remained together for an hour; but the continual presence of the municipals prevented them from opening their hearts to each other, at a moment when so many fears besieged them. At ten o'clock they had to separate; their mutual looks expressed what their lips dared not utter. The Dauphin, as usual, went down with his father; it was the hour at which the young Prince often pressed the King to play with him a game of siam:* on this occasion, he

* A game, something like skittles or nine-pins.—TRANSLATOR.

entreated so earnestly that Louis XVI., despite his anxieties, could not refuse. The child lost all the games, and twice he could not get beyond *sixteen.* "Every time I have this point of sixteen, I lose," said he, with a slight touch of ill-humour. The King made no reply, but the exclamation of his son had caused him a slight emotion; none knew better than he that this number is not fortunate!

After play came study; and Louis XVI. was already giving his son a lesson in reading, when, at eleven o'clock, two municipals came to seek the young Prince, to take him to his mother's room. The King demanded the reason for this removal; the commissaries replied that they were executing the orders of the Commune. Louis XVI. embraced his son, and charged Cléry to conduct him. On returning to the King's room, Cléry told him that he had left the young Prince in the Queen's arms; Louis seemed at this to be more satisfied. One of the commissaries returned almost at the same time to say that the mayor of Paris was in the council-room with a numerous retinue; that he was about to come up. "What does he want with me?" said Louis XVI. "I know not," replied the municipal. The King paced his chamber with hurried steps, and afterwards sat down on a chair next his bed. The door was ajar, and the municipals dared not enter, for fear of being questioned. Half an hour having elapsed thus in the most profound silence, they began to grow uneasy at not hearing the King, and went to pry into his chamber. They found him with his head resting on one of his hands. "What do you want with me?" he asked in a loud tone. "I was afraid," said the municipal, "that you were ill." "No; I am obliged to you," replied the King, with an accent of despair; "but the manner in which they have deprived me of my son has deeply afflicted me." The commissaries made no reply, and withdrew.

The deputation which had come for the royal prisoner arrived at the Temple at eleven o'clock, but the registrar of the Commune had forgotten the duplicate of the decree of the Convention, and it had been necessary to send for this document, in order to be able to proceed in a regular manner. Louis XVI. remained, during two hours' suspense, buried in his sad thoughts. It was not till one o'clock that Chambon, mayor of Paris, appeared in his chamber; he was accompanied by Chaumette, attorney-general to the Commune, by Coulombeau, registrar, several municipal officers, and Santerre, commander of the National Guard, with his aide-de-camp. The mayor announced to the King that he had come to conduct him to the Convention, in virtue of a decree, which the secretary of the Commune would read to him. Coulombeau read the decree. At the words, "Louis Capet shall be brought,"—"Capet is not my name," said the King; "one of my ancestors bore it, but it is not the name of my family." Then, addressing himself to Chambon: "I could have wished, Sir," he added, "that the commissaries had left me my son during the two hours that I have passed awaiting you; however, this treatment is only in continuation of what I have endured for the last four months. I will follow you: not in obedience to the Convention, but because my foes are the stronger." Having thus spoken, he took from Cléry his great coat and hat, and followed the mayor of Paris. A numerous escort awaited him at the foot of the tower, and, outside the enclosure of the Temple, a vast multitude. He got into the mayor's carriage with Chambon, Chaumette, and Coulombeau. On the road he spoke little, and uttered not a single word relative to his trial. He regarded, with an unmoved eye, the people that crowded on his way. A grand display of force had been ordered;* thirty

* Order of march of the troops conducting Louis Capet from the Temple to the National Convention.

"They shall pass by the Rue du Temple, the Boulevards, the Rue Neuve-des-Capucines, the Place Vendôme, and the Cours des Feuillants."

(The order commences by indicating the posts which the legions were to occupy.)

"Each section shall keep two hundred men in reserve. There shall municipals, decorated with their scarfs, surrounded the carriage;* the National Guard, ranged along the way, carried their arms reversed; the windows of the houses were closed; the people seemed in a state of mournful stupor. Having

be, besides, two hundred men at each prison and at each public place, and other depots or magazines, &c.

"*For the escort.*—Each legion shall furnish one piece of cannon, which will, together, form three pieces in front, and three behind. Each legion shall provide two captains, four lieutenants, four sub-lieutenants, and one hundred men, armed with muskets, and provided each with sixteen cartridges. They shall proceed to the Temple at eight o'clock, with the list of their names; this will form a corps of six hundred men, who, three deep, are to form a line on the two sides of the carriage.

"The gendarmerie shall provide forty-eight of their best horsemen, to form the vanguard.

"The cavalry of the military school shall likewise provide forty-eight horsemen, perfectly skilled in manœuvre, to form the rearguard; the whole shall be at the Temple at eight o'clock precisely.

"There shall be in the garden of the Tuileries, two reserves: the first, near the Château, shall consist of two hundred infantry; the second, near the Pont Tournant (swing-bridge), shall be provided with six pieces of cannon, furnished by the sixth division, eight cannoniers, forty-eight fusiliers, by each legion, and a caisson: all these shall likewise be at the Tuileries at eight o'clock.

"A third reserve shall be composed of the battalion of pikemen, and shall be placed in the court-yards of the Tuileries.

"The relieved guard of the Temple shall remain at its post, with the relieving guard, until after the sitting of the Convention.

"All the sentinels throughout the town shall be doubled.

"The guard of the Temple shall be placed at eight o'clock in the morning. Rounds will be made every hour, and whoever shall absent himself without permission shall be punished.

"The orders prohibiting the firing of any gun shall be strictly executed.

"Each legion shall provide eight cannoniers and eight fusiliers for the escort of the cannons, who shall receive a paper appointing and designating them, signed by the presidents and commanders of their legions: all to be at the Temple at eight o'clock. (National Archives, BB., No. 52.)

"After having heard the reading of the plan for the general safety of Paris at the present critical moment, which has been sent to the Commune by the executive council, the council-general approved it by acclamation, and decreed honourable mention of it to be inserted in the minute."

* "The council-general decrees that thirty of its members shall accompany the carriage of Louis Capet on horseback, when he shall be on his

remarked that Coulombeau saluted a great number of people just as the vehicle turned to the left on the Boulevard, Louis XVI. asked him whether they were all his friends: "They are," replied Coulombeau, "brave citizens of the 10th of August, whom I never see without much pleasure." A few steps further on, the carriage was detained by a slight commotion, produced by the words of a grenadier, whose royalist accents the leaders in vain essayed to stifle.*

The throng of the people again stopped the progress of the procession, between the Porte Saint-Denis and the Porte Saint-Martin. Louis cast a look at these two monuments, consecrated to the glory of his grandfather, and asked whether it was proposed to pull down these two triumphal arches. Chaumette replied that the gate of Saint-Denis being a master-piece, it might be preserved. We will not follow further the mournful carriage, which is about to convey before an exceptional jurisdiction him, in whose name France had passed the decrees of her justice for a period of eighteen years.

The pride of the Queen was disarmed by the uneasiness of the wife. For the first time, she deigned to interrogate the municipals; she could not obtain from them any information as to what was passing; they could only tell her that Louis had gone to the National Assembly. Marie Antoinette soon after-

way to the National Convention, and again on his return to the Temple. The commissaries appointed for this purpose, are citizens—

"DESTOURNELLES, ROARD, BICHARD, JALLIER, BOUTET, DU ROURE, VIGUIER, CAVAIGNAC, PAF, AVRIL, LION, CARDOT, DUMONTIER, VERON, LEGENDRE, SERMAISE, LEGENDRE DU LOUVRE, TRAVERSE, MOELLE, LAFISSE, CHAULIN, TOULAN, PERRIERE, RETOURNAT, LAUVIN, LEVASSEUR, FALLET, BERTHOLON, MICHONIS, CHENEAUX, ETIENNE, JOSSE, and GROUVELLE."

(Session of Sunday, 9th December, 1792.)

* He was named Hyvonnet, and was a clerk in the excise. See the report of General Santerre to the council general, bearing date the 11th December, on the conveyance of Louis XVI. to the Convention.

wards saw Cléry enter, conducted by a municipal. The latter did not at all resemble his colleagues, being a man of mild exterior and polished language. Left alone with Cléry, after the King's departure, he had apprised him that Louis would not see his family again, but that the Mayor of Paris had yet to consult some deputies on the subject of this separation. Cléry, profiting by the kindness of this municipal, had induced him to take him to the Dauphin, who was in the Queen's room.

The Princesses and the Prince Royal came down as usual to dinner, which was served in the King's dining-room. The meal was brief and silent. Having returned to their apartment, the captives had reason that day, by some miracle, to be pleased with their gaolers. Their misfortune had become so great, that it began to amaze their foes. There were present, on this occasion, municipals who did not insult the King,—a fortunate circumstance; and who had some respect for females,—a very rare circumstance. Only one commissary remained with the Queen after dinner; he was a young man of about four and twenty, of the section of the Temple, who was now for the first time on duty at the tower. Whilst Marie Antoinette was conversing with him, and questioning him about his condition, his parents, &c., Madame Elizabeth passed into her room, and signed to Cléry to follow her. From the first hour of their captivity, Madame Elizabeth had never had so facile and so long an interview with her brother's servant; she learned from him that the Commune had decreed the separation of the King from his family, that the Convention had not yet decided on the matter, but that the mayor was directed to put the proposition, and that, probably, the separation would take place that very evening.

"The Queen and myself," replied Madame Elizabeth, "are prepared for everything; we are under no illusion as to the fate that awaits the King; he will die, the victim of his goodness and his love for his people, whose happiness has been his aim ever since his accession to the throne. How cruelly they are deceived! The religion of the King, and his great confidence in Providence, will sustain him in this last adversity. Cléry," added Madame Elizabeth, thinking that she spoke to her confidant for the last time, "you will be alone with my brother; redouble, if it be possible, your attention to him, neglect no means of sending us news of him; but, for any other object, do not expose yourself to peril, for then we should have no one in whom we could confide."

Cléry arranged with the Princess the means of keeping up a correspondence. Turgy was named as the only person that could be admitted into the secret. It was agreed that Cléry should continue to keep the linen and clothes of the Dauphin; that every other day he should send whatever the young Prince required, and avail himself of this occasion to intimate what was passing about the King. Further, Madame Elizabeth gave him one of her handkerchiefs: "You will keep this," said she, "as long as my brother is well; if he falls ill, you will send it to me in my nephew's linen." The degree of the illness was to be indicated by the way in which it was folded. "Have you heard the municipals speak of the Queen?" asked Madame Elizabeth, with an expression of terror; "Do you know what fate is in store for her? Alas! what can they reproach her with?" "Nothing, madame," replied Cléry; "but what can they reproach the King with?" "Nothing, nothing," said Madame Elizabeth; "but perhaps, they look upon the King as a victim necessary to their safety; the Queen and her children, on the contrary, would not be an obstacle to their ambition." Cléry would fain have communicated a hope that they would merely condemn the King to banishment. "Oh! I have no hope," replied Madame Elizabeth, stifling her tears.

The fear of the arrival of the municipals put an end to this conversation. The Princess returned to the Queen's apartment. Tison and his wife, those perpetual spies, said to Cléry, "You were never before so long with Elizabeth; it is to be hoped that the municipals have not observed it." "Oh! there is nothing to fear," replied Cléry, carelessly; "Madame Elizabeth was speaking to me about her nephew, who will probably remain henceforth in his mother's room." An instant afterwards, Cléry returned to the Queen, who made him comprehend by a look that she was aware of the concerted arrangements, and by a smile testified her satisfaction. At six o'clock he was summoned to the council chamber; the municipals read to him a decree of the Commune, which forbade all communication with the three Princesses and the young Prince during the trial. They, at first, even gave him the order, for the purpose of keeping Louis XVI. in solitude, not to sleep in his apartment; to lodge in the little tower, and only to go into the King's room when he required his services. But these orders were not strictly carried out; it would have been too much trouble for the commissaries to seek him every time the King required his assistance. At half-past six the King returned to the tower, escorted as at his departure. "Sir," said he, to the mayor of Paris, just as the latter was withdrawing, "I beg you will send to me without delay the decree granting the counsel I have demanded, and which is refused to no one." "The Convention, doubtless," replied Chambon, "will acquaint you with its resolution."

Louis immediately asked to be conducted to his family; the authorities rejected his request, alleging that they had no orders to grant it; he insisted that, at all events, they should be informed of his return. It was promised, and the Queen was immediately made cognizant of his arrival. She demanded permission of the municipals to see him; and, as the municipals said that they had no authority to give their consent, she sent the request to Chambon, who was still in the council-hall. The mayor gave no answer.

Notwithstanding the agitation of the day, and the close attendance of the four commissaries who surrounded him, the King resumed his ordinary reading, which he continued till half-past eight. He had ordered Cléry to bring his supper at that hour. When it was served, he asked the municipals if his family were not coming now; they made no reply. "But at least," said he, "my son will pass the night with me, his bed and clothes are here." The silence continued. After supper, Louis XVI. repeated his desire to see his family; he was told that he must await the decision of the Convention. Cléry then gave out what was necessary for the young Prince's bed.

The King went to rest at the same hour and with the same calmness as usual. He said to his *valet-de-chambre*, who was undressing him: "I was very far from anticipating all the questions they put to me."

The same tranquillity by no means reigned in the apartment of Marie Antoinette; her son having no bed, she gave him her own, and remained up all night, in such mournful sorrow, that her daughter and sister would not leave her; but at last she made them go to bed.*

The next morning, Wednesday, the 12th December, she again demanded to see the King, and to read the journals containing an account of his trial; she insisted that, if she was not allowed to see her husband, her children should at least be permitted to see their father, These three requests were conveyed to the council-general of the Commune, and thence to the Convention.

On his part, as soon as Louis XVI. saw a municipal he asked whether they had come to a decision respecting the desire he had expressed to see his family The answer, as before, was that they waited orders with regard to that point.

Princes have a tact which rarely deceives them, accustomed as they are to observe the slightest change in the attitude, gesture, and even in the dress of those who approach them. Seldom did a new commissary come near Louis XVI. but the latter instantly divined his secret sentiment; happy when he

* See Narrative of Marie Thérèse Charlotte.

found neither hate nor ill-will: a pitying look was all the homage that this descendant of mighty kings could now receive.

Comprehending to whom, on this occasion, he was addressing himself, Louis begged the commissary to inquire after the health of the Princesses and the Dauphin, and to tell them that he himself was well. The municipal assured him, on his return, that his family were quite well. Louis XVI. directed Cléry to carry his son's bed up to the Queen's room; Cléry begged him to wait for the decision of the Convention. "I reckon on no respect," replied the King, "on no justice; but let us wait and see."

The King was right in expecting no more justice from the Convention than respect from the Commune of Paris. Pitiless, in its broader and more regular march towards regicide, the Convention left it to the Commune to exercise over the captives the petty details of tyranny. The Convention was only to demand of Louis XVI. his head: the Commune tortured him incessantly in all the fibres of his heart. It often took measures to which it had some trouble in procuring the sanction of the Assembly, which still desired to think itself sovereign.*

The same day, a deputation, consisting of Thuriot, Cambacérès, Dubois-Crancé, and Dupont de Bigorre, brought to the Temple the decree authorising the King to have counsel. The King declared that he chose M. Target, advocate, one of the principal compilers of the Constitution; in default of him, M. Tronchet; but both, if he were allowed to have them. The deputies desired him to sign his request, and added their own names. The King said, further, that he must be supplied with pens, ink, and paper, Having returned to the Assembly, the deputies immediately gave their report, and a decree ordered that the minister of justice should send forthwith a message to Target and Tronchet, acquainting them with the King's

* See the verbal-process of the sitting of the Convention of the 15th of December, 1792.

choice; that the commissaries of the Temple should allow them to communicate freely with the prisoner, and that they should furnish the latter with pens, ink, and paper.

On Thursday, the 13th December, in the morning, the deputation returned to the tower, constituted as on the previous evening, with the exception of Salicetti instead of Dubois-Crancè; they informed the King of the refusal of M. Target, who was, on account of his shattered health, incapable of accepting a task which required the most vigorous powers. They told him that they had sent in quest of M. Tronchet to his country seat of Palaiseau, and that they expected him in the course of the day. They then read to him several letters, addressed to the Convention, all soliciting the honour of defending an unfortunate prince. The first, without date, was signed Gustave Graindorge, formerly known as Ménil Durant, adjutant-general of the army; the second, bearing date the 12th December, signed Gourdat, a citizen of Troyes; the third, dated the same day, signed Huet de Guerville, formerly advocate in the late parliament of Normandy; the fourth, dated the 11th, was from M. de Malesherbes, and was to this effect:

"Paris, 11th December, 1792.

"Citizen President,—I do not know whether the Convention will grant to Louis XVI. a counsel to defend him, or whether it will leave to him the choice; if he has the choice, I desire to have Louis XVI. informed that, if he selects me for this duty, I am ready to devote myself to it. I do not ask you to acquaint the Convention with my offer, for I am far from thinking myself worthy of its notice; but I have been twice summoned to the counsels of him whom I acknowledged as my master at a time when this duty was eagerly sought by everyone. I owe him the same service when it is a duty which many persons think dangerous. If I knew any means of making known to him my wishes, I would not have taken the liberty of applying to you; but I thought that, in your position, you have better means of forwarding this intimation to him.

"I am, with respect, &c.,

"LAMOIGNON DE MALESHERBES."

A fifth letter, addressed to the Convention, also claimed the honour of defending the accused; but the deputies, not having this letter at hand, merely mentioned its purport and author, M. Guillaume, formerly advocate to the council, and member of the Constituent Assembly.

A number of other generous Frenchmen presented themselves, soliciting the glory of defending Louis XVI.—Cazalès, Necker, Nicolaï, Lally-Tollendal, Malouet, Mounier, Gin, &c. The illustrious Schiller sent to the Convention, from Germany, a memorial in favour of the King. A large number of petitions arrived from all parts of France.*

Louis XVI. replied to the envoys of the Convention: "I fully appreciate the offers made by gentlemen who wish to become my counsel, and I beg of you to testify to them my gratitude. I accept M. de Malesherbes as my counsel. If M. Tronchet cannot give me his services, I will arrange with M. de Malesherbes as to the selection of some other person."

The note of acceptance was drawn up at the tower, and read to Louis XVI., who signed it, with the deputies.

Possessed of rare qualities and great virtues, that true philosopher was animated in the highest degree by the sentiment of justice and of humanity. Holding by honour to the traditions of the past, and, by his reflections, to all useful reforms—a stranger alike to court intrigues and to parliamentary violence—Malesherbes, in the sphere of quiet and study within which he loved to confine himself, would have given everything in the world to be popular—everything, except his own self-respect. Torn by the tempest from his rural pursuits, from his books and his friends,

* The National Records contain a great number of these letters, addessed to the President of the Convention.

he came, with the same ardour with which he had formerly defended the interests of the people, to solicit the honour of defending his unfortunate sovereign; only, the perils of the latter undertaking rendered, in his eyes, this duty more sacred.

On the morning of Friday, 14th December, M. Tronchet presented himself at the Temple. Stopped, in accordance with the general order, in the palace,* which separates the courtyard from the garden, he was kept there for twenty minutes before the commissaries came to recognize him, and conduct him to the council hall, where he was searched. Thence he was introduced into the tower, where he had an interview with the King, as the decree permitted. The arrival of the jurisconsult greatly disconcerted the commissaries of the Commune. Feeling himself supported by law, Louis demanded, authoritatively, permission to see his family; the council of the Temple dared not take upon themselves the responsibility either of assent or of refusal, and they referred the request to the council-general of the Commune.

The same day, after having undergone the rude formalities to which all, without exception, were subjected at the gates of the Temple, M. de Malesherbes was also introduced. Louis XVI. ran to meet the old man, and clasping him in his arms: "Ah! it is you, my friend!" said he, his eyes filled with tears; "you see to what I have been brought by the excess of my love for the people, and by that self-abnegation which led me to consent to the removal of the troops, whose function it was to defend my power and my person against the enterprises of a factious assembly. You come to aid me with your counsel; you do not fear to expose your life to save me; yet 'twill be all in vain." "No, Sire, I do not expose my life, and I even believe your Majesty's life is in no danger. Your cause is so just, and the means of defence, therefore, so victorious."

* The French call many places *palaces* which are not royal dwellings. —TRANSLATOR.

"Ah, my friend, they will kill me; but it matters not, my cause is gained, so that I leave behind me a stainless memory."

As the King was authorized to confer freely with his counsel, Cléry, upon the arrival of M. de Malesherbes, had closed the door of his master's apartment. A municipal reproached him for this proceeding, ordered him to open the door immediately, and forbade him ever again to close it. Cléry opened the door, but the King was already in the turret with his advocate. The King was so impressed with the presentiment, or rather prescience, of his death, that he spoke on this occasion, not merely of his appearance before the men who arrogated the right to try him, but of his appearance before God. Malesherbes relates, in the notes he has left of this event, that the King took him aside in the turret, and said to him: "My sister has given me the name and address of a nonconformist priest, who may assist me in my last moments. Go to him from me, and ask him to give me his aid. This is a strange commission, M. de Malesherbes, for me to give to a philosopher; but if you should ever be doomed to die, as I must die, I wish that you may have, as I have, the support of religion. Religion will console you far better than philosophy." "Sire," replied M. de Malesherbes, "there is nothing so pressing about this commission." "There is nothing more pressing with me;" replied the King. The address on his Majesty's note was: "*A Monsieur Edgeworth de Firmont, aux Récollets, à Paris.*"

Before their first interview, Messrs. Tronchet and Malesherbes already understood each other by their common zeal for truth and for their royal client: but they could not arrange the defence, ignorant as they were of the charges. They wrote to the National Convention for these documents. On the morning of the 15th December, the Convention, after having heard the report of its commission of Twenty-one, decreed that that commission should nominate four of its own members, who were, "to proceed forthwith to the Temple, remit to Louis collated copies of the documents in proof of his crimes, draw up a statement of them, then place before his eyes the originals of the documents which had not been presented to him at the bar, and ascertain whether he recognised them." These communications were made to the King in the presence of Tronchet, and the documents, to the number of one hundred and seven, were endorsed.

The same morning, the Assembly took under its consideration the request which the King had made, to be allowed to communicate with his family. This permission was at first granted without reservation; Tallien interposed, alleging that the municipality of Paris would not execute the decree. Several members thereupon indignantly demanded that the author of an observation, so insulting to the law and to the National Convention, should be censured, and that his name should be inserted in the minutes of the sitting, which was ordered.* Several voices were then raised, demanding that the decree which permitted Louis to see his family be rescinded. After several contradictory propositions, a middle course was adopted, the terms of the authorization were modified, and, about one o'clock, the following decree was brought to the tower: "*The National Convention decrees, that Louis Capet may see his children, who shall not be permitted, till the close of his trial, to communicate with their mother or their aunt.*"

"You see," said Louis XVI. to Cléry, "the cruel alternative in which they place me. I could never make up my mind to keep my children with me; as to my daughter, it is impossible; as to my son, I am too sensible of the grief it would cause the Queen. I must, therefore, consent to this new sacrifice." Ever generous, even at the expense of his gentlest affections, the King ordered Cléry to replace his son's bed in his mother's room, which was done forthwith. The royal infant had slept for the three last nights on a mattress. Cléry kept his linen and his clothes, and, every other day, sent him all that was necessary, as had been arranged with Madame Elizabeth.

* See the sitting of the Convention, 15th December, 1792.

At half-past three in the afternoon, the deputation of the commission of Twenty-one, which we have mentioned, presented itself at the Temple; it consisted of Borie, Dufriche-Valazé, Poullain-Grandpré, and Cochon, accompanied by Gauthier, clerk in the journal office of the Convention, appointed secretary of the commission; of Varennes, usher to the Convention, and of Deveaux, quarter-master-general to the grenadiers of the National Gendarmerie, commanding the detachment which now escorted the deputies. On reaching the outer gate, the commissaries of the Temple came to receive them, and to examine their powers. One of these, named Perriac, objected to the admission of Gauthier, Varennes, and Deveaux, of whom the decree of the Convention, he said, made no mention. This obstacle having been removed by Arthur and Bodson, his colleagues, the deputation, with its retinue, was ushered into the presence of Louis XVI. Tronchet was there. Borie explained the object of the mission with which he and his colleagues were charged. After a brief conversation, the large table of the antechamber was wheeled into the centre of the King's room, and on it were placed the indictment, and all the documents relating to the trial, most of them having been found in the iron cupboard of the Tuileries. Each took his place at it, Tronchet by the side of Louis, and the Conventionals opposite. The two municipals on guard also seated themselves in the chamber; one of them was Mercereau, who, after working for some time at the Temple as a stone-mason, now made his first appearance as a member of the council-general of the Commune, attired in his ragged working dress, with a dirty round hat, worn out and discoloured, a leathern apron, and decorated with his tri-coloured scarf; this man stretched himself in the arm-chair which Louis XVI. had just left, wheeled it towards the chair in which that prince had seated himself, and there, with a careless air of importance, listened to what passed, *Thee* and *Thouing*, with his old hat on his head, all who addressed him. The members of the Convention were astounded at the more than familiar attitude of the demagogue mason; but observations thereon were postponed, and matters took their course.

Conformably with the decree, a copy was handed to Louis XVI. of the papers which had been already communicated to him at the bar, in number fifty-one, as well as a copy of the inventory of those papers. They were all endorsed, and then signed by Louis XVI. and two members of the commission, Grandpré and Cochon. The King's signature was merely a large L.

They then laid before Louis the originals of the papers, which had not been presented to him at the bar, and which were comprised in a second inventory, to the number of one hundred and seven; each of these was read by Gauthier, secretary to the commission. Valazé asked Louis: "Have you any knowledge, &c.?" the King replied "Yes" or "No," without any further explanation. Borie got him to sign them all, as also the copy, which Grandpré, each time proposed to read, with which reading the King as regularly dispensed. Cochon called them over by folio and number, and the secretary registered them as they were handed to the King.

Although commenced before four o'clock, this operation was not near its end when half-past nine arrived. Louis XVI. interrupted the procedure by asking the deputies if they would take supper. They accepted the offer. Cléry served up a cold fowl and some fruit in the dining-room. Tronchet would not take anything, and stayed with the King in his chamber. During supper, Grandpré asked Cléry several questions about Mercereau. "I used often to see him formerly," replied Cléry; "he was a clever man at Versailles, before the Revolution." "Is the Commune," resumed Grandpré, "regularly and exactly informed of the manner in which they treat the late King here?" Cléry was about to reply, when the municipal Bodson politely begged Grandpré not to ask any more questions: "It is expressly forbidden," said he, "to speak to Cléry; but we shall, in the council-hall, give the citizens, the representatives of the people, all the information they can desire." Grandpré held his peace: they soon left the dining-room, and the interrogatory of the royal defendant re-commenced. Some of the manuscripts which they submitted to him (among others, those numbered 18 and 53), contained projects for constitutions in the King's own hand; several other papers (those numbered 5, 6, 22, 31, 78), had notes also in his hand-writing, some in ink, and some in pencil; the letter numbered 30, and addressed to M. de Bouillé, was altogether written by him.* Calm, almost abstracted, he received these papers, *as a great lord receives the accounts of his steward.*† Indifferent about the mass of trashy papers whence issued so many voices which his enemies had evoked against him, he, for a long time, concentrated his attention on Tronchet's snuff-box. This snuff-box had a double face, and represented, on one side, *Aristocracy desiring the counter-revolution*, and on the other a figure, wearing the cap of liberty, with this legend: *Democracy loves Revolution.* The King turned, and pointing to the side where aristocracy was represented, "I should not have expected," said he, with a smile, "to find on the snuff-box of citizen Tronchet, a figure preaching counter-revolution." "It is a figure of ancient date," replied Tronchet, occupied with the extracts.‡ "There are also ancient dates in all they are showing me here," said the King, carelessly. His placidity, however, was disturbed when they presented to him certain denunciations and registers of police, among which were some reports made and signed by some of the servants of his household. The informers entered into minute details of all that was passing in the interior of the Tuileries, in order to communicate, by local colouring, greater probability to their calumnies. This black ingratitude, this odious malevolence, which seemed greatly to amuse Mercereau, as he lay

* The King in this letter, congratulated M. de Bouillé on his conduct at Nancy.

† Sitting of the council-general of the Commune of the 27th December, 1792.

‡ Sitting of the council-general of the Commune of the 27th December, 1792.

stretched in his arm-chair, affected Louis XVI. for a moment, but reason resumed her habitual serenity. When they presented to him the document numbered 79, he said : "I recognise my signature there," and, endorsing it, passed it on to Tronchet, adding: "You will not yourself deny the authenticity of this paper, for it bears your signature also." It was the declaration which the King had made on his return from Varennes, and was signed by the three deputies whom the Constituent Assembly had appointed to receive it.

At length, with midnight, came the termination of this long and painful sitting, to which the National Convention had contributed the cold and hypocritical phantom of its legal procedures, the Commune of Paris the insolent malignity of its tyranny, and Christian royalty its martyr gentleness.

When the deputation had withdrawn, Louis XVI. took some refreshment, and retired to rest, without making any complaint of the fatigue he had undergone. He merely asked Cléry whether the supper of his family had been delayed, and on his replying in the negative, added: "For delay would perhaps have occasioned alarm." Then, having gently reproached his servant for not having supped already, he went to sleep, turning his thoughts, doubtless, towards his captive family, towards his unhappy people, towards his God—his only consolation and his sole joy ; for his conscience was even still more serene than his heart was afflicted.

Tronchet and Lamoignon de Malesherbes were alarmed, less at the intrinsic gravity than at the number of the documents adduced in support of the prosecution, and which they had to refute one by one, without a single exception : they were still more alarmed when they heard that the Convention had decreed, that they would not hear counsel for the defence after the 26th of the then current month. Having been unable to commence their task until the 15th of that month, the two advocates were fearful both that time and their own strength would fail them. The King, however, would not consent to their soliciting any extension of time. The age and the extreme sensibility of Malesherbes rendered it almost impossible for him to address the court, and the venerable man, therefore, conceived the idea of demanding the assistance of a young advocate, then in the full enjoyment of a brilliant renown; he proposed M. Desèze to his colleague, and both proposed him to the King. The King, as yet, knew him only by reputation, but: "Do as you think proper," said he, with a smile; "physicians congregate where the danger is great. You prove to me that the malady is desperate. I will prove to you that the patient is all-enduring." The counsel, hereupon, wrote to the Convention, requesting, in consideration of the brief time allowed them, that M. Desèze might be joined with them in the defence that had been entrusted to them; this letter was read in the sitting of Monday, 17th December, and its request granted.

The same day, about five in the afternoon, the three defenders came to the tower, and from the 17th to the 26th December, Louis XVI. saw them all regularly every day. Malesherbes used to bring him, in the morning, the public papers, sit with him for an hour or two, and arrange with him the labour of the evening. At five o'clock he would return with Tronchet and Desèze; the three counsel did not leave their royal client till nine, and the remainder of the evening, and a great portion of the night they then devoted to labour, scarcely allowing themselves an interval for refreshment.

The unhappy King was solaced by the affection of Malesherbes, and encouraged by the zeal and devotion of his two other generous advocates; but his own conviction, as to the result, remained unaltered. Taking M. de Malesherbes apart, one day, he reminded him that, at their first interview in the tower, he had charged him with a pious negociation, to the success of which he attached the greatest importance. "Though I have not thought it expedient," replied Malesherbes, "to give your Majesty an earlier account of this mission, I have faithfully executed your orders. M. de Firmont does not reside at the Récollets; he has apartments in the Rue du Bac; but, since the first week in September, he has been at Choisy-le-Roi. Not knowing him personally, and unable either to receive him at my house or to go to his, I proposed to him an interview at the house of a third party, my sister, Madame Sénozan, and it was there we met. I delivered, Sire, your message, which another man would have considered a pressing invitation, but he regards it as a command. Like myself, however, he firmly thinks that human wickedness will never render it necessary for him to give you so afflicting a proof of his devotion. He charged me to express how deeply his heart was wounded at the present unhappy circumstances." "Thank him, in my name," replied the King; "and request him not to quit Paris at present."

We will endeavour to relate, under their respective dates, some conversations which should not be lost to history, leaving to each day its tears and its consolations.

Cléry had already contrived the means of communicating, through Turgy, news of the King to Madame Elizabeth. On the 17th, he was, in his turn, informed by Turgy, that this Princess, in giving him her napkin after dinner, had slipped into his hand a note, written with a needle, wherein she entreated the King to send her, if but one word written with his own hand. Cléry communicated Madame Elizabeth's wish to the King that evening; and next morning, Louis, who, since the commencement of the prosecution, had possessed pens, ink, and paper, wrote a note to his sister, which he handed, unsealed, to Cléry: "There is nothing in it," he said, "that can compromise you: read it." The discreet servant entreated the King to dispense with his obedience on the latter point, and took the note to Turgy, who brought back an answer rolled in a ball of thread, which he threw under Cléry's bed, while passing the door of his chamber. Rejoiced to have thus found a means of procuring news from his family, Louis XVI. continued the correspondence. He gave his nôtes to Cléry, who, after reducing them to as limited a compass as possible, covered them with thread, wool, or cotton. Turgy always found these little balls in the cupboard, where the dinner plates were kept, and transmitted them to Madame Elizabeth. Less cautious than his colleague, Turgy availed himself of various means for conveying the answers, and more than once, on receiving these, the King said to him, with grateful interest: "Take care; you incur too great a risk."

The candles which the commissaries sent in for the use of Louis XVI. were tied up in packets. Cléry preserved the string; and, when he had collected a sufficient length, informed his master that they might now carry on a more active correspondence. The window in Madame Elizabeth's room was exactly above that of the little corridor between the King's chamber and that of Cléry.* The Princess, by fastening her letters to a string, could easily convey them from her window to the window below, where a skylight in the form of a dosser prevented their falling into the garden. The same string that brought down the letter would take back the reply, and the same medium would convey to the Princesses a little paper and ink, resources of which they were destitute. The string removed the whole difficulty. "This is an excellent plan," said the King; "and, if our present medium fail us, we will adopt it."

Since he had been separated from his family, the King had abstained from his promenades in the garden. "I have no wish to go out by myself," said he, to those who urged him to take exercise; "a walk was very pleasant to me when accompanied by my family, but not otherwise." Though kept apart from the persons dear to his heart,—though certain of his fate, he suffered no complaints or murmurs to escape him; he had already pardoned his oppressors. Each day he derived from his books fresh strength to support his courage, and enable him to meet, without anger or annoyance, the petty

See the plans, pages 264 and 266.

vexations to which, every hour of his life, he was subjected. He treated the municipals on guard about his person as though he had no fault to find with them, and conversed with them as of old he had conversed with his subjects; he talked with them about their families, their children, the advantages and duties of their occupations. Those who listened to him were astonished at the propriety of his remarks, at the variety of his knowledge, and at the classification of that knowledge in his memory. Gentle to his enemies, he was a father to his servants. On the 18th, he learned that the domestic, Marchand, had been robbed in the Temple of the two months' wages he had just received, amounting to 200 livres, a loss of very serious moment to the father of a family. Louis XVI., observing his affliction, inquired its cause, and, upon being informed, directed Cléry to give Marchand 200 livres, and to recommend him, at the same time, not to mention the circumstance to any one: and, above all, not to manifest any gratitude towards the donor, lest he might thereby compromise himself. Marchand was touched by the benefit thus conferred upon him, but still more so by the prohibition to express his gratitude. As to Messrs. Hue and Cléry, we have seen with what affectionate consideration the King treated them. This was but just; fidelity to misfortune elevates the individual, socially as well as morally:—a *valet-de-chambre* at the Tuileries, at the Temple, Cléry was a friend.

On Wednesday, 19th, Cléry, not recollecting that it was ember-week, brought in breakfast as usual. The King, reminding him that it was a fast-day, directed him to remove the meal, untouched. The municipal on service, Dorat-Cubières, said sneeringly to Cléry; "I suppose you, too, like your master, will fast." "No, Sir," replied Cléry, calmly; "I am hungry."

At dinner, the King said to his servant, before the commissaries present: "Fourteen years ago, this day, you were up rather earlier than you were this morning." Cléry at once understood the reference. "It is my daughter's birthday," continued Louis XVI.; "poor child! and I may not see her!" The father's eyes filled with tears, and, for a moment, a respectful silence prevailed.

Having heard that his daughter had expressed a wish for an almanack, in the form of the *Petit Calendrier de la Cour*, he directed Clery to buy her one, and, at the same time, to procure for him the *Almanach de la République*, which had superseded the *Almanach Royal;* possessor of this book, he read and re-read it, and noted the various names with his pencil.

The conversation he held that day with M. de Malesherbes turned upon the war of the coalition against France. "Even were the war," said the King, "to effect the re-establishment of my throne, it would be a violent measure, which, so far from bringing back men's hearts to me, would only exasperate them still more fiercely. The throne, regained by force, would every day be subjected to fresh shocks. The exhaustion of the finances and sound policy would not permit us to maintain in the country, for any length of time, the force of foreign troops that would be required for the re-establishment of order. And, again, these troops would no sooner have departed than the factions would recommence their intrigues. There would be no security for the repose of the State, no happiness for myself, in any restoration of authority that I should owe to other causes than the love of Frenchmen."

The conversation was then directed to the various parties into which the Convention was divided. "Most of the deputies," said Louis XVI, "could have been easily bought." "Why, then, Sire, did not your Majesty purchase them, other means failing?" "It was not want of money: that was placed at my disposal; but, one day I should have had to repay it from the funds of the State, and I could not make up my mind to apply those funds to corruption. The civil list, representing merely the amount of my domains, I could, perhaps, have dealt with more freely; but the irregularity of the payments and the necessities of my expenditure interposed great obstacles."

Tronchet and Desèze now arrived and all set to work The King's strength of mind, and immoveable tranquillity, excited the admiration of his defenders. To prepare with them his justification, to proceed with the analysis of the papers and the refutation of the complaints, such was the occupation of a part of his day. More than once, Tronchet and Desèze, who knew him less intimately, struck by the justice of his observations and his coolness, testified to him their surprise. "Why are you astonished?" asked Louis XVI.; "is not misfortune man's best instructor?" At another time he said to them: "We are doing here, believe me, Penelope's work; my enemies will soon undo it all. Let us go on, however, although I am not bound to give an account of my actions to any but God." The foreign record office possessed several papers, the examination of which was indispensable; Malesherbes wrote to the minister to request an inspection of them. In its sitting of the morrow (December 20th), the National Assembly allowed this claim, ordering, at the same time, that collated copies should be remitted to the commission of Twenty-one. A number of keys, found in the lumber room, and enclosed in an envelope, on which were these words in Thierry's handwriting: "Keys which the King sent to me at the Feuillants. on the 12th August, 1792," was laid, at the same sitting, before the National Assembly, and gave the agitators a hope that some new iron closet would be discovered.

Thanks to the correspondence which had been established between Cléry and Turgy, Madame Elizabeth was advised of the new mode of correspondence which had been contrived; she received the packthread, and, on the morning of the 20th December, she informed the King that she would make use of it at eight o'clock in the evening.

Malesherbes came to the tower about eleven o'clock in the morning, bringing, as usual, some journals. He often had an opportunity of observing with what coolness Louis XVI. read the attacks directed against him from the tribune; nevertheless there was, among the epithets lavished upon him, one which always hurt the unfortunate King: it was that of tyrant. "I! a tyrant!" said he; "a tyrant looks only to himself. Have I not always regarded the interests of the people? Who hates tyranny most, they or I? They call me a tyrant, and they know, as well as you, what I am." Malesherbes brought him also a ballad, which was being sung at that time throughout Paris; it was entitled, "Louis XVI. to the French people," and took as its theme those words of the prophet: "Oh, my people, what have I done to thee?" The perusal of this gave the King a momentary consolation.

At half-past four, the deputation of the commission of Twenty-one, which came to the Temple on the 15th December, was again introduced into the tower, accompanied this time by Jean-Antoine Cousin, a clerk in the register-office of the National Convention; Coursol, one of the ushers of the Convention; and Corman d'Avignon, brigadier of the National Gendarmerie, commander of the escort. They found Louis alone with his two municipal officers. They placed themselves, as before, at the table, and read to the King fifty-one new papers, which he signed, as on the first occasion. Mercereau was not present at this sitting; but he had worthy substitutes, Legendre and Gatrey, less clownish, but as violent as the stone-mason. Among the papers read in their presence was a lieutenant's commission, signed, in the emigration, *in the name of the King*, by a French prince. Bitter observations, in an undertone, hailed this discovery. When they opened a packet of letters and invoices relating to the wheat, sugar, and coffee trade, made out in the name of Septeuil, the hitherto suppressed indignation of the two municipals burst forth; and the name of monopolist escaped their lips, in a sufficiently loud tone for Valazé, who was already tired of their whispers, to call them to order and silence by these words: "Citizens, you are not judges here."

Collated copies of all original papers, and of the inventory of them, having been handed to Louis XVI., signed by him, and by Borie and Cochon, the commission withdrew. It was half-past five. The deputies of the Convention and the King's counsel met at the foot of the tower; having descended with the one party, Mathey and a municipal went up again with the other. The matters on which his counsel wished to consult with him did not make Louis XVI. forget the intimation he had received from Madame Elizabeth. Cléry had arranged everything; he had shut the door of his own room and that of the corridor, and he was conversing quietly with the commissaries of the Commune in the antechamber. The dial-clock scarcely pointed to eight; the King rose and went out for a moment; his counsel did not suspect, in seeing him re-appear three minutes afterwards, that he had received news of his family, and that he himself had transmitted to them the expressions of his tenderness.

On Wednesday, the 21st December, the King's counsel did not come to the tower; the duties of their ministry detained them the whole day at the committee of the Convention.

The King had a slight swelling in the cheek. For some days he had greatly suffered from the length of his beard; they had asked him whether he would be shaved, but he had refused, and answered that he was in the habit of shaving himself. He often washed his face with fresh water, to soothe the irritation which he felt. Perhaps it was this excessive heat, brought on by the beard and checked by the cold water, which had produced the disease which incommoded him; or perhaps he had taken a chill at the window of the corridor. He entreated Cléry to procure him scissors and a razor, not wishing to mention the subject himself to the municipals. Cléry observed that if he appeared in that condition at the Assembly, the people would see with what barbarity the council-general treated him. "I must not," replied Louis XVI., "seek to excite compassion for my fate."

This slight indisposition did not incapacitate him for his ordinary occupations. He wrote, besides, a long letter, which he intended to entrust to the aerial post, which now brought the captives together. A few slips of paper and a pencil were also sent up to his family, to come down again in the course of the next few days in the form of consolations. Eight o'clock in the evening was always selected as the hour for the transmission of this correspondence; Cléry took care to close the door of his room, and, in one way or another, occupy the commissaries of the Commune; he frequently persuaded them to play.

On Saturday, the 22nd, the municipal Jon, being present when the King rose, inquired if he suffered much from his face-ache, and if he wished a dentist to be sent for, that he might consult him. "I suffer little," answered Louis XVI., "and should not have made the request; but I am thankful to you for proposing it, and should be glad if my dentist were allowed to see me." He named Dubois-Foucou, Rue Croix-des-Petits-Champs. The officious prompter of this request, Jon, also took upon himself to make it known to the council of the Temple, but he met with the greatest opposition; the council abstained from a decision, and referred it to the council general.* This appeal to the council-general served at once as a ground and a cloak to the refusal.

* Extract from the register of the deliberations of the council of commissaries of the Commune, on duty at the Temple.

"December 22nd, 1792; first year of the Republic.

"At half-past twelve, the council being assembled, and consisting of all its members, to the number of eight, one of them, the citizen Jon, represented that Louis Capet had, that morning, in presence of the commissaries on guard over him, testified a wish to see a dentist, in order to consult him respecting a swollen face, from which he has been suffering some days, and mentioned the citizen Dubois-Foucou for that purpose.

"The question was discussed, and several members said, that not only did humanity demand that this request should be granted to relieve Louis Capet, but that it was necessary, in order to avoid any reproaches being made to the council on that subject; other members objected that, being only a swollen face, which was a temporary inconvenience, and would not

On his part Cléry had applied to the commissaries to request that the King might be provided with razors; and the Princesses asked that scissors might be lent to them to cut their nails. The council of the Temple assembled again in the afternoon to discuss these two requests, and, after a long deliberation, referred them also for decision to the Commune, which, having considered the question, came to the following resolution:—*

"The council-general considering that, by the decree which permits the counsel for Louis Capet to communicate freely

last long, the assistance of a dentist was of no sort of use, and might perhaps only increase the evil, or be supposed to have done so, which would give rise to remarks far more to be feared than those alluded to; that, besides, Louis Capet had formerly declared that he suffered no pain from this swollen face.

"Upon which, the subject having been sufficiently discussed, the members unanimously agreed that it was proper the council should abstain from decision on such a subject, and that it was better to refer it to the council-general of the Commune, which, in its wisdom, would know how to reconcile the attentions due to Louis Capet with the prudence necessary on such an occasion.

"The register is signed by:—

"CONCEDIEU, ROBERT, GIRAUD, FIGUET, JON, CUVILLEZ, JACQUES ROUX, and DESTOURNELLES.

"Copied, according to the register, the said day, month, and year, as above.

"DESTOURNELLES, municipal officer."

* Extract from the register of the deliberations of the commissaries of the Commune, on duty at the Temple.

"22nd December, 1792; first year of the Republic.

"At six in the evening the council met to take into consideration the two following subjects:—

"1. Louis Capet seems inconvenienced by the length of his beard; he has several times notified this. It was proposed to him to allow himself to be shaved. He showed great repugnance to this, and testified a desire to shave himself.

"The council thought yesterday they could give him some hope that his request would be granted to-day, but this morning they perceived that Louis Capet's razors had not been left at the Temple. This gave rise to fresh discussion on the subject; it was thoroughly discussed, and the result was, the unanimous opinion that the question should be submitted to the council-general of the Commune, who, in case they think proper to allow Louis Capet to shave himself, will be good enough to order with him, the council-general is responsible only for the escape of the prisoners, consents to the razors and scissors asked for by the prisoners being granted to them; and agrees that the present decree, as well as that adopted by the commissaries of the Temple, shall be sent to the Convention."

In accordance with this decree the council of the Temple allowed the King two razors, on condition of his using them in presence of two commissaries, to whom they should immediately be returned, and who should declare such return to have been made. The same conditions were made with regard to the scissors which were to be lent to the Princesses.

Malesherbes, who had not come to the Temple for two days, did not arrive till six in the evening, with his colleagues. Louis XVI. was grieved to learn that the good old man and his two friends had spent thirty-six hours almost consecutively in several committees of the Convention. He remonstrated with them about this, and said to Malesherbes "My friend, why fatigue yourself in this way? I should forbid such exertions were they even useful to my cause, but then you would not obey me, I know. Let me entreat you to abstain from them, at least, when I assure you they will be

one or two razors to be allowed him, for his use in the presence of four commissaries, to whom the said razors shall be immediately returned, and who shall declare that such return has been made to them.

"2. The wife, sister, and daughter of Louis Capet have requested that scissors may be lent to them to cut their nails.

"The council, having deliberated, have decreed unanimously that this request shall also be submitted to the council-general of the Commune, who are requested, in case they give their consent, to fix the plan to be adopted in this case.

"Decided, that the present deliberation shall be sent to the council-general of the Commune, sufficiently early in the day that their answer may be known to the council of the Temple on this day.

"The register is signed by :—

"MAUBERT, DEFRASNE, JON, LANDRAGIN, ROBERT, MALIVOIR and DESTOURNELLES.

"Copied, the day, month, and year, as above.

"DESTOURNELLES, municipal officer."

utterly fruitless. The sacrifice of my life is made; preserve yours for the sake of your family, to whom you are so dear."

On the 23rd December, after his devotional reading, which on a Sunday was more especially necessary for his conscience, the public papers of the 21st and 22nd, brought by M. de Malesherbes the day before, occupied his entire morning. At ten o'clock, that of the 23rd was given him by his old minister, who spent several hours with him. "This is Sunday," said the King to him, "and, moreover, my aunt's birthday.* I will devote myself entirely to you: we will occupy ourselves entirely with our reminiscences, and indulge in our old habit of chatting. We will not talk of my cause till the evening, when those gentlemen will be here. Pleasure in the morning and business in the evening, here; at Versailles it was just the reverse."

In spite of the wish and determination to take refuge in past joys, the serious spirit of the two conversers constantly reverted, involuntarily, to the gloomy present, but without anger or bitterness, and without dismay,—the one with his gentle charity, the other with his calm philosophy. Malesherbes still clung to the illusion which Louis XVI. had lost. His first idea was that, not daring to pronounce sentence of death against the King, the Convention would condemn him to exile. In this hypothesis he asked him to what country he would retire. "To Switzerland," he answered, without hesitation. "But, Sire," continued Malesherbes, "if the French people, returning to their senses, should recall you, would your Majesty return?" "By choice, no; by duty, yes. But in the latter case, I should attach two conditions to my return,—one, that the Catholic religion should continue to be the religion of the state, without, however, excluding other creeds; the other, that if bankruptcy is inevitable, it should be declared by the usurping power, which, having rendered it necessary, should bear the shame."

The King beheld, with surprise and sorrow, men of high birth basely serving the enemies of the throne. "That I

* Madame *Victoire*-Louise-Marie-Thérèse de France.

said he to his confidant, "born in an obscure station, or even gentlemen who have had no opportunity of knowing me, should have believed and blindly followed the destroyers of my authority, does not astonish me; but, that people who have been attached to the service of my person, and for the most part been loaded with my favours, should have augmented the number of my persecutors, this is what I cannot conceive. God is my witness, however, that I bear them no feelings of hatred, and that, even now, were it in my power to do them good, I would still do so." In his confidence, the King allowed his old friend to know the extreme distress in which he had been kept during his captivity. "In the penury I am in," said he to him, "I am unable to show liberality towards any one. Your colleagues have devoted themselves to my cause; they devote all their labours to me: and, situated as I am, I have no means of acquitting my obligations to them. I have thought of leaving them a legacy; but it would not be paid, and they would be persecuted." "Sire, this legacy is already paid; the King, in choosing them for his defenders, has immortalized their names."

Recalled incessantly, in spite of themselves, to the exciting affairs of the moment, the names of the principal leaders of parties were mentioned. "I have been assured," said Louis XVI., "that the Duke of Orleans expects the Republic will give him the title of Doge or Stadtholder; that he is encouraged in these expectations by Santerre, Marat, and several others."* "Those who dare become his courtiers," answered Malesherbes, "no doubt speak to him of a still higher title." "I have been told that also," replied the King, "but I do not believe a word of it. I think my cousin is misled by his opinions, and not by his heart. I have had the most terrible accusations against him in my own hands. I could have compromised him for ever, and now I rejoice doubly that I did not do so; not because I should have feared the resentment it would have

* "Mémoires de Sénart," published by Al. Dumesnil, Paris, 1824.

incurred, but, because I would not have it said that he was acting from revenge." "The King is too generous, and I am not sufficiently distrustful. I begin to think, Sire, that we are not of this age."

Alas! yes: Malesherbes was right. True types of ancient honesty, the most Christian King and the philosopher, both of whom had desired and facilitated reforms, did not understand the Revolution; but, both were equally ready to make a sacrifice of their heads to it,—the one with the vivid faith of a martyr, the other with the tranquil gravity of a stoic.

On the next morning, Monday, December 24th, at nine o'clock, Malesherbes was shown into the King's room. He drew from his pocket a purse filled with gold: "Sire," said he, presenting it to him, "permit a family which has become rich by your favours, and those of your royal house, to lay this offering at your feet." Louis hesitated; but, yielding to the entreaties of the old man, he at last took the purse and locked it up in his desk. In a moment of leisure he made three rolls of the contents, on each of which he wrote with his own hand: "*To be returned to M. de Malesherbes.*"

At five o'clock the King, as usual, had around him his three advocates. M. Desèze, by a species of miracle, was already prepared to read to him the defence he had drawn up. Louis did full justice to the eloquence, the logic, and the loftiness of the orator's style; but he earnestly entreated him to sacrifice all those paragraphs detailing his virtues, as well as thoso passages which seemed to appeal to public commiseration. "I do not hope to persuade them," said the unhappy King; "but I would not excite their pity." Desèze, approving the wisdom and modesty of his august client's observations, complied with his suggestion. "Curtail your peroration, also; eloquent as it is, it does not become my dignity thus to seek compassion on my fate. I will excite no interest but that which should arise from the simple statement of my justification. What you suppress, my dear Desèze, would do you more harm than it would do me good." The advocate obeyed with an air of sadness; it was the part of his defence which he had most elaborated. He suppressed three parts of his speech, and left in his defence nothing but that majestic simplicity with which it has come down to us, and which should ever be the only adornment of truth. The principles, however, displayed in the commencement of this vindication, were blamed by all the monarchical men in Europe.

Louis the XVI. could undoubtedly have declined the tribunal of the Convention. This was the opinion of M. de Malesherbes, it was also the King's opinion, and his wish, but he sacrificed both, piously accepting the humiliation of justifying himself before those who had condemned him by anticipation; for they were denouncers, accusers, witnesses, and judges, and, above all, enemies. He consented then to be defended, not against death, but against calumny, and to waive the vindication by protestation and silence of the majesty of kings, so deeply wounded in his person.

On Tuesday, 25th December, Christmas-day, Louis XVI., conceiving that he might be assassinated on the way, while repairing from the Temple to the Convention, and persuaded that, at all events, his last hour was not far distant, resolved to remain for a while wholly alone, and so framed himself in that disposition of heart and mind becoming every man who is about to render to the Creator an account of the life he has received. Face to face with his conscience, alone with his heart, he wrote that immortal will, which has found so many echoes in men's souls, suffused so many eyes with tears. Though all may have read them, we cannot refrain from reproducing here those pages, so replete with ineffable piety, tenderness, and benevolence, which will live for ever, the purest and most Christian apology of dying royalty ever put forth.

In the afternoon the King showed this will to Malesherbes, and permitted him to take a copy of it; he then, with his own hand, made some corrections in the copy, which Malesherbes took away with him, and succeeded in transmitting to its destination, beyond the limits of France. The original remained in the hands of Louis XVI. till the 21st January. It is written entirely with his own hand. Soon after this matter had been transacted, Tronchet and Desèze came in; the latter had made some slight alterations in his speech, which he submitted to the King's consideration. It had been stated that the idea was, to retain Louis XVI. at the Feuillants for a day or two, so that he might be tried without going to and fro; Cléry had, in point of fact, received orders to be ready to follow his master thither. The project, however, was relinquished. The King's counsel, not knowing in what manner they were to repair the next day to the Convention, applied to the Commune for directions on the subject. "Let them go on foot or on horseback, that is no affair of ours," cried a member of the council-general, and the Commune passed on to the order of the day. This refusal was not notified to the King or his counsel, who departed in the evening without any idea where or when they were to meet next day.

Fearful that the beating of the drums and the movement of the troops might alarm Marie Antoinette, the King, at daybreak of the 26th December, requested the municipals to inform her that he was about to be led to the bar of the National Convention. The armed force took up a position in the court-yard of the Temple at eight o'clock, and at half-past nine, the mayor, the attorney-general, and registrar of the Commune, arrived, accompanied by the commandant-in-chief, surrounded by his aides-de-camp. Chaumette was unwell, but, on such an occasion, he doubtless feared that he might be suspected of a want of zeal or civism had he attended only by deputy. Ascending the tower with some of the commissaries on duty, they found the prisoner tranquil, exempt alike from agitation and from depression. The decree of the Convention was notified to him; Louis asked for his hat, and at once went down stairs. The only anxiety he manifested was with regard to the manner in which his counsel

The Will of Louis XVI.

Au nom de la tres Sainte Trinité du Pere du fils et du St Esprit Aujourd'hui vingt cinquieme jour de Decembre mil sept cent quatre vingt douze. Moi Louis XVIe du nom Roy de France, etant depuis plus de quatre mois enfermé avec ma famille dans la Tour du Temple a Paris, par ceux qui etoient mes sujets, et privé de toutte communication quelconque, meme depuis le onze du courant avec ma famille de plus impliqué dans un Proces, dont il est impossible de prevoir l'issue a cause des passions des hommes et dont on ne trouve aucun pretexte ni moyen dans aucune Loy existante n'ayant que Dieu pour temoin de mes pensées et auquel je puisse m'adresser je declare ici en sa presence mes dernieres volontés et mes sentiments

Je laisse mon ame a Dieu mon createur, je le prie de la recevoir dans sa misericorde, de ne pas la juger d'apres ses merites, mais par ceux de Notre Seigneur Jesus Christ, qui s'est offert en sacrifice a Dieu son Pere, pour nous autres hommes quelqu'indignes que nous en fussions et moi le premier.

Je meurs dans l'union de notre sainte Mere l'Eglise Catholique Apostolique et Romaine, qui tient ses pouvoirs par une succession non interrompue de St Pierre auquel J.C les avoit confiés. je crois fermement et je confesse tout ce qui est contenu dans le Symbole et les commandements de Dieu et de l'Eglise, les Sacrements et les Mysteres tels que l'Eglise Catholique les enseigne et les a toujours enseignés. je n'ai jamais pretendu me rendre juge dans les differentes manieres d'expliquer les dogmes qui dechirent l'Eglise de J.C. mais je m'en suis rapporté et rapporterai toujours si Dieu m'accorde vie, aux decisions que les superieurs Ecclesiastiques unis a la Sainte Eglise Catholique, donnent et donneront conformement a la discipline de l'Eglise suivie depuis J.C. je plains de tout mon cœur nos freres qui peuvent etre dans l'erreur, mais je ne pretends pas les juger, et je ne les aime pas moins tous en J. C. suivant ceque la charité Chrétienne nous l'enseigne.

Je prie Dieu de me pardonner tous mes peches j'ai cherché a les connaitre scrupuleusement a les detester et a m'humilier en sa presence, ne pouvant me servir du Ministere d'un Pretre Catholique je prie Dieu de recevoir la confession que je lui en ai faitte et surtout le repentir profond que j'ai d'avoir mis mon nom, (quoique cela fut contre ma volonté) a des actes qui peuvent etre contraires a la discipline et a la croyance de l'Eglise Catholique a laquelle je suis toujours resté sincerement uni de cœur. je prie Dieu de recevoir la ferme resolution ou je suis s'il m'accorde vie, de me servir aussitot que je le pourrai du Ministere d'un Pretre catholique, pour m'accuser de tous mes peches, et recevoir le Sacrement de Penitence

Je prie tous ceux que je pourrois avoir offensés par inadvertance, (car je ne me rappelle pas d'avoir fait sciemment aucune offense a personne) ou ceux a que j'aurois put avoir donné de mauvais exemples ou des scandales de me pardonner le mal qu'ils croyent que je peux leur avoir fait

Je prie tous ceux qui ont de la Charité d'unir leurs prieres aux miennes, pour obtenir de Dieu le pardon de mes peches.

Je pardonne de tout mon cœur, a ceux que se sont fait mes ennemis sans que je leur en aie donné aucun sujet, et je prie Dieu de leur pardonner, de meme que ceux qui par un faux zele, ou par un zele mal entendu m'ont faits beaucoup de mal.

Je recomande a Dieu, ma femme, mes enfants, ma Sœur, mes Tantes, mes Freres, et tous ceux qui me sont attachés par les Liens du Sang ou par quelqu'autre maniere que ce puisse etre je prie Dieu particulierement de jetter des yeux de misericorde sur ma femme mes enfants et ma Sœur qui souffrent depuis long temps avec moi, de les soutenir par sa grace s'ils viennent a me perdre et tant qu'ils resteront dans ce monde perissable.

Je recomande mes enfants a ma femme, je n'ai jamais doutté de sa tendresse maternelle pour eux; je lui recomande surtout d'en faire de bons chretiens et d'honnestes hommes, de leur faire regarder les grandeurs de ce monde ci (s'ils sont condamnés a les eprouver) que comme des biens dangereux et perissables, et de tourner leurs regards vers la seule gloire solide et durable de l'Eternité. je prie ma Sœur de vouloir bien continuer sa tendresse a mes enfants, et de leur tenir lieu de Mere, s'ils avoient le malheur de perdre la leur.

Je prie ma femme de me pardonner tous les maux qu'elle souffre pour moi, et les chagrins que je pourrois lui avoir donnés dans le cours de notre union, comme elle peut estre sure que je ne garde rien contre elle, si elle croioit avoir quelque chose a se reprocher.

Je recomande bien vivement a mes enfants, apres ce qu'ils doivent a Dieu qui doit marcher avant tout, de rester toujours unis entre eux, soumis et obeissants a leur Mere, et reconnoissants de tous les soins et les peines qu'elle se donne pour eux, et en memoire de moi. je les prie de regarder ma Sœur comme une seconde Mere.

Je recomande a mon fils s'il avoit le malheur de devenir Roy, de songer qu'il se doit tout entier au bonheur de ses Concitoyens, qu'il doit oublier toute haine et tout ressentiment, et nommement tout ce qui a rapport aux malheurs et aux chagrins que j'eprouve; qu'il ne peut faire le bonheur des Peuples qu'en regnant suivant les Lois, mais en meme temps qu'un Roy ne peut les faire respecter, et faire le Bien qui est dans son cœur qu'autant qu'il a l'autorité necessaire, et qu'autrement etant lié dans ses operations et n'inspirant point de respect, il est plus nuisible qu'utile.

Je recomande a mon fils d'avoir soin de toutes les personnes qui m'etoient attachées, autant que les circonstances ou il se trouvera lui en donneront les facultés, de songer que c'est une dette sacrée que j'ai contractée envers les enfants ou les parents de ceux qui ont peri pour moi, et ensuite de ceux qui sont malheureux pour moi. je sçai qu'il y a plusieurs personnes de celles qui m'etoient attachées qui ne se sont pas conduittes envers moi comme elles le devoient, et qui ont meme montrés de l'ingratitude, mais je leur pardonne, (souvent dans les moments de troubles et d'effervescence on n'est pas le maître de soi) et je prie mon fils s'il en trouve l'occasion de ne songer qu'à leur malheur.

Je voudrois pouvoir témoigner ici ma reconnoissance à ceux qui m'ont montrés un veritable attachement et desinteressé. d'un coté si j'etois sensiblement touché de l'ingratitude et de la deloyauté de gens à qui je n'avois jamais temoignés que des bontés, à eux à leurs parents ou amis, de l'autre j'ai eu de la consolation à voir l'attachement et l'interest gratuits que beaucoup de personnes m'ont montrés je les prie d'en recevoir tous mes remerciments, dans la situation où sont encore les choses, je craindrois de les compromettre, si je parlois plus explicitement mais je recommande specialement à mon fils de chercher les occasions de pouvoir les reconnoitre.

Je croirois calomnier cependant les sentiments de la Nation, si je ne recommandois ouvertement à mon fils M.rs de Chamilly et Hue, que leur veritable attachement pour moi, avoit porté à s'enfermer avec moi dans ce triste sejour, et qui ont pensés en estre les malheureuses victimes. je lui recommande aussi Clery des soins duquel j'ai eu tout lieu de me louer depuis qu'il est avec moi comme c'est lui qui est resté avec moi jusqu'à la fin, je prie M.rs de la Commune de lui remettre mes hardes mes livres, ma montre ma bourse, et les autres petits effets qui ont eté deposés au Conseil de la Commune.

Je pardonne encore tres volontiers à ceux qui me gardoient, les mauvais traitements et les gênes dont ils ont cru devoir user envers moi. j'ai trouvé quelques ames sensibles et compatissantes, que celles là jouissent dans leur cœur de la tranquillité que doit leur donner leur façon de penser

Je prie M.rs de Malesherbes Tronchet et de Seze, de recevoir ici tous mes remerciments et l'expression de ma sensibilité, pour tous les soins et les peines qu'ils se sont donnés pour moi.

Je finis en declarant devant Dieu et pret à paroitre devant lui que je ne me reproche aucun des crimes qui sont avancés contre moi. Fait double à la tour du Temple le 25 Decembre 1792.

Louis

would reach the Assembly. "They applied to the Convention on the subject," he said to Chambon and Chaumette; "what was your decision?" "The council considered that it was not a matter for their determination," replied the attorney-general; "your counsel must take their own course."

The King, as he passed to the carriage, gave marked attention to the detachment of the cavalry of the Ecole Militaire, of the formation of which he had not been aware. The carriage, in which were Louis XVI., Chambon, Chaumette, and Coulombeau, proceeded under the escort of this small detachment of cavalry, which advanced at a rapid pace and without any order. The people, hastening from all directions to look at the procession, contributed to the general effect of confusion; the military posts along the Boulevards conceived some distrust, and their distrust soon assumed the form of an impression that Louis XVI. was escaping from his guards; cannons were levelled to prevent the presumed flight.* It was but a momentary alarm, the truth soon became evident; the deepest silence prevailed among the innumerable battalions ranged in lines from the Temple to the Manége. Among the immense throng of citizens assembled to behold this imposing spectacle of a king driven from his throne, several remarked that Louis XVI. had a less gloomy, or, rather, a more confident and easier, air than when he first appeared at the bar; he conversed familiarly with his attendants. As it was raining hard, and the wind blew strongly, the ex-monarch requested them to put down the blinds, but this request was refused, for fear of giving rise to discontent among the spectators.

During the whole march he manifested the greatest coolness and serenity. "This man," said Coulombeau, the next day, in giving an account to the Commune of the second transit of the King to the National Convention, "Yes, this man,

* Reports made to the Commune on the second transit of Louis XVI. to the Convention.—See "*Histoire du Dernier Règne de la Monarchie.*" Vol. I., page 262.

must be fanaticised, for it is impossible to explain his calmness, in any other way, seeing that he has so many causes of apprehension. When in the carriage he joined in the conversation, which was kept up tolerably well on literature, and especially on some of the Latin authors. He gave his opinion on every subject with great justness, and seemed to me to be very desirous of showing his erudition. Some one said that he did not like Seneca, because his love of riches ill-accorded with his vaunted philosophy, and that he could never pardon his palliation, before the Senate, of Nero's crimes. This reflection did not seem to affect him. In speaking of Livy, he said that he had occupied himself in composing long speeches, which had never, surely, been delivered anywhere but in the cabinet; for, added he, it is impossible for generals to pronounce them at the head of their armies. He remarked besides, still speaking of Livy, that his style was a great contrast to that of Tacitus."*

Some imprecations, devoting him to death, reached at intervals the ears of Louis XVI. They, doubtless, afflicted him, from the contrast they exhibited to the former blessings of his people; but they did not disturb for a moment the gracious calmness of his critical observations, to which his conductors listened with equal curiosity and astonishment.

Having reached the vestibule adjoining the hall of the legislative sittings, he found his counsel, who, on the refusal of the Commune, had gone to the president of the Convention, by whose order they gained admittance. He conversed with them walking, during the twenty-three minutes that the authorities made him wait. Malesherbes, Tronchet, and Desèze, kept at a respectful distance from him, and still used, in addressing him, the words Sire and Majesty. Treilhard, member of the Convention, suddenly entered, and furious at hearing the expressions used by the King's counsel, stopped short, before

* Reports made to the Commune on the second transit of Louis XVI. to the Convention.—See "*Histoire du Dernier Regne de la Monarchie.*' Vol. I,. p. 262.

them, exclaiming: "What makes you so rash as to pronounce in this place names which the Convention has proscribed?" "Contempt for you, and contempt for life!" replied Malesherbes.

Invited to proceed to the Assembly, Louis took his place between Malesherbes and Tronchet. It was a touching spectacle to behold this Prince assisted by these two old men, sustained by them, as it were, on the border of the abyss Desèze, standing in an attitude at once modest and dignified, pronounced, with the impressive energy which he derived from his veneration for the accused, that defence, which, "from its importance, its solemnity, its brilliancy, its re-echo in future ages, would have merited many months of meditation and effort, but for which he had only been allowed eight days."* It was a fine stroke, when, slowly surveying all the members of the Assembly, the orator exclaimed: "I seek among you judges, and I see among you only accusers!" The portion of the exordium which only referred to principles was received with favour; it was not so with respect to the refutation of the charges imputed to the accused. Some royalist deputies endeavoured to manifest their applause, but their approbation was overwhelmed by an opposing manifestation. The peroration, full of warmth, was calculated to produce a great effect; but at this phrase: "The people demanded liberty, and he gave it," a murmur of disapprobation was heard in the galleries, filled with the most ardent enemies of royalty, who had installed themselves there the evening before, and had there passed the night. However, despite the hostility of so prejudiced an audience, M. Desèze had more than once moved, by the force of truth, those who listened to him; but these favourable impressions had but short existence before the resolute antagonism of hatred. The speech of the young orator lasted nearly three hours. When he had finished, Louis rose, and pronounced in a tone, firm,

* M. Desèze's own expressions, while pleading.

though full of emotion, these words, the last he ever uttered in public :—

" Gentlemen, my defence has been laid before you ; I will not recapitulate it. In speaking to you, perhaps for the last time, I declare to you that my conscience bears me no reproach, and that my counsel have only told you the truth.

" I have never feared to have my conduct publicly investigated ; but my heart is deeply pained at finding in the indictment, the imputation that I wished to shed the blood of the people, and, above all, that the calamities of the 10th August are attributable to me.

" I must own, that the repeated pledges which I have given at all times of my life for the people, and the manner in which I have ever conducted myself, appeared to me proofs that I have never feared, on the contrary, to expose myself, that I might spare my people."

Who would not be struck with these simple and noble words : " I have never feared to have my conduct publicly investigated !" Do they not make it appear that it is no longer a judicial proceeding, in which Louis XVI. considers himself implicated, but an investigation into his conduct, which he himself permits all persons to institute? Does it not appear as though the speech just delivered by his counsel was not a defence, but an account of his conduct which he did not fear to render to his people ? Yes : these words of his, without offending the pride of his accusers, seem to raise up royal majesty from the humiliations to which it was subjected, and to cover, with a sacred ægis, the rights and the dignity of the crown.

As soon as the King had done speaking, one of the secretaries of the Convention presented to him a bunch of keys, that lay on the table, with the note written by Thierry, and the president asked him if he recognised the keys and the note. He replied, that he had given some keys to Thierry at the Feuillants, because, his drawers and boxes having been forced open, he had no further occasion for keys; but he did not know whether these were the same keys. The president asked him whether he had anything further to offer in his defence; he replied in the negative. The president told him he might withdraw, and he withdrew accordingly with his counsel.

Having quitted the Assembly, which he was never again to revisit, and returned to the hall for the reception of deputations, he took M. Desèze in his arms, and earnestly embraced him; then, fulfilling the office of a friend, he asked whether there were no means of enabling him to change his linen, for that he was in a complete bath of perspiration. M. Desèze entered an adjoining cabinet, and put on a clean shirt, which the King himself aired for him.*

The municipality now came to convey Louis XVI. back to the Temple. Let us hear Coulombeau narrate the circumstances.

"We got into the coach; he preserved the same calmness, the same serenity, as though he had been in an ordinary position. On passing before the depôt of the late *Gardes-Françaises*, he remarked, with astonishment, the splendid house that was being erected on the site.†

"A little further on, he said to me, jocosely, on observing that I had my hat on, 'The last time you came, you had forgotten your hat; you have been more careful on this occasion.' Perhaps he made this observation without any particular application; but perhaps, also, recalling to mind his old privileges, he wished to let me know that, in his opinion, I ought to remain uncovered in his presence. Chaumette nudged me with his elbow, at the remark, probably making in his own mind the same reflection upon it that I had made.

* This incident, related by M. Hue in his "*Dernieres Annèes de Louis XVI.*," p. 394, has been confirmed to me by Balza, a messenger to the Convention, who was present, and who brought the shirt.

† Between the Chaussée d'Antin and the Rue du Helder. It forms the corner of the Boulevard and of the Rue du Mont-Blanc, of which it is No. 2.

"Speaking of the indisposition of the attorney-general of the Commune, the conversation turned upon the hospitals of Paris. He made observations on the expense of these establishments, and said that it would be useful to institute one in each section, so that the poor might be better and more immediately cared for. He then asked several questions about Chaumette, what part of the country he came from, what were his occupations, and even what family he had.

"Next, seeing me, as in coming, salute several of my comrades whom I saw in the streets, he said to me: 'Are these persons whom you salute of your section?' 'No,' I replied, 'they are members of the late council-general, whom I am happy to see engaged in the preservation of order.' Thereupon he said to me that there was one of them who had not remained long in; he meant Lemeunié. 'When he was employed at the Temple,' he told me, 'a gesture of emotion had often escaped him on hearing musket shots—it seemed as if he was alarmed at them.' I replied that this was less the effect of fear than of surprise, at finding that the council's order against discharging muskets in the streets was not attended to. 'He died a very miserable death," answered he. I do not know whence he obtains such correct information, but, as you see, he is acquainted with almost every particular connected with the members of the council.

"After this he took up the mayor's box, and asked him whether the portrait engraved on one side was that of his wife; but, before the mayor could reply, the conversation was interrupted, by cries of 'Shut the windows! shut the windows!' ("*Fermez les fenêtres!*") He said 'This is abominable.' 'It is a precautionary measure,' replied Chaumette; 'orders have been given against opening the windows.' 'I thought they were shouting '*Vive Lafayette!*' returned he, 'which would have been absurd.' No doubt, at that moment, the mind of Louis Capet was running on the difference between the brilliant guard of Lafayette and his own escort, which was composed, in great part, of *sans-culottes*."*

It was five o'clock when the carriage re-entered the Temple. The municipal officers who accompanied the prisoner to the bar remitted him to the commissaries on duty, and retired.

Once more in his own apartment the King, well knowing the anxiety of his family, took up his pen, doubtless with a sorrowful reflection that the words thus hastily written by himself for their encouragement would not reach them before eight o'clock at night, though but the thickness of the ceiling separated them from him. This done, he passed into the dining-room, the meal there prepared, serving that day for dinner and supper in one. Malesherbes, Tronchet, and Desèze arrived just as the cloth was removed: he offered them some refreshments, which were accepted only by Desèze. The King renewed his expressions of gratitude, and they then went all together into the bed-room. As soon as they were alone, "Are you convinced now," said he to them, "that even before I was heard, my death had been sworn?" "No, Sire," replied Tronchet, "we are not at all convinced; and the Convention themselves do not know what the vote of the majority among them will be. When the King was gone, they gave orders that his defence should be signed by himself as well as by us, and we have therefore brought it with us; they gave orders that this defence and the King's speech, also to be signed by himself, should be laid on the table, printed, and circulated; and, lastly, they gave orders that the discussion of this subject should be carried on, to the exclusion of all other business, till judgment be given."

"Mere forms," returned Louis XVI.; "this day has deprived me of all hope, and that is the reason you find me so calm,—the struggle is over. They have sent me back to the Temple because time was required, in order to give a judicial

* Report to the Commune of the 27th December.—See *Histoire du Dernier Règne de la Monarchie*." Vol. I., p. 265.

appearance to their sentence, which is already fully resolved on. I did not, like Charles I., demand by what authority I was brought before them; but I may truly say, in the words of my predecessor:—'It is long since I have been deprived of all save that which is dearer to me than life—my conscience and my honour.'"

The speeches called for by the Convention were returned to them signed. Desèze had taken care to erase from his manuscript the words which, in his speech, had excited murmurs of dissatisfaction—"The people demand liberty, and he gave it." The Convention ordered this phrase to be re-inserted.

On this, the counsel for the defence made the following declaration:—"One of our number had erased this phrase from his manuscript, out of respect for the Convention, and because it had occasioned some murmuring in the galleries; but, that omission having become the subject of a decree, we deem it our duty to state that, in using the word 'gave,' our sole intention was to recall to mind that Louis had provided for the safety of France by convoking the states-general; and our idea was taken from the national decree of the 4th August, 1789, which proclaimed Louis the 'Restorer of the liberty of France.'"

At eight o'clock in the evening a note was conveyed, by an invisible thread, from the second to the third story of the tower.

During the day of the 27th December, Desèze transmitted to the King a certain number of copies of his defence, which he had had printed. A municipal guard, named Vincent, engaged to convey one secretly to the Queen. Of a kind and brave nature, this man had rendered more than one service already to the royal family, and this time he seized the moment, when the King was expressing his gratitude towards him, to ask for some little thing that had once been his as a remembrance. So, in the primitive ages of heroic Christianity, the martyrs of the faith, on the eve of their death, were entreated to bestow some part of their dress on those they left behind.

Louis took off his cravat, and presented it to this commissary.* Some minutes afterwards, the two municipal guards were speaking, in the King's presence, of Desèze's defence, and their own desire to read it. "I am very willing to let you have it," said the prince; "but may I not give a copy to Cléry too?" "We see no objection to that," replied the guards; and thus it was that the faithful Cléry also became possessed of a copy.

The King was right; he had studied the countenances of his accusers but too accurately on the preceding day. In fact, no sooner had he quitted the Assembly than his blood was demanded with such vehemence, and so greedily, that, to use the words of some of the journals of the period, the sanctuary of legislation seemed turned into an arena of gladiators. All that could be effected by those few who were horror-stricken at the precipitation with which the grave was already preparing for the victim, was to obtain the boon, that to the exclusion of all other business, his trial alone should be discussed. The motion, carried at the tribune, for reserving the right of appeal to the people after the verdict, was laid aside, under the pretext that to attempt this would be to court a civil war.

On that day, the conversation of the King and his three counsel was protracted until past nine o'clock. His mind and heart acquired fresh vigour from this confidential discourse. Louis XVI. regretted neither crown nor life; he lamented only the deplorable errors in public opinion, and the bloody calamities which would ensue. "What will become of you, my friends?" he said to them: "Perhaps it will be imputed to you as a crime that you have defended, and consoled me. What a situation is mine! I leave my people distracted, my country miserable, my family in captivity, my friends menaced with impending dangers! Will my blood alone suffice to appease the

* We reproduce this fact under the date of the 27th December, indicated by Cléry, although the register of the Commune does not name Vincent as having been on duty at the Temple till the 4th January. Vincent was a builder.

wrath of Heaven? How gladly would I make the sacrifice, if, by so doing, peace, concord, and justice were restored to France!"

On the 28th, 29th, and 30th December, those whom Louis called his friends came to the tower as usual; but, those three days were unmarked by any new incident, and no remarkable conversation is recorded in any of the memoirs which I have consulted

On the evening of the 31st, the conversation in the Temple turned less upon the fierce declamations continually taking place at the national tribunal, than upon a denunciation of the minister Roland, made, that same day, by Marat.

Mention was made, in particular, of the agitation going on throughout the whole country, and in neighbouring nations. Accounts from Geneva stated that the *sans-culottes* of that town had expelled the great and lesser council composing the government, and had formed themselves into popular committees. Tronchet had remarked: "Wise and durable reforms will never be the result of anarchy." "I attempted to make them by other means," returned Louis XVI.; "I took the first step by abolishing statute-labour, of my own accord, on my domains. I endeavoured to carry on my government, paying strict regard to economy and the correction of abuses. It is now six years since, on this same day, and almost at this very same hour, I convoked the first assembly of notables, to consult with them for the relief and liberty of my people.* My desire to do good was disbelieved, and my plans not understood or ill-executed. The time when I had hoped to see my country happy grows sadly gloomy round her: this year, at its close, sees her in commotion, and myself in prison! and what will that which begins to-morrow bring forth?" "Let us hope the best, Sire," replied the confidants of the royal prisoner, as they presented him the homage of their respect and devotion. "It is long," said the King, "since

* In fact, it was on the 31st December, 1786, that the King had convoked an assembly of notables, from which he expected the most favourable results.

I have lost all faith in happiness; I have every confidence in your zeal and affection, but I have no hope save in God."

On Tuesday, the 1st January, 1793, Cléry came into his master's room before it was light; approaching the bed, he, in a low tone, begged leave to offer him his ardent wishes for the termination of his misfortunes. "I thank you for your kind wishes," said Louis affectionately, stretching out his hand to him, which Cléry kissed and bathed with his tears. The King, as soon as he was up, pushed his room door half open, and begged a municipal guard to go and inquire from him after his family, and offer them his best wishes for the new year. The commissaries were moved by the tone in which these simple words were uttered, and which were rendered so touching by the King's situation. "Why does not the King ask to see his family?" said one of them to Cléry, when the King had gone back into his room; "now the interrogatories are over, there could be no more difficulty in the matter. Application should be made to the Convention."

The municipal guard who had gone up to the Queen's apartment came back, and informed Louis that his family thanked him for his good wishes, and presented theirs to him. "What a new year's day!" said the King.

The only persons in all France who were allowed to enter the Temple—Malesherbes, Tronchet, and Desèze—could not fail to come on such a day; but Louis XVI. would not allow them to remain long. "You have relations," he said to them, "friends, business, which require your presence to-day. I could never forgive myself were I to take you away from the duties you owe to society, and still less from your family ties." And when old Malesherbes endeavoured to resist: "As for you, my dear Malesherbes," said he, "I should be still more inexcusable were I to detain you; for, as you are more advanced in life than any of us, you have three generations of descendants to cherish you and expect your presence; do not make them angry with me. Adieu, adieu, then, till to-morrow!

And the generous prince, preferring the sadness of his own thoughts to any selfish amusement, spent the day alone, in a solitude that was yet surrounded by crowds of spies.

At night, while he was undressing, Cléry told him that he thought himself sure of the consent of the Convention, if the King would apply for permission to see his family. "In a few days more," replied Louis, "they will not refuse me that comfort. We must wait."

Next day, Wednesday, 2nd January, at about nine o'clock, Malesherbes, waiting in the council-room to be admitted into the tower, was looking through some periodical papers, when a municipal guard came to summon him. "How can you, the friend of Louis, venture to show him these writings, in which he is so constantly abused?" asked the guard. "Louis XVI.," replied Malesherbes, "is not like other men!" Indeed, vacillating as the King had shown himself, while on the throne, his fortitude and imperturbable composure ever since his first appearance at the bar of the Convention, excited in an eminent degree the admiration of his counsel. The frenzied declamations of the tribune, the sanguinary orgies of the press, shocked him, not as outbursts of hatred and menace against himself, but rather as a shame and a disgrace to humanity at large. He read all the speeches of the Convention relating to his trial, and frequently gave some of them to Cléry to read. "What do you think," he would say, "of Thirion's opinion, of Chazal's, of Raffron's, of Lakanal's?" "I have no words to express my indignation sufficiently,' Cléry replied; "but you, Sire, how can you read all this without horror?" "I see," returned Louis XVI., calmly, "how far the wickedness of men can go, and I never could have imagined there were such in the world." The King never went to bed without reading these various papers, and, having done so, he carefully burned them himself in the stove in his closet, that they might not compromise Malesherbes.

A journal of that same day had related the anecdote of

Louis's refusal to break his fast on one of the ember days,* representing the circumstance in a distorted and ludicrous light. "Read it," said the King to his valet, giving him the paper; "you are mentioned also; they call you a roguish wight, but, had they been able, they would certainly have preferred representing you as a hypocrite."

Meantime, however, public opinion seemed once more becoming favourable to the King; this was shown at night at the Théâtre Français, when the first representation of the "*Ami des Lois*" (Friend of the Laws), was given. The brave and noble author of this comedy, M. Laya, while dedicating it to the representatives of the nation, said, in his preface (in which, under the peculiar style of the period, we perceive sentiments most honourable to his heart): "How imposing is that mass of opinions, so energetically and unanimously expressed, for the sacred love of law, of order, and good morals! How overpowering is its weight for the open and secret enemies of liberty! You who calumniate Paris, seek her now! She is not to be found in tumultuous assemblies, where intrigue and crime reign triumphant, where the wildest and most ferocious carry the day; she is to be found in this concourse of citizens, devoted to liberty, but at the same time to laws without which liberty cannot exist,—kindling at its sacred name, burning with civic fire, their eyes and hearts steadfastly fixed upon that *friend of law*, who reflects in himself the sentiments of every individual of this mass."

At the Vaudeville was represented, at the same time, the play of "*La Chaste Suzanne.*" One of the characters says to the two old men, "How can you be accusers and judges at once?" These words, and other allusions to the trial of Louis XVI., were received with transports of applause. As the time for Louis's sentence drew near, popular emotion grew more and more vivid; agitation reigned everywhere, save in the heart

* Wednesday, 19th December.

of the accused. His three counsel coming into his room in the evening, he said to them: "Did you meet the White Lady, gentlemen, in the neighbourhood of the Temple?" "No, Sire," replied Malesherbes, in considerable surprise. "What," returned the King, with a smile, "do you not know that, according to popular tradition, whenever a prince of my race is about to die, a lady, clad all in white, wanders round the palace?"

On the 3rd of January, Madame Cléry came to see her husband, and told him of the happy reaction observable in the minds of men, of which the great success of the "*Ami des Lois*" was a fresh symptom.* She also gave him a message from several persons devoted to the royal cause, informing him that a considerable sum of money, deposited with M. Pariseau, a dramatic writer, and editor of a paper called the "*Feuille du Jour*," was at the King's disposal; begging Cléry to take his orders, and stating that, with the King's permission, the amount would be remitted to M. Malesherbes. Cléry informed his master accordingly. "Give my best thanks to those persons," answered the King, "but I cannot accept their generous

* We find another symptom of this disposition of mind in the continually increasing difficulty, experienced by the council-general in finding commissaries to take the Temple duty; far from that service being courted, it was shunned by all. As early as the 19th December, we read in the registers of the Commune, that a decree was made for sending an order to a commissary, named Favanne, who, having been selected for that duty, had failed to perform it. On the 31st of the same month, the council, "indignant at the obstinate and uncitizen-like refusal of Favanne, decrees that he be reprimanded, and the reprimand be made public by printing and handbills, and sent to the four sections." Lastly, during the sitting of the 31st January, after having deliberated on the difficulty of procuring persons for this service, the council-general decrees, that all such as have not served in the Temple for the space of a week be selected for that employment. A member moves that a fine be laid upon such as, having been named for the Temple, should fail to proceed thither; and this motion is carried. The procurator-syndic is appointed to bring the recusants before the police tribunal, and to pronounce their condemnation on the simple minutes of the trial; the amount of the fine not to exceed £10.

offer, for it would expose them to danger." "At least, then," said Cléry, "I entreat your Majesty to speak with M. Malesherbes on the subject." "I will see about it," said the King; which meant, "I shall do nothing of the kind;" for he always considered the welfare of others before his own. He did not mention the circumstance to Malesherbes, and matters rested as they were.

From the correspondence carried on nightly, Louis XVI. had learned that his daughter was ill, and he became very uneasy about her. Political considerations entirely disappeared before his paternal anxiety. At night, in his conversation with his three counsel, his words, as well as his thoughts, constantly reverted to his family. "In the midst of all my sorrows," said he, "Providence has given me many kind and tender consolations: much of the happiness of my life I owe to my children, my Queen, and my sister. I will not speak of my children, unfortunate as they are already,—at their age!" he continued, with emotion; "nor of my sister, whose life has been one unvaried course of devotion, courage, and affection. Her alliance was sought by Spain and Piedmont; and, at the death of Christina of Saxony, the canonesses of Piedmont wished to elect her their abbess;* but nothing could separate her from me; she clung to me in my misfortunes, as others attached themselves to my prosperity. But, I wish to speak on a subject that gives the keenest pain to my heart; I mean, the unjust opinion of the Queen entertained by my subjects. If they only knew her value, if they knew to what a degree of excellence she has attained since our misfortunes, they would revere and cherish her; but, for a long time back, by spreading calumnies among the people, her enemies and mine have been artful enough to turn the love, of which she was so long the object, to general hatred.

"You saw her," continued he, "when, scarcely more than

* July 24th, 1786. It was on her refusal that Mademoiselle Condé was elected.

a child, she first arrived at court. My mother and grand mother were no more, and my aunts, though they were still alive, had not the same right to control her. Day after day, placed by her position in the very centre of a brilliant court, beside a woman, whom intrigue alone supported there,* the Queen had an example of display and extravagance constantly before her eyes. What sort of opinion must she not necessarily have formed of her authority and her rights, with such manifold advantages centreing on her head?

"It was not proper for the Dauphiness to associate with the favourite; and, thus obliged to live partly in retirement, she adopted a mode of life free from constraint and etiquette, and she continued the same habits on the throne. These manners, foreign to the court, were too congenial to my natural taste for me to oppose their introduction. I did not then know how dangerous it is for monarchs to allow of too near an approach to their persons. Familiar intercourse lessens that respect which ought always to surround those who rule. At first, this departure from ancient customs was applauded by the multitude: afterwards, they made it a crime.

"The Queen desired female friends; the Princess de Lamballe was the lady most distinguished by her mistress's affection, and, throughout the course of our misfortunes, her conduct has fully justified the choice. The Countess Jules de Polignac was also a favourite; and she beame her friend. At the Queen's request, I granted some extraordinary favours to the Countess (since Duchess de Polignac) and her family, which excited the envy of others: the Queen and her friend are the objects of most unmerited censure.

"Not even her affection for her brother, the Emperor Joseph II., could escape the tongue of calumny. At first a vague report was spread, then it was published in the newspapers, and finally asserted from the tribune of the National

* Madame la Comtesse du Barri.

Assembly, that the Queen had bestowed numberless millions on the Emperor, and had transmitted them to Vienna; an atrocious calumny, which was triumphantly disproved by one of the deputies.

"The eager attempts made by the factions to slander the Queen and injure her character, have been made for no other purpose than to prepare the people for her destruction. Yes, my friends, her death is determined; for, were her life spared, they fear she would avenge my death. Unfortunate Princess! in espousing me she had the prospect of a throne; and now, what a future lies before her!" As he uttered these last words the King's eyes filled with tears, and his hand, as it dropped from his head, rested mournfully on that of M. de Malesherbes.

On Monday, the 7th of January, a municipal guard, named Ragoneau, finding himself for a moment alone with Louis XVI., said to the monarch, "I should be greatly distressed were my presence to disturb you much; I must do my duty: but, Sire, do not think I could ever wish to offer any insult to one who has been the sovereign of France, and who has it still in his power to render me happy." "I can do nothing for you," replied Louis XVI. "Excuse me, Sire," returned Ragoneau, in a low tone, and bowing respectfully; "the least thing that had once been yours would be most precious to me." Louis XVI. took his gloves and gave them to him. The scaffold was not yet erected, and, as we have related already, even the most trifling things that had belonged to the victim were regarded as sacred relics; and Ragoneau, in this division of the royal saint's garments, was happy in his share as Vincent had been in his.

Long after this period, Ragoneau, repeating this anecdote of his stay in the Temple, told with what sentiments he entered upon his service in the tower, and with what impressions he quitted it. "I had a horror of the tyrant," said he; "I had formed many resolutions to reproach him with his crimes; but every time I encountered the paternal glance of the tyrant, I felt my civism dispelled. Indeed, more than once, after hearing him speak, my eyes overflowed with tears. I learned to feel that I was not born to be a republican. I have kissed the tyrant's hand; and I would not give up his pair of gloves for all the treasures in the world!"

Some days passed without any occurrence worthy of re mark. The King employed himself almost all day in reading the speeches of the Convention. He perused them with the touching serenity of one who knows himself innocent, who has a witness in heaven, and who sees a bright prospect of reward in the future. Cléry had procured him a copy of the "*Ami des Lois*," the extensive circulation of which had excited the most violent opposition. Louis was affected by some generous words relating to his own situation. He said to Cléry, "It is more than a clever comedy, it is an act of great courage."

On Monday, the 14th January, the representation of this piece was the cause of a great disturbance at the Théâtre-Français. As the time for pronouncing the King's sentence approached, the public mind became more and more prone to seek aliment for its emotions. At the lines:—

"The welfare of the people is the only real law.—
Most true. But then your remedy, this salutary fear,
Can only be legitimate so long as 'tis sincere;
And even should the interest of the people seem to claim it,
If guiltless blood be shed for this, 'tis murder we must name it—"

a burst of applause resounded from every corner of the theatre; but this was instantly opposed by a thunder peal of groans, mingled with hisses. Hot words, threats, and mutual defiance were exchanged; but, the authorities interfering, the theatre was cleared.

The King had been very uneasy for several days about his daughter's health; the account he received every night at eight o'clock did not entirely satisfy him. On the 13th, as he was undressing, he said to Clery: "Try to find out my daughter's real state. I am afraid they conceal the extent of the malady from me, that I may not be pained."

On the 14th, Cléry was not able to hold any communication with Turgy. A municipal guard, who had been implored to make inquiries, brought back no intelligence, and this silence increased the anxiety of the unhappy father. His pre-occupation was remarked by his counsel at night, and he confided to them the cause. They promised to make a complaint to the council of this neglect; but about eight o'clock, the King, having left them for a few minutes, came in again, and, with difficulty restraining the joy of his heart, "Gentlemen," he said to them before they went away, "I have reflected upon the step you are about to take, and beg you to put it off until to-morrow—nay, not even to attempt it until you have seen me again."

As soon as they arrived next day he hastened to tell them, "I know now that my daughter is better, that Brunier is to see her, and the Queen's mind is at rest. God be praised!"*

On Tuesday, the 15th, a decree of the National Convention declared "Louis Capet guilty of conspiring against the liberty of the nation, and of having assailed the general security of the state." Another decree afterwards appeared, declaring that: "The sentence pronounced by the Convention should not be subjected to the sanction of the people." It was time! Time for his wife, for his sister, for his children, pining under a load of suspense, still more cruel than the certainty of a blow,

* "The council-general, on the report of the Temple committee, which mentions that Marie Antoinette wishes to call in the citizen Brunier, residing at Versailles, to see her daughter, who has been attacked by a serious indisposition,

"Decrees that Brunier be permitted to visit and bleed the daughter of Antoinette.

"The council-general decrees, further, that the citizen Brunier may hold no communication with Marie Antoinette, except in the presence of the commissary on duty, and that all the drugs administered be examined by the apothecary.

"Sitting of the council-general of the Commune,
"Sunday, 13th January, 1793."

irreparable as it was inevitable! Time for himself, whose hope was entirely gone! For a month he had rather defended his honour against the accumulated calumnies directed against it, than his life from the revolutionary scaffold. His actions, his writings, nay, even his thoughts, were imputed to him as crimes; but his true crime consisted in being King,—an unpardonable offence in the eyes of men who asserted that republicanism was of natural right. In fact, the Revolution immolated its conquered and captive foe, just as savages do their victims after a battle gained,—and this was what they called trying him! He had but three men and his own virtues to defend him against a host of pamphleteers, against myriads of spies, and a parliament of assassins.

Calm, amid the universal excitement and agitation, Louis XVI., formed for misfortune rather than for command, was as great in another way at the Temple as he had been at Versailles, and became more and more worthy of the throne as, one by one, he descended its steps, that bristled all around with bloody steel. He looked upon his sorrow as his true kingdom, and the nearer he approached the fatal close, the more radiant grew the brightness of his virtues and the glory of his martyrdom.

That evening he was visited as usual by his three counsel. M. Tronchet and M. Desèze apprised him of their necessary absence on the ensuing day.

During the morning of the 16th, M. Malesherbes passed some hours at the tower, while his colleagues were at the Convention. As he went away, he said to the King, that he would let him know as to the nominal appeal so soon as he should learn the result. "I have one more request to make to you," said Louis XVI.; "it is, that you will beg M. de Firmont, from me, to hold himself in readiness; the day is fast approaching!" Thus, while M. de Malesherbes, thinking of his King, felt all his thoughts cling fast to earth, the King's turned to Heaven alone, for he had bidden adieu to life!

Malesherbes was on his way to the Convention: he met an Englishman of his acquaintance, who said to him:—"What reassures all good citizens, is that the most unfortunate of kings has the best of men as his defender." "If Louis XVI. fall," replied Malesherbes, "the defender of the most virtuous of kings will be the most unfortunate of men!"

At six o'clock in the evening, four municipal guards (among whom was Du Roure) came into the room, and read aloud to the King a decree, the substance of which was, "That he was to be guarded, day and night, by four commissaries, who were never to let him out of their sight; and that two of them should pass the night at his bed-side."

"Is my sentence pronounced?" said Louis XVI. "Faith, I know nothing about it," replied Du Roure, sitting down in Louis's elbow-chair (for the King had remained standing); "I don't trouble myself with what goes on at the Convention; but I think I heard they were still at the nominal appeal."

Some minutes after M. de Malesherbes returned; he informed the King that the sitting was in fact not yet over, and that it would probably be prolonged till far into the night.

At this moment, the chimney of a room inhabited by the wood-carrier belonging to the château of the Temple took fire; a considerable crowd of people entered the court, and a municipal guard, looking quite scared, came and ordered M. de Malesherbes to retire immediately. M. de Malesherbes withdrew accordingly, after having promised the King to return and inform him of his sentence, whenever it should be given.

"What alarms you so much?" asked Cléry of the municipal guard. "They have set fire to the Temple," replied the commissary vehemently; "it has been done on purpose to save Capet in the confusion; but I have had the walls surrounded by a strong guard." It was soon, however, ascertained that the fire was out, and that it owed its origin to accident alone.

By Thursday morning, the 17th January, all Paris knew that the work of iniquity was complete; but as yet the victim himself was not aware of his doom, and the melancholy task of acquainting him with it devolved upon M. de Malesherbes. It was nine o'clock in the morning when the three defenders of the King reached the Temple. M. de Malesherbes entered first, and Cléry going to meet him—"All is lost!" said the old man to him; "the King is condemned to death!"

Louis XVI. was seated with his back to the door, his elbows resting on the table, and his face covered with his hands; the noise made by the entrance of his counsel roused him from his reverie. He rose to receive them, and said, "For the last two hours I have been taxing my memory to find whether, in the course of my reign, I ever voluntarily gave my subjects a just cause of complaint against me. Well! I can swear to you, in all sincerity of heart, as a man who is soon to appear before God, that I always desired the welfare of my people, and that I never formed a single wish opposed to it!"

The terrible duty which his three visitors had to perform, the contrast between the mild words of the King and the sentence of death they must announce to him, filled them with anguish to the very innermost core. Malesherbes could not contain his grief, and throwing himself at the King's feet, remained some moments, his voice so choked with sobbing that he could not articulate a word. Louis XVI. raised him, and warmly embracing him; "I expected what your tears announce," said he, "compose yourself, then, dear Malesherbes. It is better, yes, far better to be relieved at last from such suspense. If you love me, instead of mourning for it, you will not envy me the only refuge now remaining." "Sire, all hope is not yet lost; they are going to deliberate as to a delay; and, even if this be refused, we have still the appeal to the nation. The nation is generous, and you a good prince!" Louis motioned with his head that he expected nothing from these two last resources. "No, no!" he said, "there is no hope whatever now. The nation is misled, and I am ready to sacrifice myself for it. May the blood for which they thirst so much save the people from all the horrors I fear for them!" The King made his counsel sit down, and Malesherbes, having recovered himself, gave him an account of the result of the nominal appeal. Accusers, personal enemies, ecclesiastics, laymen, absent deputies—all had voted: yet, notwithstanding this violation of all legal forms, those who had voted for the King's death—some because they really thought him guilty, and others merely as a political measure—had obtained a majority of five voices only; some had declared for death, with a stipulation for delay. A second nominal appeal on this question had been decreed, and it was to be hoped that the voices of those who had wished to delay the King's death, joined with the suffrages against the capital punishment, might make up a majority. But round the doors of the Assembly were crowds of assassins, devoted to the deputies of Paris; and the revolutionary mob, inured as it was to crime by every species of excess, and steeled to murder by the massacres of September, terrified by their cries, and threatened with their weapons, whoever refused to become their accomplice in guilt; and, whether from stupor or indifference, Paris either dared not or would not make any attempt to save Louis XVI., who was thus left to perish by the fury of one party and the cowardice of the other.

Nevertheless, Malesherbes observed to the King: "As I was leaving the Convention I was accosted by several persons, in the corridors leading to the hall, and was assured by them, that the King should yet be snatched from the hands of his murderers by some of his faithful subjects, or they would perish in the attempt with their royal master." "Do you know them?" asked Louis. "No, Sire; but I could find them if necessary." "Well, then, try to do so, and assure them of my gratitude for their zeal; but any attempt in my favour would only expose their lives without saving mine. I would not make use of force when my doing so might have preserved my crown and my life; would I now wish the blood of Frenchmen to be shed for me?"

"At least," said Tronchet, "the King cannot prevent our making use of every means consistent with law; and we must therefore beg him to write and sign this declaration with his own hand." Thus urged by the entreaties of his three friends, Louis copied the following lines, which Tronchet had just prepared at a corner of the table, and affixed his signature to them.

"I owe it to my honour, I owe it to my family, not to submit to a sentence which lays a crime to my charge of which I know myself innocent: and, therefore, I declare that I appeal to the nation itself from the sentence given by its representatives. By this present writing I give my counsel the special charge, and depend expressly on their fidelity, to acquaint the National Convention with this appeal by every means in their power, and to demand that it be mentioned in the minutes of its sitting.

"Given at the Temple tower, this 16th January, 1793.*

"LOUIS."

Even after having written these lines, Louis XVI. seemed to hesitate whether or not to entrust them to his counsel. "It is much more for the people's interest," said Desèze, "than for the King's, that we desire this declaration." "No," returned the King, with a benevolent smile, impossible to describe, "you desire to have it much more for my interest than for the people s; but I give it to you much more for their sake than for my own—the sacrifice of my life is of so little consequence compared with their glory or welfare! And do not think,

* The reader will observe it is dated the 16th, and not the 17th. As sentence was pronounced at eleven o'clock the preceding night, did Tronchet wish to affix the same date to this declaration, or was it merely as error, very likely to be made at a time when all his attention was engrossed by matters of such moment?

gentlemen, that the Queen and my sister will display less fortitude and resignation than myself. Death is far preferable to their lot!"

The three counsel rising to go, Louis detained M. de Malesherbes, and, as the municipal guards made no objection, he took him into his closet, and, closing the door, remained nearly an hour alone with him. When he parted from the King, Malesherbes could not restrain his tears. "Kind-hearted old man," said Louis XVI. to him, pressing his hand; "do not weep for me; we shall meet again in a better world. I regret leaving a friend such as you are. Adieu! As you go out of my room, command yourself, for it is necessary. Consider that you will be observed." Then, having conducted him once more to the outer door, he said to him again: "Come back early this evening, for I want to see you frequently at tnis critical moment. Adieu! Adieu!"

Malesherbes withdrew, overwhelmed with grief, and no less convinced than his colleagues, that they had all seen the King for the last time.

"That good old man's sorrow affected me very much," said Louis XVI., as he re-entered the room, where Cléry was waiting for him. Ever since he had heard of the fatal sentence, Cléry had been suffering from an aguish trembling. However, he had made every preparation for the King to shave himself. The Prince put on the lather. "Standing before him," says Cléry, "I was holding his bason, and, as I was obliged to check my grief, I had not yet ventured to look at my unfortunate master; but now, as I raised my eyes to his face, my tears burst forth in spite of myself. I do not know whether the state in which I was, recalled to the King's mind his situation, but a sudden paleness overspread his countenance, his nose and ears becoming white in a moment. At this sight, I felt my knees failing beneath me. The King perceiving that I was turning faint, took hold of my two hands, and, pressing them warmly, said to me in a low voice: 'Come, come! a little more courage!' He was observed. I expressed my distress by the mute language of glance and sign. He appeared to understand me, and his countenance brightening again, he shaved with great composure, after which I dressed him.

"His Majesty remained in his room till his dinner-hour, either reading, or walking up and down. During the evening I saw him go towards his reading-closet, and followed him thither. 'You have heard the account of my sentence.' said the King to me. 'Ah! Sire,' replied I, 'let us hope for a delay; M. de Malesherbes does not think it will be refused.' 'I have not any hope,' returned the King; 'but I am much distressed that my relative, M. d'Orléans, should have voted for my death. Read this list,' and he gave me the list of the votes which he held in his hand. 'The public,' said I, 'murmur loudly. Dumouriez is at Paris, and it is said he brings the protest of his army against your Majesty's trial. The people are shocked at the conduct of M. d'Orléans; and there is a report that the ministers of foreign powers intend to go in a body to the Assembly. Besides, it is confidently asserted that the Convention are afraid of a popular insurrection.' 'I should be very sorry were it to take place,' replied the King; 'it would but furnish fresh victims. I do not fear death, but I cannot contemplate without a shudder the cruel fate to which I leave my family, the Queen and our unfortunate children; and those faithful servants who have not deserted me, those aged men who had no other means of support than the trifling pensions I allowed them—who will help them now? I see my people given up to anarchy, becoming the prey of every faction; crime succeeding crime, and protracted dissensions desolating France!' Then, after a moment's silence, he went on: 'Oh, my God! was this the reward I should have received for all my sacrifices? Did I not try by every means to secure the welfare of my people?' As he uttered these words he pressed my hands, and, filled with pious reverence for the martyr-king, I bathed his own with my tears. I was compelled to quit him in this state.

"The King waited in vain for M. de Malesherbes. In the evening he asked me whether he had sought for admission. I had made the same inquiry of the commissaries who had all replied in the negative."

One would have thought the strange prophetic spirit, sometimes accorded to the dying, had been given by Heaven to the King, as his last hour drew near. He saw the abyss about to yawn for France beneath the scaffold raised for him; dissension, crime, and anarchy seemed to him as ghastly reapers, sickle in hand, ready to enter the field of desolation that bore the name of France; and the prospect of the dreadful future he left to his country embittered the last moments he had to pass on earth.

On Friday, the 18th, the King's counsel did not make their appearance at the tower.* Louis XVI. was especially disturbed at the absence of M. de Malesherbes. In an old

* Commune de Paris, 18th January, 1793.

Extract from the register of the deliberations of the council-general:—

"In reference to the account given by citizens Garrin, Yon, and Bruneau, the commissaries named in the sitting of to-day, that they presented themselves this morning at the National Convention, and persisted in demanding admission to the bar, but without being permitted to do so:

"The council-general, taking into consideration that the office of counsel to Louis Capet ceased to exist the moment sentence was pronounced by the Convention; that, by a decree of the executive authorities of this day, the municipality of Paris are expressly charged to take every precautionary measure; and that it is of importance for public tranquility that Louis Capet should have no communication beyond the walls:

"The procurator of the Commune having been heard, and without stopping to discuss his requisition: decrees that all communication between Louis Capet and his ex-counsel be suspended, and directs its president to inform the National Convention of the present decree:

"Also decrees, that the commissaries employed in the Temple be directed to enter upon a diligent search through the apartments of Louis Capet.

(Signed) "BEAUDRAIS, Vice-President.
"COULOMBEAU, Secretary-Registrar."

"*Mercure de France*" that had come into his hands, he met with a riddle, which he gave Cléry to guess. Cléry tried in vain to find out the word. "What, cannot you make it out?" said the King; "yet it is very applicable to me at this moment, for the word is *sacrifice*. However, these are not the books I ought to study now; go, and bring me from the library the volume of the History of England that contains the account of Charles I.'s death." On this occasion, Cléry learned that, since his entering the Temple, Louis had read two hundred and fifty volumes.

The evening was long and sad. The King received accounts as usual from his family, but the kind messages exchanged every night between the two stories, were turned to expressions of the deepest grief. The town-crier had apprised the Queen of the King's condemnation, and wife, sister, and children, were all overwhelmed with despair.

The King mentioned the name of M. de Malesherbes several times, and Cléry took the liberty of observing to him, that he could not be deprived of his counsel except by a decree of the Convention; that the council of the Commune could not take upon it to deny them access to the Temple, and that he would do well to complain. Always patient and resigned, Louis only replied, "Let us wait till to-morrow."

On Saturday, the 19th, at nine o'clock in the morning, a municipal (his name was Gobeau) entered with a paper in his hand, and accompanied by Mathey, door-keeper of the tower, carrying writing materials. The commissary informed the King that he had orders to make an inventory of the furniture and other effects. By the way in which the King was treated, it would have been supposed he was no more; they came into his room as if it were the chamber of death, to make out an inventory of everything. Louis XVI., leaving Cléry with the two visitors, retired into his turret to read the account of Charles I.

Under the pretence of making an inventory, the municipal guard began to search with the most minute care, to make sure that no weapon or instrument of danger was concealed in the rooms. In order to open the little desk in which the King kept his papers locked, and of which he had the key, they were obliged to disturb him. He came, without displaying a single mark of opposition, opened all the drawers himself, taking out and showing every paper in succession. There were the parcels of money at the bottom of one of the drawers. Gobeau desired to see the contents. "The money is not mine," said the King, "it belongs to M. de Malesherbes; and it was to give it him that I got it ready." We have said elsewhere, that, as early as the end of December, the prince had had the precaution to write on each of these parcels: "To be given to M. de Malesherbes."

When the search was over in the bed-room, it began in the turret, and the King, coming back into his room, drew near the fire. At that moment Mathey was standing just in front of the fire-place, with his back to the fire, squaring his elbows, and holding his coat-tails back. Thus Louis XVI. could only warm himself, and that but little, by standing at one of the sides. The door-keeper remaining ostentatiously immoveable in the same place, the King said to him with dignity, "Move aside!" Mathey retired, and the municipal guards, having completed their investigations, withdrew also.

In the course of the evening, the King desired the commissaries to demand the reasons of the Commune for refusing his counsel admission to the tower, adding, that he wished to speak with M. de Malesherbes at least. They promised to mention it, but one of them confessed that they had been forbidden to carry any request of Louis to the council-general, unless it were written and signed by his own hand. "And why," replied Louis XVI., "was I for two whole days left in ignorance of this change?" He immediately took up his pen, and wrote the following note:

"I request the commissaries of the Commune to transmit

my complaints to the council: 1st, as to the decree of Friday, which directs that I am never to be lost sight of, by day or by night; it must be evident that, in my situation, it is distressing not to be allowed to be alone, and to have the tranquillity necessary for me to collect myself, and that at night repose is requisite; 2nd, as to the decree which prevents my seeing my counsel. I was permitted by a decree of the National Assembly to have free intercourse with them, without any limit being assigned for the indulgence, and I am not aware of that decree having been repealed.

"LOUIS."

This note, though it was given immediately to the commissaries, was not carried to the Commune till the next morning (Sunday, 20th January).* Hébert, a witness of what took place at the Temple, remarked to the council that this letter was written before his sentence was announced to him; and that, in consequence, no attention should be paid to it.†

* See the reports made to the council-general of the Commune.

† Ibid.

BOOK TENTH.

THE REGICIDE.

Notification of the decrees of the Convention—The King's letter—Hébert's Account—The Abbé Edgeworth at the Temple—Last meeting of the King with his family—Oath required by the King of his son—Last night—Mass at the Temple—Morning of the 21st January—Departure from the Temple—Appearance of Paris—The Place de la Révolution—The Scaffold—Last words of the King—His head shown to the people—Letter of the executioner, Sanson—Paris after the execution—Remarks—The Abbé Le Duc demands the body of Louis XVI.—Interment.

On Sunday, the 20th January, as soon as he was dressed, Louis XVI. asked the municipal guards whether his demand had been transmitted to the council-general of the Commune, and they assured him that it had been taken immediately after it was written. At about ten o'clock, he said to Cléry, who had approached him: "I do not see M. de Malesherbes!" "Sire," replied Cléry, "I have just heard that he has presented himself several times at the door, but has always been refused access to the tower."

"I shall soon know the reason," returned the King, "why he is refused admission. The Commune has most likely decided upon my letter."* Alas! it was more than three days since the Commune had closed the doors of the Temple; and, to give a legal appearance to this rigorous measure, they had obtained the sanction of the National Convention.

* Reports made to the council-general of the Commune, upon the measures taken for the execution of the decrees of the Convention, which sentenced Louis XVI. to death.

It was in their power still to deceive Louis XVI., but not to provoke him. Composed, though unhappy, he walked up and down his room for a few moments, and then returning to the study of Charles I., he wrote, and otherwise employed himself all the morning.

Two o'clock had just struck, when the door was suddenly opened; it was the executive council. Twelve or fifteen persons presented themselves at once: Garat, minister of justice; Lebrun, minister for foreign affairs; Grouvelle, secretary to the council; the president and the procurator-general, syndic of the department; the mayor and the deputy-attorney of the Commune; the president and public accuser of the criminal tribunal. Santerre, who preceded them, said to Cléry—"Announce the executive council." The King, who had heard a great stir, had risen and advanced several paces, but, at sight of this train of people he stopped, and stood still, in a most dignified attitude, between the door of his room and that of the entrance. Garat, with his hat on his head, began: "Louis, the National Convention has directed the provisional executive council to acquaint you with the decrees of the 15th, 16th, 17th 19th, and 20th January. The secretary to the council will read them to you."* Then Grouvelle, opening a paper, read, in a feeble and trembling voice:—

DECREES OF THE NATIONAL CONVENTION

OF THE 15TH, 16TH, 17TH, 19TH, AND 20TH JANUARY.

"ARTICLE 1ST.

"The National Convention declares Louis Capet, last King of the French, guilty of conspiring against the liberty of the nation, and of assailing the general security of the state.

* Report to the National Convention by the minister of justice.

"ARTICLE 2ND.

"The National Convention decrees that Louis Capet suffer the punishment of death.

"ARTICLE 3RD.

"The National Convention declares null and void the act of Louis Capet, brought to the bar by his counsel, in the form of an appeal to the nation from the sentence pronounced against him by the Convention; and decrees that any person whatsoever attending to the same be prosecuted and punished, as guilty of assailing the general safety of the Republic.

"ARTICLE 4TH.

"The provisional executive council will notify the present decree in the course of the day to Louis Capet, and will take all measures of police and precaution necessary to insure its execution within twenty-four hours* of its notification, and will give

* We read in the *Moniteur Universel*, of the 21st January, 1793:—

"Proclamation of the provisional executive council of the 20th January.

"The provisional executive council after deliberating on the measures to be taken for the execution of the decrees of the National Convention of the 15th, 17th, 19th, and 20th January, 1793, decrees the following arrangements:

"1st. The execution of Louis Capet will take place to-morrow, Monday, 21st.

"2nd. The place of execution will be the Place de la Révolution (formerly the Place de Louis-Quinze), between the pedestal and the Champs-Elysées.

"3rd. Louis Capet will leave the Temple at eight o'clock, A.M., so that the execution may take place at noon.

"4th. There will be present at the execution some commissaries of the department of Paris, some of the municipality, and two members of the criminal tribunal. The secretary-registrar of that tribunal will give an exact account of the proceedings, and the said commissaries and members of the tribunal will come, as soon as the execution is over, and report the same to the executive council, which will remain sitting during the whole of that day.

"Provisional Executive Council."

an account of the whole to the National Convention immediately after the execution."

"During the reading of the decree," says Cléry, "no change was visible in the King's countenance; only I observed that, when the words 'conspiring against' were pronounced, in the 1st Article, an indignant smile curled the corner of his lips; but at the words, 'will suffer the punishment of death,' a look of angelic mildness, as he regarded those around him, seemed to say, the word is void of terror to the innocent."

The King, moving towards Grouvelle, took the decree out of his hand, folded it, and placed in his pocket-book; then drawing a paper from the same pocket-book, he said to Garat: "M. le Ministre de Justice, I beg you will forward this letter for me to the National Convention immediately." The minister appearing to hesitate, the King added: "I will read it to you;" and, without any perceptible change in his voice, he read as follows:

"I demand a delay of three days, to prepare myself to appear before God. During that time I request permission to hold free communion with the person whom I shall point out to the commissaries of the Commune, and that the latter be not exposed to fear or molestation for this act of charity to me.

"I request to be freed from the constant watch kept over me for several days by the Commune. During this period I request permission to see my family whenever I wish, and without witnesses. I am very anxious that the National Convention should take the ultimate destiny of my family under their immediate consideration, and permit them to retire unmolested to whatever place that Assembly may think proper to direct.

"I recommend to the kind care of the nation all the persons who were attached to me. Many of them had invested their whole fortune in their places, and now, having lost their situations, must be in actual want; as must be others who had no means of support beyond their salaries. Among those who were allowed pensions, there are many old men, women, and children, who had no other subsistence whatever.

"At the Temple tower, 20th January, 1793.

"Louis."

Garat took the King's letter, assuring him that he would take it immediately to the Convention. As he went out, Louis XVI. said to him: "Sir, if the Convention grant my request to see the person I wish, here is his address." Then opening his pocket-book again, he took out a paper, on which were written these words: "M. Edgeworth de Firmont, 483, Rue du Bac." The King gave the address to a municipal guard, and then drew several paces back; and the minister retired with those who had accompanied him thither.*

In order to exhibit the scene we have just presented to our readers in its full grandeur, we need only have recourse to a testimony which will not be doubted, that of Louis XVI.'s enemies themselves. We may remark, that almost all the pamphleteers and journalists, notwithstanding some assertions collected for the purpose of steeling their readers' hearts against pity, rendered justice to the fortitude with which this prince supported the last terrible trials of that long career of misfortune. We give the account by Hébert, deputy attorney-general of the Commune.

"I wished to be among those who were to be present at the reading of Louis's sentence. He listened to it with a marvellous coolness; and when it was over, he desired to see his family, a confessor,—in short he requested whatever could tend to solace his parting hour. There was so much unction, so much dignity, nobleness, and grandeur in his words and bearing, that I could not contain myself, and tears of rage moistened my eyelids,—in his glance, and in his manner, was something visibly supernatural. I retired, vainly endeavouring to restrain the tears that flowed in spite of every effort to the

* Report to the Convention by the minister of justice.

contrary, and firmly resolved that my part in the proceedings should terminate there. I opened my feelings to a colleague, whose firmness was no more proof than my own, and said to him with my usual frankness: 'My good friend, the priests who belong to the Convention and voted for his death, although the sanctity of their character should have prevented their doing so, made up the majority by which we are delivered from the tyrant. Well, then, let it be also by constitutional priests that he is led to the scaffold, for only constitutional priests could have ferocity of nature sufficient to perform such a deed.' Accordingly my colleague and I contrived that the two priests who were municipal guards, Jacques Roux and Jacques-Claude Bernard, should be selected to conduct Louis to his death."*

What a confession, and what a page in history, is this testimony of "Père Duchêne!"

Still, we believe in this emotion of pity expressed by Hébert; human nature is thus formed: at the very time when it is sunk to the lowest depth of iniquity, it is occasionally susceptible of an involuntary and invincible sentiment of admiration, on beholding the sublime picture of that virtue for which it was itself created. We believe in the sincerity of Hébert's resolution to terminate then his public life; but revolutions do not thus give up the men who have embarked in them. Those who will not withdraw when they ought, are no longer able to do so when they would. When once Revolution has laid her hand on the shoulder of a man, and marked him with her seal, she never relinquishes her prey.

The King desired to be alone. He walked up and down

* "Conformably with the arrangement made by the proclamation of the provisional executive council, the council decrees that two commissaries be named to be present at Louis Capet's execution. It was proposed to choose them by lot, but this motion, at first adopted, was afterwards rejected, and Jacques Roux and Jacques-Claude Bernard were named with one voice by the council for this service.

"Council-general of the Commune, Sunday, 20th January, 1793."

for a few moments in his room, then passed into that of the commissaries, the door of which had remained open, and without taking any particular direction, moved all about the room. His glance having fallen on the Declaration of the Rights of Man, he said to Mercereau, pointing with his finger to the 8th article: "If this article had been attended to, much disorder would have been avoided." "True," replied the stonecutter. "Sir," said Louis XVI., "while I am waiting for the return of the minister of justice, I desire leave to go upstairs to my family."

"We have no orders," replied Mercereau. "It seems to me, Sir," returned the King, "that what the law does not forbid is permitted to take place; if I have a right to see my wife and children, why do you assume that of preventing my doing so?" Saying these words, he went back into his room. Cléry had remained there, leaning against the door as he stood with his arms folded, as it were deprived of motion. Louis XVI., approaching him, said: "Cléry, ask for my dinner." Cléry obeyed, and a few moments after was summoned into the dining-room by two municipal guards, who read him a decree, of which the substance was as follows:—"That Louis should be allowed to use neither knife nor fork at his meals; that a knife might be entrusted to his valet, who should cut up his bread and meat for him in presence of two commissaries, and after this was done, that the knife must be taken away." The two municipals desired Cléry to acquaint the King with this decree, but he refused to do so.

As he went into the dining-room, Louis saw the basket in which was the Queen's dinner. "Why did they keep my family an hour waiting?" asked he: "the delay must have made them uneasy." He sat down to table. "I have no knife," said he, looking at Cléry. On this, a municipal, named Minier, informed him of the decree. "Do they think me so cowardly as to attempt my own life?" said the King· "they have imputed crimes to me, but knowing myself innocent of having committed them, I shall die without fear. Would that my death might secure the welfare of France, and prevent the miseries that I foresee!"

Still the same prophetic view of the future, so terribly realised in after days! There was a deep silence; Louis XVI. ate but little, breaking his bread with his fingers, and cutting the beef with his spoon: his dinner lasted only a few minutes.

Garat had made no delay, however; he had communicated the last wishes of Louis XVI. to his colleagues; he had invoked the decision of the Convention, and had sent for the priest, whose presence had been requested.

'Several days had passed away," says the Abbé Edgeworth, "since my interview with Malesherbes, and hearing nothing further, I indulged the hope that the King would only be banished, or that, at least, his fate would be deferred for some time; when, on the 20th January, at four o'clock in the afternoon, a stranger called on me, and presented to me a note containing these words: 'The executive council, having business of the highest importance to communicate to citizen Edgeworth de Firmont, invites him to come instantly to its sitting.' The stranger added that he had orders to accompany me, and that a carriage waited for us in the street. I went with him to the Tuileries, where the council held its meetings. I found all the ministers assembled. Consternation appeared in their countenances. As soon as I entered they arose, and all surrounded me with eagerness. The minister of justice first addressed me. 'Are you,' said he, 'the citizen Edgeworth de Firmont?' I replied that I was. 'Louis Capet,' continued the minister, 'having expressed to us his desire to have you near him at his last moments, we have sent to you to know whether you consent to the service he requires of you.' I replied that, since the King had signified his wishes, and named me, it became my duty to attend him. 'Then,' pursued the minister, 'you will go with me to the Temple, whither I will conduct you!" And immediately taking a bundle of papers from the table, he whispered a moment with the other ministers, and, going out in haste, ordered me to follow him. An escort of horse waited for us at the door, with the minister's carriage, into which I got, and he followed me. At this time, all the Catholic clergy of Paris were dressed like other citizens, so that I was not in a clerical dress; but, recollecting what I owed to the King, who had not been accustomed to such a costume, and to religion itself, which received for the first time a sort of homage from the new government, I thought I ought, on this occasion, to resume the exterior marks of my station; at least, to make the attempt appeared to me a duty. I mentioned it to the minister before we quitted the Tuileries, but he rejected my proposition in terms that prevented my further insisting upon it, though without using any offensive language towards me.

"Our drive to the Temple passed in gloomy silence. Two or three times however, the minister made an attempt to break it; he drew up the carriage windows and exclaimed: 'Great God! with what a dreadful commission am I charged! What a man!' added he, speaking of the King: 'what resignation! what courage! No; human nature alone could not give such fortitude; he possesses something beyond it.' Such expressions gave me an excellent opportunity for speaking some unwelcome truths, but I hesitated an instant what course I should pursue; for I reflected that my first duty was to afford the King the religious consolation he had so earnestly desired, and that by giving vent to the indignation the conduct of my companion and his associates had inspired me with, I should probably be forbidden to approach my royal master. I therefore resolved on absolute silence. The minister seemed to comprehend my motives, and said not a word during the remainder of our drive. We arrived at the Temple, and the first gate was instantly opened to us; but when we reached the building which separates the court-yard from the garden, we were stopped, and before we could proceed, it was necessary that the commissaries of the tower should come and examine us, and ascertain our business; even the minister seemed subject to this form. We waited for the commissaries near a quarter of an hour, without speaking to each other; at last they appeared; one of them was a young man of about seventeen or eighteen. They saluted the minister as an acquaintance; he told them in a few words who I was, and the nature of my mission; they made a sign to me to follow them, and we crossed the garden all together to enter the tower. Here the scene became horrible beyond description; the door of the tower, though very narrow and very low, opened with a terrible noise; it was loaded with iron bolts and bars. We passed through a hall, filled with guards, into a still larger hall, which appeared from its shape to have been once a chapel. There the commissaries of the Commune, who had the custody of the King, were assembled. I could not distinguish in their countenances that embarrassment or consternation which had struck me in the ministers. There were about twelve of them, mostly in the dress of Jacobins. Among them was Mercereau, who, when he came on duty the evening before, had said: 'Everybody refused to come, but I would not give up this day's enjoyment for any money;" and a young man, named Bodson, aged twenty-two, but who looked scarcely seventeen, so soft and feminine was his beardless face, had exclaimed: 'And I, too, asked to come to the Temple, to see the grimace he'll make.'

"Their air, their manners, their *sang-froid*, all denoted them to be men of desperate minds, who did not shrink from the contemplation of the blackest crimes.

"But, in justice, I ought to say, that this is not a portrait of them all; and I thought I could discover some who had been induced, from the meekness of their character, to associate with the rest. Whatever might be their respective feelings, they were all taken indiscriminately by the minister into a corner of the apartment, where he read to them, in a low voice, the papers which he had brought from the Tuileries. When he had done, he turned suddenly to me, and desired me to follow him, but this the council opposed by acclamation. Again they assembled in a corner of the hall, deliberating some time in whispers; the result was that one half of the assembly accompanied the minister, who went up stairs to the King, while the other half remained to guard me. When the doors were carefully closed, the oldest of the commissaries approached me with a polite but embarrassed air, spoke of the terrible responsibility he was under, and begged a thousand pardons for the liberty he was obliged to take. I guessed that this preamble was to end in my being searched, so I anticipated him by saying, that since the reputation of M. de Malesherbes could not excuse him from this formality, I could not flatter myself that when I came to the Temple an exception would be made in my favour. I assured him that I had nothing about me that could be suspected, but added that he was welcome to satisfy himself. Notwithstanding this declaration, the search was made with rigour; my snuff-box was opened, the snuff examined, and a little steel pencil-case, which happened to be found in my pocket, was carefully inspected, to discover whether it concealed a poniard. This done, they repeated the excuses made in the first instance, and invited me to sit down.

While this scene was passing in the council-hall Garat ascended to the second floor, leaving the Abbé in the council-room. Cléry, overpowered with grief, was in his own room; but coming out at the noise he heard, he announced to Louis XVI. the return of the minister of justice. Santerre, who preceded Garat, drew close to the King, and said in a low tone, "Here is the executive council." The minister, advancing, informed the King that he had carried his letter to the Convention, and had been desired by that Asssembly to notify the following reply:

"That Louis was free to summon any minister of his religion he chose, and to see his family unrestrainedly, and without witnesses; that the nation, always great, and always just, would take the case of his family under its consideration; that the creditors of his establishment should be indemnified according to their just rights; and that the National Convention had proceeded to the order of the day without considering the three days' delay."

The King heard this answer read without making any remark; but, going back into his room, he said to Cléry: "I thought, from Santerre's manner, they were going to announce that the delay was granted." Bodson, seeing Louis XVI. speak to Cléry, came near him. "You have seemed to feel for me," said the King to him; "let me thank you for it." The young municipal was confounded, and knew not what to answer; he must have thought the word of gratitude was addressed to him ironically, so little had he deserved it. Yet it was not said ironically. The unfortunate prince seeing that face, so gentle and so young, had thought its expression betokened a generous mind; the cruelty with which he was treated by some men seemed to him so improbable to be genuine at that moment, that even though he found it was real he could scarcely believe it.

After the reply of the Convention had been read, the municipals drew the minister of justice aside, and asked him in what manner Louis was to see his family. "In private," replied Garat; "such was the intention of the Convention." On this the commissaries acquainted him with the decree of the Commune, ordering them not to let him out of their sight either by day or by night; and it was agreed between the municipals and the minister, that in order to reconcile these contradictory decrees, Louis XVI. should receive his family in the dining-room, so as to be seen through the glass partition; but that the door should be closed, so that their conversation should not be overheard.

The King called back the minister of justice to inquire

whether he had let M. de Firmont know. Garat replied that he had brought him with him in his carriage, and that he was coming up; on which two municipals immediately went down stairs to bring him to the King.

Louis XVI. taking from his desk the three rouleaux which he had kept there, gave them in charge to a municipal named Baudrais, who was chatting with the minister, saying, "There are three thousand livres in gold, Sir, belonging to M. de Malesherbes: I beg you will remit them to him." This the commissary promised; but the precaution taken by the honest prince was useless; the sum was immediately carried by Baudrais to the council, who sent it to the municipality:* it never reached M. de Malesherbes.

"I was scarcely seated," says M. Edgeworth, "when two of the commissaries who had gone up to the King, came to tell me that I was allowed to see him. They conducted me by a winding staircase, which was so narrow that two persons could hardly pass each other; at certain intervals barriers were placed across the stairs, and at every barrier stood a sentinel; the men were actually *sans-culottes*, and almost all drunk; the shouts they made, re-echoing through the vaults of the Temple, were quite horrible.

"When we reached the apartment of the King, all the doors of which were open, I perceived him in a group of eight or ten persons; it consisted of the minister of justice, accompanied by some members of the Commune, who came to read to him the fatal decree *which sentenced him to death on the following day.* He was calm and tranquil, with even an aspect

* Commune of Paris.

"I, the undersigned, registrar to the municipality, acknowledge that the citizen Flechelle, of the horse artillery, remitted to me the sum of three thousand livres (125 louis d'or), received by him from the commissaries forming the council of the Temple.

"Done at the hall of the Commune, this 20th January, 1793, the 2nd year of the Republic, at a quarter before ten o'clock.

"COULOMBEAU, Registrar."

of benignity, while not one of those who stood around him had an air of composure.

"As soon as he saw me he waved his hand for them to retire; they obeyed in silence; he himself shut the door after them, and I found myself alone with my sovereign.

"Till this moment I had been able to command the various emotions with which I had been agitated; but, at the sight of a prince who had been once so powerful, and who now was so unfortunate, I was no longer master of myself, I could not restrain my tears, and I fell at his feet without the power of utterance. This touched him more than the decree which he had just heard. He answered my tears only by his own; but soon resuming all his firmness: 'Forgive me,' said the King, 'forgive me, Sir, a moment's *weakness*, if such it may be called; for a long time I have lived among my enemies, and habit has in some degree familiarized me to them, but when I behold a faithful subject, this is to me a new sight, a different language reaches my heart, and, in spite of my utmost efforts, I am unmanned.' Saying these words, he kindly raised me from the ground, and led me into his closet, that he might speak more freely, for, from his chamber, all he said was overheard. This closet or cabinet was built in one of the turrets of the Temple, it had neither hangings nor ornament, a bad stove served for a fire-place, and the only furniture was one table and three chairs. There making me sit down beside him: 'Now, sir,' said he, 'the great business of my salvation is the only one which ought to occupy my thoughts, the only business of real importance! What are all other subjects compared with this? This must, however, be delayed for a few moments, because my family are coming to take leave of me for ever; in the meanwhile here is a paper that I wish you to read.' As he spoke he drew from his pocket a sealed paper, and broke it open; it was his will, which he had written in the month of December, at a period when he was uncertain whether any religious consolation would be allowed to him in his last moments.

"All those who have read this paper, so interesting and so worthy of a Christian king, can easily judge of the deep impression it must have made on me. But, what most astonished me was, that the monarch had fortitude sufficient to read it himself, which he did nearly twice over. His voice was firm, and no change was to be seen in his countenance, except when he read names most dear to him, then all his tenderness was awakened; he was obliged to pause a moment, and his tears flowed, notwithstanding his efforts to restrain them; but when he read passages that concerned himself alone, and that related only to his personal calamities, he seemed no more affected than if he had heard the misfortunes of an indifferent person related.

"Perceiving, when he had finished reading, that the royal family were not coming, the King hastened to inquire from me the state of the clergy and of the French Church. Some things he had learned, notwithstanding the rigour of his confinement; he knew, in general, that the French ecclesiastics had been obliged to flee their country, and had been received in England, but he was entirely ignorant of particulars. The little that I thought it my duty to tell him seemed to make a great impression upon his Majesty's mind; he deplored the fate of his clergy, and he expressed the greatest admiration for the people of England, who had mitigated their sufferings. But he did not confine himself to these general inquiries; he entered into particulars that surprised me; he wished to know what had become of many of the clergy in whose welfare he took a peculiar interest. The Cardinal de la Rochefoucauld and the Bishop de Clermont seemed to fix his attention, but his eager ness redoubled at the name of the Archbishop of Paris; he inquired where he was, what he was doing, and whether I had the power of corresponding with him. 'Tell him,' said the King, 'that I die in his communion, and that I never have acknowledged any pastor but him. Alas! I am afraid he is offended at my not answering his last letter. I was then at the Tuileries, but in fact my enemies kept so close to me at that period that I had not time to write; at all events, he has so much goodness of heart that I am sure he will pardon me." His Majesty spoke also of the Abbé Floirac, whom he had never seen; but he was well acquainted with the services which this respectable divine had rendered to the diocese of Paris in times of the greatest difficulties; his Majesty asked me what had been his fate, and when I told him that he had the good fortune to escape, he spoke of him in terms which evinced the value he attached to his services, and the esteem in which he held his virtues. I do not know by what chance the conversation fell on the Duke of Orleans; the King seemed to be well acquainted with his intrigues, and with the horrid part he had taken at the Convention, but he spoke of him without any bitterness, and with pity rather than with anger; "What have I done to my cousin,' he exclaimed, 'that he should so persecute me? What object can he have? Oh! he is more to be pitied than I am! My lot is melancholy, no doubt, but his is much more so. Oh! I would not change with him.'

"This most interesting conversation was interrupted by one of the commissaries, who came to inform the King that his family was come down, and that he was at length permitted to see them. At these words, he appeared extremely agitated, and he broke from me with precipitation."

"You heard," said the King to the commissary, "that by the decree of the Convention I was to be allowed to see them without witnesses." "That is true," said the municipal, "you will be in private. We will shut the door; but, through the glass partition, we must still keep an eye upon you."

While his family was descending, Louis XVI. went into the dining-room. Cléry followed him thither: he pushed the table on one side, and placed the chairs at the back of the room to give more space. "You must bring a little water and a glass," said the King to him. There was a decanter of iced water on the table, and Cléry only brought a tumbler, placing it near the decanter. "Bring some water not iced," said the

King; "for if the Queen were to drink that it might make her ill. You will tell M. de Firmont not to come out of my closet. I am afraid the sight of him would distress my family too much."

More than a quarter of an hour elapsed from the time when the commissary went to summon the royal family. Louis XVI., walking up and down the room, stopped every moment before the door, with marks of strong agitation visible in his manner. At last, at half-past eight o'clock, the door opened; the Queen appeared first, holding her son by the hand; then came Marie Thérèse and Madame Elizabeth. All rushed into the King's arms; a mournful silence reigned for some minutes, broken only by sobs. Marie Antoinette making a motion as if she wished to draw the King into his own room: "No," said Louis XVI., "let us pass into this chamber; I may only see you there." They went into the dining-room, and the municipals closed the door, which, as well as the partition, was of glass. The King sat down, the Queen placed herself on his left hand, Madame Elizabeth on his right, Marie Thérèse just before him, and the young Prince stood between his father's knees, and, leaning all towards him, they frequently embraced him.

Louis XVI. described his trial, excusing those who had sentenced him, gave some religious advice to his children, enjoined them to forgive his death, and blessed them. The Queen ardently desiring that the royal family should pass the whole night with him, he refused, alleging that he had need of quiet and repose. This mournful scene lasted an hour and three quarters. When it was nearly over, the King wishing to impress strongly on his son's heart the pardon which he had left in his will, employed a touching expedient, transmitted to posterity by Madame Royale, herself an afflicted witness of the circumstance. "My father," she says, "at the moment he was leaving us for ever, made us promise never to think of avenging his death. He was well assured that we should consider as sacred the fulfilment of his last wishes; but my brother's extreme youth made him desirous of making a stronger impression on the boy's mind. He took him upon his knee, and said to him: 'My son, you have heard what I have just said; but, as oaths are something more sacred still than words, swear, with your hands held up to Heaven, that you will obey your father's dying injunction.' My brother, bursting into tears, obeyed, and this most affecting goodness redoubled our own grief."

The Abbé Edgeworth's narrative proceeds thus:*

"Even I, though shut up in the cabinet where the King had left me, could easily distinguish their voices, and I was involuntarily, in some degree, witness to the most touching scene I had ever beheld. It would be impossible for me to describe this agonizing interview; not only tears were shed, and sobs were heard, but piercing cries, which reached the outer court of the Temple. The King, the Queen, Monseigneur the Dauphin, Madame Elizabeth, Madame Royale,—all were bewailing at once, and their voices were confounded. At length their tears ceased, for their strength was exhausted; they then spoke in a low voice, and with some degree of tranquillity. The King was the first to rise, and all followed him. Cléry opened the door. The Queen held the King's right arm, both giving a hand to the Dauphin; Madame Royale, on his left, had her arms clasped round her father's waist; Madame Elizabeth, on the same side, but behind her, had seized her brother's left arm; and they moved in this manner towards the entrance-door, uttering the most piercing cries and lamentations. 'I assure you,' said Louis XVI. to them, 'that I will see you to-morrow morning at eight o'clock.' 'You promise us that?' they repeated all at once. 'Yes, I promise it you.' 'Why not at seven o'clock?' said the Queen. 'Well, then, yes, at seven o'clock,' replied the King; 'Adieu!' He uttered the word in so expressive a manner that their sobs

* Fragment from the unpublished memoirs of Madame la Duchesse de Tourzel.

redoubled. Madame Royale fell down in a swoon, at the feet of the King, her arms still clasped around him; Cléry raised her up, and assisted Madame Elizabeth to support her The King, desirous of putting an end to this heart-rending scene, embraced them again and again with the utmost tenderness; then tearing himself from their arms by force—'Adieu! adieu!' said he, and retired into his room."

The Princesses went up again to their apartments, and Cléry wishing to support Madame Royale thither, the municipals stopped him on the second step, and obliged him to go back again. Both doors were closed, but the cries and groans of the Princesses, and the exclamation, "The murderers!" uttered by the Queen, were audible still on the staircase.

"He returned immediately to me," writes M. Edgeworth, "but in a state of agitation that showed he was wounded to the soul. 'Oh, Sir,' cried he, throwing himself into a chair, 'what an interview have I gone through! Why should I love so tenderly, and why should I be so tenderly beloved? But it is past. Let us forget everything else to turn my thoughts to that alone which is now of importance,—to that which should at this moment concentrate all my feelings.'

Half an hour had elapsed when Cléry came to invite the King to sup; he hesitated for a moment, and then, on consideration, accepted the offer. He ate little, but appeared to relish his food. There were more municipals than usual in the anteroom on that evening, and, although they conversed in a low tone, the King caught the words: "It is time that the people should avenge themselves!" "The people," said Louis XVI. calmly, without looking at the two commissaries who were standing near the table,—"the people will do justice to my memory when they know the truth, and have regained the power of being just; but, alas! till that time arrives they will be very unhappy."

The supper had not lasted more than five minutes, and

the King, retiring into his closet, begged M. Edgeworth to take some refreshment, which offer he accepted, after some hesitation. The Abbé thus continues his narrative:—

"One thought had strongly weighed upon my mind since I had been with the King. I determined to procure the means of administering the sacrament to his Majesty, at any risk to myself, since he had been so long deprived of the opportunity of receiving it. I should have brought the holy viaticum with me, as we do to all Christians who are detained in their own houses, but the strict search it was necessary to submit to in coming to the Temple, and the profanation which would have infallibly followed, were motives more than sufficient to prevent me. There remained no other resource than for me to say mass in the King's chamber, if I could find the means. I proposed it to him; but, though he desired it most ardently, he seemed afraid of compromising my safety. I entreated him to grant me his consent, promising that I would conduct myself with prudence and discretion, and he at length yielded. 'Go, Sir,' said he, 'but I very much fear you will not succeed; I know the men with whom you have to deal, they will grant nothing which they can refuse.' Fortified by this permission, I desired to be conducted to the hall of council, and there I made my demand in the name of the King. This proposal, for which the commissaries of the tower were not prepared, disconcerted them extremely, and they sought for different pretexts to elude it. How could they find a priest at that hour; and when they had got one, how obtain all that was necessary? 'The priest is already found,' I replied, 'for I am he; and, as for the rest, the nearest church will supply all that is necessary. You must consider that my request is just, and that it would be against your own principles to refuse me.' One of the commissaries then, though in rather guarded terms, insinuated that my request was only a snare, and that, under the pretence of giving the communion to the King, I intended to poison him. 'History,' he said, 'has furnished us with examples enough of this kind to make us circumspect.' I looked steadily in the face of this man, and replied: 'The strict search I underwent when I came in here ought to con vince you that I do not carry poison. If, then, to-morrow any is found, it will be from you I shall have received it; all that I require for the celebration of mass must pass through your hands.' He would have replied, but the rest commanded him to be silent; and, for a last subterfuge, they said that, as the council was incomplete, they could not decide upon anything; but that they would seek the absent members, and then let me know the result of their deliberations.

"A quarter of an hour passed, and I was again brought into their chamber, where the president thus addressed me: 'Citizen, minister of religion, the council have taken into consideration the request that you have made in the name of Louis Capet, and, since they deem his request conformable with the law, which declares that all forms of worship are free, they consent, but on two conditions: first, that you draw up a memorial setting forth your demand, signed by yourself; secondly, that your religious ceremonies shall be concluded by to-morrow morning at seven o'clock, at the latest, for, at eight o'clock precisely, Louis Capet must set out for the place of execution.' These last words were said, like all the rest, with that degree of cold-blooded indifference which characterises an atrocious mind. I put my request in writing, and left it on the table. They reconducted me to the King, who had been awaiting, with anxiety, the conclusion of this affair. The summary I gave him, in which I suppressed all particulars, pleased him extremely.

"It was now past ten o'clock, and I remained with the King till the night was far advanced, when, perceiving that he was fatigued, I requested him to take some repose; he complied with his usual kindness, and charged me to lie down also."

Cléry helped the King to undress. When he was preparing to roll his hair, the King said, "It is not worth the trouble." At these simple words, the tears of Cléry flowed more abundantly. "Courage, Cléry!" said Louis XVI.; "should not those who love me desire a term to be put to my long sufferings?" He added, as he lay down: "Cléry, you will awaken me at five o'clock." The Abbé Edgeworth, who, a prey to the most distracting thoughts, had thrown himself on Cléry's bed, heard the King through the partition, as he thus quietly gave his orders for the morrow.

No sooner had he laid down than Louis XVI. sank into a profound sleep. Cléry passed the night in a chair in his master's room, imploring Heaven to preserve the King's strength and courage.

Hearing five o'clock strike, he lighted the fire: the King awoke at the noise, and said, drawing his curtain back: "Has five o'clock struck?" "Sire, it has, by several clocks, but not yet by the time-piece." The King rose immediately. "I have slept well and uninterruptedly," said he; "I was in great need of it, for the occurrences of yesterday had fatigued me very much. Where is M. de Firmont?" "On my bed." "And where did you pass the night yourself?" "In this chair." "I am sorry for it," said the King. "Ah, Sire! could I think of myself at such a moment?" The King gave him his hand, and pressed his affectionately.

Cléry dressed the King, and arranged his hair. While this was going on, the prince detached a seal from his watch, and put it into the pocket of a white waistcoat which he had worn the day before; he laid his watch down on the mantel-piece, after which, taking a ring from his finger, he looked at it for some time, and then put it into the same pocket in which was the seal; he changed his shirt, put on the waistcoat in which were deposited his two farewell tokens, and passed his arms into his coat, from the pockets of which he took out his pocket-book, his eye-glass, his snuff-box, his purse, and some other little matters, which he placed beside his watch on the mantel-piece; all this in silence, and in the presence of several municipals. When his toilet was complete, he told Cléry to let M. de Firmont know it, and Cléry went and informed him. M. de Firmont being ready dressed, he came, and, following the King into his closet, remained shut up with him there for half an hour.

Meantime, Cléry moved a chest of drawers into the middle of the room, arranging it like an altar, covered it with a white cloth, and adorned it with a little silver crucifix; two common torches took the place of candelabra, and the wax candles served for tapers; he brought the priest's canonicals into the room, as well as the chalice, and all that was necessary for divine service, which had been brought, at the demand of the municipals, at two o'clock in the morning, from the old church of the Capucins du Marais (Rue d'Orléans), which had become the parish church of Saint-François d'Assises. All being thus prepared, he went to tell Louis XVI. The King asked him if he could aid in performing mass. Cléry replied in the affirmative; but added, that he did not know the responses by heart. The King had a book in his hand, and, opening it at the service of mass, he gave it to him, and took another book for himself. Cléry had placed an arm-chair before the altar, and laid a large cushion on the ground. The King made him take away that cushion, and, going into his closet, brought another smaller one, covered with horse-hair, which he was in the habit of using in saying his prayers. The priest, who had been meanwhile putting on his robes, now came in, bearing the cup; the municipals withdrew into the ante-room, leaving open one half of the folding-doors. The mass began as the hour-hand of the time-piece pointed to six o'clock. A deep silence reigned throughout the tower, which seemed as if taking part in the august ceremony. Louis XVI., on his knees the whole time, heard mass, and took the sacrament with a composure of mind most holy and devout.

The priest went back into Cléry's room to divest himself of his robes, and the King retired into his cabinet, having completed his religious duties. Thither he was followed by his valet. Taking hold of his two hands: "Cléry," said Louis XVI.

to him, with a most penetrating emphasis, "Clery, I am satisfied with your services." Cléry, much affected, threw himself at his master's feet, bidding him yet have hope. "Sire, they will not dare to strike you!" "I am not afraid of death, Clery," replied the King, quietly; "I am quite prepared for it But do not you expose yourself to danger. I am about to beg that you may remain with my son; give him all your care in this terrible abode; tell him often of all the grief I suffered for the misfortunes he experiences. One day, perhaps, he may be able to requite your zeal." "The only reward I desire," exclaimed Cléry, who was still kneeling, "is to receive your Majesty's blessing. Do not refuse it, Sire, to the only Frenchman still with you." The Christian King gave his faithful servant his blessing; then raising him, and pressing him to his bosom, "Carry the same," he said, "to all who are attached to me, and tell Turgy also that I am satisfied with him. Now, go back again, that they may have no reason for suspecting you." Then, suddenly recalling him, "Stay," he said to him, giving him a paper which he had laid upon the table; "here is a letter which Pétion wrote to me when you first entered the Temple. It may be of service to you for remaining here." Cléry seized the King's hand once more, kissed it, and retired. "Adieu!" said Louis XVI. to him.

Cléry, going back into his room, found M. de Firmont praying at his bed-side. "What a prince!" said the priest, rising; "with what resignation and courage he goes to his death! He is as composed as if he had just heard mass in his palace, in the midst of his court." "He has just taken leave of me in the most affecting manner," said Cléry; "he has deigned to say, he will ask for me to remain in the tower, in attendance on his son. I beg you, sir, to remind him of it when he is going out, for I shall not again have the happiness of seeing him in private." "Make yourself easy," said M. Edgeworth, and he returned to Louis XVI.

He found him seated near his stove, where he could scarcely

warm himself. "My God," said he, "how happy am I in the possession of my religious principles! Without them, what should I be now? But, with them, how sweet does death appear to me. Yes, there dwelleth on high an incorruptible Judge, from whom I shall receive the justice refused to me on earth!" "The sacred office I held at this time," adds M. Edgeworth, "prevents my relating more than a few sentences out of many interesting conversations I held with the King during the last sixteen hours of his life. But, from the little I have told, it may be seen how much might be added, if it were consistent with my duty to say more."

The day began to dawn, and the drums were already beating to arms in all the divisions of Paris. The night had been rainy and cold; and the streets were obstructed by the melting snow.* The day broke so gloomy, and so wrapped in fog,

* Archives of Paris.—Commune of Paris.—Department of Police.

"20th January, 1793; second year of the French Republic, one and indivisible.

"We have to beg of you, citizen president, to acquaint the council-general with the murder that has just been committed at the Egalité garden.

"Pelletier Saint-Fargeau was the unhappy victim, and it is said that one Pâris, an old garde-du-corps, is the assassin. We have just despatched a peace officer to search for the murderer.

"From another quarter we learn, that a conspiracy is to break out to-night, and that the market-men have been summoned to assemble in great strength to-morrow, on Louis Capet's route, and assassinate him.

"We have written to the inspector to have the streets cleared, which are choked with the melting snow. Notwithstanding the measures that have been adopted to make people illuminate, it is reported to us that the fronts of the houses are ill-lighted, and that few patrols are to be met with.

"We beg you will invite the different sections, by means of the commissaries among you, to redouble their zeal and activity at a moment when the enemies of the Republic are driven to the rage of despair.

"We remain sitting permanently, to execute the orders transmitted to us by the council-general, and to answer the deputations of the sections.

"The administrators of the department of police.

"Vigner.

"Brusle."

that it seemed as if the night were prolonged. A thick and icy mist spread a melancholy tint over mourning nature. The piercing sound of the trumpet, and the rolling of the drum, awoke the people; all was stir, agitation, and commotion within the houses. Women and children, with anguish in their hearts, and terror on their brows, withdrew to the most retired chambers; grown men and youths armed themselves, for the most part murmuring and moaning, to form a line along the streets, and maintain order in the movements of the people, while the enormous moral crime, the murder of a king, slain by his own subjects, should be perpetrated on the scaffold of the 21st January. The Revolution issued her command, and fear obeyed—fear, the accomplice of crimes it detests in secret, and, while detesting, commits them—for it is fear alone that renders them practicable. Ruffians of the *lanterne*, bullies from the clubs, cut-throats of the Revolution, butchers thirsting for human blood,—in short, men versed in every imaginable villany, all were early out in the Faubourgs, with menace on their lips, as they uttered shouts of triumph. All were in motion, the good as well as the bad; the former stricken with grief and terror, the latter animated with joy and impatience. In all Paris, calm and peace rested only on the brow of that saintly man who was so soon to die.

The stir in the town was very distinctly audible in the tower; the sound froze the blood in the veins of the servant and the priest, the last friends of the last King of France. Louis XVI., listening a moment, said, without betraying the least emotion: "Most likely it is the National Guard beginning to assemble."

And, true enough it was assembling! Shortly afterwards detachments of cavalry entered the court-yard of the Temple, and the voices of officers, and the trampling of horses, were distinctly heard. The King listened again, and said to me, with the same composure: "They seem to be approaching."

"On taking leave of the Queen, the evening before, he had

promised to see her again the next day, and he wished earnestly to keep his word; but I entreated him not to put the Queen to a trial, under which she must sink. He hesitated for a moment, and then, with an expression of profound grief, said: 'You are right, Sir, it would kill her. I must deprive myself of this melancholy consolation, and let her indulge in hope a few minutes longer.'"

Coming out of his cabinet, the King called Cléry, and, drawing him into the recess of the window, said to him: "Give this seal to my son, and this ring to the Queen; tell her with what pain I leave her. In this little packet is inclosed the hair of every one of my family,—give that to her also. Say to the Queen, to my dear children, and to my sister, that I had indeed promised to see them this morning, but that I wished to spare them the pain of so cruel a separation. Oh! what does it not cost me, to go without receiving their last embraces!" Having dried a few tears, he added, in a most heart-rending tone: "I charge you to give them my last farewell!" and went back into his closet.

The municipals, who had approached on hearing the King speak, had seen him give Cléry the various articles, which he was still holding in his hands. They ordered him to give them up; but one of their number proposed to let him have them in his keeping until the council should decide on the subject, and his proposition was adopted.

A quarter of an hour afterwards, Louis XVI. came out of his closet: "Ask if I may have a pair of scissors," said he to Cléry, and then went in again. Cléry asked the commissaries, accordingly. "Do you know what he wants with them?" "I know nothing about it." "We must know." Cléry knocked at the closet door, and the municipals, who were with him, said to the King, as he presented himself: "You wished for a pair of scissors; but, before asking the council's permission, we must know for what purpose you want them." "For Cléry to cut my hair," replied Louis XVI.

The commissaries then withdrew: one of them went down to the council-room, and, after half an hour's deliberation, the scissors were refused. It was Mercereau who came this time to knock at the closet-door, and announce this decision to the King. "I will not touch the scissors myself," said the prince; "I wish Cléry to cut my hair in your presence; go again to your colleagues, Sir, for my request cannot be rejected when thus made and explained." "Oh! that was all very well while you were King, but you are not King now." Louis made no reply: he closed the door again, and coming back to M. de Firmont, who had overheard Mercereau's words, contented himself with saying to him: "You see how these people use me; but I must bear everything."

After the lapse of a few minutes the King was again disturbed by a municipal, who informed him of the obstinate and formal refusal of the council. He went back into his closet, and said, smiling, to M. Edgeworth: "These people see daggers and poison everywhere. They are afraid of my killing myself. Alas! they know me very little! To kill myself would be an act of great weakness. I shall have fortitude enough to die."

Meanwhile, Cléry was told by two municipals that he must get ready to accompany Louis XVI., in order to undress him on the scaffold. At this announcement, Cléry was struck with horror; but, collecting all his energy, he prepared to pay this last service to his master (who shrank from the performance of this office by the executioner), when another commissary, coming up from the council-room, said to him: "Cléry, you are not to go: the headsman is good enough for him."

Each time the King was disturbed in his closet M. Edgeworth, who had been shut up with him ever since seven o'clock, had been seized with an indescribable shudder, trembling with fear that every time might be the last.

Every moment, as it passed away, increased and justified

his terror. It was nearly nine o'clock; the din of arms and the trampling of horses, together with the incessant removal of cannon backwards and forwards—all this noise re-echoed through the tower as an ominous prelude The large doors of the King's apartment opened with a great crash. M. Edgeworth shuddered again at the sound, and this time he had good cause,—Santerre was come.

Accompanied by Jacques-Claude Bernard and Jacques Roux, —priests who had taken the oaths, and become municipal officers, and who had been recommended to the Commune, by Hébert, as fit persons to conduct the King to the scaffold,— the commander of the forces entered at the head of ten gendarmes, who ranged themselves in two lines; five or six municipals, besides, were grouped about the room. Louis XVI. opened his closet door. "You are come for me?" he said to Santerre. "Yes." "I am busy," said the King, authoritatively; "I ask one minute; wait for me there!" Then closing the door again, and kneeling before the Abbé Edgeworth: "All is nearly over, Sir," he said; "give me your blessing, and pray God to support me to the end!" Rising again quickly, and coming out of his closet, he advanced towards the group who had stopped in the middle of the bed-room. All had their hats on, which the King perceiving immediately asked for his own. While Cléry, drowned in tears, was gone to bring it, the King said: "Is there a member of the Commune among you?" And, on Jacques Roux coming forward: "I beg of you, Sir," said Louis XVI. to him, "to deposit this paper with the president of the council-general." It was his will. "I cannot take charge of any packet," replied Jacques Roux; "my duty is simply to conduct you to the scaffold." "Ah! just so," said the King, without betraying any indignation. He addressed the same question to a commissary on guard at the Temple, named Baudrais, who took charge of his will, and, having countersigned it, remitted it to the council-general of the

Commune.* Then, addressing himself to another municipal:† "Will you be good enough to give this paper to my wife?" he said: "you are at liberty to read it; there are some arrangements of which I wish the Commune to be informed."

Cléry was standing behind the King near the fire-place, and, on his turning round, presented him with his great-coat. "I do not require it," said Louis XVI.; "give me my hat only." Cléry gave it to him. In doing so the King's hand met that of his servant, which he pressed for the last time. "Gentlemen," said he, addressing the municipals, "I recommend also to the Commune, Cléry, my valet, whose services I cannot sufficiently praise. Let care be taken to give him my watch and all my effects, as well what I have here as what was deposited with the Commune. I should wish Cléry to remain with my son, who is used to him. I hope that, as a reward for the attachment he has shown me, he will be left in the service of the Queen—of my wife," he added hastily. "I also recommend my old servants at the Tuileries and Versailles to the care of the Commune." No one answering him, the King looked at Santerre, and said, in a firm voice: "Let us go!"

At these words, the last he spoke in his room, they began the march. At the head of the staircase, Louis XVI. met Mathey, and said to him: "I was a little hasty with you, the day before yesterday; do not be angry with me for it!" Mathey turned his head away, and answered nothing; affecting even to draw back when the King spoke to him.

* As stated in the registers of the council-general.

† Cléry calls him Gobeau; the name is not to be found in the list of commissaries appointed to do duty in the Temple on the 19th and 20th January. The registers of the Commune give us the following names:— "For Saturday, the 19th, Pelletier, Mercereau, Minier, Baudrais, Cailleux, Turlot; for Sunday, the 20th, Gilet Marie, Dome, Yon, Grouvelle, Bourdier, Destournelles."

However, Gobeau, who had come to the Temple, as we have seen, on the 19th, charged with a special duty, was there still no doubt.

They went down—Santerre and the municipals surrounding the King, his confessor following him, and the gendarmes filing behind. The roll of drums announced his departure. Louis crossed the first court-yard on foot, between two lines bristling with pikes and bayonets. Turning round twice towards the tower, he bade adieu to all he loved in this world, and by his gesture it was seen he was gathering strength and courage.

At the entrance of the second court-yard the carriage of the mayor of Paris* was standing, with two gendarmes at the door; on the approach of the King one of them got in before him and took the front seat. Louis XVI. had thought, up to that moment, that the assistance of his confessor would end when he left the Temple; but now, with surprise, that soon became pleasure, he saw there was no intention of removing him. He got into the carriage, and sat down at the back with the

* Not a hackney-coach, as has been pretended. The following is the order of the executive council :—

"Archives of the Hôtel de Ville.

"To the citizens administrators of the police department.

"Paris, 20th January, 1793, the 2nd year of the French Republic.

"Citizens,—Your deliberations, dated this day, at eleven o'clock at night, and the letter of the executive officer of justice which was attached to it, having been read, theCouncil makes the following decrees, in answer to the observations contained in that letter :

"1st. Louis Capet shall be brought to the place of execution from the Temple in the mayor's carriage.

"2nd. With respect to the interment, the curé of Madeleine-la-Ville-l'Evèque will take measures with the deputy-attorney-general, syndic of the department, according to the council's resolution, of which a copy has been given to the said curé, and of which citizen Lefèvre is cognizant.

"3rd. The executive officer of justice and his assistants shall attend only at the place of execution.

"Every difficulty will thus, we think, be removed.

"The provisional executive council.
"LE BRUN, President.
"By the council.
"GROUVELLE."

the Abbé Edgeworth ; the second gendarme jumped in last, sat down beside his comrade, and shut the carriage-door. It has been asserted that these men had orders to assassinate Louis XVI. on the least commotion being remarked among the people. It has also been pretended that one of them was a priest in disguise, but it is an account for which there is no authority.*

Still, this fear of a disturbance was not entirely unfounded. A great number of persons devoted to the royal cause had formed the design of snatching the King by main force from the hands of his assassins. The Baron de Batz, the soul of the plot, who had returned to France a few days before, perceiving the impracticability of making an attempt upon the Temple, for the rescue of the royal family, had been incredibly active in organizing an association of all the persons who were ready to sacrifice their own lives to save the King's. The descendant of that glorious companion in arms of Henri IV., Manaud de Batz, who saved his master's life at the taking of Eauze, and would not, at the battles of Cahors and Coutras, leave his side further than the *length of his halberd*, sought to revive the example of his ancestor's devotion by saving the descendant of that noble king. A secret appeal had been made to the young men who were hostile to the Convention, in all the quarters of Paris, and M. de Batz reckoned on from fifteen hundred to two thousand adherents among them ; besides which, he thought a much smaller force would be sufficient to excite, by their generous example, the sympathy of a populace prone to excitement, armed against their will, and, against their will, witnessing a crime in which those in power were anxious they should appear to participate. In the long transit from the Temple to the Place Louis XV., where the royal immolation was destined to take place, he

* The other was named Jean-Maurice-François Lebrasse. He was a lieutenant of gendarmes in attendance on the tribunals when, on the 24th Germinal, 2nd year (13th April, 1794), he was guillotined, together with Arthur Dillon, Chaumette, Gobel, Duret, Beysser, &c.

had selected the very spot most favourable for the execution of his design. He knew that, however numerous the escort might be, the regicides would be afraid of passing through the streets, and would rather choose the Boulevards, as had been the case both times that Louis XVI. had been brought before the Convention; and that, taking this route, the party must ascend from the Porte Saint-Denis to the Boulevard Bonne-Nouvelle. In this place the road suddenly widens, a great number of streets leading to it, by which the assailants might approach almost unperceived, and crown the height in a moment. There, too, the ordnance, which the escort would have in their rear, and which must, from the nature of the ground, be pointed with an upward aim, would be of scarcely any service against the attacking party, while the latter would have the advantage of the side streets for engaging the flanks of the party as soon as the onset should begin in that place. These various reasons decided the head of the enterprise to make choice of this spot, as offering the best chances for the attack of the escort, and the rescue of the victim. He hoped, and perhaps there was some cause for his even expecting, to meet with that exasperation and horror that was likely to be more and more excited by the crime of the Convention, and that the mass of spectators would instantly join the assailants who should give the bold signal; nay, he even dared to hope, from the enthusiasm of the moment, that, after having rescued the King, they would all unite to bear him to the very heart of the Convention, and re-erect his throne there.

This was the dream of M. de Batz; but it was well known by the committees that the death of Louis XVI. was no more desired by the city of Paris than by the rest of France; they had been informed that for several days papers, exhorting the women, invoking the men, to save the King, had been, by means of every available channel, circulated among the people; that ladies of rank, and the wives of wealthy tradesmen, had visited the market-women, now become an influential body in the Revolution, to implore mercy for Louis XVI.

The members of the Convention were equally aware of the fact, that the youth of the town were active, and that some commotion was in contemplation ; and, therefore, to prevent the execution of the plots that threatened them, they took such measures as fear might dictate to men intoxicated with power and frenzied with rage.

Favras had been executed on the Place de Grève, whither also had been transported the bleeding remains of Flesselles and Delaunay. Laporte, late superintendant of the civil list, had been guillotined on the Place du Carrousel. But the Convention, wishing to surround the scaffold of the King with a vast display of force, selected the Place de la Concorde, which was about to be called the Place de la Révolution.

The Commune had arranged the formidable array, which was to shroud the King so thoroughly from view that the headsman alone could approach him. By their orders, all young men were forced to appear in their own quarter at such an hour, in such a place, on the morning of the fatal day; and notice was given that two lists would be kept, one, of those who were present, and another, of those who were absent; and these last, without any other examination, should be held as conspirators, while fathers were declared responsible for the conduct of their children. All who were capable of bearing arms, except the public functionaries, were to be at the post assigned them before daybreak;* and there they were severally enjoined to keep the most profound silence, and remain in the most rigid state of inaction, as long as the escort was in sight. All other persons were forbidden to appear in the streets of Paris, or to show themselves at the doors and windows as the condemned was passing. It was forbidden to cross the line, or move forward upon the route intended for the procession, under pain

* Extract from the deliberations of the council-general of the department.

of being treated as a conspirator—that is, under pain of death. Every carriage was forbidden to run on that day; all the cavalry corps were forbidden to leave the posts assigned them, until their captains should receive the special order for their departure, lest their marching might occasion some confusion favourable to the plan in agitation for saving Louis XVI.

As a complement to these measures, Santerre sent a sufficient force of horse and foot to all the barriers, to prevent any number of persons, armed or unarmed, from entering or leaving Paris.* Yet more—the market-women were forbidden, by a decree of the police, to take their places in the market until the execution should be over. The clubs were brought into action in aid of the committees; they roused the zeal of the latter, and watched their operations.† The police commissioners excited the activity of the sections;‡ and lastly,

* Extract from the registers of the deliberations of the council-general of the department.

† "Society of the friends of Liberty and Equality.

"Live free or die!"

"Paris, 20th January, 2nd year of the French Republic.

"The society decrees that a deputation of twelve of its members shall proceed immediately to the executive council of the department, and to the council-general of the Commune, in order to invite them to redouble their vigilance, and to take all measures necessary to prevent the execution of designs formed by the enemies of liberty.

"Decrees, that one citizen out of each section shall proceed thither immediately, to request the committees and the guard to exercise the most active vigilance, and to be on their guard against all alarming reports that may be brought them, and that all members of the society unite their efforts to prevent any movement.

"The society further decrees, that it remains sitting permanently until after the execution of the final decree issued against the tyrant.

"F. Desfieux, Vice-President.

"Auvrest, Mittie, jun., Secretaries.

"Monestier, Member for Puy-de-Dôme."

(Archives of the Hôtel-de-Ville.)

‡ Letter of the police commissioners Vigner and Baulé. (Archives of the Hôtel-de-Ville.)

false reports were circulated: "The spies of the committees are in all ranks; enormous rewards are promised to informers; whoever shall stir will be condemned to death."

Such were the feeble projects formed for the rescue of the King, and such the powerful measures taken to complete his destruction. While sorrow and indignation, depicted on the countenances of a few, encouraged some to hope that so great a disgrace might be spared to the Revolution, artfully combined precautions made others certain of rendering the 21st January the most execrable day in the national history.

The gloomy roll of the drums was prolonged, and announced the departure from the Temple. The street, in the short space reaching to the Boulevard, was lined with ten thousand armed men. All the doors and windows were closed. The Boulevard, by which the procession passed, was bordered on each side by a double line of men, four ranks deep, so close together as to be like a wall, and armed with muskets and pikes. The Place de la Révolution was, in like manner, hemmed in on all sides by a force of above twenty thousand men. All the people able to bear arms were thus pressed together in a line, forming a camp of a league in extent; while the other quarters of the capital were like vast solitudes, depopulated by the wrath of an avenging God.

The coach in which the victim was borne was preceded and followed by a great number of pieces of ordnance, and escorted by a considerable body of horse and foot, composed of federates, called "Marseillais," of the assassins of September, and other resolute men. An immense number of drummers preceded the carriage, in order to drown, by their noise, any cries to the rescue that might be uttered.

At short distances were posted strong detachments, armed in every kind of manner, with orders, in case of anything occurring, to repair to the point attacked. The day was dark and unsettled, and the sun, hidden behind a thick fog, seemed to withhold its light from the crime about to be committed, and which nature appeared to feel more than man.

Louis XVI., shut up as he was, with his confessor, in a carriage, where he could neither speak nor listen without witnesses, betook himself to silence. M. de Firmont presented him with his breviary; the King seemed to accept it gratefully, and even expressed a wish to be shown the psalms best adapted to his situation, which he repeated alternately with him. The two gendarmes, without uttering a word, seemed confounded and charmed with the calm piety of the King who was about to die.

Meanwhile, two groups, not numerous it is true, formed, one on the right, the other on the left of the Boulevard, behind the quadruple row of men. The carriage reached the Porte Saint-Denis, on the height of the Boulevard Bonne-Nouvelle, and was caught sight of, in the midst of the formidable escort, by M. de Batz. He looked up the side streets, where the attack should have commenced, for his companions in the enterprise, but in vain. The streets were deserted, the houses shut up, and through an icy fog there was nothing but solitude to be seen. Maddened by this desertion, he was afraid of being obliged to retire as the carriage approached, but, at the sight of the two groups we have mentioned, his hopes revived. Two young men immediately detached themselves from one of these groups and joined him. Accompanied by them and by his friend Devaux,* he sprang forward, sword in hand, opened himself a way through the line, and all four cried out, again and again, with all their strength, "To our help, Frenchmen!—all who would save their King!" But, in that confused mass of people, not one responded to their cry Mutual distrust and suspicion reigned throughout the ranks, each individual feared his neighbour, and thought he saw in

* Devaux was employed at the national treasury. He was condemned to death on the 20th Prairial, 2nd year (8th June, 1794), after having refused to betray the retreat of M. de Batz to Fouquier Tinville.

him an informer or an assassin; every heart was frozen by terror, and the silence of death was on the whole line.

De Batz and his friends, seeing no stir in their favour, passed again through the midst of those half-stupified men; they called to the two groups, and the latter were hastening to their aid, but at that very moment, having been apprised by a vidette, one of the corps in reserve rushed upon the intrepid De Batz and his companions. The two young men tried to take refuge in a house, but it was closed against them: they were cut to pieces at the door, and their names perished with them. De Batz and Devaux disappeared.

This incident created no disturbance in the train that accompanied the King. Nothing had been seen or heard of it in the carriage. Still M. de Firmont, though entirely occupied with the duties of his holy ministry, was not free from worldly anxiety; two young men, who were to take part in the plot, had acquainted him with it on the preceding evening, and, without quite believing in the possibility of success, a slight feeling of hope still agitated his mind in spite of his better judgment. As for Louis XVI., he was no longer of this earth; he saw nothing of the innumerable army that bore him along, he perceived none of the terrible precautions that had been taken to stifle any cry of pity before it left the lip; he calmly read the prayers for the dying, and gave himself entirely up to the feelings awakened in his breast by those sublime and affecting compositions.

From this time there was not even the shadow of any manifestation of feeling on the route; the escort moved on in silence the most profound. An hour had elapsed since their leaving the Temple. At every step, with every moment, M. de Firmont's hope grew fainter, and then was utterly extinguished. The fatal carriage reached, at last, the Place de la Révolution, and stopped in the midst of an empty space that had been left around the scaffold, which was erected between the pedestal of the statue of Louis XV. and the avenue of the Champs Elysées. It was now twenty minutes past ten o'clock.*

The King finding that the carriage had stopped, raised his eyes and closed the breviary, keeping the place with his finger: then turning to the Abbé Edgeworth, he said to him in a whisper: "We are arrived, if I mistake not." The priest's silent bow replied in the affirmative. One of the guards came to open the carriage door, and the gendarmes would have jumped out but the King stopped them, and, leaning his arm on the Abbé's knee: "Gentlemen," said he, with a tone of majesty, "I recommend to you this good man, take care that, after my death, no insult be offered him. I charge you to prevent it." The two men answering not a word, the King was continuing in a louder tone, but one of them stopped him, saying, "Yes, yes, we will take care; leave him to us;" and the accent in which these words were uttered must have overwhelmed M. Edgeworth, had it been possible for him, at such a moment, to think of himself. As soon as the King had left the carriage, three guards surrounded him, and would have removed his upper garments; but he repulsed them, took off his coat, untied his neckcloth, and opened his shirt. The guards, whom the determined countenance of the King had for a moment disconcerted, seemed to recover their audacity; they surrounded him again, and would have seized his hands. "What are you attempting?" said the King, drawing back his hands. "To bind you," said these wretches. "To bind *me!*" exclaimed the King, with an indignant air; "no, I will never consent to that; do what you have been ordered to do in other respects, but you shall never bind me." The guards insisted, they raised their voices, and seemed to wish to call on others to assist them.

"Perhaps," says M. Edgeworth, "this was the most terrible moment of this most dreadful morning; another instant, and the best of kings would have received from his rebellious subjects indignities too horrid to mention, indignities

* Miuutes of the execution. (National Archives.)

that would have been to him more insupportable than death Such was the feeling expressed on his countenance. Turning towards me, he looked at me steadily, as if to ask my advice. I replied: 'Sire, in this new insult I only see another trait of resemblance between your Majesty and the Saviour who is about to recompense you.' At these words he raised his eyes to heaven, with an expression that can never be described.

"'Certainly,' said he 'nothing less than the example of One greater could induce me to submit to such an affront.' Then, turning to the executioners. 'Do as you will,' he said; 'I will drink the cup to the dregs.'"

His hands were then bound, but with his handkerchief. and not with a rope, and his hair fell beneath the shears. "I hope now they will allow me to speak," said he, and ascended the scaffold, the steps of which were extremely uneven. Being deprived of the use of his hands, he leaned with his elbow on his confessor, and by the difficulty with which he moved, M. Edgeworth, for one moment, feared that his courage was failing him. But what was his astonishment, when, having reached the last step, he saw the King make his escape—so to speak—from his hands, pass across the whole width of the scaffold with a firm step, silence with a glance the noise of fifteen or twenty drums placed opposite to him, and, in a voice so strong as to be heard as far as the swing-bridge, pronounced the following ever-memorable words:—

"I die innocent of all the crimes imputed to me. I forgive the authors of my death, and I pray God that the blood you are about to shed may never be required of France! And you, unhappy people!——"

Then a powerful voice exclaimed, "Do not allow him to speak." And Santerre added, "I brought you here to die, and not to make speeches." A cavalry officer rushed towards the drummers, and obliged them to beat their drums. At the same time the cries of the assassins of September, surrounding the scaffold, were heard encouraging the executioners. The latter seemed to rouse themselves, and violently seizing hold of the King they pushed him under the axe, and his head was severed from his body.

On hearing the fatal blow, the Abbé Edgeworth had thrown himself on his knees. The deepest silence reigned among the spectators, who, in spite of themselves, were seized with unconquerable horror. The youngest executioner (he seemed not more than eighteen), immediately raised the bleeding head that had borne the crown of France, and showed it to the people, going all round the scaffold with it in his hand. M. de Firmont, who was below him, having remained kneeling on the steps of the guillotine, felt his bowed head moistened, as he passed, by drops of blood:—it was the blood of the martyr, which a second time consecrated the brow of the priest.*

A few cries of "*Vive la Nation!*" "*Vive la République!*" were soon audible. By degrees more voices joined in the cry, and, in a few minutes, the shout was universal among the multitude, and every hat was off. M. Edgeworth, having succeeded in forcing his way through the thousand ranks of pikes and bayonets that closed around him, retired from the scene, to hide in retirement a life preserved by a miracle, and thenceforth marked with an imperishable glory. The two commissaries of the executive council, the two delegates of the directory of the department, the two deputies of the municipality, specially named, who were stationed at the Hôtel de la Marine to witness the death of

* It is remarkable that, in his account of the last moments of Louis XVI., the Abbé Edgeworth has omitted to relate that fine apostrophe which every one has heard, and which everybody believes that he addressed to his King at the moment of execution:

"*Fils de St. Louis! Montez au ciel!*" (Son of St. Louis! Ascend to Heaven!)

The Abbé Edgeworth was asked if he recollected to have uttered this exclamation. He replied that he could neither deny nor affirm that he had spoken the words. "It was possible," he added, "that I might have pronounced them, without afterwards recollecting the fact, for I retain no memory of anything that happened relative to myself at the awful moment."

Louis Capet, immediately prepared the official report of his execution.*

The shouts in the Place Louis XV. resounded to the very midst of the Convention. The deputies of the Mountain, ghastly pale as they sat, responded by their clamours, and the

* Report.

"The year 1793, 2nd year of the French Republic, and on the 21st January:

"We, the undersigned, Jean-Antoine-Lefèvre, deputy attorney-general, syndic of the department, and Antoine-François Momoro, both members of the directory of the said department, named to the duties to be hereafter stated by the council-general of the department:

"And François-Pierre Sallais, and François-Germain Isabeau, both commissaries, named by the provisionary executive council to the duties also hereafter stated:

"We repaired to the Hôtel de la Marine, Rue and Place de la Révolution, the place indicated by our commission, at nine o'clock, A.M., of this day, where we waited until ten o'clock precisely for the presence of the commissaries named by the municipality of Paris, as well as the judges and the sheriff of the criminal tribunal of the department, in whose absence one of our number prepared this report:

"We assembled in order to see, from the place where we still are, the execution of the decree of the Convention, of the 15th, 17th, 19th, and 20th January, the present month, and of the proclamation of the executive council of the same day, 20th January, whose orders are attached to the report:

"And at a quarter past ten, A.M., precisely, citizens Jacques-Claude Bernard and Jacques Roux, both municipal officers and commissaries of the municipality, arrived, bearing their credentials, who, together with ourselves, have been present at the events noted herein:

"And at the same hour the procession, commanded by the commander of the forces, Santerre, arrived at the Rue and Place de la Révolution, bringing Louis Capet in a four-wheeled carriage, and approaching the scaffold erected in the said Place de la Révolution, between the pedestal of the statue of Louis XV. and the Avenue of the Champs Elysées:

"At twenty minutes past ten o'clock, Louis Capet, having reached the foot of the scaffold, left the carriage:

"At twenty-two minutes past ten he ascended the scaffold. The execution was instantly performed, and his head shown to the people.

"Hereto witness our hands,

"LEFEVRE, MOMORO, SALLAIS, ISABEAU, BERNARD, JACQUES ROUX."

(National Archives.)

impatient Assembly, even while the victim's blood was yet warm, hastened to decree an address to the French nation, excusing the crime and extolling the regicide.

By degrees the troops quitted the fatal square. The lowest dregs of the populace rushed towards the scaffold; grown men and children dyed their weapons in the blood yet running—some bathed their hands in it, some dyed their clothes, others even smeared their faces with it. Cries of savage joy resounded through the air, while a dance, like that of wild cannibals, was formed round the altar of the sacrifice. Meantime, one wretch* ascended it, fixed the victim's coat upon a pike, and shouted to the infuriated people, howling and dancing below: "This is the coat of a tyrant!"

Immediately the coat was torn in pieces. The victim's hat, which had remained on the first step of the scaffold, was also rent in strips, of which the possession was disputed by a thousand hands at once, for each desired to carry away some token of the scene he had witnessed.†

Alas! as in recording the actions of the martyred King Louis XVI., we see that human nature may bring heaven down to earth; so, when we read of the crimes, the fury, the hideous joys of his murderers, we see that human iniquity is capable of turning earth into hell.

Ocular witnesses of the scene have slightly varied in the accounts they have given; but, on the whole, their testimony agrees. The descendant of Louis the Bold, Saint Louis, and Louis the Great, displayed throughout this terrible trial courage without ostentation, mildness without meanness, and the composure of countenance resulting from a mind at ease. We have still, however, to lay before posterity a testimony of yet more weight than the account of a spectator,—that of one of

* His name was Heuzé.

† Report made to the council-general of the Commune by the police authorities, in the sitting of the 29th April, 1793

the actors in that terrible drama in which there are but two performers—the slayer and the slain!

The following is the declaration which the executioner, incited by an article in a newspaper of that period, addressed to that paper.* We give this letter exactly as it was written:—

"Citizen,—A short journey has prevented my having hitherto had the honour of replying to your request concerning Louis Capet. According to my promise, I now send you the following, which is the exact truth of all that passed:—As he left the carriage to be executed, he was told that he must take off his coat, and made some difficulty about it, saying that he could be executed as he was. On its having been represented that this was impossible, he himself helped to take it off. He made the same difficulty about having his hands tied; but gave them of his own accord, when the person who accompanied him

* The *Thermomètre du Jour* (of the 13th February, 1793, No. 410, p. 356) contained the following article, under the head of "A well-authenticated anecdote of Louis Capet's execution:—"

"'The moment the *condemned* mounted the scaffold (Sanson, the state executioner, relates this circumstance, and the word *condemned* is used by himself), I was surprised at his intrepidity and firmness; but, at the roll of the drums, which interrupted his harangue, and the simultaneous movement for his seizure made by my assistants, his countenance suddenly changed, and he cried out very hastily, three times over: "I am lost!"' This circumstance, together with another, also related by Sanson, that the condemned had supped plentifully the night before, and made a very good breakfast that morning, show us that Louis Capet had been under a delusion up to the very moment of his death, and had reckoned upon being reprieved. The persons who had encouraged him in this belief had, doubtless, done so in order to give him a boldness of countenance that should impose on the spectators as well as on posterity; but the roll of the drums dissolved the charm of that borrowed firmness, and our contemporaries, as well as posterity, will now possess a guide by which to judge of the last moments of the condemned tyrant."

Sanson, having read this article, protested against the words put into his mouth, and, on the editor's begging him to correct a report which he declared to be entirely false, he wrote the letter we republish, and which appeared in the *Thermomètre* of Thursday, 21st February, 1793.

observed it was a last sacrifice. Farther, he asked whether the drums would go on beating, and was answered that it was not known,—and it was the truth. He ascended the scaffold, and would push to the front, because he wished to speak. But, on its being again represented that the thing was impossible, he allowed himself to be conducted to the place where he was bound, and where he cried out very loud: 'People, I die innocent!' Then, turning towards us, he said to us: 'Gen tlemen, I am innocent of what I am accused. I wish my blood may cement the welfare of the French.' These, citizen, are his real last words.

"The sort of little altercation, at the foot of the scaffold, was occasioned by his not thinking it necessary to take off his coat and have his hands tied; he also proposed to cut his own hair.

"And, to pay regard to truth, he bore all with a coolness and firmness that astonished us all. I am fully convinced that he derived this firmness from religious principle, with which no one could seem more deeply imbued and affected than himself.

"You may rest assured, citizen, that this is the truth in its most perfect purity. I have the honour to be, citizen,

"Your fellow-citizen,

"SANSON.

"Paris, 20th February, 1793, 2nd year of the French Republic."

This homage paid to the martyr by the murderer, by Sanson to Louis XVI., a few days after the sacrifice of the 21st January, is one of the most important documents in history. The man of the guillotine, accustomed to slay and to look upon death, was astonished at this royal death. He felt that the moral courage displayed by the King had something superhuman in its greatness; and, on seeing Louis XVI. die, he, too, cried out, after his manner, "He is a God!"

This was not all; the blow he had been doomed to strike touched himself, and he came down from the scaffold never again to ascend it. The executioner was seized with remorse, —a new occurrence in his fearful office,—and his remorse was so acute that it abridged his life; he died at the end of six months, directing by his will that an expiatory mass should be annually said at his expense, every 21st January, foi the repose of the soul of Louis XVI.* Thus, the first attempt to expiate the murder of the 21st January was made by the executioner; and when the solemn service, instituted for that purpose in 1815, was suspended, the mass founded by Sanson survived the ceremonies it had preceded, and still continued, year by year, a protest before God ol the virtues of the victim and of the repentance of the assassin

Does it not seem as if the will of Heaven had been that no single trait of resemblance should be wanting between the royal martyrdom and that of our blessed Lord? The King's clothes were divided after his death like the garments of Christ; and Sanson, performing, after his manner, the part of the centurion, withdrew, after the execution, beating his breast, and repeating, "*Vere hic homo erat justus!*"

All was over! As if haunted by a gloomy terror, the greater part of the crowd that blocked up the square gradually dispersed. One by one they withdrew, each head bowed down; and, returned to their several homes, they shut themselves in with their families, there to relate all that had passed, while even the victim's enemies did not dare rejoice at the deed.

A mournful stillness settled down on Paris. It seemed as if life were extinct in the regicidal city, her houses standing silent all, as if deserted by their tenants; but the minds of

* His son and successor (Henri Sanson), who died 22nd August, 1840, at the age of 73, religiously performed this duty throughout a long career employing the curé of St. Laurent (his own parish), to repeat the annual mass.

men were in fearful agitation, every faculty absorbed in, every thought directed to, one object alone. If human eye had been permitted to penetrate the retreat of each inhabitant of the mighty city, what scenes of terror, of grief, of regret,—perhaps even of remorse,—would not have been disclosed! What stifled moans, and silent tears! Fathers and mothers of families struck down by a mortal blow! Vergniaud himself, his very soul bowed down, trembling with burning fever, and his voice almost choked, told one of his friends how, on the night before, the bleeding form of the King had appeared to him—a fearful spectre!—"*whose severed head murmured words of reproach and forgiveness!*"

Two o'clock came. The fog grew thicker, and not a single shop was opened yet. The most melancholy silence still prevailed in the streets and public squares, only interrupted, and that at long intervals, by the passing of a few wretches, whose sanguinary cries and savage dances celebrated that dreadful day, and who were pursuing with their howlings the few citizens to be seen in the streets, and who fled as they drew near. The patrols went round: Paris was as if dead.

The news of the murder, that detracted so much from the honour of the Republic, and, perhaps, will yet be the cause of much misery to future generations, circulated beyond the town. Mourning was in all the provinces, as if one vast funereal pall had covered France; the soldier loudly vented in the camp his astonishment and his grief; women trembled with horror; while France, motionless with affright, and participating by her inaction in the crime,—France, indignant and disgraced, saw the bloody shadow of that scaffold falling upon her history, perhaps for many long years.

But she had not yet sounded the depth of the abyss that yawned for her beneath the fallen head of the King. She had not reckoned the seas of human blood, the countless corses that would sink into that gulf before it could be filled. The greatest poet of England,—speaking here as a philosopher and politician,—has said:

> "That spirit, upon whose weal depend and rest
> The lives of many. The cease of majesty
> Dies not alone; but, like a gulf, doth draw
> What's near it with it."
>
> *Hamlet*, Act III., Scene 3.

France was about to experience this; not for the King was she to weep, but for herself. When the Son of God expirea, nature seemed convulsed to dissolution; and thus, also, France, sustained through ages by the strong hand of royalty, must be convulsed in her turn before the scaffold of her King. His destroyers were soon to devour each other. All who had taken the principal parts in this bloody deed had the fatal mark impressed upon their brow, that doomed them to the headsman's hand. The Girondists,—those courtiers, alarmed into acquiescence by their dread of revolutionary fury, regicides from ambition and from fear,—they were not to escape. The hour of the Mountain was approaching, and they failed not to respond to the fatal call. The scaffold of Louis XVI. was not to be overthrown; it stood there firmly, awaiting the judge, and, like a terrible magnet, drew a whole generation to destruction. Woe to the hands that were not raised to prevent the crime, though they moved not to share it! The death of the King was to become a signal for the most frightful tyranny that ever scourged a nation and weighed down a people! The death of the King was the inaguration of terror: on that scaffold disappeared all that was noble and admirable eloquent and illustrious! How many fathers were to weep for their children! How many children to mourn for their fathers! Old men who had lived too long, children yet unborn, women—hitherto spared in the revolutions—all were food for *death!* Woe to that liberty under whose name such crimes are committed! In time to come, long after, it will be paid for. In the far future the cry will still be heard,— "Woe to you! You call yourselves the *Republic*, and you bear on your brow the stain of King Louis XVI.'s blood!"

The prediction of the martyred saint involuntarily recurs to our pen: "The people will restore my memory when they know the truth, when they recover power to be just; but, alas! until that time comes they will be very miserable!"

Yes, their misfortunes have been great, their trials long and severe, and they are not over yet! The recollection of the judicial murder of the 21st January, 1793, committed in France, unimpeded by France, weighs upon her conscience, perhaps upon her destiny! Vainly does she seek to forget that inauspicious day in the hurry of affairs, in the din of war, in the arms of victory, in the sophistry of those rhetoricians who, forgetting the words of an ancient writer: "It is more difficult to justify a parricide than to commit it," have pleaded necessity as an extenuating circumstance in favour of this great crime! Vainly have some historians, dying their pens in a miry sea of blood, and prostituting their genius to the defence of crime, sought to convert into a pedestal the scaffold of the judges of Louis XVI. Their lives condemned them, and the stoicism of their death will avail but little with posterity. From that day the principles of government and the idea of order seemed to forsake the nation, while old Europe trembled upon her foundations, as if convulsed by volcanic fire! Alas! revolutionary blood, before it can be tamed, must pass through the veins of many generations, and the ground that drank the martyr's blood has moved more than once of its own accord, to show the world that the passions of men cannot be substituted for the laws of God with impunity! Before Heaven can be appeased by the devotion of the great expiatory sacrifice, the whole nation must acknowledge that King who loved them so well, and confess that the execution of the 21st January was a sacrifice, and the scaffold an altar!

The murder of Louis XVI. was begun by calumny and

completed by the knife. The roll of the drums was but a continuation of that universal murmur that, for a long time back, had concealed the virtues and drowned the words of the King. The devotion of individuals had vainly protested against the injustice of his death, and the devotion of one isolated being had vainly sought to shield his remains from the insult of being buried in the place set aside for criminals. As soon as he had heard of the King's condemnation, the Abbé Benoît le Duc, the former head of the abbey of Saint-Martin de Paris,* had hastened to the Prince de Conti, the only prince of the blood royal then at Paris, and had asked him whether he did not intend to demand the body of Louis XVI. "I should like to do so," replied the timid prince; "but they would not grant my request, and it would be only exposing myself to no purpose." "Will you allow me," returned the Abbé le Duc, "to take this step?" "I make no objection, and I wish you may succeed; but I do not think you will."

Early on the fatal morning, the Abbé le Duc (he related these details himself)† put on an old brown coat, which was sufficiently like the costume of the Jacobins, and, with a double-barrelled pistol in his pocket, left his residence. He soon learned that, in order to have the right of appearing in the street, it would be necessary to join the ranks of the armed multitude; but he was without weapons, his concealed pistol not being a permitted one. Suddenly, making up his mind what to do, he sprang upon one of the citizens who were hastening to the scene, and snatched away his musket. The man from whom he had taken it was completely bewildered by the suddenness of the action; he knew not to what to attribute the movement—rapid as lightning—nor had he time to ask its meaning. He was fain to hide his shame and provide for

* He was a brother of the Abbé de Bourbon, and, like him, was descended from Louis XV.

† "*Les Augustes Victimes du Temple*," by Madame Guénard de Méré, Vol. II., page 159.

his personal safety by flight, for the aggressor was already far away, and had slipped among the ranks of the armed population. By means of this stratagem, justified, in his opinion, by the plan he had so near his heart, the Abbé le Duc moved on with the crowd to the Convention. There he left the ranks, and attempted to force his way into the hall, but found all the approaches lined with cannon.* At this moment a deputy passed by, and the Abbé le Duc joining him, told him he had a petition of the utmost importance to present to the Assembly. Struck with the truthful accent and decided tone of the man who thus adjured him, the deputy agreed to admit him into one of the vestibules, and took upon him to present the president with the petition, in which Le Duc demanded the body of Louis, under the law which grants this boon to the relations of the condemned. Unknown to the greater part of, if not to all, the representatives of the people, this claim of relationship with the condemned called forth much ironical laughter from the audience. However, as the demand was of a serious nature, the Assembly heard it to the end, and were thus informed that Benoît le Duc demanded the remains of Louis, in order to lay them in the cathedral church of Sens, beside those of his father, the great Dauphin. While two deputies were speaking against this petition, and causing it to be rejected, some others, attracted into the vestibule by the singularity of the petitioner's claims of relationship, were carrying on a conversation with him, which closed with a threat of putting him under arrest.

"Do not think of it," said the Abbé le Duc to the most violent of the deputies; "I have here a double-barrelled pistol. If you say one word, the first shot will be for you, and I shall rid the earth of a monster; the second for myself, and I shall thus escape the scaffold!" The confusion produced by this

* Orders given by Santerre. Report made to the council-general of the Commune on the 18th January.

scene, and the universal agitation of the moment, gave the Abbé le Duc an opportunity to retire.*

The Republic decided upon interring the tyrant at its own expense, and the function of consuming his remains was entrusted to quick-lime. The evening before, the curé of the Madeleine de la Ville-l'Evèque had been sent for by the executive authorities, and had consulted with the deputy-attorney-general, syndic of the department, and with the delegated officers.† Orders were given to dig a grave ten feet deep, in the cemetery of La Madeleine, ten feet from the inclosure, and to bring a certain quantity of quick-lime, to be placed near the grave, that it might be thrown in at the moment of interment. Was the Revolution distrustful of itself, and anxious to destroy these remains lest posterity should collect them and bring them to honour?

On the 21st January, at nine o'clock, A.M., before the victim had got half way from the Temple to the Place de la Révolution, citizens Le Blanc and Dubois, administrators of the department of Paris, and armed with all the power of the council-general of the department, repaired to the house of citizen Picavez, curé of Saint-Madeleine, to satisfy themselves that the orders given the evening before had been executed. Thence, accompanied by citizens Renard and Damoureau, curates of that parish,—who were sent by the curé (rector or vicar), he himself being prevented by illness from assisting at the obsequies of Louis Capet,—the two administrators repaired to the cemetery of the parish, in the Rue d'Anjou, where they

* The Abbé le Duc retired to an estate near the Château Thierry, where he was arrested and put in prison for having demanded the body of Louis Capet. Being transferred to Soissons, he was carried thence by the commissary of the executive power and brought to the prisons of Paris, 25th December, 1793, where he remained until the death of Robespierre. His name was on the list of those who were to have perished on the 10th Thermidor.

† Letter of the provisionary executive council to the administrators of police. (Archives of the Hôtel de Ville.)

ascertained that every preparation had been made according to the orders given.*

Towards eleven o'clock a carriage, escorted by a detachment of foot gendarmerie, stopped in the Rue d'Anjou. A crowd of people instantly rushed into the cemetery, surrounding a new-made grave, beside which, in presence of the two administrators and the two vicars, the gendarmerie deposited an open bier, bearing the dead body of Louis Capet, which the former declared perfect in all its members, the head being severed from the trunk, and lying between the legs.† The hair was shaved off at the back of the head. The body was dressed in a shirt, a white waistcoat, a pair of grey silk breeches, with stockings also of grey silk, and no shoes. The priests chaunted the vespers, and recited the prayers for the burial of the dead; and the same populace who, a quarter of an hour before, were surrounding the scaffold of the victim, deafening him with their cries, listened, in silence the most devout, to the prayers for the repose of his soul.‡

Before the body was lowered into the grave, a bed of lime was laid down, and then the open bier, that left the mortal remains all uncovered, was lowered. Another layer of quick-lime was next spread on this bier and the body, covering them entirely. Then the grave was filled up with earth, and beaten down hard. After this, the delegates of the executive authorities retired to the residence of the curé, where they prepared the report, which was then signed by the curé and his two curates. The crowd dispersed in silence.

The Revolution was now satisfied that all vestige of royalty was thus entirely destroyed. After having dethroned the King and killed the man, his very dead body was destroyed with the utmost care. In this fell rage there was a secret

* See, in Document No. IX., the report of the interment.

† Deposition by M. Danjou, ex-advocate, who witnessed the interment.

‡ Deposition by M. Renard, curate of La Madeleine, who officiated at the interment.

presentiment of impotence; in this hope, a great ignorance of the nature of things, and of the durability of those fundamental institutions which, like the sturdy oaks, acquire new vigour from the sweeping violence of the axe. Revolutionary eternities are but of short duration, and royalty, *abolished for ever*, was not silenced in France; while the earth itself, notwithstanding the corrosive assistance of quick-lime, was one day to restore the remains of the martyred King for solemn interment in the vaults of Saint-Denis.

END OF THE FIRST VOLUME.

DOCUMENTS

AND

CONFIRMATORY PAPERS.

I.

French Republic.

TOWN OF VERSAILLES.

LIBERTY, EQUALITY, FRATERNITY.

Extract from the Register of Births of the Town of Versailles, for the year of grace 1785, *Parish of Notre Dame.*

In the year seventeen hundred and eighty-five, the twenty-seventh of March, the very high and very mighty Prince, Monseigneur Louis-Charles of France, Duke of Normandy, born on this day, son of the very high, mighty, and excellent Prince Louis-Auguste, King of France and Navarre, and of the very high, mighty, and excellent Princess Marie-Antoinette-Josèphe-Jeanne, Archduchess of Austria, Queen of France and Navarre, his consort, was baptised in the King's chapel by Monseigneur the Prince Louis-René-Edouard, Cardinal of the Holy Roman Church, Bishop and Prince of Strasbourg, Landgrave of Alsace, Prince of the Empire, Grand Almoner of France, in presence of the undersigned Curé; the godfather, the very high and mighty Prince Louis-Stanislas-Xavier of France, Monsieur, brother to the King, and the godmother, the very high, mighty, and excellent Princess Marie Charlotte-Louise of Lorraine, Archduchess of Austria, Queen of the Two Sicilies, sister of the Queen, represented by the very high and mighty Princess Elisabeth-Philippine-Marie-Hélène of France, sister of the King, in the presence of His Majesty: and in testimony whereof we have hereunto affixed our signatures. Louis-Stanislas-Xavier, Marie-Joséphine-Louise, Charles-Philippe, Marie-Thérèse, Elisabeth-Marie-Hélène-Philippine, Marie-Adélaïde, Victoire-Louise, L.-P.-J. d'Orléans, Cardinal de Rohan, and Brocqueville, Curé.

Exact copy, this 26th February, 1852.

THE MAYOR OF SAINT-GERMAIN.

We, President of the Tribunal of the First Instance, sitting at Versailles, declare the above signature of M. de Saint-Germain, Mayor of this town, to be really his.

PONSINET.

Versailles, 26th February, 1852.

Order from the King to General de Bouillé. №. 2.

De par le Roy

mon intention etant de me rendre à Montmedy le vingt juin prochain, il est ordonné au S.r de Boüillé, lieutenant général en mes armées, de placer des troupes ainsiqu'il le jugera convenable pour la sureté de ma personne et celle de ma famille sur la route de chaâlons sur marne à Montmédy, voulant que les troupes qui seront employées à cet effet éxécutent tout ce qui leur sera prescrit par le dit S.r de Bouillé les rendant responsables de l'éxécution des ordres qu'il leur donnera fait à paris le 15 juin 1791.

Louis

il est enjoint à monsieur de Mandel, aux officiers sous officiers et cavaliers du regt royal allemand, d'executer et de faire executer le present ordre. Stenay ce 21. juin 1791. Bouillé

III.

Deposition of Balthazar Sapel.

In the year seventeen hundred and ninety-one, on Friday, the twenty-fourth of June, at seven o'clock in the evening, appeared before us, the commissaries of the Section du Roule, assembled in committee, the commissary of police being present:

Balthazar Sapel, coachman and postilion of M. the ex-Count de Fersen, colonel of the Royal Swiss Regiment, the said M. de Fersen residing in the Rue du Faubourg Saint-Honoré, at the corner of the Rue Matignon, and said Sapel living in the Rue du Faubourg Saint-Honoré, at the corner of the Petite Rue Verte, at the house of a greengrocer:

Said Balthazar informs us, that the ex-Count de Fersen, his master, being on Monday last in his house in the Rue du Faubourg Saint-Honoré, sent for him, the deponent, by a little boy, and told him to keep the horses ready to be put to the carriage at half-past eleven o'clock at night; that, half an hour after giving him this order, he sent to him, the deponent, two men, one dressed in a blue great coat, of from five feet seven to five feet eight inches in height, and stout; the other of from five feet four to five feet five inches; that they found him in the stable, and desired him to be as quick as possible, and have the horses ready at midnight precisely; that, by M. de Fersen's orders he gave a pair of spurs to the tallest of the two men; that, at about five or six o'clock in the afternoon, by order of M. de Fersen, he had driven a four-wheeled vehicle, the carriage of which was painted yellow and the body puce-colour, from his master's house to that of Lord Grafford, Rue du Clichy, near the barrier, the last house on the right; that the carriage doors were locked, and he had not seen the inside; that he knows this carriage, said to be for Madame Kolf, was built by one M. Louis, a saddler, and that the latter, having expressed a wish to know where the said carriage would be driven, he had promised to let him know; that, after having driven it to the Rue du Clichy, he told the saddler, accordingly; and that he did not see the carriage arrive at M. de Fersen's. Said Sapel assures us he would know the carriage very well again, were he to see it. He says, further, that these two individuals did not leave him from the time they joined him, at about nine o'clock at night, until they all set out; that, at about half-past eleven, still accompanied by these two individuals, he took four carriage-horses, and that one of the men took another, a saddle-horse, at an Englishman's, in the Petite Rue Verte, and that they had all gone together to the Rue du Clichy, to the house of Lord Grafford; that, immediately on his arrival, he harnessed his horses to the berlin he had driven thither in the afternoon; that these two men hurried him to make haste with the utmost eagerness—nay, even that, when one of his reins snapped, and he wanted to go back to M. de Fersen's to change it, these two men objected to his doing so; that, having harnessed the horses, he, the deponent, mounted one as postilion, while the taller of the two men got on the box, and the other mounted the saddle-horse; that, pursuant to the orders he had received from M. de Fersen, he followed the rider in front; that they proceeded along the outer Boulevards from the barriers as far as that of the Faubourg Saint-Martin, where they stopped upon the high road, and waited till near two o'clock in the morning; that, during this time, growing impatient, and not knowing what was the meaning of this stopping, the two men not speaking to him at all, nor dismounting any more than himself, and being armed, he asked them who the gentlemen were whom he was going to drive, and they replied that he should know by-and-by; that, at the end of this long waiting, a carriage, drawn by two horses at full gallop, came up very close to that where he, the deponent, was the postilion; that both the coach doors were opened, and four or five persons got out from the carriage which had just arrived, and whom he could not distinguish sufficiently to know whether they were men or women; that they got into the other carriage, the door of which was locked, and that he rode as postilion to this carriage as far as the first post-house; that the same man who had led him on horseback to the place where the other carriage joined them, had ridden on as fast as possible, when he saw it coming, saying he would go on; that the one who had acted as coachman had remained on the box, helping him, the deponent, to drive, which they did, at the utmost speed of the horses, to the first post-house. The deponent further declares that, when the carriage arrived, and while the people inside were getting out of the one into the other, driven by himself, he saw his master, M. de Fersen;

that he does not know from which of the two carriages he alighted; that the same De Fersen got upon the box, beside the coachman, and that they drove the carriage to the post-town of Bondi, where they hurried the postilions; that there M. de Fersen got off the coach-box, mounted the saddle-horse which had gone before the carriage since it left Lord Grafford's house, and, approaching the coach-door, said, "Adieu, Madame Kolf;" after which he gave him, the deponent, orders to start immediately for Bourget, by the Valenciennes road, without taking time to sup, nor to cool the horses; that he was to proceed by short stages to the latter town; and he, the deponent, was informed that, when he should reach the post-town of Bourget, the saddle-horse should be given him back; that he was especially ordered by his master, at Bondi, to sell this last horse, together with a black one belonging to the carriage; to return six hundred francs to him out of the price, and keep the surplus for himself; but that he was particularly enjoined not to drive them to Valenciennes; also, he was told if he was in need of money, to address himself to the manager, and he should have some; that he, the deponent, had observed to his master that he had no passport, and that the latter had replied that he had no occasion for one, and that, besides, if he were stopped he had only to say he belonged to the colonel of the Royal Swiss Regiment, and that he was not going beyond Valenciennes—or to write to the regiment; that, after this, the said M. de Fersen had gone off in the direction of Bourget, and he has not seen him since; that, agreeably to the orders his master had given him, he had followed the Valenciennes road as far as Roye; that, when he reached Bourget, the post-house postilions returned him the saddle-horse left there by M. de Fersen, and told him his master had desired them to give the said horse to a man who would come for it in about three hours' time; that when he, the deponent, reached Quivilliers, being apprehensive of being arrested, he had recourse to the mayor of the village, demanding a passport; that that officer being then just starting for Compiegne, ordered the horses to be left at the inn, and took him, the deponent, thither with him, when the mayor of Quivilliers having been told that he might give passports to persons whom he knew, and he, deponent, being known to the said mayor of Quivilliers, and not intending to leave the kingdom, said mayor gave him two passports, one for himself and two short-tailed horses, and the other for the two horses he was to sell; after which he, deponent, followed the Valenciennes road as far as Roye; that, on reaching this town, his passport, not being given at Paris, was thought insufficient; his horses were therefore put in the pound, and a passport was given him for himself, with an order for him to have a post-horse and and a guide to Paris, whither he accordingly came, having left the post-horse at La Chapelle because he was too much fatigued to go any further.

We, ourselves, committed the present report to writing, and read it to the said M. Balthazar Sapel: he declares it to contain the exact truth, and, persisting in his statement, assured us that he did not know how to sign his name when required to do so according to rule. Just as we were about to sign, said Sapel told us he had forgotten to state that, on the said day, last Monday, he had gone, by his master's orders, at about six o'clock in the evening, for two horses that his said master had purchased of an English horse-dealer, in Petite Rue Verte; that he afterwards took these two horses to M. Louis, a saddler, in the Rue de la Planche, to bring thence an old berline, for six persons, of which the carriage was vermillion colour, and the body red, and drove the said carriage to the Avenue de Marigny, Faubourg Saint-Honoré, where he stopped; that, waiting in this manner, as he had been ordered, M. de Fersen appeared a moment after with a bridle in his hand, and accompanied by his chasseur; that his master ordered him, deponent, to leave the carriage, saying he intended it as a present to an elderly lady; that he gave the bridle he was holding to him, deponent, desiring him to carry it to the place where the saddle-horse was, and to tell the groom to be ready to mount at the appointed hour; that he, deponent, did as he was ordered, and went home. He observed that he should know that old carriage and the horses perfectly well. And said Sapel also informed us that his master's English out-rider had, about a fortnight or three weeks before, bought four very expensive English saddle-horses, which were to have been brought to Sedan by a dragoon belonging to a regiment in garrison in that town.

This addition to his declaration having been read to said Balthazar Sapel, he says it contains the exact truth, persists in his statement, and again declared, on being required to do so according to rule, that he did not know how to sign his name.

Stainville, Commissary.
Jonchery, Commissary.
Petit, Commissary of Police.
De Tremouilles, President.
Langlois, S. G.

Supplementary Deposition.

In the year seventeen hundred and ninety-one, on Sunday, the 25th June, at half-past two o'clock in the afternoon, Balthazar Sapel, coachman and postilion in the service of M. the Count de Fersen, colonel of the Royal Swiss Regiment, came before us, and declared that he had forgotten to make affirmation, in the deposition made by him yesterday, now in the hands of the commissary of police of this quarter, that the said Count de Fersen, his master, had had, besides the articles mentioned in the former declaration, two vehicles made for him by M. Louis, saddler, Rue de la Planche, Paris,—one, a travelling carriage, painted red, and the other a post chaise, the carriage of which was painted yellow and the body green; that these two vehicles left Paris with the Count de Fersen, his master, but that he does not know where they were loaded. This was all he had to declare; and his declaration being read to him, he said it contained the exact truth, persisted in his statement, and declared he did not know how to sign his name.

Fontaine de Saint-Freville, Commissary.
Labillois, Commissary.
Plantier, Commissary

V.

We find the following written in the minutes of the sitting of the Council-General of the Commune of Paris, of the 3rd September, 1792:—

The Council-General reports to the Committee of Surveillance the examination of what was found in one of Madame de Lamballe's pockets, taken from her at the moment of her immolation.

The result of this examination was:—Deposit of trifling effects found in one of the pockets of Madame de Lamballe, at the time of her death at the Hôtel de la Force.

Two documents from the account given by Citizen Mareux:—

Municipality of Paris.

Year 1792, 4th of Liberty, 1st of Equality, 3rd day of September, at a quarter to two o'clock in the afternoon.

We, Commissaries of the Council-General, were named in a decree of to-day to examine a letter found in the pocket of Madame de Lamballe, who was confined in the prison of the Hôtel de la Force, where she has just perished by the hands of the people. This letter was conveyed accordingly to the Commune, and laid upon the desk, together with a gold ring bearing a motto inside and out, a bunch of nine little keys on one steel ring, and a seal-skin case, containing a pair of steel mounted spectacles; all were brought by Pierre Robbe, one of the herculean market-porters, residing No. 10, Rue de la Muette, Faubourg Saint-Antoine, and François Pernet, a tradesman and officer, No. 347, Rue Saint-Antoine, volunteer gunner in the armed division of the Rights of Man, who desired to be discharged by us, the Commissaries, and subscribed themselves—

Pernet.
Robbe.

Then proceeding to examine the said letter, we found nothing

Nº IV.

A tous Officiers civils et militaires, chargés de surveiller et de maintenir l'ordre public dans les différents Départements du Royaume, et à tous autres qu'il appartiendra, Salut. Nous vous mandons et ordonnons que vous ayiez à laisser librement passer la Baronne de Korff allant à Francfort avec deux enfants, une femme et un valet de chambre et trois domestiques

sans lui donner ni souffrir qu'il lui soit donné aucun empêchement. le présent Passeport valable pour un Mois seulement.

Donné à Paris le 5. Juin 1791

Montmorin

Gratis

suspicious in it, for which reason we have decided that this document be added to the act authorizing the removal of the seals at Madame de Lamballe's, as well as the keys and other things here mentioned, the which we have subscribed with our signatures, after having deposited said effects with the secretary,

LEGRAY, Municipal Officer.
MAREUX, Municipal Officer.

The following letter is spotted with blood.

(Addressed) To Madame,
Madame la Princesse de Lamballe, Paris.

I have just heard, my dear Princess, of all the new disasters that have taken place at Paris. I wished to go and visit the King and Queen in these afflicting circumstances, but have been prevented from doing so by the fear of being detained there were I to venture. Will you, my dear Princess, be so kind as to let them know the contents of my letter, and to send me some account of all the royal family, and of yourself. I will say no more, for language is too weak to describe all that the heart must feel under such circumstances.

L.-M.-T.-B. D'ORLEANS.*

* Louise-Marie-Thérèse-Bathilde d'Orléans, Duchess of Bourbon, and mother of the Duke d'Enghien.

VI.

General Archives of the Kingdom.

COMMISSION NAMED BY THE COMMITTEE OF GENERAL SECURITY, OF THE NATIONAL CONVENTION, TO OVERLOOK THE GUARD OF THE PRISONERS IN THE TEMPLE.

Report of 1st *Nov.*, 1792, 1*st year of the French Republic, given in to the Minister of Justice* at *noon, on the* 23*rd November*, 1792.

The Commissaries named by the Committee of General Security to make a personal investigation into the state of Louis Capet and his family, confined in the Temple Tower, and to examine into the measures of security taken by the Council-General of the Commune and the Commander-in-chief of the National Guard of Paris, for the care of the hostages committed to their charge, repaired to the Temple to-day, 1st Nov., at about 10 o'clock, A.M. After having shown our credentials to the proper authorities, we desired the Commissaries of the Council-General of the Commune to acquaint us with the means they employed for the safe keeping of the individuals for whom they were responsible. In reply to our questions, they stated that eight members of the said Commune were on service daily within the Temple:—viz., one in the apartment of the ex-King, one in his wife's, and six composing the council guard of the Temple. These eight members are relieved in the following manner:—four members are chosen by lot to be on service one day, and the next day four others are chosen in the same way. The persons on service, in the rooms of the different prisoners, are allowed to reply only to such questions addressed to them as are trivial and unimportant, and their answers must be very short.

We also desired the Commander-in-chief of the National Guard to give us an account of his method of arranging the duty of the

Temple guard, and he gave us the orders of the day, by which it appears that the guard is composed of a commander-in-chief, a head of a legion, sub-adjutant-general, a commandant of battalion, an adjutant-major, an ensign, a colour-serjeant, and twenty gunners,—in all, 287 men ; and two pieces of cannon.

We asked the Commissaries how many persons were employed in domestic attendance on the prisoners. They replied that there were four in all,—Cléry, Tison and his wife, and Louis, a man who only came in to rub the floors.

After we had made these inquiries, we desired the Commissaries to open the doors of the tower of the Temple. We went up to the second floor, into a suite of apartments occupied by Louis Capet and his son, consisting of four rooms. After a strict examination of all the furniture, we came to the conclusion that he was lodged comfortably, and in a healthful manner; we also saw that neither pen, ink, pencil, nor paper was left at his disposal. We asked him if he wanted any comfort, and if he was satisfied with his food. To which he replied, that he was content with the manner in which he was treated, only he would wish to be allowed to live again with his family.

Thence we repaired to the third floor, and went into a suite of apartments, consisting of four rooms, inhabited by Louis's wife and daughter, and Madame Elizabeth : we satisfied ourselves that they had no writing materials, and that the same salubrity and comfort existed there as in the former apartments.

Then we proceeded to the kitchen, to inquire into the mode of preparing the food served up at the prisoners' table. We saw that it was all good, and enough of it, and that every measure was taken to prevent the possibility of any paper being introduced into the tower, either in the linen, or in the bread, or in any other way; and that the Commissaries of the Commune tried, and carefully tasted, all the food and drink, so that no foreign and deleterious drug could be mixed with them.

We had an account given in to us of the daily food provided, and we add to it these two original writings by the hand of the purveyor himself; by reading which the truth will be admitted of what we have advanced, with respect to the quality of the provisions intended for the support of Louis Capet and his family. This is a victorious answer to the miserable calumnies propagated against the Commune, regarding the manner in which the ex-King is lodged and fed.

We questioned the labourers and heads of workshops on the works now in progress at the Temple, as to the necessity for said works (*sic*): by their answers we have been convinced that these works were indispensable for the safe keeping of the prisoners. We asked them if they were regularly paid; to which they replied that they were satisfied on that score. The contractors declared that they had given their estimates to the architects, and that an ordinance ought to issue to-morrow, so that they may be enabled to receive some money to pay the workmen on Saturday; and, for the rest, they assured us the works would be completed in a month.

Done and closed at the office of the Temple guard, in presence of the Commissaries and Commander-in-chief, who signed with us, after it had been read; 1st November, 1792, 1st year of the French Republic.

DROUET; FRANCOIS CHABOT; DU PRAT; SANTERRE, Provisional Commander-in-Chief; BAILLY, Commissary of the Commune; CARON, Commissary of the Commune; VIVIER, Commissary of the Commune; ———, Commissary of the Commune; LARCHER, Commissary of the Commune.

VII.

Commune of Paris.

November 23rd, 1792, 4th year of Liberty, 1st of the French Republic, and 1st of Equality. Extract from the Register of the Deliberations of the Council-General.

The Council-General, with respect to the requisition made by Louis Capet for some books for his son, the list of which is here affixed, and the expense of the same, amounting to the sum of 104 francs 12 sous:

Decrees:

That the Temple Council is at liberty to give them.

(Signed) BOUCHER RENE, President.
In the Mayor's absence.
COULOMBEAU, Secretary Registrar, pro tem.

Copy, agreeing with this minute,
METZEE, Secretary Registrar, pro tem.

Louis Capet demands the books here named for his own use, and that of his son.

		fr.	s.
1.	Appendix de diis, &c., heroibus, Poet. cum notis Gallicis, a Pere Juvencio, in 24mo.		15
2.	The same, or an abridgment of the history Poet. by Father Juvencii; new edition, translated, Latin and French in 1783	1	4
3.	Aurelius Victor, in 24mo.		15
4.	Cesaris Comment. cum notis, in 24mo., 1788 . . .	1	4
5.	Cornelius Nepos, ed. in 24mo., 1772		15

		fr.	s.
6.	Dictionarium Universale, in 8vo., 1786 . . .	6	0
7.	Eutropius cum notis Gallicis, in 24mo.		15
8.	Lafontaine's fables, 2 vols., in 12mo., illustrated, 1787	10	0
9.	Florus, in 24mo.		15
10.	Latin Grammar for the use of Schools, by Lhomond	1	4
11.	A similar French Grammar, 18mo.		15
12.	General Principles of the French Language, by Vailly, 2nd ed., 1786	2	10
13.	Poetry, to understand the Poets, by Father Gautruche, edit. 1759	1	4
14.	Horace, cum interpret. cum notis Juvencii, 2 vols. in 12mo., 1785	5	0
15.	Quadragintaviris, &c., in 32mo., with frame, in morocco	2	10
16.	Justinus, cum excerptionibus, in 24mo., 1788 . .	1	5
17.	Maxims from the Bible, in 32mo., 1786.		12
18.	Ovid's Metamorphoses, Latin and French, 2 vols., in 12mo., 1788, by Barrette	5	0
19	Phædrus's Fables, in Latin, notes, 12mo. ed., 1786 .	1	4
20.	Curtius, cum notis, in 24mo.	1	5
21.	Remarks on the French Language, by the Abbé d'Olivier	2	10
22.	Rudiments, new method, for schools, 15th ed., 18mo.		15
23.	Sallustius, cum notis Gallicis, in 24mo., 1788 .	1	0
24.	Suetonius, cum notis, in 24mo, ed. Elzevir . . .	3	0
25.	Tacitus (Cornel.), juxta 1789	2	10
26.	The Adventures of Telemachus, ed. 1791	6	0
27.	Terentius, cum notis Juvencii	2	10
28.	Titus Livius, cum notis, 6 vols.	18	0
29.	Treatise on Studies, by Rolin, 4 vols.	12	0
30.	Lives of the Saints, by Messang, 7 vols.	2	10
31.	Velleius Paterculus, in 24mo.		15
32.	Virgilius, idem, cum notis, tantum, in 12mo., 1792.	2	10
33.	The same, translated into French, with the Latin beside it, by M. Barrette, 2 vols., in 12mo., 1787. .	6	0
	Total	104	12

Thirty-three works, Latin and French. At the Temple Council, the 21st November, 1792, 1st year of the French Republic.

CLERY, serving in the Tower.

The Temple Council, taking into consideration that the above demand, for several reasons, should be submitted to the Council-General of the Commune, has decreed that the granting it be suspended until it be considered and decreed by the said Council-General.

21st November, 1792, 1st year of the French Republic.

Maillet, Commissary on duty at the Temple.
D. Jolly Berthault, Commissary on duty.
Thomas, Commissary on duty.

VIII.

National Archives.

List of instruments for cutting, and arms, offensive and defensive, belonging to the prisoners of the Temple, delivered up by Citizens Cléry and Tison, in the service of the prisoners at the Temple.

Belonging to Louis Capet, by Citizen Cléry :—

1st. A case of green shagreen, with lock and key, containing six razors with tortoise-shell handles, and gold-tipped, a pair of fine scissors, and a leather.

2nd. A knife with a tortoise-shell handle, with five blades.

3rd. A knife with a mother-of-pearl handle, the blade and ornamental work of gold.

4th. Another little knife to get rid of powder, the handle of mother-of-pearl, clasp of gold or gilt, and flat blade.

5th. Two pair of scissors, one large, for cutting hair, and the other smaller.

6th. A lancet, enclosed between two steel plates.

7th. A little steel compass.

8th. A pair of curling tongs.

9th. A little box made of oak-wood, lined with tanned leather, with copper braces and a clasp, containing another little box of green shagreen, lined with cherry-coloured velvet, and ornamented with nine gold pieces, the lock and hinges included, the other parts wanting, and the lid of the box being broken, in which there were nine instruments for the feet, all with mother-of-pearl and gold handles; eight with steel blades of different shapes, and one with a gold blade.

In the false bottom of the box there were three pairs of scissors, of different sizes, and a pair of round nippers, all of steel, and fit for the feet.

10th. Also a little pair of scissors, with one end rounded, in a sheath, belonging to L uis-Charles.

Which are all the objects Louis Capet and his son had in their possession that said Cléry knew of.

CLERY, serving Louis Capet and his son in the Temple.

By Pierre Joseph Tison, attendant on the women:—

Belonging to Marie Antoinette—

1st. Two pair of scissors, one large and one smaller, chased steel.

2nd. A knife for getting rid of powder, with a mother-of-pearl handle.

3rd. A steel toothpick.

To her daughter—

1st. A knife with two blades and a mother-of-pearl handle, one blade of gold, and its top also set in gold, inclosed in a green seal-skin case.

2nd. A small pair of steel scissors, with their case.

To Elizabeth, the sister—

1st. A seal-skin case, containing two knives, both with mother-of-pearl handles, and one with a gold blade.

2nd. Another little knife, or penknife, with two blades and horn handle.

3rd. And lastly, a small pair of scissors, in a shabby case.

Which are all that said Tison knows to belong to the women, of defensive weapons.

TISON.

Further Citizen Cléry reports a morocco companion, containing a gun worm and an instrument to break stones, a pair of tweezers, a needle, a bodkin, an ammunition bag, and a little case containing needle and thread.

Which are additional effects, acknowledged by Citizen Cléry as belonging to Louis Capet, and which he had about him; he submitted to give into the Council everything of the kind which Louis Capet may still have, and that are not yet given in voluntarily and immediately, on reading the said decree, and signed,

CLERY.

Certified by us, the undersigned municipal officers, conformably to the decree of to-day, to which the present is joined. At the Temple, Friday, 7th December, 1792, 1st of the French Republic.

MOELLE. GUILLAUME SERMAIZE.
CHANSLAY. ESTIENNE.
FIGUET. QUENIAR.

And, on the 7th December of the same year, Citizen Cléry, named above, laid upon the table, in obedience to the decree of the Provisional Council-General, a pair of curling tongs and a toothpick; which effects are a part of those sent to him for the use of Louis Capet in the earlier days of his confinement, and which, together with the linen, are to be confided to the storekeeper, of which he has required an acknowledgement from us, under the same reserve as above, and signed himself,

CLERY.

SERMAIZE. CHENAUX, Municipal officer.
QUENIAR, Commissary. CHANSLAY.
FIGUET.

IX.

National Archives.

INTERMENT.

Report.

21st January, 1793, 2nd year of the French Republic.

We, the undersigned, Administrators of the Department of Paris, being entrusted with powers from the Executive Council of the French Republic:

Repaired, at nine o'clock in the morning, to the residence of Citizen Picavez, Curé of Saint-Madeleine, and having found him at home, asked him if he had provided for the execution of those measures which had been recommended to him, the day before, by the Executive Council and by the Department, for the interment of Louis Capet. He replied, that he had rigidly executed all that had been ordered by the Executive Council and by the Department, with out a moment's delay.

Thence, accompanied by Citizens Renard and Damoureau, both Curates of the parish of Saint-Madeleine, charged by the Citizen Curé to act at the interment of Louis Capet, we repaired to the cemetery of the said parish, in the Rue d'Anjou-Saint-Honoré; having reached it, we saw that the Citizen Curé had executed the orders which we had transmitted to him the night before, in virtue of the commission received by us from the Council-General of the Department.

Soon after, the dead body of Louis Capet was laid down in our presence, by a detachment of gendarmerie, and we hereby declare that it was perfect in all its members, the head separated from the trunk. We remarked that the hair was cut off at the back of the head, and that the body was without cravat, coat, and shoes. It was dressed in a shirt, a white vest, like a waistcoat, a pair of breeches of grey silk, and a pair of stockings, also of grey silk. In this attire it was laid upon a bier, which, being lowered into the grave, was covered immediately.

The whole was arranged and executed conformably to the orders given by the Executive Council of the French Republic. And we hereby sign, together with Citizens Picavez, Renard, and Damoureau, Vicar and Curates of Saint-Madeleine.

PICAVEZ, RENARD, DAMOUREAU, LEBLANC, and DUBOIS.

Two months later, the execution of Louis XVI. was entered in the Register of Civil Acts of the Commune of Paris, in the following terms. The words in italics are the printed form :—

REGISTER OF DECEASE.

On Monday, 18th March, *in the year seventeen hundred and ninety-three, 2nd of the French Republic. Register of Decease of* Louis Capet, 21st January ult., at 22 minutes past ten, A.M., *Profession,* last King of the French, *Age,* thirty-nine *years, Native of* Versailles, parish of Nôtre-Dâme, *Residing at* Paris, Temple Tower, *Married to* Marie-Antoinette of Austria. Said Louis Capet was executed on the Place de la Révolution, in virtue of the decrees of the National Convention, of the 15th, 16th, 19th, and 20th of the said month of January, in presence of—1st, Jean-Antoine Lefèvre, Deputy Attorney-General, Syndic of the Department of Paris, and Antoine Momoro, both members of the Directory of the said department, and Commissaries in that district of the Council-General of the said department; 2ndly, of François-Pierre Sallais, and François-Germain Ysabeau, Commissaries named by the Provisional Executive Council to be present at the said execution, and to draw up the report, which they did; and 3rdly, of Jacques-Claude Bernard and Jacques Roux, both Commissaries of the Municipality of Paris, named by it to be present at this execution. See the report of said execution of said 21st January last, signed "Grouvelle," Secretary to the Provisional Executive Council, sent to the public officers of the Municipality of Paris, this day, upon a demand previously made by them to the officers of justice; and said report being deposited in the Archives of the Civil Branch of the Administration.

PIERRE-JACQUES LEGRAND, Public Officer.

END OF THE APPENDIX.

www.ingramcontent.com/pod-product-compliance
Lightning Source LLC
LaVergne TN
LVHW020934110826
845150LV00004B/856

9781425552602